MICHAEL JACKSON'S
BEER COMPANION

(Above) Detail from *The Guinness Alice*, Dublin, 1933.
(Previous page) Label design (1947) by Jean Cocteau,
for the Fischer/Pêcheur brewery in Alsace.

MICHAEL JACKSON'S
BEER COMPANION

Mitchell Beazley

Dedication

To Paddy, for the quiet pints at the end of the road.

Michael Jackson's Beer Companion

First published in Great Britain in 1993
by Mitchell Beazley
an imprint of Reed Consumer Books Limited
Michelin House, 81 Fulham Road
London SW3 6RB
and Auckland, Melbourne, Singapore and Toronto

A CIP catalogue record for this book is available from the British
Library.

A DBP book,
created and designed by
Duncan Baird Publishers
Highlight House
57 Margaret Street
London W1N 7FG

Edited by Segrave Foulkes
Editor: *Maggie Ramsay*
Designer: *Paul Reid*
Commissioned photography: *Sally Cushing, Ian Howes,*
 Richard McConnell, Alan Williams
Maps: *Sue Sharples*
Type formatted by: *MacGuru*

Typeset in Ehrhardt
Colour reproduction by Colourscan, Singapore
Printed by Imago, Singapore

The author and publishers will be grateful for any information
which will assist them in keeping future editions up to date.
Although all reasonable care has been taken in the preparation of
this book, neither the publishers nor the author can accept any
liability for any consequences arising from the uses thereof, or
from the information contained therein.

ISBN 1 85732 181 2

Contents

Never ask for 'a beer'…

No one goes into a restaurant and requests 'a plate of food, please.' People do not ask simply for 'a glass of wine', without specifying, at the very least, whether they fancy red or white, dry or sweet, perhaps sparkling or still. More often, they trouble to decide whether the red should be American or Australian, Italian or French, from Burgundy or Bordeaux, and choose a vineyard and year. When their mood switches from the grape to the grain, these same discerning folk often ask simply for 'a beer', or perhaps name a brand, without thinking about its suitability for the mood or moment.

What the British call 'plonk' and the Americans 'jug wine' is often well-made and good value, but there is more to the grape than that. It is well understood that there are 'fine wines', but less widely appreciated that beer can be equally varied, complex and noble.

The similarities between wines and beers are far greater than the differences. Wines begin with fruit (usually, but not always, the grape), while beers start with grain (customarily, but not necessarily, barley); both are made by fermentation; and many of the flavour compounds naturally formed are shared between them. Distil wine and you have brandy. Distil beer and you make whisky.

In many European countries, wine is taken for granted. 'Wine is for peasants in Calabria,' a yuppie in a beer-bar in Milan once told me. 'Wine is what my parents drink – I prefer beer.' One's own heritage is never quite as much fun as something that comes from elsewhere. I believe that is one of the principal reasons for wine snobbism. The Italians, French and Spanish make wine; the Germans and Belgians, British and Americans revere it.

A more significant factor might be that warm southern European countries grow the grape, and other round, soft, squashy fruits such as tomatoes and peppers. Cool northern lands grow resilient grains and underground vegetables such as the potato and turnip. Wine is at home with a more sensuous cuisine than beer.

Femininity and elegance were considered a fitting backdrop for beer in the days of Vienna waltzes and Imperial splendour.

THE WINE-LOVER'S GUIDE TO BEER
You love wine, but fancy a beer. If this is the wine you would choose, consider the beer that follows. It will not taste like a wine (you asked for beer, after all), but you may enjoy it.

Dry white: an authentic, hoppy Pilsner
Gewürztraminer: a spicy, malty Vienna-style lager, or a darker Munich-style lager
Champagne: a wheat beer
Blush Zinfandel or pink champagne: a framboise (raspberry beer)
Cabernet Sauvignon: a fruity English-style ale, or an oaky American IPA (India Pale Ale)
Pinot Noir: a richer Scottish or Belgian ale
Fino sherry: a lambic
Amontillado sherry: a porter or dry stout
Port: a dark Trappist ale, with some bottle-age

Today's fashionable beers are more likely to embrace post-modernism or industrial chic. The Gordon Biersch brewpubs are in northern California, where beers and wines are part of America's new cuisine.

Which style of beer suits the moment? Old World classics at Stoudt, in Pennsylvania.

Wine was not born with a vocabulary; that came later, with the help of writers such as Saintsbury and Simon, Lichine and Johnson. Any wine-writer who has ever enjoyed beers (and most have) will confirm that some are drier, others sweeter; this one firm-bodied, that soft; one hints at pears or oranges, another at coffee or chocolate. This is not a difficult language; anyone with an interest in the tastes of foods and drinks already has a smattering of it, and it is the easiest way in which to appreciate beer. Wine-makers and brewers often prefer chemical descriptors, but those hardly reflect drink as a pleasure.

'Do you ever drink wine?' people ask me, as though beer were a prison rather than a playground. A day may pass when I do not drink wine, but never a week. Whatever is argued about other pleasures, it is not necessary to be monogamous in the choice of drink. Beer is by far the more extensively consumed, but less adequately honoured. In a small way, I want to help put right that injustice.

The uses of beer

People who drink only the most conventional beers have failed to understand that there are different brews for each mood, moment or purpose.

Some people drink beer to get drunk, though it is an inefficient means of doing so. Although there are far stronger beers, the great majority worldwide have an alcohol content of 3–4 percent by weight, 4–5 by volume. At those strengths, beer is the least potent of the world's alcoholic drinks, less than half as strong as most wines and with little more than a tenth of the potency of most spirits. In several countries, beer has been promoted as a drink of moderation.

Beer's greatest use is as a sociable relaxant. The best beers for this purpose are a gentle south German Helles, a rounded north German Altbier, a Belgian ale, an English bitter, or something similar from the New World. A sociable beer must not be too strong, and needs a touch of hoppy dryness to make it moreish.

Other people drink beer to quench a thirst. Wheat beers or Belgian tart 'red' ales such as Rodenbach are the most refreshing. Standard lagers are often put to this use, but do the job less well because they are too sweet and too gassy, and therefore bloating.

Anyone who has done a hard day's work knows that a beer is a restorative. Medical opinion may vary on the scientific justification of this view, but a great many doctors appear to enjoy a beer after work. A sweeter beer, for example a dark lager or mild ale, or one of the creamier stouts, seems to do the job.

Some beers sharpen the appetite, others are well suited to accompany foods. I have discussed some of these uses on page 252.

The renaissance of beer

Wine was not always as widely appreciated and discussed as it is today, and beer was praised by countless European writers from the time of the Nordic sagas to Shakespeare and Goethe.

The fragility of the grape, and wine's traditional reliance on wild yeasts, has rooted it in place. Grain travels more easily, and beer has become more universal, perhaps more commonplace. Wine-makers make a merit of their product's differences from one year to the next, brewers are excessively preoccupied with a consistent product. Many wines develop in the bottle over the years; fewer beers are made in this way, though a handful are.

The countries where beers have traditionally been least consistent are Britain and Belgium. In Britain, the classic ales are put into the cask unfiltered, often with a dosage of yeast and sugar, and allowed to have a secondary fermentation in the vessel. They are still 'alive' and evolving in the cask, in the cellar of the pub, and the first pint drawn will taste different from the last. Ordering a pint of cask-conditioned ale is like opening a bottle of a fine wine. You know the character of the vineyard, but each bottle will have its own delights or disappointments.

In Belgium, there is a strong tradition of either bottling beer unfiltered, or adding yeast and sugar. These 'bottle-conditioned' beers also continue to develop, and gain in complexity.

In 1971, at a time when cask-conditioning was in decline in Britain, a consumer movement called the Campaign for Real Ale was started to protect the practice. The Press began to run articles on beer, and demonstrations by the campaign made news. Today, the campaign has more members than ever, and there are similar organizations in Belgium, the Netherlands, Scandinavia and Canada. The American Homebrewers' Association, while not a consumerist movement, has provided a focus for the appreciation of beer (for addresses, see page 272).

The growing interest in beer led to the establishment, for the first time since the two World Wars, of new, small breweries in Britain. While serving in Britain in the military, the young American Jack McAuliffe became interested in the idea and in 1976 set up his country's first microbrewery, New Albion, in Sonoma, California. The movement began to spread internationally, notably to Canada, Australia, New Zealand and South Africa.

With their massive capacities, big national brewers like Sapporo of Japan must concentrate on easy-to-drink beers for the mass market, but some do produce additional specialities. Sapporo has a hoppy Pils, a Dortmunder-style lager, a Düsseldorf-style Altbier and a black beer. Sapporo turned its original brewery (right) into a beer garden and restaurant to help promote the cultural traditions of its products.

This is Cooper's Ale House in Seattle, with a row of taps offering different styles of beer. Many of these are made by microbrewers, whose small kettles render it easier to produce specialities.

'The little brewhouse' is a brewpub, making its own beer on the premises, in Munich.

Sizes of brewery

The smallest of the new generation of breweries are those that serve only one pub or restaurant. Once, most breweries were like this; Germany still has scores of old-established 'house breweries', but since 1977 it has gained 150–200 new ones, many of them specializing in unfiltered beers. Typically, a brewpub might produce 1,000 to 6,000 hectolitres a year.

The next size is the true microbrewery. This is a very small brewery selling its beer to a variety of outlets. Germany has produced brewpubs, rather than micros. Britain seems to have at any one time 50 or 60 of each, though they are forever opening and closing. The United States has both, totalling more than 300.

Only in the United States have there been attempts formally to define a micro, at first suggesting an output of fewer than 10,000 US barrels and more recently 15,000 (17,600 hectolitres). I would argue for the inclusion of some twice that size, such as Sierra Nevada and Redhook, on the basis that they are in chronology and philosophy part of the new brewery movement.

A further development has been the contract brewer. He is the entrepreneur who raises money, hires a consultant (frequently a retired brewer) and has beer made to his specification on someone else's plant, under contract. People who have built their own breweries sometimes look askance at this practice, but it has produced one or two very good beers.

Old-established regional breweries often count their production in hundreds of thousands of hectolitres, and can find themselves in a difficult area of the industry, neither small nor big.

Most countries have national brewing companies, though Germany is to some degree an exception. (There are national ownership groups, and some widely available products, but nothing like the concentration that exists elsewhere.) A national brewer is likely to count his hectolitres in millions, most of them accounted for by standard, international-style lagers, but several of these companies have in recent years begun to give more attention to specialities.

A big brewery has all the skills to make speciality beer, but finds it hard to think small in terms of volume. A small brewer does not have that worry. The best of the artisanal producers, the micros and brewpubs offer a new diversity of beer for the devotee.

The world's classic pastries, cheeses and wines were each born in a particular place as a result of local materials, circumstances and the ideas of the original creator. The same is true of the classic styles of beer. If there is a clear original, I review it in this book. Otherwise, and more often, I discuss brewers who show a particular interest in the style.

A civilized drink

Beer deserves to be treated as a civilized drink; it may even have been the cause of civilization. Although wild grapes and grain were probably both turned into drinks before either was cultivated, the latter seems to have been the beginning of farming, between 13,000 and 8,000 years ago. Humans ceased to be nomadic hunters and gatherers, and settled in organized communities to grow grain, but why?

In the *Museum Magazine of Archaeology and Anthropology* produced by the University of Pennsylvania, Professor Solomon Katz in 1986 described as 'the world's oldest recipe' a series of tablets in the Sumerian language. These early accounts, with pictograms of what is recognizably barley, show bread being baked, then crumbled into water to make a mash, which is then made into a drink that is recorded as having made people feel 'exhilarated, wonderful and blissful'.

The brewery of Weihanstephan ('holy Stephen') to the northeast of Munich in Germany claims to be the world's oldest.

The baking rendered the barley soluble, and was employed before man knew how to turn the grain into malt. Was the bread never eaten, but always made into beer? Did a diet of bread come first, or did man live by beer alone?

Katz points out that it is difficult to make appetizing bread out of barley. Perhaps the bread was never intended as anything other than an intermediate step in the production of beer, a nutritious and pleasant drink. By baking the grains into hard loaves, the ancients had created a partly processed resource that could be conveniently stored for later use, and easily transported, whereas fruits were edible only when they had been freshly picked, during their short season. The fruits could be turned into wine, but that lacks the protein value of beer.

Remnants of breweries, or relics showing or describing in detail the making and drinking of beer, sometimes listing a selection of different types, have been found in several parts of the fertile crescent that stretches around the converging valleys of the Rivers Euphrates and Tigris, between which lay ancient Mesopotamia, the region of Sumer and city-states such as Ur and Babylon. Similar relics have been found in other areas of ancient civilization, from the Nile Valley to Mount Ararat; and from modern Egypt to Iraq and Iran.

A seal around 4,000 years old is a hymn to a goddess of brewing, called Ninkasi (translated by Miguel Civil, of the Oriental Institute of Chicago), and suggests that the Sumerians by then knew how to make malt. Much of the evidence concerns beer as a drink of the gods and priests. A collection of these items is on show at the University of Pennsylvania Museum.

Work there by Patrick McGovern and others identified as traces of beer the residue found on a clay jar more than 5,000 years old. The vessel had been unearthed at a site in Iran by archaeologists from the Royal Ontario Museum of Toronto. The site was a Sumerian outpost on the ancient trade route that became the Silk Road between East and West. This research was described in the British magazine *Nature* in 1992. Similar evidence 4,000 years old has been found on the western Scottish island of Rhum.

The hymn to Ninkasi has been used by the Anchor brewery of San Francisco for an essay into Sumerian

Each month, a new beer is left for the deity at this shrine at a brewery in Japan. All Japanese breweries and distilleries have such shrines. Beer's close links with religious belief echo through the ages. The word 'ale' is thought to derive from 'alu', an Old Saxon invocation of religious ecstasy.

An unholy drinker: Pistol, crony of Shakespeare's Falstaff, in turn-of-the-century tiling at the White Horse pub, Parson's Green, London.

beer-making techniques. Anchor's Ninkasi Beer, made from specially baked bread, and flavoured with dates and honey, was fermented with a modern brewing yeast. It emerged with a russet colour and a sherryish, nutty flavour, with late notes of honey. No hops were used. The ancient beer of Rhum has also been recreated experimentally, by the Glenfiddich distillery laboratory in Scotland.

The baking of bread as an intermediate material from which to brew has continued in Russia, with the production of kvass.

As the cultivation of barley spread north and west, brewing went with it. Romans such as Tacitus and Caesar, more accustomed to wine, noted that the peoples of the North drank beer. Several of today's brewing strongholds are in areas of early Celtic settlement, from central Europe to Ireland.

After the Dark Ages, Christian abbeys, as centres of agriculture, knowledge and science, refined brewing methods, initially in the making of beer for the brothers and for visiting pilgrims, later as a means of financing their communities. The modern abbeys that make beer today are all Roman Catholic. Christian, usually Protestant, disapproval of drinking is a relatively recent phenomenon.

In most of the traditional brewing countries, beer is seen as a part of the national identity. Royal courts assumed brewing rights in medieval times as a means of raising revenue, and some noble families are still in the business. Farmers and private brewers served their own taverns, then formed trade guilds. Finally, industrial capitalism gave the brewing business the shape it has today.

During this long history, wine and beer had no competition in Europe until the spread of tea from Asia and coffee from the Arab world between the 15th and 17th centuries.

The first extensive written work on brewing was produced in 1585 by the Bohemian Thaddeus Hajek, physician to the German Emperor Rudolf II. Most of the subsequent advances were in Bohemia, Germany, France, Belgium, the Netherlands, Denmark, Britain and Ireland.

The last major style of beer to be introduced was Pilsner, in Bohemia (then a part of the Austrian Empire), in 1842. The greatest milestone since has been the isolation of a pure-culture yeast, in Copenhagen in 1883. As an agricultural industry, and a form of cooking, brewing remains a craft and an art, as well as a science, despite technological developments.

Taking a world view

The classic beer styles all originate from the northern part of central and western Europe: Pilsner from Bohemia; Vienna lagers from Austria; a wide variety from Germany and Belgium; many types of ale from Britain; and dry stouts from Ireland. There are also local traditions in bordering regions such as Poland, Switzerland, northern France, the south of the Netherlands and Scandinavia.

Many of these classic styles are now being made by brewpubs and microbreweries in North America and Australasia, and in a small way by the big Japanese brewers. In a blind tasting, some of the European specialities might find their character exceeded by that of the newcomers.

Outside of the temperate regions, there are many perfectly well-made lagers but few of any distinction (the hoppy Singha from Thailand, and the Maibock of Namibia, are examples of the odd splendid exception). There are also a good many stouts, especially in Africa and the Caribbean, but not much else. Hot countries do not grow barley or hops, have to import them, and tend to make straightforward, light-tasting lagers intended as nothing more than simple thirst-quenchers. Developing nations and intermediate economies often buy barley, malt and hops by barter, and cannot choose varieties.

Nor is there any reason why a country without a northern European beer tradition should make classic styles unfamiliar to its consumers. Many of these countries have 'traditional beers' made from millet, cassava root, coconut sap, or whatever raw material is local. These ancient products, often milky-looking and soapy-tasting, are of great interest to anyone who enjoys unusual drinks and their social history, but they do not in any way resemble beer in the western understanding of the word.

The big international brand-owners license local breweries to make their products in distant lands. In theory, a licensed version could be very close to the original. The malt, hops and yeast could be exported, and the local water treated, though the brewery plant cannot be identical. In practice, compromises are gradually made, and often only the yeast is identical. Most of the products made under licence are standard international lagers. Try the local brew – at least it is something you could not buy at home.

Homes of the classic beer styles

SCOTLAND

NORTHERN IRELAND

Belfast

Edinburgh

Newcastle

REPUBLIC OF IRELAND

Dublin

ENGLAND

Cork

Burton

WALES

London

FRANCE

NORWAY

Oslo

FINLAND

Helsinki

Stockholm

SWEDEN

ESTONIA

DENMARK

Copenhagen

THE NETHERLANDS

Amsterdam

Berlin

Grodzisk

Warsaw

Einbeck

POLAND

Antwerp

Dortmund

Düsseldorf

GERMANY

Brussels

Cologne

Oudenaarde

BELGIUM

Bad Köstritz

BOHEMIA

Lille

Kulmbach

Prague

Bamberg

Pilsen (Plzeň)

LUXEMBOURG

Budweis
(České Budějovice)

Paris

Vienna

Munich

AUSTRIA

Zurich

Bern

SWITZERLAND

ITALY

N

0 km   100   200   300

0 miles   100   200

Malt

Everyone knows that wine is made from grapes, and occasionally other fruits, but even regular consumers are often unaware that beer is produced from barley, and sometimes wheat or other cereals. All cereals are members of the grass family, and their grains or kernels are technically fruits. Barley and wheat are the two oldest cultivated food plants, and their domestication seems to date from the same time.

Turning grain into malt
While grapes can simply be crushed to yield the juices that contain their fermentable sugars, grains are more stubborn. They have to be steeped in water for a couple of days, then allowed to germinate for around a week. When the kernel's development has reached an optimum stage but it has not sprouted and begun to live off its own sugars (as it would if it were reseeding in the ground), events are brought to a halt by a drying process. The grain has now become malt.

Barley, wheat, oats and rye can all be malted; other brewing grains such as maize, rice or (in some tropical countries) sorghum, are rendered soluble by being cooked. As well as making the grain soluble, malting also releases enzymes that will be required in mashing and fermentation. The grains do not greatly change in appearance during malting, although they do become drier and perhaps darker. To the layperson, the more obvious difference is that grains are hard before malting and can be crunched and eaten afterward. A maltster walking past the finished product will often scoop up a handful to chew; so will a brewer. As well as being the basis for beer and whiskies, malt is turned into a dark, syrupy extract as a tonic (it contains vitamin B and iron), and is used to make milk drinks, breads, cakes and other foods.

Methods of malting
In western Norway, I have seen farmer-brewers steep their grain by tying a sackful to a rock in a fast-flowing river. Commercial maltsters simply use large metal tanks.

The most traditional method of germination used in commercial maltings is to spread the moist grains on a stone floor. They must then be raked regularly, to aerate them and prevent them becoming stuck together as they begin to sprout. The raking is still sometimes done by hand, but more often by a tiny, electrically-powered tractor, or perhaps a device moving on rails above the grains. Floor-malting is very labour-intensive, but some brewers feel that it produces a cleanness and dryness of flavour that is not quite matched by other methods. Of necessity, the layer of grain is shallow, and this influences moisture and temperature.

Other, much more widely used techniques employ ventilated boxes or rotating drums.

Germination and drying were probably once a continuous process. In Einbeck, Germany, many houses have shuttered gables that could be opened to allow in the wind to dry malt for domestic brewers. I have

Barley suitable for malting grows in temperate but cool places, among them Bohemia, Bavaria, Champagne, Britain, Ireland, Oregon, Washington and Tasmania.

The grains are first steeped in water. Most maltings today are freestanding, but some are still at breweries, such as this one, at the Paulaner brewery in Munich.

heard of this method being used within living memory in the region of Leuven, Belgium.

A more predictable method of drying is to spread the grains on a sieved floor over a fire. This method is still used by some farmer-brewers in Scandinavia. In the Danish-related language spoken on the Faroe Islands, *sodnhus* is the word for a malt-kiln. The etymology is uncertain, but suggests that the Faroese may have kilned their malt over 'sods' of grass, or turf, in other words peat – as used in Scotland for the drying of whisky malt. Some home-brewers in western Norway use wood, always alder, and this method has in recent years been taken up by some microbreweries in the United States (see page 238). In Franconia, the northern part of Bavaria, Germany, beechwood is used. Malt dried by these means produces smoky-tasting beers.

More sophisticated procedures became possible in the 1800s, with the use of coke (see Porters and Stouts, page 171) and indirect heat. Most malt today is dried over warm or hot air, or in roasting drums, without any exposure to smoke.

The choice of grains

Just as the wine-maker can choose between grapes, elderberries, rhubarb, or whatever fruit he fancies, the brewer must decide which grain to use. Sometimes he will employ more than one. Barley produces soft, sweetish, clean flavours; wheat makes for tarter notes; oats seem to give an oily, silky smoothness (although they are used in very small proportions, and only in speciality beers); rye (an even rarer grain in the brewery) has a hint of spiciness. The microbrewery on the Scottish island of Orkney has experimented with bere, a primitive barley that produces a thinnish beer. Some German and Austrian brewers have from time to time used spelt, a species of wheat that creates a very fine flour and perhaps a more refined-tasting beer. In Minneapolis, the James Page brewery makes a crisp, slightly grainy beer called Boundary Waters with wild rice.

Corn and rice are now extensively used, but the practice is especially associated with the United States, where both grains are widely grown. Their original appeal was probably their availability, thus reducing the price of beer. They also make for a beer

The sun and the earth unite their power to bring forth the grains that are kilned to produce this chocolaty-tasting beer from Köstritz, Thuringia.

lighter in taste and body. Rice, the more expensive of the two, makes for a cleaner, crisper flavour. Corn, used in the form of grits (flakes) or syrups, can impart an unpleasant 'chicken-feed' character.

In some countries, sugars made from beet or cane are used. Sugar is highly soluble, and might be expected to ferment completely. Highly refined sugars used in large proportions do – making for thin-tasting beers. Some of the less well refined types offer a more interesting contribution. In their very strong beers, Belgian brewers often use a less-refined 'candy sugar', which imparts an intriguing rummy taste. Candy sugar is also used to prime champagne. Many British brewers use small proportions of sugar, and these have become a part of the flavour of some ales.

Grain must be the base of anything called beer, but I have heard of fruits being used as an additional fermentable material. Belgian producers of 'white' beer sometimes – and until quite recently – put figs to this purpose. Some American microbrewers have made a pumpkin beer at Hallowe'en. An Australian home-brewer once sent me a flowery-tasting, dryish beer that he made with the help of malted lupin seeds.

The Anchor brewery of San Francisco insists upon a Californian barley for its Christmas beer. Tulelake

is unmistakably in the west, land of wide open spaces, on the Californian border with Oregon.

More often, such materials – although they do contribute to the fermentation process – are added to impart extra flavours.

The choice of barleys

No modern wine-maker, or drinker, doubts that the grape variety is a huge influence on the character of the finished product. Some brewers (not only in the Czech Republic, but also in America) insist that a barley from a strain of Moravian origin is essential to make a good Pilsner lager. Many German brewers favour a variety called Alexis.

Bohemians and Germans tend to feel strongly that barley sown in the spring provides the soft, clean, malty note they seek. Some Belgian and British brewers consider that barleys sown in winter, being hardier and more robust, provide them with a firmness they like in their ales.

Most brewers feel they get the softest, cleanest flavours from varieties of barley that have two rows of grains in each ear. Others argue in favour of the six-row variety that grows in warmer climes. Six-row barley is tougher, and can impart a slightly sharp, 'husky' flavour.

Because farmers wish to grow varieties that produce the most grain per acre, and some big brewers want strains that yield the most fermentable sugar per ton, several of the finest barleys are becoming difficult to find. This is especially true in England of Maris Otter and in Scotland of Golden Promise. Having tasted a product made in exactly the same way from two different strains, I have no doubt that these farmers and brewers are taking a very foolhardy view. More means less. It is as true of barley as it is of tomatoes or strawberries.

The choice of malts

The wine-maker must determine how long to leave the juices on the skins (where they will pick up not only colour, but also tannin and other flavours); the maltster has similar decisions to make about kilning.

There are several classic styles of malt, some of which can be divided into further sub-categories according to the precise regime of steeping, germination and drying. Grains that have been very gently kilned will produce golden beers such as Pilsners, with a soft, clean, lightly sweet malt character. The classic British pale ale malt is kilned at slightly higher temperatures, to impart a tinge of colour and a hint of drier, cracker-like flavour. In Continental Europe, a similar process is used to make the slightly redder, sweeter Vienna malt. The traditional Munich malt has a yet more intense kilning, making for considerably more colour and a suggestion of fresh bread.

If the grains are moister when they begin the process, and are 'cooked', they will partly caramelize (like the grape juices in Madeira) or crystallize, developing luscious aromas and gaining reddish-brown colours and nutty flavours. Roasted malts ascend in intensity through types known as biscuit, chocolate and black, the last being heated to the point of carbonization. Grains of roasted malt look like tiny coffee beans. There are many variations on these styles of malt, including some where a Pilsner or Vienna type is partially caramelized. Where patented processes are used, some malts are sold under trade names.

Just as some wines are made from only one variety of grape and others from several, the same is true of beers and malts. Some beers are made only from Pilsner or pale ale malt, while others contain two or three styles, or even seven or eight. With crystal and roasted malts, a little goes a long way in adding colour, aroma, flavour and body. The blending of malts is a good example of the brewer's art.

Colours of beer

So that brewers can specify the colours of malt they require, a scale has been devised and agreed by the European Brewing Convention. The EBC scale can be applied to the malt or the finished beer. A typically golden Pilsner beer will, for example, be in single figures, perhaps 6–8 units EBC; an amber-red English pale ale will count its colour in tens (20–40); while porters and stouts will be in hundreds (150–300 or more). These figures cannot explain the attractive subtleties of colour, but they are of interest to some connoisseurs and brewers, and are therefore provided in this book when the occasion seems to merit.

All-malt beers

When they arrive at the brewery, the malt grains are cracked in a mill. Because of this grinding, they are known as grist. (The expression should surely be 'grist from the mill'?) Around 35 percent of the grist of many beers, especially light lagers, comprises non-traditional grains, such as corn or rice, or other sugars. Even with such a high proportion of 'adjuncts', there is sufficient malt to provide the enzymes required.

The Belgians use a lot of wheat, a traditional grain, but in unmalted form. They regard that as beyond reproach, but the Germans would insist that it should be malted.

Most serious beer-lovers want to recognize the clean, delicious flavours of malt. German brewers in their home market cleave to the Bavarian Beer Purity law of 1516, the *Reinheitsgebot*, which specifies that only malted grains may be used. There are arguments for and against this measure, but it does have the merit of defining beer and telling the consumer

Rice may be the grain of *sake* and sustenance in Japan, but this Suntory beer is proud to be made of barley malt.

A typical floor maltings in Bohemia. The grains are turned (to keep them separate) by a machine resembling an electric lawnmower.

exactly what the drink contains. It did not become law beyond Bavaria until the beginning of this century.

An 'all-malt' beer does, of course, also contain water, hops and yeast. Although the hops are not usually milled, some brewers refer to them as a 'grist'.

Infusion and decoction

After being milled, the malt is mixed with hot water. The simplest method employs just one vessel, in which the malt sugars infuse in the water for a period of one or two hours.

Temperature regimes in this mashing procedure have a significant influence on the body and flavour of the finished beer, and are another aspect of the brewer's art. The temperature may be raised, or lowered, by the addition of warmer or cooler water.

When the mash is complete, the bottom of the vessel is opened onto a sieve-like base, so that the 'malt juices' can run through like coffee draining through a filter. The traditional mash tun has a deep bed of malt, turned by rotating rakes. The more modern lauter tun uses a more intensive system of knife-like blades. After the mash, the 'malt juices' that emerge (actually, they are a solution of grain sugars in water) are known as wort.

Many brewers, especially in Britain, maintain that the cell walls of the barley are so broken down during malting that no more complex system of mashing is required. Perhaps because they stayed longer with the gentler floor-malting system, and because their

warmer summers make for a harder barley, some brewers in Continental Europe (especially Bavaria and Bohemia) prefer the more exhaustive decoction system of mashing.

This system employs a second, and sometimes a third, vessel, and can last for as long as seven hours. Proportions of the mash are transferred to the second vessel, brought to the boil, then returned to the original tun to adjust the temperature of its contents.

Brewers argue as to the merits of the Continental barleys versus the 'maritime' strains, and of infusion as against decoction. The best lagers of Bohemia and Bavaria have a softness, sweetness and cleanness of malt character that can be found nowhere else.

There is also a question of emphasis here. Many Bohemian and Bavarian brewers stress the significance of the mashing procedure as a key to fine beer. Some Belgian brewers seem to focus more heavily on the aromatic qualities of their malts and other brewing sugars. To some extent the English, and certainly the new generation of American brewers, are very oriented toward the hop. The Belgians again, and the northern French, are often very keen on long boiling times – and on the use of unusual yeasts.

If there were a 'best' way to make beer, everyone would use the same techniques. In these regional differences, the beers of Bohemia or Bavaria, Flanders or Wallonia, Britain or Ireland, and the East Coast, Midwest and Northwest of America are as varied as the food, the people, the architecture and the landscape.

At Paulaner, the grains are spread in long ventilated boxes, and turned by a machine that runs above on fixed tracks. These are called malting 'streets', and Paulaner has ten of them. The grains spend a week here, beginning to germinate.

Water

Once, every community in Europe's beer belt brewed for its own use. In the days when much water was not safe to drink, beer had the health benefit of having been boiled.

No community can live without water, but it requires a far greater, and constant, supply to brew beer in any quantity. In the days before mains water, the availability of a very clean river or of springs, or the possibility of sinking boreholes into a reliable underground source, was essential if a town was to produce beer worthy of a reputation, and in sufficient volume eventually to trade. This was one reason why, from the 12th and 13th centuries, some towns began to be known for their beer.

Most of the oldest-established famous brewing towns were the sites of monastic communities, in or near regions where barley (and sometimes hops) grew well, but they were also distinguished by the availability and quality of their water. Long before the influence of different waters in brewing was understood, they were contributing to the evolution of these cities' brewing styles.

This is true of České Budějovice (Budweis), Pilsen, Munich, Dortmund, London, Burton, Dublin and many other great brewing cities. Many breweries still have their own private sources, usually boreholes. I have encountered only one brewery, Lapin Kulta in Lapland, that takes its water from a river. In Belgium, the Rodenbach brewery pumps its supply from a lake that is filled by underground springs. On the Mediterranean island of Malta, where water is in short supply, the Farsons brewery has reservoirs on the roof to catch rain. At least one brewery in the Caribbean desalinates sea water.

A brewery is very happy if it has a private supply of water that is ideal for its style of beer, but that is no longer essential. Available water may have helped shape particular styles, but today, minerals can be removed from, or added to, the municipal water to produce any style of beer. Sadly, even some breweries with their own supplies are switching to town water. Wells and springs are being polluted, especially by farmers who use fertilizers. Some breweries take the precaution of filtering their water to neutrality, or even boiling off any minerals, then adding back such salts as they require.

Underground springs feed this ornamental lake, which in turn supplies the Rodenbach brewery, seen peeping through the trees.

The softness and delicacy of Bohemian lagers, and to a great extent those of Bavaria, are enhanced by the very low percentages of dissolved salts in the waters of those regions. The firmness of some Dortmunder lagers may be due to harder waters. Waters do differ greatly. The total salts in Pilsen's water amount to 30.8 parts per million. At the opposite extreme, the figure for Burton-upon-Trent is 1,226.

Among salts that often occur in water, calcium, sulphate and chloride are of the most positive interest to brewers. Calcium increases the extract from both malt and hops during mashing and boiling, reduces haze, and decreases colour. Sulphate enhances hop bitterness and dryness. Calcium sulphate in the water of Burton helped to shape pale ale as a style.

Chloride makes for a fuller texture and enhances sweetness. Chlorides are relatively high in London and Dublin, the original porter and stout capitals.

Herbs, spices and hops

Wine-makers once aromatized their product with herbs, spices and fruits. Some still do – using juniper berries, thistle and camomile flowers, and more exotic ingredients such as ginger, grains of paradise, quinine bark, coriander or orange peel – and call the result vermouth. Most of these aromatic ingredients, along with yarrow, rosemary and others, have also been used in beer, but the brewer's favourite is the leafy cone, sometimes known as the flower or blossom (technically, the strobile), of the hop vine, a member of the nettle family and first cousin to cannabis.

Hops and cannabis were both mentioned by Pliny in his *Natural History*. The ancients noted that the hop grew 'wild among the willows, like a wolf among sheep,' and it came to be known as *Humulus lupus* (*lupus* being Latin for wolf).

Hops have been used for a variety of purposes: their shoots can be eaten as a salad; their blossoms work as a sedative (in hop pillows); their resins and oils in shampoos and as a preservative in tanning. Recent research at the University of Minnesota has found that some components of hops may help the body get rid of poisons, pollutants and drugs.

When wine-makers switched from clay amphorae to wooden casks, they eventually discovered empirically that the fruity flavours of the grape no longer needed balancing with drier herbs and spices; the 'juices' in the oak would do the job instead. Some beers are aged in unlined oak, but most today are too light in flavour to stand up to the wood.

Herbs and spices can also in some instances act as preservatives. In this respect, the hop performs especially well, and that is probably one reason why it became the usual choice for brewers.

It is not clear when hops were first employed in beer. Although there is strong circumstantial evidence from the eighth century, the first definite reference is by the Benedictine nun Hildegarde (1098–1179), abbess of Rupertsberg, near Bingen, which is not far from Mainz, Germany. Her writings on natural history mentioned the use of hops and ash leaves in beer (and cannabis as a cure for headaches).

Most of the early references concern abbeys, and they arise from Bohemia, southern Germany, northern France and Flanders.

The use of hops in beer did not reach Britain until the 15th and 16th centuries, but a century later they were being grown for this purpose in the New Netherlands in America. They are now cultivated on a considerable scale in Australia and New Zealand and to a lesser extent in Japan and China.

In several parts of the world, adjoining swathes of countryside with progressively cooler climates cultivate wine grapes, apples, cherries, hops and barley. In

The cones or flowers of East Kent Goldings hops, rich in aromatic oils, resins and acids.

As powerful as the wolf? The hop has to be contained by a frame of strings suspended between poles. The shoots peep through the ground in winter, and reach 15 feet (4.5 metres) or more by autumn.

In winter, the reddish earth of Bohemia seems to be growing hop-poles. On the green hills of Catholic Bavaria, they are often seen silhouetted against the sky like looming crucifixes.

Europe, it is possible to map out a wine belt, followed in a northerly direction by cider, beer (where both hops and barley grow) and spirits (grain alone – and weather needing a 'warmer' drink).

Herbs and spices

Long before the word holistic was fashionable, this philosophy was evident in brewing in the Nordic region. The farmer-brewers of western Norway typically have a wooden cabin with a fire in the middle, over which they brew beer, bake crispbread and smoke meats. At the beginning of the new brewing and livestock-slaughtering season in October, I have been required to drink a juniper beer as an accompaniment to a sheep's head, within which the eyes are regarded as the delicacy.

The juniper is applied in holistic fashion, too. Branches bushy with twigs and berries are placed in the kettle, along with hops, as both a flavour and a preservative, but they are also used to filter the mash. The result is a beer full of malt and juniper flavours.

In commercial brewing, the use of herbs and spices other than the hop almost died out, but never quite. The Till brewing company, in the north of Sweden, made a beer lightly spiced with juniper, bog myrtle (another traditional ingredient, also known as sweet willow) and angelica until around the time it was taken over by Falken in 1989. The local brewery in

Thisted, Denmark, makes a beer with bog myrtle. Across the Baltic, a brewery in Gdansk, Poland, made a beer with rosehips until around 1910.

Even in America, I remember the now-defunct Schmidt brewery in Philadelphia making a juniper beer in the 1980s, albeit as a novelty. It was only in the 1950s and 1960s that some sizable British brewers stopped using ginger and licorice.

The Belgians, with their artisanal approach to brewing, and their gastronomic inclinations, never stopped employing herbs and spices. A conventional Belgian lager is unlikely to contain such ingredients, but many specialities do, and some are specifically identified as herb beer (*kruidenbier*).

Any such additions would contravene the German Beer Purity Law, although essence of woodruff is frequently added to a Berliner Weissbier in the glass. (Their logic is that the drinker should know what he is getting from the brewery, but can add anything he likes himself.)

With revivalist breweries such as Hoegaarden in Belgium and Anchor in the United States, and the brewpub and micro movement, beers using herbs and spices are now becoming much more widespread. From the new generation of brewers I have tasted several beers made with chili peppers, which dominate the flavour in a similar way to fruit such as cherries and raspberries.

Fruits, spices and herbs such as dried orange peels of various types, aniseed and coriander are still employed in speciality beers in some countries, and the use of such exotic ingredients is enjoying a considerable revival at the hands of new microbrewers and brewpubs. This selection is offered by Belgian herbalist Robert Meyskens in Quievrain, who supplies many brewers.

Hops

Samples of ground cumin seeds, fennel, juniper berries and thyme have all been used as comparison by specialists trying to monitor and identify the flavour characteristics of particular varieties of hop on behalf of the brewing industry. Most working brewers love hops, and would use at least twice as many of the flowers in each batch if the market researchers were not afraid of frightening the consumer.

The aromas and flowery, herbal bitterness of hops arise from resins and essential oils produced by glands at the base of the petals. The resins no doubt contribute the pine note that is one characteristic of the hop. Does this sound an odd flavour for a drink or food? Not to anyone who has ever eaten pine kernels or enjoyed retsina or balsamic vinegars (some of which are matured in juniper, ash or cherry wood).

The petals of the hops also contain tannins, which help to settle and preserve beer. One brewer who insists upon using hop blossoms (as opposed to a pelletized form, or an extract) told me he felt they better imparted those tannins. Others consider that the resins and oils are disturbed in the process of compacting hops into pellets. Some brewers argue that,

because pelletization removes the air from between the petals, pellets are less likely to oxidize. (Oxygen can give hops, and beer, flavours that are stale, cardboardy or cheesy.) Hop pellets are vacuum-packed, like coffee. Hop extracts (which look like green jam) have improved in recent years, but in my view still impart synthetic, essence-like flavours. Some brewers use elements of all three techniques.

Some varieties of hop are used primarily to confer aroma, others to impart dryness and bitterness. Several are employed for both purposes.

Varieties of hop

The most delicate, flowery aroma variety is the Saaz, named after the region around the town of Žatec, Bohemia, and classically used in Pilsner-style lagers.

Germany also has a famously delicate aroma hop, the Hallertau Mittelfrüh, traditionally grown in the Hallertau district of Bavaria, between Munich and Regensburg. Today, Hallertau hops are also grown in the Hersbruck region north of Nuremberg. Hersbruck additionally has its own variety of aroma hop, slightly more robust. Between the two is another growing region, at Spalt, south of Nuremberg. The

Spalt aroma hop is very complex in character. Tettnang, just across the Bavarian border into Baden-Württemberg, also has its own aroma variety, again delicately flowery. There are also newer hybrid varieties such as Hüller and the more bitter Perle.

Bittering varieties include the robust Northern Brewer and the sweeter Brewers' Gold, both originating from Britain.

Belgium grows Brewers' Gold, Record (a hybrid of Saaz and Northern Brewer) and several other non-native varieties. Where a variety is transplanted to another country or region, it will assume a slightly different character in its new home.

Britain's most famous varieties are Goldings and Fuggles, named after the farmers who selected and propagated them, in 1790 and 1875 respectively. Goldings have a rich, earthy, rounded aroma; Fuggles are less rounded, and are used both as an aroma and a bittering hop.

The United States' principal areas of cultivation are the Willamette Valley of Oregon, the Yakima Valley of Washington state, and the Snake River Valley of Idaho. Hops are also grown in British Columbia, Canada. European brewers are often critical of American hops as being too 'catty'; they are certainly different, and have their own character. American hops are very assertive in their pine, floral, fruity, citric characteristics. The classic bittering hop is the Cluster, and the aroma type the Cascade.

Australia long managed with only a bittering hop, a resiny variety called Pride of Ringwood, but is beginning to experiment with others. New Zealand has already won admirers for new varieties such as Sticklebract and Green Bullet.

The act of brewing

The 'juices' of the malt first meet the hop in the brew-kettle, where the two are boiled together. The boil is the actual act of brewing. Its duration varies, but one and a half hours is typical. Hops added at the beginning of the boil impart dryness and bitterness; those given at the end are more influential in aroma. If hop extract is used, there are no leaves to remove afterward. Pellets or flowers deposit leaves that must be taken out of the brew by a centrifugal whirlpool or a strainer called a 'hop back'. Some brewers add more flowers into the hop back so that the brew is strained through them. Others add further hops in muslin bags during maturation, or to the finished casks of beer. These procedures, known as 'dry-hopping', are intended to heighten the aroma. I believe dry-hopping also heightens flavour.

Units of bitterness

The ability of hops to impart dryness and bitterness can be measured in their content of acids. By a sum of this and the quantity used, a brewer can judge the likely bitterness of his beer according to an internationally agreed scale. This does not provide any information about subtleties of flavour, but it is a general guide to intensity. This also has to be judged against the gravity, maltiness and body of the beer. The fuller it is, the more hop is required simply to balance the sweetness of the malt.

The blandest of beers may have 10–15 units of bitterness. International brands tend to hover around 20. Around 35, a pleasant hop emphasis begins to emerge. Above 40, there is real hop character. Even the hoppiest products rarely exceed the 60s, although the American brewpub Buffalo Bill's, in Hayward, California, makes one of around 100, called Alimony Ale, 'the most bitter beer in America'.

Birra Perfetto is made by adding a dash of oregano to a pale ale. It is a product of the Pike Place brewery, in Seattle. The pungency of oregano melds with the earthy hop, spicy malt and fruity yeast.

Yeast

Like wine, bread, cheese, various pickles and sauces, and many other foods and drinks, beer depends upon yeast, a microorganism which as a single cell is invisible to the naked eye. The yeast consumes sugars and converts them into alcohol and carbon dioxide. Without it, wine would be grape juice and beer barley water.

The first wine-makers did not know that their work was made possible by the yeast on the skins of their grapes. Neither did beer-makers understand that their brew, when it was cooling, invited the attentions of airborne yeasts.

This method – spontaneous fermentation – is still used by brewers of porridge-like 'traditional beers' made from native grains, roots and saps in Asia, Africa and Latin America. No doubt the wooden tubs often used as fermenting vessels also harbour resident yeasts. In Mexico, where *pulque* is made from the juice of a cactus-like plant, I have seen orange-skins added to the mash. The producers must have discovered empirically that the skins carry wild yeasts.

A farmhouse brewer in western Norway showed me a wooden stirring stick that was something of an heirloom; it had been used and reused over decades, and perhaps centuries, in the course of which its tip had become home to an endlessly refreshed community of yeast cells. Early brewers must have thought such sticks had magic properties; a good stir, and the mash came to life and started producing alcohol. The farmhouse brewer liked to think his yeast dated from Viking times. I took a sample for analysis by a brewing scientist, who told me that it was 'extremely robust', and resembled none other that he had seen.

The lambic family

The oldest fermentation method used by commercial brewers in the developed world is the system employed by the most traditional makers of lambic, in the Zenne Valley of Belgium. They leave open their windows, so that the wild yeasts may settle on the cooling brew, and they feel that they achieve their best results on a cool autumn evening. Some also prefer not to disturb cobwebs and moulds on the walls and casks where their beer ferments. Within any given habitat, certain yeast strains will adapt best and emerge as the strongest. So long as the habitat is not changed, the pecking order of yeasts should remain the same. If there are changes, the beer might not ferment, or may run wild.

Wild yeasts, being barely domesticated or trained, are inefficient and undisciplined. They leave many sugars and volatile flavour compounds (esters) in the beer. This is why lambic beers are full of vinous, fruity, and sometimes phenolic, complexity.

Ales and wheat beers

During fermentation with wild yeasts, many cells will rise to the top of the vessel, forming a foamy head.

The last massive scientific advance in beer-making techniques, and probably the biggest ever, was Emil Hansen's work on the isolation and cultivation of single-cell, pure-culture yeasts at the Carlsberg brewery in Denmark in the late 1800s. Hansen finally 'tamed' yeast, and took the uncertainties out of brewing. This painting of Hansen in his laboratory was made around the turn of the century. The old lab is preserved for the sake of history.

Although early brewers did not know this head was made up of yeast cells, they observed that residual foam from one batch would help start the fermentation of the next. By skimming this foam and using it as a starter, they began to select what are now known as top-fermenting or ale strains of yeast, taxonomically identified as *Saccharomyces cerevisiae*. All true ales, and most wheat beers, are fermented with variations on this type of yeast.

Top-fermenting cultures represent an intermediate stage in the history of yeast-selection by brewers. They are not totally 'efficient', in that they still leave behind certain sugars and esters; these create the fruity complexity always found in a true ale, and sometimes a buttery sweetness.

If the yeast is to work in this way, it requires a temperate environment. The top-fermentation method evolved before the development of artificial refrigeration, and even today temperature control is used only to avoid extremes. The yeast is pitched into the vessels at an ambient temperature (around 15°C/59°F) and the heat created by fermentation may take it as high as 25°C/77°F.

Traditionalist ale brewers use open fermenters, in which the yeast can still be skimmed from above. Modernists have tall, cylindrical vessels, in which the yeast learns to compact in the conical base, whence it is collected. As its behaviour changes, the yeast will eventually cease to produce the typical ale flavours;

after four or five batches, the brewer will propagate more yeast from his original source to ensure that the character is not lost.

Ale spends at most a week in primary fermentation. After this, the bulk of the yeast will be removed and the brew may have a week or two of secondary fermentation, either at an ambient temperature or in a cooled vessel, or first one and then the other. During this period, some harsh flavours will volatilize, carbonation develop, and the remaining yeast settle. Warm conditioning will further develop the complex of fruity flavours; cold maturation will make the beer cleaner and rounder. Sometimes a priming of sugar and an extra dosage of yeast is added prior to the maturation, whether it is to be in cask or bottle, to stimulate secondary fermentation and therefore encourage natural carbonation.

Lagers

Brewers in the Munich area understood in the 1400s that a stock of beer stored in icy caves in the foothills of the Alps would remain good through the warm Bavarian summer, but they did not know why. One reason was that the cold was not a welcoming environment for additional wild yeasts. Another was that the yeast already in the vessel eventually sank to the bottom, where it could not interbreed with intruders. This storage (*Lagerung* in German) empirically selected bottom-fermenting yeasts.

Fermenting beer is aroused to a fury by the living organism yeast. It swirls, foams and develops its own heat. Even with modern yeasts, the process can be somewhat unpredictable. The brewer keeps a practised eye on the foam as it progresses through rocky, flowery, creamy and almost cappucino-like stages. Adjustments to times and temperatures may be necessary to prevent it running wild. He measures attenuation of sugars with a floating instrument called a saccharometer or hydrometer.

This was a beginning to the taming of the yeast, but that could not be completed until artificial refrigeration was developed through the work of the German Carl von Linde (1842–1934) and the Scot William Kelvin (1824–1907). Nor until brewers realized that yeast was not simply a magic foam (sometimes known to them as 'God is Good') but a mass of living cells. This understanding came gradually, with the development of the microscope, and its use in research by scientists from the Dutchman Anton van Leeuwenhoek (1632–1723) to the Frenchman Louis Pasteur (1822–95). Pasteur advised several Continental European brewers and the British company Whitbread. In the head brewer's office at the monastery of Chimay, I once noticed, crowded among books on the shelves, an 1876 edition of Pasteur's *Etudes sur la Bière*.

During the early 1800s, some lager-brewers in Bavaria began to practice bottom-fermentation more methodically. Early work during that period is credited to a monk named Benno Scharl, at a small brewery near Munich, around 1810, and then to Gabriel Sedlmayr the Younger, at the Spaten brewery in the city. One of Sedlmayr's students was Jacob Christian Jacobsen, who founded Carlsberg in Copenhagen, Denmark, in 1845. A sample of the Spaten yeast was taken to Copenhagen by Jacobsen, who is said to have kept the container cool by shielding it under his stovepipe hat during the 600-mile journey. At Carlsberg, a single-cell, pure-culture yeast was finally isolated in 1883 by a young brewery scientist called Emil Hansen. Bottom-fermenting, or lager, yeast is still widely known as *Saccharomyces carlsbergensis*, although scientists now classify it as uvarum.

Bottom-fermenting yeasts work at colder temperatures than ale yeasts, and more slowly, nibbling away until they have eaten more sugars, leaving the beer more attenuated, potentially drier, cleaner and rounder, with less obvious fruity characteristics, and often with a faintly sulphury note reminiscent of new-mown hay. Knowledgable drinkers who enjoy a 'traditional lager' character look for this.

Classically, primary fermentation is at 5–9°C/41–48°F, for as long as two weeks, although many breweries use slightly warmer temperatures. Lagering will be at close to 0°C/32°F. Some lager brewers mature their beers for only two or three weeks, but four to six is more respectable, and three months not unknown. The odd very strong lager may be matured for the best part of a year.

Sometimes a small proportion of a partly fermented brew is added during lagering to stimulate secondary fermentation. This is known as *kräusening*, and imparts a crisp, spritzy character.

The importance of yeast

Brewers dread more than anything the moment when their yeast might change in character for no obvious reason, mutate, or become infected by another microorganism. Most keep their breweries hospital-clean for that reason, but disasters still happen, causing the beer to change in taste, become vinegary or develop other unpleasant characteristics. If this happens, everything in the vessels has to be dumped, and the brewery sterilized from head to toe. I have heard

The turn-of-the-century brewhouse at Carlsberg in Copenhagen evidences the prosperity and pride brought by the work of Jacobsen and Hansen.

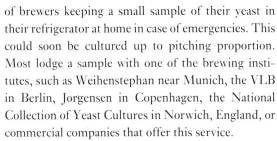

Skimming the yeast off top-fermenting beer in Belgium. The foam of yeast cells rises to the top and stays there until it is removed. Lager yeasts sink.

Farmhouse brewery, bakery and smokery operated by two sisters near Voss, Norway. The yeast used has thus far not revealed the secret of its distant origins.

of brewers keeping a small sample of their yeast in their refrigerator at home in case of emergencies. This could soon be cultured up to pitching proportion. Most lodge a sample with one of the brewing institutes, such as Weihenstephan near Munich, the VLB in Berlin, Jorgensen in Copenhagen, the National Collection of Yeast Cultures in Norwich, England, or commercial companies that offer this service.

In the days before such arrangements existed, a brewery that had yeast problems would obtain a fresh sample, as a favour, from a nearby competitor. This led to some breweries becoming famous as commercial suppliers of proven, resilient yeast strains. Many lager-breweries use a yeast culture originating from Hürlimann of Switzerland. Several North American microbreweries use a Whitbread ale yeast, while others have Labatt's ale yeast from Canada.

If a brewer changes his yeast strain today, he will not do it casually. If his yeast performs well, and has been in the brewery for decades, he will be a happy man. This is because, in recent years, brewers have finally come to understand just how significant is their yeast strain in giving their beer its own house character. The yeast's contribution to sweetness, dryness, texture, fruity and grassy notes, is subtle but as complex and individualistic as a fingerprint.

Yeast and strength

In some countries, brewers label their beer with a figure indicating the measure of its 'original gravity', rather than its alcoholic strength. This practice arose when brewers knew how to measure the gravity (the density of malt and other sugars used), but could not be sure what proportion of this the yeast would consume and turn into alcohol during fermentation (this is known as the extent of attenuation). Today, the nature of yeasts, and the factors that influence their performance, are better understood.

The measure of original sugars best known outside the drinks industry is Brix, which is applied to wine grapes. This was based on work in the brewing industry in 1843 by the Bohemian Carl Joseph Napoleon Balling. The system was later perfected by Dr Fritz Plato for a commission in imperial Germany.

Other scales are used in different countries. In areas of British influence, a system based on a factor of 1000 is used. The Balling or Plato figure multiplied by four will approximate with the last two figures of British original gravity. For example, a typical beer of 12 Plato has a British 'o g' of 1048. These last two figures provide a general idea of alcohol by volume. The beer will probably have around 4.8 percent, but that can vary depending upon the extent of attenuation.

Alcohol by volume is marked on labels in the European Community and elsewhere. In the United States, where strength is not currently indicated, regulations deal in alcohol by weight. Because alcohol is lighter than water, this produces lower figures. A beer marked 4 percent in Europe or Canada is deemed 3.2 percent in the United States, not because it is lower in alcohol, but because the first measure is according to volume and the second by weight.

A beer-lover's calendar

Just as the wine-maker's year has its seasons, so does the brewer's. Barley and hops are harvested in the autumn, and were traditionally turned into beer throughout the winter. Until the invention of refrigeration, there was no brewing during summer. This suited farmer-brewers, who were busy on the land. When the darker days came, they could turn to producing beer again.

Seasonal traditions still influence the styles of beer available. So does the weather: lighter-bodied, more quenching beers best suit the summer; heavier, sustaining ones warm the winter.

Here, with a few light-hearted suggestions, is a beer-lover's calendar of appropriate brews and events, or at least some of the best-known.

JANUARY
Some Slavic countries make strong porters for winter. German brewers often introduce a Doppelbock or a Dunkelweizen at this time. The Belgians are especially fond of extra-strong Scottish-style ales in the New Year. The British have a variety of strong ales, often dark, for the colder months; some are described as 'winter warmers'. In North America, spiced seasonal ales are popular.

FEBRUARY
St Valentine's Day demands something romantic. The prettiest and most delicate of beers are the Belgian raspberry brews known as frambozen or framboise. Beers containing honey – supposedly an aphrodisiac – also have their moment. It's a little early for Belgium's honey-primed Boskeun ('Easter Bunny' beer), but in Britain, Ridley's of Chelmsford, Essex, has on occasion produced a Honey Mead Ale, and the tiny Enville brewery,

near Stourbridge in the West Midlands, has an example. In North America, Grant's of Yakima, Washington, puts honey into its Imperial Stout, and several micros and brewpubs have been known to use the nectar; the Calistoga brewpub in California even has a Honey Pilsner.

February usually sees the pre-Lenten Fasching, Carnival or Mardi Gras in Roman Catholic – and beery – European cities such as Munich, Cologne and Maastricht. Revellers in less obviously beery places can still find a worthwhile brew. Look out for Abita's Mardi Gras Bock in New Orleans.

MARCH
Once the end of the brewing season, signalled by strong beers meant to last the summer. Some Bavarian breweries make a Märzenbier and several French ones have a bière de mars. The Munich brewery Paulaner usually launches its new season's Salvator in mid-March. The middle of the month also sees a 'Blessing of the

Bock' festival organized by the Lakefront Brewery in Milwaukee. Hop shoots are in season, and especially celebrated in Belgium (see page 258). Saint Patrick's Day (the 17th) demands plain porter or dry stout, but not cheap beer coloured green with food dye.

APRIL
The Munich brewery Hofbräuhaus launches its 'May' Bock, usually on the Wednesday of the last week. At the end of April at the opposite corner of Europe, the bars of Tromsø, Norway, start selling seagulls' eggs with the local Mack beer. The brew is a conventional golden lager, with a hint of grassy graininess; the eggs, which are boiled, taste nutty, sometimes with a suggestion of seaweed.

MAY
The first sees the launch of Maibock in Einbeck, Germany, though with no great ceremony. This month is the height of the asparagus season, celebrated throughout northern France, southern Germany and Switzerland. In the New World, Cinco de Mayo is the most important of Mexico's various national days; bring out the Negra Modelo or Dos Equis.

JUNE

The summer months are full of village celebrations in Bavaria and the Rhineland, always with a beer tent and often with a Festbier. This is also the season for refreshing wheat beers, and for sharply sour, quenching specialities in Belgium.

JULY

Raise a glass of an American brew on the fourth (Independence Day) and a French one on the 14th (Bastille Day). In Britain, the Campaign for Real Ale takes up the independence theme to promote privately owned breweries. In San Francisco a major festival of American and imported beers is held by the TV station KQED, usually on the second Saturday. The city of Portland, Oregon, hosts America's biggest regional beer festival, usually on the last weekend.

AUGUST

Early in the month, the Great British Beer Festival, with several hundred cask-conditioned British ales under one roof, is organized by the Campaign for Real Ale. Often held in London, but sometimes in other cities. It's the season for a harvest mild such as Fuller's Hock.

SEPTEMBER

Every third year, a beer and hop festival is held at Poperinge, near Ypres, Belgium. From mid-September, Munich has its Oktoberfest, reaching its finale on the first weekend of the new month. This month or next usually sees a weekend festival of speciality beers (on a different theme each year) in Antwerp, Belgium, organized by the Objective Beer-Tasters (De Objectieve Bierproevers).

OCTOBER

The Great American Beer Festival is organized by the Association of Brewers. Usually the first weekend of the month, in Denver, Colorado.

For Hallowe'en, try the French lager Bière du Demon, the Belgian ale Duvel ('devil'), the English bitter Pendle Witches' Brew (from Moorhouse's in Lancashire), or Blackened Voodoo lager (from New Orleans).

NOVEMBER

Festival of Bock beers organized by the Dutch consumerist group PINT, usually in Amsterdam, on the first or second weekend. In London, a small celebration of old ales is held at the White Horse pub, Parson's Green, usually on the last weekend. Winter beers begin to appear, some timed for Thanksgiving, on the fourth Thursday. Try a Vienna lager with the turkey, a brown ale with the pecan pie.

DECEMBER

Samichlaus ('Santa Claus') beer, from Hürlimann, of Zurich, Switzerland, becomes available on 6 December. At a post office at Rovaniemi, on the Arctic Circle, Father Christmas answers letters from children worldwide. He told me that he drinks the Yule beer (a malty, amber lager) of the nearby Lapin Kulta brewery. With English Christmas pudding, there is nothing like an imperial stout.

THE LAMBIC FAMILY

It is the use of wild yeasts that gives such a vinous aroma and palate (reminiscent of fino sherry, or vermouth) to the lambic family of beers. No other style of beer in the developed world is intentionally made with wild strains as the principal yeasts, and it is this procedure, where fermentation occurs spontaneously, that defines a lambic. All beer – and wine – was once made in this way, with the wild yeasts producing a slightly different result each time.

Its definition also insists that lambic be made with a proportion of at least 30 percent raw wheat, the rest of the grist being malted barley.

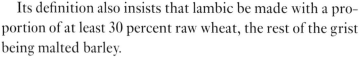

These beers were originally the local brews in the mainly Flemish valley of the small River Zenne (spelled with an initial 'S' in French), to either side of the city of Brussels, Belgium. The surviving producers in this area, ten or a dozen at the most, are all on the west side of Brussels, in a district known as Payottenland.

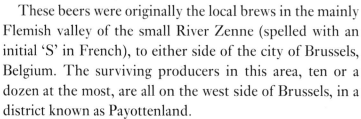

Beers of the lambic family became the dominant local style of Brussels itself from the 1750s to World War I, and they are still the speciality of some cafés there. They are now widely known elsewhere in Belgium, and to some extent in the bordering nations of the Netherlands and France. Only recently have they become available in countries further afield, in some of which they have developed a small but devoted following.

Efforts are being made to establish a European Community *appellation contrôlée* that would restrict the term lambic to brewers working with wild yeasts in the traditional area. One brewer in France (Brasserie du Bobtail, at St

Séverin, in the Perigord) and one in Britain (All Saints, in Stamford, Lincolnshire) have in recent years experimented with spontaneous fermentation.

In its basic form, lambic is almost still, something between a fino sherry and a hard cider. This version is sold in some cafés in the Zenne Valley, but even there is not always easy to find. A more widely available member of the lambic family is gueuze (spellings vary). This is a naturally carbonated, champagne-like blend of young and old lambic beers. A lambic sweetened with candy sugar is known as a faro. A diluted version of this was called mars. It vanished some decades ago, but may well reappear as traditions are revived.

Among the immense complex of flavours to be found in many of the lambic family is one reminiscent of rhubarb. This flavour is created in fermentation; rhubarb is not added to lambic (although it is an ingredient of some vermouths – which may explain that note). Other fruits often are added, especially cherries or raspberries. In Belgium, if a lambic is used as the base for a fruit beer, this will be indicated on the label. A kriek lambic is made with cherries, a frambozen (or framboise) lambic with raspberries.

Because lambics are the base for many of the classic fruit beers, the two elements are discussed together in this section of the book. It should be noted, however, that not all fruit beers are lambics. In Belgium, the term lambic is not used if another style of brew is the base for a fruit beer. Many fit into this category; among Belgium's best-known kriek and frambozen beers are those from Liefmans, for example, both based on a brown ale. Liefmans therefore does not describe these as lambics – they are not. The confusion in terminology has arisen as fruit beers have become popular in the English-speaking world. Lambic is not the base for the Boston Beer Company's cranberry brew, for example, and in that instance the use of the term on the label results from a misunderstanding.

Lambics are an esoteric speciality but, like other wheat beers and many of the top-fermenting styles, they have an individuality that is beginning to attract a new generation of beer-lovers.

Lambic

To sample lambic is not only to encounter one of the world's most complex drinks, it is also to experience a taste of life 400 years ago. No other commercially brewed beer can trace its history back so far. Nor, in its production process, has any changed so little.

Lambic is the beer the lusty villagers were drinking in the paintings of Bruegel. He depicted stoneware pitchers like those still used today, pouring the local beer of that same, onion-skin, colour. I have sat in a café in the countryside near the town of Lembeek, been fetched a lambic in a crock from the cellar, and enjoyed it with local people whose faces seem to have changed not a whisker from those of their forebears as portrayed by Bruegel.

The town of Lembeek

Although no one is sure of its derivation, the name of this family of beers (also spelled lambiek) seems most likely to be a corruption of Lembeek, one of the producing towns. Today, it has only one brewery, but it was historically an important centre of production. It had its own Guild of Brewers as early as the 1400s.

Unblended lambic is hard to find, though it is offered by some cafés in the producing region. This is an ancient, elemental style of beer. To the drinker used to more conventional styles, lambic scarcely seems like a beer, with its shock of earthy aromas, its profound stillness and tartness. Think of it as the beer world's counterpart to a fino sherry or dry vermouth. Serve it with an equally challenging sharp cheese.

Even today, the townspeople make an annual pilgrimage (on Easter Monday) to the Celtic fort of Saint Veronus, adopted as patron saint of lambic brewers.

Lembeek is a town of only 4,000 people, but its easily defended site, perched on a hill and moated by a bend in the River Zenne, made it an important border point between the old duchies of Brabant and Hainaut. For a time, it was an independent 'city state'.

During its period of independence, Lembeek granted its farmers the unusual right to combine brewing and distilling (of genever gin). A farmer would have used the same part of his premises for both activities. Another theory about the name lambic is that the occupying Spanish, during their rule in the 1500s and 1600s, called such premises simply a distillery, an *alembic*. There are several further theories, and I doubt anyone will ever be sure.

Because of its political position, Lembeek was a commercial centre in the agricultural valley that fed and watered Brussels. When brewing spread beyond village level, the lambic beers of the valley began to establish themselves as the local style of the big city.

Lembeek's importance declined with a series of restrictions on distilled spirits, culminating in tough laws in the early 1900s, at a time when the whole of the developed world was going through a temperance phase. This was doubly difficult for Lembeek, because frustrated spirit drinkers did not turn to lambic beers, whose spontaneous fermentations make for modest alcohol contents (typically 4–4.8 percent by weight, 5–6 by volume). Instead, the restrictions on

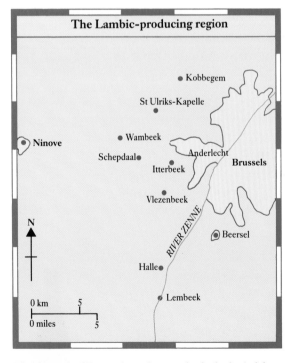

The sprawl of Brussels embraces Anderlecht (with a couple of lambic breweries). The encircling towns and villages comprise Payottenland.

Of the three Bruegels, it was Pieter the Elder (1525–69) who seems to have dipped his brushes in lambic beer. On the left is a detail from his painting *The Wedding Feast*. Bruegel's vivid depictions of pleasure and its supposed price have made him a Flemish national hero. Beery scenes were painted by several Flemish masters, including the aptly named Adriaen Brouwer or 'Brewer', (1605–38).

spirits popularized stronger styles of beer such as Trappist and Scotch ales. Soon afterward, Pilsner-style beers were introduced in Belgium.

In the villages of Payottenland, and in several famous cafés of Brussels, beers of the lambic family remain as a speciality. There were also lambic breweries to the east of Brussels; they faded in the 1960s, but the lambic family is remembered in the gueuze served at the pavement cafés in the one-street village of Jezus-Eik. This village, 'Jesus Oak', is on the edge of the forest of Soignes, a popular spot for a Sunday afternoon stroll.

The production process

The process starts at a conventional enough gravity, typically 11.75–13.5 Plato (1047–54). Why is unmalted wheat used, as it is in some other Belgian specialities? Wheat grows in the area, so it is a natural choice. Perhaps originally it was unmalted to save time and cost. The saving may have been significant to farmer-brewers. The production of lambic is the best surviving example of commercial brewing as an agricultural industry. Perhaps the producers learned empirically that the wheat used need not be malted so long as the barley is (the barley produces sufficient enzymes for fermentation). Perhaps the raw wheat was their own and the barley bought from maltsters.

The unmalted grains produce a milky-white mash, rather than the clear, amber liquid run off in a more orthodox brewery. The mash tuns are often open and made from cast-iron, as in many artisanal breweries in Belgium. The turbid wort requires a very long boil; three hours or more is not uncommon.

The hopping is unusual, too. Traditionally, lambic is brewed with aged hops. Some lambic-makers buy old stocks of excess hops from merchants and other brewers, but economy is not their motivation. This being such an old method of brewing, the hops are employed as a preservative. I know of no other commercially brewed beer in which this is still their principal role. In this function, large quantities are required, and the aging, typically of around three years, reduces their flavour and prevents them from intruding on the palate. Assertive hop flavours do not combine well with the tartness of wheat beers or the intentionally sour notes in some very old styles.

After the boil comes the most remarkable feature, the one central to lambic brewing. The brew is run into a 'cool ship', an open vessel like a shallow swimming pool made of copper. This is in the attic of the brewery. The windows are left open, and there may be the odd slate missing from the roof. As the brew cools overnight, it is visited by wild yeasts.

Even a brewer who bends the rules by pitching in a

little cultured yeast (top-fermenting) may still leave his beer to spend more than three years undergoing a chain reaction of fermentations in wooden barrels. Many of these barrels were made in Portugal, Spain or France. They were either discarded in the 1920s, when the *bodegas* or châteaux began to use stainless steel, or they were used to transport wines to Belgium. Once, all beers were fermented in wooden barrels. Today, lambic is the only style in which this is still the normal procedure.

There are 70-odd microorganisms at work in the valley's breweries, two of which have been given taxonomic names identified with the area: *lambicus* and *bruxellensis*. These are both *Brettanomyces*, the type of yeast that is said to give leathery or 'horse blanket' aroma and flavours. There are also four oxidative yeasts not unlike the *flor* which appears on sherry. Several styles of sherry seem to be echoed in a number of different beers, but it is more than chance that compares finos with lambics.

The winy dryness of the two drinks lends them to similar purposes. In Spain, especially Andalusia, I have been served lightly chilled fino sherry with *tapas*, a snack often featuring local seafood. In Belgium, it would have been a lambic or gueuze with cheeses such as the salty Brusselsekaas, the fresh-curd Plattekaas or the acidic Pottekaas with silverskin onions, radishes, sausages and brown bread.

The brewers

Lambic of less than one summer in the cask may be served as 'young' or *vos* ('foxy'), the latter indicating its hazy, rusty colour. This can be quite sharp and lactic. 'Old' lambic, of two or three summers or more, becomes clearer, pinkish, and more complex.

Because breweries are apt to release vintages when they feel so inclined, and sometimes at more than one age, it is difficult to be precise about the numbers available. In recent years, I have found around a dozen on the market at any one time.

In metropolitan Brussels, not far from the Midi railway station, the western district of Anderlecht has two lambic breweries. One, making a classic lambic in a very tart style, is the tiny Cantillon, in Rue Gheude (see page 37). In the same district, at 58–60 Rue Delaunoy, is a much larger, but still traditional, lambic brewery owned by Vandenstock, now controlled by Interbrew. After some years of a low profile, this brewery is being opened to the public (Tel: 02-522 19 35). It is to be hoped that the excellent lambics produced here will eventually be made available to the consumer in their natural form, but at present they are blended with lesser beers to make the sweetish, mass-market Belle Vue gueuze and fruit variations.

The same company owns the proud old lambic brewery De Neve, of Schepdaal, but there is doubt about its future. De Neve made a crisp, clean, slightly

In Brussels and the nearby countryside of Payottenland, it is not always easy to spot the small River Zenne, but there are rustic glimpses. Here, it flows near the town of Lembeek, probably the ancestral home of lambic beer. The stone tower provides a reminder of this town's history as a meeting point between two duchies. Of such encounters are great drinks and foods born.

The café De Drie Fonteinen blends its own gueuze – served here with a tangy beer snack.

Frank Boon knows that to brush away cobwebs would be to disturb the all-important wild yeasts.

citric-tasting lambic, and for a time supplied casks to various negociants, and to cafés, for maturation. For the moment, there is talk of Vandenstock making brews for De Neve to mature.

Traditionally, negociants ordered either wort or beer to their specification, and did their own maturation and blending. The only freestanding blender left seems to be Hanssens of Dworp, although at least one café, De Drie Fonteinen (The Three Fountains) in Beersel, makes its own kriek and gueuze. This tradition of negociants was another manifestation of lambic as a meeting point of beer and wine cultures.

Because lambic is a rustic product, offering low volumes, the (relatively) bigger producers are all concentrating on blending gueuzes and fruit beers. These are generally sweetened to make them more accessible to an audience weaned on soft drinks.

Kronenbourg, of France, owns Alken-Maes, the other giant of Belgian brewing. Alken-Maes acquired Schepdaal's other producer, Eylenbosch, famous for its nutty lambic, but has not brewed there for some years. Alken-Maes also controls the Kobbegem brewery De Keersmaeker, whose hyssop-tasting pure lambic is difficult to find, although its Mort Subite gueuze and fruit beers are widely available.

Similarly elusive are the delicate, complex, lightly acidic pure lambic from Timmermans of Itterbeek, and the more sherry-like example from Lindemans of Vlezenbeek.

In Lembeek itself, the tradition is being not only protected but also fostered by Frank Boon (see page 37). His pure lambic is perfumed and fruity, almost

reminiscent in aroma of lemon skins. In Halle, the Vander Linden brewery has a tart lambic with some ale-like notes. There is an ale-like character, too, to Vandervelden's lambic, brewed in Beersel. It also has some pine notes. In Wambeek, the De Troch brewery includes in its range a traditional lambic, fairly full-bodied and dry. A very intense example is made by Girardin, at St Ulriks-Kapelle (see page 38) and the same product is available as a house lambic from the merchant Wets, in St Genesius-Rode.

Strictly local

Payottenland is in the province of Brabant. Immediately beyond it lies East Flanders, where no one produces anything under the name of lambic or gueuze. Curiously, the province beyond, West Flanders, has two breweries whose ranges include beers described as gueuze (see page 42). Presumably they buy a proportion of lambic and blend it into a more conventional beer, or they have cultured up a yeast with some of the typical characteristics.

The term lambic should be restricted to the Zenne Valley, but it is not. Experimental lambics have been made in other parts of Belgium, notably as part of research by the University of Leuven. Spontaneous fermentation has been achieved, but the beers have not developed the same characteristics as those made in the Zenne Valley. It is not that the valley really has a magic, just that the microbiological climate of every region is different. Furthermore, the microbiology of the breweries has been built by the accretion of decades, if not centuries.

The proportion of wheat to be used in lambic, and the employment of spontaneous fermentation, are laid down in a Royal Decree of 1965. Both lambic and gueuze are protected as exclusively Belgian terms under a European Community ordinance of 1992 on regional products. The Confederation of Belgian Brewers talked with the relevant authorities in Japan to prevent a 'lambic' being brewed there, and may try to stop the term being used in the United States.

In the Netherlands in the mid-1980s, a beer very reminiscent of a lambic was made at Gulpen, which adjoins the city of Maastricht. The Gulpener brewery, better known for its Pilsner-style lager, decided to revive an old Maastricht style that had vanished in the 1920s or '30s.

The brewery made a mash, gave it a primary fermentation, then took it to an undisclosed 'special place' (in the words of the senior manager who told me about it), and exposed it to the atmosphere. Lactobacilli and *Brettanomyces*, and perhaps other organisms, entered the wort, which was then given 14–16 months' secondary fermentation in wooden barrels.

After three years of experimenting with secondary fermentations, with a view to developing the right mix of cultures and persuading them to take up residence, the brewers were satisfied. The beer was thoroughly filtered, then blended 25:75 with Gulpener's dark lager. The two flavours, sour and sweet, combined beautifully in the bottle, and the product was released as Mestreechs Aajt. Some beer-lovers in the Netherlands felt that I overrated this beer, but I regarded it as being not only a tasty summer quencher but also, at the time, a much-needed contribution to tradition and variety in Dutch brewing.

The brewery continued to make Mestreechs Aajt for some years, but not long enough for it to benefit from the city's fame as host to the controversial political negotiations in 1991. By then, the brewery had decided it was too much trouble, and arranged for its production at the Belle Vue brewery in Belgium.

In 1992, a company in Britain began to experiment with the production of fruit beers fermented with cultures from a brewery in the lambic region of Belgium. The All Saints brewery in the historic town of Stamford, Lincolnshire, was founded in 1825, rebuilt in 1876 and finally closed in the 1970s, when it was acquired by Samuel Smith's. With its wooden mash tun and leather pulleys, it became a museum of brewing, until its antiquity suggested it for a new role as a home for rambling yeasts.

Inside the Boon brewery ... the belt-driven machine in the background is the mill that cracks the wheat and barley malt to expose the grains. They are then funnelled into the mash tun.

The grains are made into an infusion, or mash, in hot water in this tun. In the centre is a mechanical stirrer or rake. In artisanal breweries such as the one shown here, the mash tun is sometimes made of wood or cast-iron, and is open at the top. In more modern establishments it is usually a closed vessel of copper or stainless steel, resembling a brew-kettle.

Lambic producers

Many Belgian brewers, and even more blenders, sell versions of lambic, gueuze and the fruit variations. From those producers who make authentic lambic using traditional methods, I have profiled three whose beers I have found especially memorable.

BOON
Brouwerij Frank Boon, 65 Fontein Straat, 1520 Lembeek, Belgium Tel: (02) 356 66 44

The sparkling version deserves a champagne bottle.

Like every other Belgian, Frank Boon (pronounced as in 'bone' or, for the wine-lover, Beaune) was born with family connections in the brewing industry. At college, he ran a student bar, and he eventually found himself in the wholesale beer business, then blending lambics, and finally brewing them as well.

While many lambic-brewers' children seek jobs with faster, richer returns, less musty surroundings and more obvious glamour, Boon came into the industry as a young outsider, and has tried hard to breathe new life into it. When local breweries and blenders closed, such as Van Malder or Mosselmans, he bought their casks. When he had no more beer to blend, he bought stocks from Girardin and Lindemans.

In the world of lambic, Boon's inspiration was René De Vits, a veteran producer. De Vits blended lambic beers on a site in Lembeek that had accommodated a farmhouse brewery and distillery as far back as 1680. His buildings dated from 1810, and he lived in the brewery's former café and beer-and-grocery shop.

When De Vits retired in 1977, Boon acquired the brewery.

I met the inspirational Mr De Vits in 1986, and he was pottering about his house still wearing the leather apron of the brewer. That year, Frank Boon moved out of the former De Vits brewery into more spacious premises, formerly an iron foundry, close to the River Zenne.

Boon sells unblended Lambic, and makes Faro, Geuze (his spelling) Kriek and Framboise. The Geuze has a good, well-rounded, earthy, 'dry sherry' character, and he blends his best lambics in a range subtitled Mariage Parfait. His individualistic 'double' faro, Pertotale (4.8 percent alcohol by weight, 6 by volume), is a minor classic. It has a soft body and a full palate, with both lambic and ale-like flavours, is sweetened with candy sugar, hopped with Styrian Goldings and Saaz, and spiced with Curaçao orange peel and gentian. It is bottled and pasteurized.

His Lembeek's 2% is the extreme example of a beer that is low in alcohol but full of flavour, based on an extinct branch of the lambic family, the mars beers. It is made from a mash of 9.5–10 Plato (1038–40), containing 15 percent raw wheat and 85 percent malted barley. Three strains of yeast are cultured up from the lambic galleries, but fermentation is in stainless steel vessels. The beer is spiced, and has suggestions of lemon and ginger. Its alcohol content is 1.6 percent by weight, 2 by volume, the latter figure giving the beer its name. It is marketed by Boon's partners in the venture, the Palm ale brewery, best known for its Speciale Palm, the biggest-selling ale in Belgium (see page 115).

CANTILLON
Brasserie Cantillon, 56 Rue Gheude, Anderlecht, 1070 Brussels, Belgium Tel: (02) 521 49 28

Cantillon's Jean-Pierre Van Roy guards his brew-kettle.

In a small street, and looking from the outside more like a garage, this little brewery also bills itself as a working museum. The Cantillon family were brewers in Lembeek from the 1700s. In 1900, they came to the big city, initially as lambic merchants. In 1937, they started to brew. Since 1970, the brewery has been run by Jean-Pierre Van Roy, a member of the family who is an intensely proud and assertive propagandist for his products.

With its whitewashed brewhouse, its wood-clad, cast-iron mash tun and copper kettle, Cantillon is a classic example of a lambic brewery. Most are very similar. Its open cooler, a shallow copper vessel some five or six yards long, perhaps four wide and less than a foot deep, is in the gable of the roof, in the traditional fashion. There are slatted ventilators in the roof, and the odd missing tile. In its urban location, Cantillon fringes the Zenne Valley, and seems to attract the appropriate wild yeasts. Or perhaps the microorganisms resident in the building, and especially on the casks, are more important.

There are stone floors and wooden ceilings in the dusty galleries where several hundred barrels bubble, sigh or sleep: 'Brussels tuns' of 250 litres, 'pipes' of 650 litres, and various larger barrels known as *foudre* (the name derives from thunder).

The brewery is unusual in that it

occasionally bottles a lambic in its unblended, still form. Typically, these have three years in the wood and have an astonishingly light, clean dryness after a further 12 months in the bottle.

Some competitors argue that Cantillon's beers are too acidic and dry. 'Sweet lambic doesn't exist,' Van Roy once told me, railing against brewers who add sugar or saccharin.

To my palate, his beers have an almost creamy smoothness, before a dry, sharp, fruity finish. They are beers of great complexity. Van Roy remembers his family having made framboise in the 1950s, and he did much to promote the style in the early 1980s. He has even added Muscat grapes (from Hoeilaart-Overijse, east of Brussels) to make a Druivenlambik, although I find that the fruit's flavour seems largely to be lost in the subsequent fermentation. One of his classics is the superbly aromatic, smooth, delicate, dry Rosé de Gambrinus, made from 75 percent raspberries, 25 percent cherries, and a dash of vanilla. In this instance, there is a wonderful late efflorescence of raspberry character.

Although Cantillon produces only from mid-October to May, the 'brewery museum' is open all year to visitors and for the sale of beer, much of it in champagne bottles. I once declared a case as beer on leaving Belgium and entering Germany. 'Nobody brings beer to Germany,' said the customs man, outraged. When he saw the bottles, his tone changed: 'Oh, that's okay…this stuff isn't beer, it's wine.'

GIRARDIN

Brouwerij Girardin, 10 Lindenberg, 1744 St Ulriks-Kapelle, Belgium
Tel: (02) 452 64 19

Louis Girardin and his sons Paul and Jan grow wheat and use it to produce their own lambic beers in a classic farmhouse brewery.

Like many farmhouse producers, especially in the lambic region, they have bricked-in kettles, fired by direct flame (in their case, gas), although they are gradually installing a more conventional, German-designed small brewhouse. They still use the open-cooler method, and have wooden casks as fermenters. A cylindro-conical fermenter makes a small proportion of the beer.

Girardin's beers (unblended lambic, classic gueuze and kriek) are big and firm in body, fruity and dry, with the attack of a good Brie cheese.

OTHER PRODUCERS OF UNBLENDED LAMBIC

De Keersmaeker (Mort Subite), *1 Brussel Straat, 1703 Kobbegem, Belgium*
Tel: (02) 452 47 47

De Neve, *52 Isabella Straat, 1750 Schepdaal, Belgium*
Tel: (02) 569 09 02

De Troch, *20 Lange Straat, 1741 Wambeek, Belgium*
Tel: (02) 582 10 27

Lindemans, *257 Lenniksebaan, 1712 Vlezenbeek, Belgium*
Tel: (02) 569 03 90

Timmermans, *11 Kerk Straat, 1711 Itterbeek, Belgium*
Tel: (02) 569 03 58

Vander Linden, *2 Brouwerij Straat, 1500 Halle, Belgium*
Tel: (02) 356 50 59

Vandervelden, *230 Laarheide Straat, 1650 Beersel, Belgium*
Tel: (02) 380 33 96

Kriek is the Flemish word for the dry cherry often used in lambic-based fruit beers. This cherry tree features in one of many eye-catching labels used by Cantillon, a brewery of artisanal, rustic style, despite its urban location.

All lambics are winy, but this fruit beer brings together grape, grain and hop. An old symbol of the alchemist, the six-pointed star was a traditional emblem of the brewery. It has no religious meaning, although legend has King David as a brewer.

Gueuze

With its champagne mousse (sustained for far longer); its roseate subtleties of colour; its insistent, tiny bead; its toastiness and delicate acidity, intricate complexity and enduring length, gueuze at its best deserves a name that is easier on the ear, and arguably the tongue. The making of a classic gueuze rests wholly on the judgment of the blender, yet its name sounds almost like the cursor of the computer age.

Unlike champagne, a genuine gueuze is made without even the help of additional sugar and yeast in the bottle. It is the product of a marriage between youth and experience. When a young lambic (still containing some of its residual sugars), is married with a mature example (advanced in its interplay of wild yeasts and other microorganisms), a further fermentation will ensue, and a new carbonation be created.

This lively fermentation may have led to the name gueuze, which some people believe derives from geyser (a similar story is told about the Steam Beer of the Anchor brewery in California – see page 233).

> **Gueuze is a blend of young and old lambic beers. It undergoes a secondary fermentation in the bottle, and like champagne, has a sparkle, a toasty aroma, and enduring length. It is intended to be acidic, although the bigger brewers make sweeter interpretations.**

Another suggestion is that the Belgian name originates from the Geus, the dissidents and liberals who opposed Spanish Imperial rule and favoured the Dutch connection during the 16th and 17th centuries.

As the blending and controlled carbonation of champagne probably predates the work of Dom Pérignon in the late 1600s, it seems likely that similar techniques were known to the lambic brewers at that

Breweries such as Cantillon are not much given to corporate identity, but in Belgium every beer has its own glass. The fluted tumbler is traditional for beers of the lambic family.

Lindemans' beers are widely exported, but many a visitor from overseas has been shocked by the dusty galleries at the Lindemans brewery.

time, especially given the trading links between the two regions. Blending is used in the production of many drinks, and for several reasons: to balance flavours, to cover unfavourable characteristics and, in wines and beers like gueuze, to create a second fermentation. This will, of course, also create extra alcohol. Lambics of 4 percent alcohol by weight, 5 by volume or a little more, might produce a gueuze closer to 4.8 percent by weight, 6 by volume.

It may be that the use of blending was originally a way of giving a rather flat lambic a little more life in the cask. This form of gueuze can still be found, but the classic method is to allow the further fermentation to take place over a period of months or years in the bottle, producing a beer of great style. It has been suggested that this method was introduced in 1870, by a mayor of Lembeek who was a political Liberal. This seems late, but might be supported by the fact that beer was much more commonly shipped in casks than bottles until the mid-1800s.

Brewers of most beer styles know from the outset that their beer will have certain characteristics. Once the beer has fermented, it will spend a fixed period in cask or bottle before it is ready to be sold. Each cask in a traditional lambic brewery is subject to a complex and continual process of decision-making. The brewer has to decide whether he should sell it as unblended lambic or keep it for blending into gueuze. In both instances, he also has to determine at what age it should be tapped.

The casks that seem to be developing best are

usually destined to be kept longest. Traditional lambic wisdom has it that the beers with the best start in life are those brewed in cool weather, when the action of the wild yeasts is at its most restrained. But the temperature will continue to affect the beer for the next year or so. Other influences on the nature of the fermentation, and the consequent results, are the origin of the casks, their size, and their locations within the cellars or attics of the brewer, blender or negociant. There are good and bad years for lambic, not so much because the wheat and barley differ (although they do, to some extent), but because of the weather during brewing and maturation.

All breweries have to deal with the unpredictability of yeast's behaviour, but most need to concern themselves with just one strain, over a period of weeks or, at most, months. The lambic-maker is working with a menagerie of yeasts, sometimes interacting for years.

Once a lambic brewer has decided to blend the contents of some of his casks to make a gueuze, the proportion of young lambic to old becomes crucial. It is obviously less expensive to make a gueuze containing a high proportion of young lambic, perhaps 70 percent, but this can make for a lactic-tasting blend. There may be as little as 15 percent young lambic, just enough to confer life and freshness, in a truly great gueuze. The larger proportion of old lambic will add aroma, depth and length.

One producer told me that his gueuze was always a blend of between 40 and 50 casks (as many malts as there are in some blended Scotch whiskies), but number depends upon the style to be made and the size of the vessels.

The lambic may be centrifuged or filtered to remove cask sediments and excess dead yeast, but sufficient live cells will be left to continue fermentation. After being blended, a traditional gueuze will be bottled and conditioned at the brewery for anything from five or six to 18 months. Cafés, restaurants and private consumers often lay down their gueuze for a further 18 months, two or three years or even longer. One of the best examples I ever tasted was a Cantillon I had kept for five years.

Gueuze made in the traditional way is often, though not always, labelled as having refermentation in the bottle. The bigger brewers may blend their beers in tanks, allow a conditioning to take place, then filter, bottle and pasteurize. These products are less complex, often sweeter and 'easier' to drink, and will not develop with bottle-age.

Almost all lambic brewers also produce at least one style of gueuze. The house characteristics of their lambics will generally carry through into their blended products. Cantillon, Boon, Girardin and De Troch are all good examples. A sweeter version of Boon's gueuze is available in Britain under the Sainsbury's supermarket label.

Timmermans has a medium-sweet gueuze and a drier version labelled Caveau. Lindemans has a sweetish example, with some sherry-like complexity.

Mort Subite makes a sweet gueuze with a dash of tartness in the finish; it is available at the classic Mort Subite café, not far from the Grand' Place in Brussels.

De Neve has traditionally produced a much-admired, clean, firm, dry gueuze. Its parent company Vandenstock blends a soft, sweetish range of lambic variations for the Café Bécasse in Brussels.

The gueuze blended by Hanssens of Dworp has a refreshingly fruity, rhubarby flavour. In Beersel, the café De Drie Fonteinen blends a drier, firmer gueuze, and offers traditional beer snacks and more elaborate meals.

Drinking in Belgium ... the grand and the rustic. La Brouette (left) is one of several terrace cafés that line the gilded, gabled Grand' Place of Brussels. On the same breathtaking square, the visitor should seek out the Brewers' Guild House, which is topped by a golden horseman. Inside is a small museum. A smaller house altogether (above) is the café De Oude Pruim, in Beersel, where gueuze and kriek are dispensed under the gaze of a saint. The café's name means 'The Old Prune', but *pruim* is also a vulgar expression for the female anatomy.

The Old Beersel Beer House (top) is what the British would call the 'tap' and the Germans the *Ausschank*, for the Vandervelden brewery. Although the café has a postwar look, the brewery was founded in 1882. Mussels steamed in gueuze and served hot in the kettle (above) are typical fare at the café In De Rare Vos in Schepdaal, and in beer taverns from Brussels to Paris.

Then there are the two brewers outside the classic region, in West Flanders. Jacobins, the gueuze from the Bockor brewery in Bellegem, has some of the nutty richness of Madeira. The Van Honsebrouck brewery of Ingelmunster makes an even sweeter example, called St Louis.

With its acidity and its complex flavours, the best of gueuze performs very well in the kitchen. It is surely the ideal beer with which to prepare mussels. I have seen a recipe in which the beer is combined with crème fraîche, an egg yolk and saffron, as a sauce to accompany mussels and scallops. The more basic classic is mussels steamed in gueuze (see page 260), which I have relished straight from a black iron kettle at the café In De Rare Vos in Schepdaal.

Gueuze can also be used as the liquid in which to stew tripe, perhaps with thyme, mustard and leeks. In De Rare Vos has weekends devoted to the consumption of mussels, and of tripe. The café's other specialities include horse and pigeon, and after a glass or two of Girardin's or De Neve's gueuze, I have often felt as if I could eat a horse.

Faro

The rustic lambic family, the local brews, enjoyed an unrivalled popularity in metropolitan Brussels until the two World Wars. While the finest lambics were held back for blending, much of the output of young lambic was sweetened with candy sugar, caramel or molasses, spiced, or even diluted with water, to make everyday, easy-drinking beers, the weaker of which could be served to families and children.

Some runnings from the mash tun may have been too weak or strong, and some finished beer too tart. Sometimes first and later runnings (the 'small beer') were blended to make the lambic that was to be sweetened. The object of these exercises was to produce refreshing, restorative beers. The beer was sent in the cask to the city, and there would be a little refermentation. On other occasions, the beer met the sugar in the café. The sugar was crushed, stirred and dissolved with a muddler like that used in cocktail bars. This procedure can still occasionally be seen.

In other countries, all that blending, sweetening and spicing might be regarded as adulteration; in Belgium, it is seen as an art. Lambic that has been sweetened is called faro. If a fine lambic is reminiscent of a fino, faro has something of the character of a sweet or cream sherry: a mid-afternoon pick-me-up.

Does the name derive from the Latin *farina*, meaning flour? Perhaps, if the occupying Spanish considered it a grain wine. In Spanish, *faro* means a lighthouse or, colloquially, a bright idea. In English, the expression 'lit up' means drunk. Any of these theories could be expounded, but no one knows.

What was once an everyday beer has now become a rarity, but two or three brewers still make it, sometimes as a traditional classic. Where these examples are bottled, they are pasteurized so that the sugar will not ferment; this procedure locks in the sweetness.

Faro is the sweetened version of lambic. A few brewers sell bottled faro, but in some Belgian cafés you will be invited to make your own by stirring sugar into a sour lambic beer.

Lindemans has a rather sweet faro. The brewery itself is a blend of ancient and modern; it has a new brewhouse, but still clings to some of its traditions.

Among the brewers in the traditional lambic district, Cantillon, Boon and Lindemans have all in recent years included a faro in their ranges. Vander Linden has even made a regular faro at 3.2 percent alcohol by weight, 4 by volume and a 'double' at 4.8 percent alcohol by weight, 6 by volume. Half a dozen approximations have been made outside the district, including the odd dark, sweetened, low-gravity lager.

Faro is suggested as the base for a 'fruit soup' dessert by the Belgian chef Michel David in his book *Cuisine légère à toutes les bières* (published in 1989 by Les Editeurs d'Art Associés, Brussels).

When the 'small beer' was diluted, it was called mars, probably after the month of March. If spring had sprung in March, and the weather was warm, a lighter beer might have been welcomed. In other countries, references to March imply the opposite: stronger beers, brewed at this time to be laid down as a provision because wild yeasts rendered brewing impossible in summer. Perhaps in Payottenland the weaker worts made the mars, while the stronger ones went forward as the provision.

Mars seems completely to have died out, but the Boon brewery (see page 37) makes a beer with a similar lightness, called Lembeek's 2%.

Fruit beer

A beer made with fruit sounds like a contradiction. Surely it is a wine? The explanation is that these are beers, produced from grain, with fruit added as a further fermentable material or flavouring. They are traditional in Belgium, where they are often based on lambic beers, and usually made with cherries or raspberries. Inspired by the success of these products in recent years, other fruits and more countries have made an entrance.

The best of Belgium's artisan-made, lambic-based, whole-fruit cherry kriek and raspberry frambozen beers have a great complexity and delicacy, and are dry. They are the beer world's elegant response to pink champagne, and make a pretty, unusual and appetizing drink with which to welcome guests at a barbecue or summer party. I have also used frambozen beer in a raspberry vinaigrette and in marmalades or sauces to accompany pâtés or game. The best examples are from Cantillon and Boon.

Some of the more commercial fruit beers, relying to varying degrees on fruit syrups or essences, are much sweeter, and better suited to being served with a sorbet or dessert (cherry jubilee, or a soufflé, perhaps?). They are also a useful ingredient in such dishes. The same is true of Belgium's newer, catchpenny confections based on other fruits. Among them, peach lambic seems to me to be the most acceptable, while banana and blackcurrant are difficult to take seriously.

The lambic brewer René Lindemans has done much to popularize fruit beers internationally. He has over the years made some magnificently dry traditional examples, full of oaky, fruity character, but his marketplace has demanded a much sweeter style.

While fruits are both a fermentable material and a flavouring, I believe their use in beer was originally for the second purpose. When employed with care, they work well as an aromatic, although they lack the preservative benefit of the hop or, for example, the juniper berry.

Among the many materials used to aromatize beer before the universal adoption of the hop, the juniper berry does not seem a thousand miles from the small, flat-headed, dark, relatively bitter, almost stalkless type of cherry known in Flemish as the *kriek*. The fruit is especially associated with the village, now a

> Fruit beers are often, though not always, based on lambic beers, whose winy dryness welcomes the aromatic tartness of the traditional raspberries and cherries. Some brewers are now making more commercial products from less suitable fruits.

suburb, called Schaarbeek, to the immediate northeast of Brussels. The traditional growing region stretches westward toward Ninove, almost enwrapping the lambic region.

Cherry trees are to be seen everywhere on the north side of Brussels, and although commercial cultivation has diminished, some householders allow small brewers to pick the fruit from their gardens. The most traditionalist of lambic brewers prefer the cherries to be dried, like prunes, while still on the tree: the fruity flavours are strengthened (as in sun-dried tomatoes), and the fermentable sugars are concentrated (as in the overripe, 'nobly rotten' grapes used in fine dessert wines). Unfortunately for the brewers, such cherries are also a favourite snack of the local birds. As Schaarbeek cherries have become rarer, some brewers have replaced or augmented them with a variety called Northern, grown in Belgium's province of Limburg and in Germany and Denmark. The Northern cherry is larger, and has a less intense dryness.

Parallel with this old-established geographical link, there is another qualification: lambic is a wheat beer. While the naturally apple-like or plummy fruitiness of wheat beers does not seem to marry well with the hop, it combines beautifully with fruit. Because they revere their Purity Law, many Germans become purple-faced with outrage at the suggestion that fruit might be used in the brewing of beer, but they have no qualms about adding raspberry syrup to the finished product if it happens to be a wheat style such as Berliner Weisse. Nor, in the past, did they hesitate to add slices of lemon to the South German style of wheat beer.

The winyness of lambic lends itself especially well

to fruit. So does the fact that this is a beer with a long period of maturation, during which it can rest on the fruit. Cherries work well in this situation, because they have stones. As the fermentation consumes the flesh of the fruit, it eventually reaches the stone, and picks up the almondy notes that make a good kriek especially complex. Raspberries do not have this advantage, but they are appetizingly aromatic and refreshingly tart.

Outside Belgium, some beer-makers have put the fruit in the brew-kettle, reasoning that the boil will sterilize it and prevent it from adding wild yeasts (found on the fruit's skin) to the brew. Lambics contain such a wild bunch of yeasts already that they are well able to protect themselves. The lambic method is to put the cherries into casks of finished beer, and then allow it a further fermentation.

A lambic brewed in March and matured through the spring and summer might be the base, although older brews are also used. Sometimes there is a blend

André De Keersmaeker, of Mort Subite, taps a sample of kriek (above). His family have been brewers since the 1700s. Today, Mort Subite – along with the lambic cellars at the former Eylenbosch brewery – is part of the Alken-Maes group owned by Kronenbourg of France. Mort Subite's kriek is sufficiently sweet not to frighten a newcomer to the style. Cantillon's fruit beer, such as the framboise below, are much tarter, and favoured by purists.

Frank Boon brings home the Lembeek provenance on a recent glass for his fragrant kriek. The snifter, popular in Belgium, does an excellent job of presenting the bouquet in this or any aromatic beer.

Damsons are in the same family as cherries. This beer, made at the Masons Arms brewpub in the English Lake District, has a deep colour and very full, fruity flavours, with lots of length and dryness.

Whether the lightly peppery Cerveza Rosanna qualifies as a fruit beer depends on the definition of the chili. It goes wonderfully well with a chili-flavoured stew.

of base beers, to impart different degrees of acidity and yeast activity. The cherries are taken from the trees at the end of July or beginning of August. The traditional proportion is one kilo of cherries to every five litres of beer, although some brewers today would regard that as generous. Several producers indicate on the label or cork the date when the beer was brewed and the season of the cherry harvest.

By the time the beer has been on the fruit for one or two months, it has picked up a strong flavour of cherries. If that is what the brewer wants, he may bottle in October. In other breweries, the beer is kept on the fruit for much longer, to benefit from the stronger yeast activity as the weather warms in March, April and May. If it has been a good harvest, the brewer may have batches of kriek at several stages of development. He will want to blend the fruitier casks with the yeastier ones, to achieve a good balance of flavours and a lively fermentation in the bottle. Occasionally, he may still have kriek from a previous year, although he will try to avoid keeping it on the fruit this long for fear that it will have picked up too much bitterness from the stones. One batch can be decanted off the fruit and a further charge of beer added to pick up a second extract, perhaps with a view to the two being blended.

Not a lambic, despite the label, but certainly a fruit beer. Samuel Adams, of Boston, chooses cranberry, very much a fruit of the region. Cranberry juice is used in several old East Coast cocktails. This product, which also contains maple syrup, is based on a wheat beer. It has an orangey-pink colour, a light but smooth palate, and an appetizing tartness.

Some producers add a dash of young lambic, for extra liveliness, just before bottling. Some add elderberry for colour, and at least one (Cantillon) flavours the beer with a little vanilla. A traditional kriek is then matured in the bottle for one summer and released the next spring, for the warm weather.

Apart from lambics, the best-known bases for cherry and raspberry flavours are brown ales such as Liefmans (see page 121), although many other styles have been used. In the Ardennes, near Houffalize, the brewery d'Achouffe uses something on the lines of a saison or a bière de garde as a base for a fresh-tasting, fruity Framboise.

Several other European countries have begun to make fruit beers, and I have especially enjoyed the delicate Framboise of La Choulette, in northern France, and the profound damson beer of the Masons Arms brewpub of Cartmel Fell, in the Lake District of England. The latter was seen as a way of utilizing a local crop, and the same philosophy motivated Maclay, of Alloa, Scotland, to make a beer using the raspberries of Perthshire. Any beer that restates the agricultural traditions of brewing, and its local and seasonal nature, can only be welcome.

North America has, since the late 1980s, produced many fruit beers. Despite a misleading name, the Samuel Adams Cranberry Lambic, made in September by the Boston Beer Company, is both charming and appropriate to the region. In Milwaukee, the Lakefront microbrewery has each August used the cherries of Door County, Wisconsin, to make a tart, lightly almondy beer based on its lager.

On an early sampling tour, in 1990, I enjoyed a fresh-tasting raspberry ale at the Strathcona microbrewery in Edmonton, Alberta; found a great depth of flavour in a Dunkel Krieken Weizen at Spinnakers, in Victoria, British Columbia; and much appreciated a fragrant raspberry wheat beer at the Marin Brewing Company of Larkspur Landing, California. Since then, examples have proliferated, and fruit beers are now judged in a class of their own at the Great American Beer Festival.

Also in 1990, at a tiny brewery in Embudo, New Mexico, I tasted a pungent, spicily dry new beer 'dry-hopped' with green chilies. Chilies are hot-tasting members of the family known popularly as 'peppers' and botanically as Capsicums. Botanists consider them a berry, horticulturists a fruit, and New Mexico deems them the state vegetable. I have since tasted several chili beers, the most delicately flavoured being the Cerveza Rosanna (named after the proprietor's wife) made by Pike Place in Seattle, Washington.

WHEAT BEERS

Some of the most refreshing beers are those made with a substantial proportion of wheat in addition to the normal barley. There is a quenching tartness to classic wheat beers that is not found in most other styles.

Wheat is a very old ingredient in brewing; it has probably been used since the days of early farming and fields of mixed grains. In several periods, it seems almost to have vanished from breweries, but has always reappeared. Given the thirst-quenching beers it produces, why has it not been better appreciated?

One reason is that brewers find it difficult to work with wheat. Being huskless, it easily clogs the mashing vessel; barley, on the other hand, has husks that form their own natural filter bed. This is why beers are rarely made exclusively from wheat; it is normally used together with a proportion of barley.

There is another side to this equation. Because it does not combine well, and bakes hard, barley has a limited usefulness in the making of bread. For the opposite reasons, wheat is friendly to the baker. Wheat and barley grow in similar climates, and their countries of habitat are likely in consequence to be lands where beer and bread are traditional staples. If the brewer and the baker have to share the grain crop, the one naturally chooses barley, the other wheat.

In several brewing regions of Europe, the term 'white' was traditionally used to describe beers made to be consumed immediately, without a significant period of maturation; today the term is used to describe wheat beers generally. Traditional wheat beers in Europe are all top-fermenting, and do not have a long lagering. One explanation of the word 'white' is that these beers produce

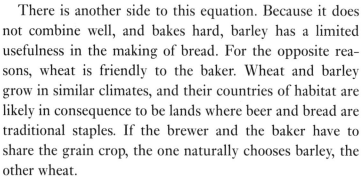

a very pale foam when they are fermenting, while that on lager beers is darker. Another possible origin is that wheat produces paler beers than barley does, and that these have traditionally also been cloudy. Before the development of filtration and refrigeration, a top-fermenting brew would remain cloudy, while one lagered in icy caves would 'drop bright' naturally.

By far the most widely produced examples are wheat beers of the style typically made in South Germany (Bavaria and, to a lesser extent, Baden-Württemberg) and increasingly imitated elsewhere in the world. They are sometimes identified by the description Weizenbier ('wheat beer') and on other occasions described as Weisse ('white'). These beers are made with at least 50 percent wheat, and often have a clove-like aroma and palate deriving from the action of the yeasts typically used. This is especially marked in Bavarian wheat beers that have secondary fermentation in the bottle.

The origin of these cultures is lost in the mists of time, but they are now available from yeast banks. In fermentation, the yeast produces natural compounds – phenols and more especially guaiacols – that resemble those in the balsamic or pine-like sap derived from tropical evergreens as an ingredient for chewing gum. South German wheat beers are a more adult taste, but they may conjure memories of childhood Juicy Fruit gum. Both products are, to their respective generations, very refreshing.

The distinct style of wheat beer made in northern Germany (specifically in Berlin) is always known as Weisse. This ultra-refreshing style is characterized by a low alcohol content, a lactic fermentation and a sharp acidity.

The Belgians also use the designation white, *witbier* or *bière blanche* to describe brews made with a proportion of unmalted wheat and spiced with Curaçao orange peel, coriander and other 'botanicals', and again sometimes a degree (though lesser) of lactic fermentation.

Belgium's lambic beers also contain a proportion of unmalted wheat, but are additionally distinguished by spontaneous fermentation, and have been considered as a family in their own right.

Berliner Weisse

While most wheat beers are refreshing, none can in this quality match the Berlin style, with its modest alcohol content, very slender body, sparkling character and an acidity worthy of Dorothy Parker. This style is said to have been much appreciated by Napoleon's troops in Berlin as 'the champagne of the north,' and it is the beer most reminiscent of the wine of Rheims and Epernay. During maturation in a cool, dark place, the beer gains in its flowery, delicately fruity complexity, for anything from two or three months to four or five years.

Although it may have a relatively low wheat content, a distinctively pale colour, and no perceptible hop bitterness, the special feature of Berliner Weisse is its fermentation with, in addition to a top-fermenting yeast, a blend of selected lactic cultures. This may sound odd, but it has parallels with the malolactic fermentation used in the production of many wines, including some champagnes. With that technique, harsh 'green apple' acids are transformed into softer, 'milky' ones like those found in Berliner Weisse.

The type of lactic cultures now used in Berliner Weisse were isolated at the turn of the century by Professor Max Delbrück, one of the founders of the university research institute and college of brewing known as the VLB (*Versuchs- und Lehranstalt für Brauerei*), in Berlin. *Lactobacillus delbrückii* may be used in several strains, or as a pure culture. *Lactobacillus delbrückii* is not used in the fermentation of south German wheat beers, or other styles, although it is sometimes employed at the brewhouse stage to modify levels of acidity.

The early history of the style is vague. Wheat beers were made widely, and lactic fermentations would have been common in the days of open wooden vessels and no refrigeration, but why did the two become fused in Berlin?

A brewer of Berliner Weisse once suggested to me that the style had been introduced, or developed, by Huguenots, but the evidence is circumstantial: the style is first mentioned in the 1600s, at a time when Berlin and the Brandenburg area accepted a great many Protestant refugees. The Huguenot movement had begun in Switzerland and the adjoining part of France; had the Huguenots picked up brewing skills in Flanders as they migrated north? Or was it simply that their mercantile activities made Berliner Weisse better known? There were said to be 700 Weissbier breweries in the Berlin area at that time.

Like a sparkling wine, Berliner Weisse tends to

The striking interior of the Berliner Kindl brewhouse is reminiscent of the public architecture of the 1930s ... cinemas, railway stations, Berlin's Tempelhof airport. The building's graceful curved lines seem particularly suitable as a setting for these brew-kettles in the traditional shape. The mash tuns and kettles are the heart of a brewery, and the place where its pride surges along with its boiling wort.

foam quickly then lose its head. Sparkling wines (and soft drinks) do not generally have the protein structure to form a lasting head, and that is also true of this beer, due to its acidity.

This style of beer can reflect two of Berlin's moods: the witty, artistic or just plain decadent might drink it from a *Molle* (a short tumbler like that used in America for the rye or Bourbon cocktail called an Old Fashioned) in a *Kneipe* (a student bar or dive); more visibly, it is served as an apéritif or summer refresher, from an oversized champagne saucer, on an elegant terrace at one of the city's many lakes.

The Berlin Museum has a collection of these huge glasses, some from the 1700s, adjoining its café, the Weissbierstube. There, I have enjoyed Berliner Weisse with pickled and grilled herring, and with a dessert of seasonal red berries (*Rote Grütze*). Among the other Berlin specialities on the beautifully displayed buffet may be 'fig and coward' (*Feige Saw*), with a sauce of cream, vodka and green peppercorns. The acidic beer goes well with both pickled savouries and tart fruits, but what about creamy concoctions? Yogurt, perhaps. During a health craze before World War I, a brewer made a Weissbier with *Lactobacillus bulgaricus*. A Balkan touch, but Berlin was always a cosmopolitan city. The Baltic touch is more usual: beer with pickled fish, berry fruits, or clear spirits such as vodka…

I have heard of Berliner Weisse being laced with Kümmel (caraway) schnapps, or being served hot with lemon juice during winter, although I have only ever seen the summer versions, with a dash of the herbal essence of woodruff (*Waldmeister*) or raspberry syrup. This is the familiar face of Berliner Weisse.

The syrup colours the head as well as the beer, the woodruff making for a vivid lime-cordial hue and the raspberry looking more like peach. Everyone knows the flavour of raspberry, but what about essence of woodruff? Sampled on its own, it is heavily fragrant, with notes of hay, lemon grass and cough candy. The herb grows in the forests around Berlin, and is also used to make a soft drink and to flavour mineral water. When Berliner Weisse is served in this way, the idea is that the drinker first tastes the sweetness of the syrup, then senses the acidity of the beer.

Whenever I have asked for a Weissbier in Berlin,

The red, amber and green versions of Berliner Weissbier were once promoted with allusions to traffic lights. Today, even a beer of such modest strength is kept away from the wheel.

Berliner Weisse beers are exceptionally thirstquenching, in much the same way as freshly squeezed lemon juice in Mediterranean countries, or lime juice in Florida. Some people find them too tart, and it has become traditional in Berlin to serve them with a dash of fruit or herbal syrup.

the server has demanded: 'Red or green?' If I have requested it without either, to sample the beer in its natural state, I have sometimes been viewed as a madman. The syrups are considered necessary to moderate the intensity of the acid, although it has its own charm to the adult palate, albeit sometimes puckering the cheeks like a *citron pressé*.

Kindl, one of the two remaining producers in Berlin (see page 53), issues a booklet of recipes for mixed drinks based on Weissbier. These include variations on the Buck's Fizz (with fresh orange juice) and the champagne cocktail, while other mixes employ cassis and grenadine. Beer cocktails may offend purists, but some of these work well, and they are a commendable effort to add excitement to an old classic.

Like most speciality styles, Berliner Weisse was originally made in a variety of gravities and strengths. Nor was it always so lightly hopped, although the flowers may have originally been added to the mash tun, as a preservative, and not to the kettle.

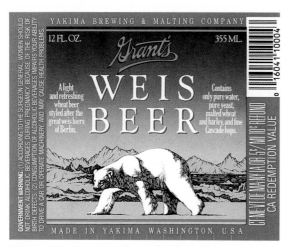

The spelling is eccentric, and so is the bear.

The style was already losing sales to Pilsner beers before the two World Wars devastated and then divided Berlin, and the beer settled into its present form when peace returned. Paradoxically, unification cost the city the former Schultheiss Weissbier brewery in the East. This brewery, founded in 1880, in Pankow, and operated under state ownership during the period of Communist Government, was acquired and closed by Schultheiss in June 1990.

In the days of a divided Berlin, I tasted the Pankow product and enjoyed its intense dryness. A bottle from one of the last batches, kept by a member of the Brewery History Society of Berlin, was presented to me on a visit to Germany in November 1992. I tasted it a month later, and rediscovered that intensity. It had the fruitiness of lemons, and I thought perhaps some of the 'horse blanket' character that derives from wild *Brettanomyces* yeasts.

In comparison, a Schultheiss Berliner Weisse made in the West seemed lighter, fresher and more flowery (almost a celery taste), and I do feel that a freshness of attack characterizes Schultheiss Berliner Weisse. The Berliner Kindl Weisse is more restrained, with less acidity and complexity, and more fruitiness.

If Berlin's last remaining Weisse beers are to survive, a new incursion of Huguenot mercantile skills may be needed. In big, volume-driven breweries, regional specialities often become endangered. This poses a problem in Berlin, dominated by two giants. Although the style can be produced elsewhere, it may not be identified as Berliner Weisse.

Northern Germany once made similar wheat beers in cities such as Brunswick (Braunschweig) and Hanover. Bremen still has an example, brewed as a speciality by Beck's. This is called Bremer Weisse. It is very much in the style of Berliner Weisse, though fractionally less attenuated, decidedly less lactic, and marginally more hoppy. Also in the north, Münster's Pinkus Weizen is very faintly lactic, although it has a more conventional strength, at around 11.5 Plato (1046) and 4 percent alcohol by weight, 5 by volume.

Beers in this style were once widely made in North America, and the custom is being revived by some of the new generation of brewers. The Vermont Pub and Brewery, in Burlington (144 College Street, Tel: 802-865-0500), has been known to produce a wheat beer with a *Lactobacillus* culture, although I have never been there when the product was available. At the Rotterdam brewpub in Toronto (600 King Street, Tel: 416-868-6882), I have sampled an earthy, lactic Weiss; again, this is not always available.

In the Chicago suburb of Berwyn, the Weinkeller (6417 West Roosevelt, Tel: 708-749-2276) is actually a brewpub; its products include both a plummy, sweetish, Bavarian-style wheat beer and a quenchingly tart, but well-balanced, and very drinkable, Berliner Weisse. Owner Udo Harttung is a German, albeit from Hamburg, with a voluble pride in his products. He might have shown more propriety by calling his beer Berwyner Weisse.

Bert Grant, a Scottish-Canadian, set up his brewery in 1981 in the old opera house in Yakima, Washington state. Grant, a brewing scientist, has since moved to purpose-built premises (see page 109). Meanwhile, he has developed a range of brews in classic styles, each with his own stubbornly idiosyncratic twist. His Weis Beer (11 Plato; 1044; just under 4 percent alcohol by weight, 5 by volume) has a delicate, lightly fruity, plummy character, some honeyed notes, and a refreshingly dry, tart finish. This beer is made with only 25–30 percent wheat, but a lactic culture is not used. The label describes the beer as being styled after those of Berlin, and shows a bear. The city's name is sometimes held to be derived from the German for bear, and a bear appears in its coat of arms. Whimsically, Grant has made his a polar bear.

Berliner Weisse producers

While Berlin-style wheat beers are increasingly being made in North America, and appear in one or two other north German cities, only two classic producers remain in Berlin itself.

KINDL

Berliner Kindl Brauerei, 50 Werbellin Strasse, Neu Kölln, 1000 Berlin 44, Germany
Tel: (030) 689 920

Doll's house models of the original 1872 brewery are displayed in the reception area of the present 1920s' building, which itself has the stylishly clean lines of its period. The entrance to the brewhouse is a narrowed arch that might suit a modern monastery. The 1920s' brewhouse was said to be one of the most beautiful in the world, but was taken to Russia in reparation after World War II, never to be seen again. The present handsome brewhouse, with copper vessels set into marble tiles, dates from the 1950s.

The brewery has its own wells, although the water is hard and has to be softened. Kindl is coy about the amount of wheat used in its Weisse, but the percentage seems to be something less than 30. The beer has a colour of 4–5 EBC, and a gravity of 7.5 Plato (1030; 2; 2.5). The hops are Northern Brewer, from Hallertau, added in one 'gift' (less than 10 units of bitterness). Being low in protein and hops, Berliner Weisse beers in general do not require a long boil. Kindl's has only 15 minutes. In fact, the brewers need to carry some protein over for fermentation.

Both the top-fermenting yeast and the *Lactobacillus delbrückii* are pure cultures. The acidification begins first, and the yeast is added later. The fermenting beer has a week in a stainless steel cylindro-conical tank, at 20°C/68°F, before spending two days being dropped to 0°C/32°F. It remains at this temperature for two to three days before filtration. A very small amount of yeast and *Kräusen*, but no *lactobacillus*, is added prior to bottling. The beer is not pasteurized.

The brewery starts production of Weissbier each February, with a view to the beer being consumed when the warm weather starts, probably from May. The period of production each year depends upon the way in which summer seems to be developing. If it turns out that too much has been made, the beer will be stored through the following winter, no doubt becoming more flowery during its extended maturation.

This is a large brewery, making a variety of styles and, as a percentage of total output, Berliner Weisse is in single figures. Kindl is nonetheless the biggest producer of the style. Kindl has subsidiaries in other cities and is part of a national group that includes Binding of Frankfurt and Dortmunder Actien Brauerei.

SCHULTHEISS

Schultheiss-Brauerei, 28-48 Methfessel Strasse, Kreuzberg, 1000 Berlin 61, Germany
Tel: (030) 780 030

An apothecary founded the 1840s' brewery, originally called Tivoli[1], that has for a hundred years been known as Schultheiss, and is today the company's headquarters, in the hippie-yuppie district of Kreuzberg. It is a magnificent, rambling building topped with castellation and turrets. The former Tivoli makes Pils and other styles, while the nearby Schoneberg produces only Weisse, and the company has regained a third brewery in the former East. Schultheiss is part of a national group, with Dortmunder Union.

The Schoneberg brewery is on a quiet, tree-lined street called Bessemer Strasse, near the company's maltings. It uses equal parts of wheat and barley malt, to a gravity of 7.6 Plato (1030.4; 2; 3, or a little more). The brew is hopped with Hallertau extract (4–8 units of bitterness), and heated to a point where unwanted solids will coagulate. It is not taken all the way to boiling point.

A multistrain top-fermenting yeast and a mixture of *Lactobacilli delbrückii* are used, with a proportion of wort that is three to six months old. This mixture ensures a good fermentation. At the brewery's quality-control lab, I was told that there had been experimental attempts to select down the yeast strains. 'We stopped counting after seven or eight, and fermentations with selected yeasts did not produce a better beer.'

Fermentation, at 20–25°C/68–77°F, lasts for three to four days, but the brew may spend from three to six months in warm maturation (15–25°C/59–77°F). The brew is then centrifuged and given a dosage of *Kräusen*, with *Lactobacillus delbrückii*, before being bottled. It is warm-conditioned in the bottle for three to four weeks, at a minimum of 20°C/68°F, before being released.

As a truly bottle-conditioned beer, it lends itself well to being cellared.

1 Several ornate breweries built in the 1800s in Germany and elsewhere took the name Tivoli. The soubriquet was presumably inspired by the paintings of Rococo artists such as Jean-Honoré Fragonard (1732-1806) of the villas at the Italian hillside town of Tivoli, near Rome.

A cosier Berlin is remembered in a brewery the size of a doll's house, on display in the reception area of the Kindl brewery.

South German Weizenbier

When people in Germany refer to the champagne-like qualities of wheat brews, they may be thinking simply of these beers' fine, insistent bead, sparkle and fruity acidity. 'We do not use the *méthode champenoise*,' a Bavarian brewer once said to me, referring to the fact that many wheat beers have a secondary fermentation in the bottle, but without a *dégorgement*. 'We prefer the *méthode bavaroise*.'

Anyone who enjoys champagne for breakfast might try the Bavarian custom of a morning wheat beer to wash down a snack of veal sausages (*Weisswurst*). Wheat brews are often described as 'breakfast beers' in Bavaria. Or 'after church' beers. On a Sunday in summer, devotions may be followed by a stroll from the church to the beer garden for a refreshing glass.

These are the most summery of beers. At the Ayinger brewery (see page 203), southeast of Munich, I was served wheat beer with elderflower fritters, something of a local delicacy. Some of the more clove-like wheat beers, especially the darker type with

a sweeter malt character, can accompany a spicy apple strudel. Others have fruity notes that suit them perfectly to a plum dish or a banana bavarois.

The recognition of wheat beers as a distinct style may have originated in Bohemia, and spread from there to Bavaria, looping around the city of Munich. The areas to the east and north of Munich are still heartlands of the style. Wheat beers are not made in Bohemia now (at least, not at the moment),

> South German wheat beers are, above all, summer drinks. Light and sparkling, they have the fruity acidity of apples and plums, often with a clove spiciness. Clear or cloudy, dark or pale, this style of wheat beer crops up all over the world.

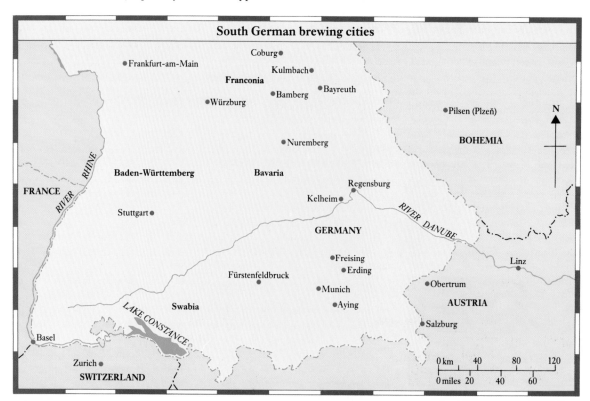

South German brewing cities

The south of Germany is a beer heaven. Bavaria, with its sub-regions of Swabia and Franconia, has ten times as many breweries as any other state of any other country. Its styles range from wheat beers through Märzenbier, pale and dark lagers, double bock beers, smoked beers and countless variations.

and this account is given scant credence in Bavaria.

Just to the northeast of Munich, the brewery which claims to be the oldest in the world, Weihenstephan, is well known for its fruity-tasting wheat beers (I have noted apples, and perhaps blackcurrant). Weihenstephan is on a steep hill, girded by the River Amper, at the small town of Freising. There was a Benedictine settlement there in 725, and beer may have been brewed then (hops were cultivated in Freising in 768). The brewery claims that there has certainly been brewing on the site since 1040. It is not clear to what extent brewing has been interrupted over the centuries, or how wheat beer has ebbed and flowed there. Weihenstephan was sacked more than once, but in parts still has the feel of a medieval cloister.

The monastic brewery was later secularized and came into the hands of the Bavarian royal family, the House of Wittelsbach. During that period, courses of study began on the site, which now also houses the world's most famous university faculty for brewers. The commercially operated brewery (with stainless steel vessels, but rather older cellars), and the faculty, are now owned by the State of Bavaria. The faculty is part of the Technical University of Munich. (There are similar university faculties or departments in Berlin, Leuven, Edinburgh and Davis, California.)

On the next hill to Weihenstephan, half a mile away, is the Hofbräuhaus Freising, also known for very fruity wheat beers (banana, spices, malt…). Its well-regarded Huber Weisses takes its name from an old-established local brewpub, which long ago ceased production. This beer is quite yeasty, and relatively low in carbonation for the style. Its puzzling polar-bear label was mockingly adopted after the town of Freising refused to allow the original brewer to use its civic symbol. Freising is represented by a more European bear which in legend ate the horse of its local saint, Korbinian, when he was on a pilgrimage to Rome. After that, Korbinian made the bear carry his baggage.

Hofbräuhaus Freising dates from at least the 1100s. It was for 400 years the brewery of the Bishop's household and court (*Hof* means court). At the time of secularization, it passed into royal hands and through marriage to the Count of Moy (the title derives from a site near St Quentin, in Picardy),

Franz Inselkammer samples the well-made Weizenbier produced for his Ayinger brewery by a wheat beer specialist in nearby Traunstein.

whose family had fled France at the time of the Revolution. When I had dinner with the present Count, one of the new generation of cosmopolitan Bavarian brewers, he served me a fish dish poached in his darker style of wheat beer. The fish was zander, a member of the perch family resembling the American wall-eye pike. The combination sounded unlikely but worked well – like Escoffier's salmon poached in Chambertin, I suppose.

Hofbräuhaus Freising is admired not only for its beers but also for its *Jugendstil* brewery building. The company also owns a brewery east of Munich, at Haag in Upper Bavaria. This produces a less yeasty, more carbonated interpretation of wheat beer. The same town has very tasty, yeasty wheat beer from the Unertl brewery.

The royal connection

Enthusiasts who make lofty claims for Bavarian wheat beers may be subconsciously echoing the style's royal heritage. Not only does Germany have a Beer Purity Law based on Bavarian tradition, and citing barley as the grain of the brewer, that state also had for a few hundred years an ordination reserving wheat for royal beer-makers.

It is always argued that the Purity Law was introduced to protect consumers, but did these various measures not also assist farmers, allot resources and provide means of patronage, or sources of levies and taxes? Politics, economics and trade were surely no different then?

In the 1400s, the Barons of Degenberg, Bavaria, seem to have appropriated the right to brew wheat beer, and this later passed to the royal family Wittelsbach. Not long after its establishment, in 1589, the Royal Court Brewery (the Hofbräuhaus) in Munich was in the early 1600s producing wheat beer on what was for the day a massive scale. At one stage, there were around 30 royal brewhouses elsewhere in Bavaria making wheat beers, and publicans were obliged to sell their products alongside independently produced barley brews. Neither government monopolies nor chain operations are new ideas.

The royal family gradually withdrew from their monopoly in the 1800s, at a time when wheat beer was having a lull in its popularity, but the present Prince Luitpold of Bavaria has in recent years aggressively promoted the style. His wheat beers (with a lightly spicy, vanilla-and-cloves character) are primarily made not at his castle of Kaltenberg (which concentrates on dark lager, see page 201) but at his additional brewery in the nearby town of Fürstenfeldbruck. The Prince's brewpub Das Kleine Brauhaus, set in Munich's Luitpold Park (named after an ancestor), also makes a rather yeastier wheat beer.

In 1918–19, Bavaria had a brief Communist interlude before joining the Republic of Germany. The Hofbräuhaus in Munich, the world's most famous tavern and beer garden, passed into state ownership, where it still resides. Its brewery was moved to a separate site in the city long ago. It still includes three wheat beers in its range.

In the 1850s, the royal family leased the Hofbräuhaus to brewer Georg Schneider, who eventually acquired the rights to produce wheat beer on his own account. The Schneider family subsequently established their own brewery nearby in the street called Tal ('dale'). Although the brewery is no longer there, the beer-hall and restaurant is one of the best known in Munich, and the only large one specializing in wheat beer. With its wood panelling and rustic theme, it is also the most old-world and least touristic.

The Schneider family had at one point owned several of the former royal wheat-beer breweries, and after the war concentrated their efforts at the one at Kelheim (see page 62), where the valleys of the Danube and Altmühl meet, near Regensburg. The brewery is currently in the hands of the fifth and sixth Georg Schneiders. It produces only wheat beers, although the family also owns a smaller brewery at Straubing, beyond Regensburg, to make lagers.

The family's faith in wheat beer has been well rewarded. Having once been a royal beer for the

Harmonious snack ... the beer and the *Weisswurst* have similar names because both are deemed to be white.

Hanging signs, smartly gilded, often announce taverns in Germany. This one proclaims itself the Schneider brewery tap.

Prince Luitpold, of Kaltenberg, makes a speciality of his dark brews, including a delicious, spicy Dunkelweizen.

aspiring drinker, it became commonplace and then old-fashioned, especially when Munich brewers perfected their dark lagers in the mid-1800s and popularized pale lagers in the 1900s. When I first encountered this style of wheat beer, in the early 1960s, it seemed to be the preserve of elderly ladies. Its share of the Bavarian market at the time could be counted in single figures. Schneider was able to rely on the style only because it was the specialist in the field. Some time in the late 1960s or early 1970s, wheat beer was discovered by a new generation. It now has 25–30 percent of the Bavarian market, with a considerable following elsewhere.

Today's wheat beers

As an old style, wheat beer had continued often to have its secondary fermentation in bottle, and thus to be served unfiltered. Before the development of filtration, all bottled beer was made in this way. This requires a great deal of skill in ensuring that the levels of fermentable sugar and yeast are just right at the bottling stage. Too little of either, and the beer will not carbonate. (It needs the carbonation not only to provide a refreshing sparkle, but also to protect it against oxidation.) Too much, and the bottle will blow its top or explode.

Today, more elaborate techniques are used. One is to centrifuge the beer, removing the original yeast and adding a new culture, in a precisely measured proportion, for the secondary fermentation in the bottle. Some brewers, among them Schneider, use the same (top-fermenting) wheat-beer yeast for both primary and secondary fermentations. This is the best way to sustain the true wheat-beer character.

Others, including Prince Luitpold, use a bottom-fermenting yeast for the secondary fermentation. This creates a more stable product, with the yeast precipitating to the bottom of the bottle. Drinkers who like a bottle-conditioned wheat beer that is nonetheless clear, can pour gently, leaving the yeast behind. Those who like a yeasty beer can, after pouring most of the brew, swirl the bottle, so that the last ounce or two of beer picks up the yeast. This last shot of yeasty beer is then dumped into the glass.

A third method is to centrifuge, perhaps even pasteurize, then add a dash of the protein sediment that

had earlier been precipitated by the malt in the brew-kettle. The drinker may assume that the haze in the bottle is yeast, but it is more like the lees in wine. Wheat beers made in this way have an almost gritty texture, but little of the classical fruitiness or clove-like complexity.

Sedimented wheat beers are today overwhelmingly the most popular type in Bavaria. Younger people, who are the greatest devotees, seem to regard a wheat beer with a sediment in much the same light as a bread with visible grains or seeds. These are the beer world's answer to 'wholefood'.

Variations on the theme

When a wheat beer is bottled with a sediment, it is most often described as a Weisse ('white'), although even in this context, the word Weizen ('wheat') is sometimes used. These two terms are regarded in Bavaria as being interchangeable, both simply indicating a wheat beer.

On the label of the sedimented type, the words *mit Hefe* ('with yeast') may be added. The filtered type was sometimes known as Champagner Weizen until the French understandably objected. Today, if a qualification is thought necessary, it is most often Kristall Weizen. Although this type lacks the extra fruitiness delivered by bottle-fermentation, the absence of yeast or protein on the tongue can lead to a smoother, cleaner, more delicate flavour. It is a trade-off; you pays your money…

A dark wheat beer may be identified as a Dunkelweizen ('dark white' might sound odd). The combination of wheaty tartness and the lusciousness of dark malts makes this style full of flavour and complexity.

Perhaps because they are an older style, Bavarian wheat beers are traditionally a little stronger than other everyday brews. Most are in the bracket 12–13.5 Plato (1048–54), with alcohol ranging from 4–4.5 percent by weight, 5–5.6 by volume. A strong one, of more than 16 Plato (1064) may be described as a Weizenbock. This strong style is often offered as a winter wheat beer.

Many breweries have wheat beers in each of these categories. The spelling of the designations on the label may vary according to the grammar of what is being said (the same word may take slightly different

In the leaded glass, the hoe symbol makes a joke of the earthy name Erding. The small town of Erding, Bavaria, is home to Germany's largest wheat beer brewery.

The German Beer Purity Law, the *Reinheitsgebot*, scrolls itself in the tiling of the brewhouse wall.

forms as a noun or adjective, for example), and to local custom or the brewer's preference.

The lemon question

When I first encountered South German wheat beers, they were often served with a slice of lemon floating in the glass. I have heard many explanations for this, none convincing.

Some brewers believe that it goes back to the days when top-fermenting beers, being less stable than lagers, were of very varying quality: the lemon was there to disguise eccentric flavours. I think that story was originally put about by lager-brewers.

Another argument says the lemon was there to restrain the carbonation. Why do this in a style of beer that is known for its highly carbonated, refreshing character? The very rocky, brightly white head (deriving from the use of wheat) and the high carbonation (partly a function of the style of fermentation, but also a tradition in wheat beers) are part of the signature of this Bavarian style.

My own feeling is that the slice of lemon is linked to the same tradition as the raspberry juice or essence of woodruff with which Berlin wheat beer is laced, or the raspberries or cherries added during the maturation of lambic. Such additions seem more common in wheat beers, with their low hop character, than in lagers, although those styles are often laced with an apéritif bitters in Alsace, and were once commonly sweetened with non-alcoholic lime cordial in Britain.

I always felt that the lemon accentuated the spritzy 'bite' and acidity of the wheat beer, as well as visually highlighting the refreshing character of the drink, but the practice has diminished in Germany. The lemon is never seen in the sedimented version of the beer, and only occasionally in the filtered type. I have even heard it argued that there might be pesticides on the skin. Can they not be removed by washing? Were there ever enough to harm a drinker of wheat beer? Meanwhile, the slice of lime in the neck of the Mexican beer bottle, a practice I have never seen south of the border, has become an effective marketing tool for brews far less worthy of popularity.

The spread of the style

Apart from the specialists, many Bavarian brewers have wheat beers in their range, often added since the revived popularity of the style. The fruity examples made by Ayinger's separate wheat beer brewery at Traunstein, the dryish interpretations from Spaten, the well-rounded entrants from Paulaner, the plummy offerings from Würzburger Hofbrau and the apple-tinged quenchers from Maisel of Bayreuth are all popular.

Elsewhere in Germany, brewers who produce wheat beers in this southern style sometimes label them with images that suggest Bavarian origin.

Across south Germany's borders, two or three Austrian and Swiss breweries produce relatively light, crisp wheat beers in this style. In the Austrian province of Salzburg, at Obertrum, the Sigl brewery produces Weizengold, clean and soft, with a pear-like fruitiness. The brewery also makes a similar product called Weizenfest for the Finnish market. There is also the odd German-style wheat beer in the Netherlands, Belgium and northern France.

In 1988, the British regional brewer Vaux of Sunderland experimentally produced two versions of a filtered Weizenbier. One was made with a wheat-beer yeast, and had a clove character, albeit very light. The other, made with a conventional top-fermenting yeast and with a pleasantly refreshing light fruitiness, was made available in a limited selection of pubs, but on a somewhat sporadic basis. In 1991, Bunce's microbrewery in Netheravon, near Salisbury, Wiltshire, produced a wheat beer, again using a conventional ale yeast, as a summer speciality. This beer has continued to be offered since as a seasonal brew. It is very soft, but with a distinct apple acidity. The beer is not filtered, but drops bright. The brewery has adapted the pronunciation of Weiss, and calls the beer Bunce's Vice. The same theme was taken up with more credibility by a brewery in Florida.

Wheat beers were produced by hundreds of breweries in Germanic parts of the United States, notably Pennsylvania and Wisconsin, before Prohibition. In recent years, they have been revived by North America's new micros and brewpubs. On the East Coast, I have greatly enjoyed Samuel Adams' lightly clove-tasting Wheat Beer and the same label's Dunkelweizen, but never been in Pennsylvania in the right months to sample Stoudt's highly regarded summertime ventures into this style. In the Midwest, well-established examples include the soft but tart Weisse of the Frankenmuth brewery in Michigan; the apple-tasting Weiss, in both bright and unfiltered versions, from Sprecher of Milwaukee; and the spicy Gartenbrau Weizen from Capital of Middleton, near Madison, Wisconsin; there are many others.

Just across the Continental Divide, I have enjoyed the fruity, honeyed Mountain Wheat of Breckenridge, Colorado. The West Coast is frothing with fine examples, among them Thomas Kemper's yeasty, soft, light, fruity HefeWeizen, from Poulsbo, Washington; the pioneering Pyramid Wheaten Ale, slightly perfumy, tart and refreshing, from Kalama, in the same state (see page 61); Widmer's dry Weizenbier and yeasty Hefe-Weizen, from Portland, Oregon; the foamy, firm-bodied, well-balanced Hubsch Weizen from Davis, California; and, with a hint of apples and honey, the delicate Anchor Wheat Beer from San Francisco. The grist of this beer is more than two-thirds wheat, an unusually high percentage, but fermentation is with a yeast that does not produce the typical clove character. Anchor first released its Wheat Beer in 1984, and made two or three summer batches before it became a permanent fixture. It was the first of the new generation of American wheat beers.

Across the Pacific, several Japanese breweries have experimented with wheat beers. I have tasted an example with a very good clove character at Suntory's Musashino brewery in Fuchu City. This was made from 60 percent wheat, with a very long boil, and fermented with a Weihenstephan yeast.

In Christchurch, New Zealand, I have tasted a very pale, light, slightly grainy Weiss Bier (60 percent wheat) with a tart finish, from the Plains Brewing Company, served at the adjoining Loaded Hog bar.

In Australia, in addition to the well-known Redback (see page 61), I very much enjoyed a soft, dry, hoppy wheat beer called Yellow Mongrel at the Geebung Polo Club brewpub in Melbourne. A beer called Copperhead has on occasion been brewed entirely from wheat, although it usually contains 55 percent. The brand belongs to Lion, of Adelaide, but the beer has been made at several microbreweries. The method was developed by Lion's biggest shareholder, the consultancy firm Thimble Breweries. Brewer Graham Howard, one of the principal partners in Thimble, told me that he had developed a regime of mashing, and a modification of equipment, that enabled him to brew using only wheat. I have sampled the all-wheat version, and found it very clean, with an interesting balance of dessert-fruit character (sweet pears in syrup?) and acidity.

Weizenbier producers

The classics among south German wheat beers are still made to the northeast of Munich by such historic breweries as Erdinger and Schneider. The style is clearly recognizable in Pyramid's Wheaten Ale, from Washington state, and under various aliases from new small breweries as far apart as Australia, Switzerland and Canada.

ERDINGER

Erdinger Weissbräu, 1–20 Franz Brombach Strasse, 8058 Erding, Bavaria, Germany
Tel: (08122) 4090

The town of Erding is dotted with the onion-domed churches typical of rural Bavaria, depicted in a mural at the brewery.

The biggest producer of wheat beer in Germany, and therefore the world, is Erdinger, which makes nothing else. From Munich, the brewery is about 20 miles to the northeast, though still on the suburban railway, in the town of Erding.

Erding was originally the seat of a duke in the late 700s. The town centre, in pastel-coloured and timbered buildings, is punctuated with onion-domed church towers. Much of the town was built in the 1600s and 1700s, after the Thirty Years' War. Before World War II, there were nine breweries in Erding; two remain, albeit under the same ownership. The Erdinger Stiftungs brewery now specializes in malty lagers, its own robust wheat beers withdrawn to leave the way clear the way for its

rival. The Stiftungs beers can be sampled at the brewery's tap, built in 1698 and reconstructed in 1816, which can be found at the corner of Haager and München streets.

A building dating from 1537 was the original site of the Erdinger brewery, and is still its 'tap' in the town centre (1 Lange Zeile). This chunky building, with walls and ceilings planked in oak, may have been a tavern long before the official foundation date of the Erdinger brewery in 1853. The brewery originally made a variety of styles, and is said to have introduced wheat beers in the 1890s. It came into the present family in 1935, and subsequently began to specialize. In 1983, the company moved to a green-field site on the edge of the town, and in 1991–92 doubled the size of its brewery there to two million hectolitres a year.

Local farmers are supplied with seed and contracted to produce much of the barley, and all of the wheat, for the brewery. The wheat has an unusually low protein level, making for an especially soft, clean-tasting beer. The brewery has its own borehole, and its water is softened. A double-decoction mash is used, in a regime where temperatures are controlled to one-tenth of a degree, and about which the company is somewhat coy. The hops are Perle and Tettnang, in three additions, with an emphasis on aroma.

Primary fermentation is in horizontal tanks in which the brew sits only 2.8 metres high. 'People say I am crazy not to have cylindro-conicals in such a modern brewery, but I think that kind of vessel can cause a convection that makes for dirty-tasting beer,' owner Werner Brombach told me. The Erdinger beers are lightly fruity

(a dash of dessert apple?), with some residual sweetness, but more delicate and somewhat less spicy than some of their competitors.

The brew has a secondary fermentation at the brewery if it is to be filtered. The Kristall (12.7 Plato; 1050-1; 4.3; 5.3; 18 BU) has a very bright gold colour, and an aromatic suggestion of vanilla. The version *mit feiner Hefe* is reyeasted with a bottom-fermenting culture, primed with wort, and given two to four weeks' warm conditioning at temperatures of up to 15°C/59°F, emerging with more fruitiness.

In 1991, the brewery launched a Dunkel, with a fractionally higher gravity and alcohol, tawny but bright, with a hint of chocolate in the aroma and palate. Each of the grains, barley and wheat, is represented by both pale and dark malts in this style.

Erdinger also has a Weizenbock, called Pikantus, available all year round. This has a very deep tawny colour, but is still bright, with a hint of licorice in the aroma and palate. It is very smooth, but only medium-bodied. Gravity is 17.3 Plato (1070), with 5.8 percent alcohol by weight, 7.3 by volume.

A marginally fuller-bodied version of the *mit Hefe* is served as a Festbier at Erding's autumn festival, which starts on the last Friday of August and lasts for ten days.

FISCHER/UELI

Brauerei Fischerstube, 45 Rhein Gasse, 4058 Basel, Switzerland
Tel: (061) 329495

A doctor of medicine, Hans Nidecker is also a beer-lover and café-owner. In the 1970s, he built a small brewery in the back room of his café, with the help of Otto Binding, whose family once owned the brewery of the same name in Frankfurt, Germany.

Doctor Nidecker's café was already called the Fischerstube, but he gave his beers the brand name Ueli, meaning jester. They include a pale lager, a marginally stronger example called Reverenz, in broadly the Dortmunder style, a lightly toffeeish dark lager and a Weizenbier. The latter has a gravity of 12 Plato (1048; 4; 5), and is made from 60 percent wheat, 40 percent barley malt. It has a very dense head; a brassy colour, with some yeasty cloudiness; a bananas-and-plums aroma and palate, 'ripe' at the start and becoming tarter in the finish.

The café is on a side street close to the centre of town. It resembles a coffee-shop, although it serves full meals. The handsome copper brew-kettle can be seen through a window at the rear, and there are open fermenters.

PYRAMID

Hart Brewing Company, 110 West Marine Drive, Kalama, Washington 98625, USA
Tel: (206) 637 2962

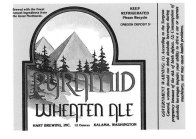

Was it because the Ancient Egyptians brewed beer, or does one of the Cascade peaks resemble a pyramid? Several explanations have been offered for the memorable brand name, which seems to have come to

founders Beth Hartwell and Tom Baune in a flash of inspiration. The couple, who previously ran a delicatessen, founded the brewery in 1984. It has since been sold to new owners, and expanded.

Pyramid, just over the state line from Portland, Oregon, makes several styles but has become especially well known for its Wheaten Ale. This is another odd-but-memorable name created by Hartwell and Baune, and it did much to popularize the new generation of wheat beers in the West.

The Wheaten Ale (10.5–11; 1042–4; just over 3.2; 4) has a dense head; a bright golden colour; a firm, smooth body; a perfumy, tart, clean palate; and a light, refreshing finish. It is a very well attenuated beer, and the same is true of the brewery's newer Amber Wheaten. Despite a fuller colour that suggests some crystal malt, this is a very crisp brew.

REDBACK

Matilda Bay Brewing Company, 130 Stirling Highway, North Fremantle, Western Australia 6159, Australia
Tel: (09) 430-6222

It all began when brewer Philip Sexton left Western Australia's regional giant Swan in order to set up, with partners, the country's first brewpub, the Sail and Anchor, in the port town of Fremantle, in 1984. This was followed by a microbrewery, Matilda Bay – making, among other beers, Redback.

I have seen no historical mention of any previous wheat beer in Australia, and there were certainly no others being made when Redback was introduced. Although it was an unfamiliar style, it became a great success. The thirst-quenching qualities of wheat beers should make them ideal for a hot country like Australia, and the name Redback – belonging to an indigenous highly poisonous spider – packed its own whimsical appeal to the young. The Matilda Bay micro

grew quickly, moved to larger premises after four or five years, and sprouted offshoots in other parts of Australia. This demanded new investment, and the company finally fell into the hands of the Carlton/Foster's group.

The original microbrewery was between Fremantle and the neighbouring city of Perth, and the present premises are nearby, on the road that runs along the coast, linking the two. The brewery is in a mid-1930s' building that was once a Ford assembly plant. With its wood-panelled offices, the building has adapted handsomely to its new role. Up a brass-railed stairway, the brewhouse is fitted with copper vessels from the former Brasserie De Clerck, in the hop-growing town of Hazebrouck, northern France. From the brewhouse windows, the view is of the sea and shipping.

Because there is now a Redback Light, the principal beer is prefixed Original. This is a misnomer, as this beer is filtered. The true 'original' Redback was bottle-conditioned, but that version is now made only in the company's brewpub on the opposite coast, in Melbourne.

Redback Original is made from equal proportions of wheat and malt, to a gravity of 11.3 Plato (1045.2) and 3.8 percent alcohol by weight, 4.7 by volume, with a colour of 8 EBC. The wheat is all of the Tincurrin variety, grown nearby, in the Avon Valley. The hops are Australian Pride of Ringwood and European Saaz, with only one addition (18 units of bitterness). The yeast, which is very non-flocculent, originally came from the Stolz brewery at Isny, in the Allgäu region just north of Lake Constance and the Tettnang hop country, on Baden-Württemberg's border with Bavaria.

The brewery claims that most Redback is fermented in shallow, horizontal cylinders. There are also tall, upright cylindro-conical vessels, but these are said to be used for Foster's

Lager and other products. Redback is centrifuged before being given two weeks' tank-conditioning, and is then sterile-filtered.

The beer has a fruity suggestion of dessert apples, quite sweet at first, but becoming tarter and more refreshing in the finish. It seems to me that it has lost some of its spiciness since its early days.

SCHNEIDER
Privatbrauerei G Schneider & Sohn,
1-5 Emil Ott Strasse, 8420 Kelheim,
Bavaria, Germany
Tel: (09441) 7050

The distinctive Aventinus glass gets a garland of hop vines... although wheat beers are not heavily hopped.

When the Schneider family acquired the brewery in Kelheim, the premises had already been making wheat beer since 1607. They believe it is the oldest brewery to have always produced this style.

A 1650s' building, vaguely Spanish in style, now provides a home for the sixth Schneider, whose parents Georg V and Margaret run the business. Other buildings are neo-Gothic, including the brewery tap, the Weisses Bräuhaus (open all months except November). Hop wreaths made by Margaret Schneider soften the entrance to the modern brewhouse block. The whole site is partially moated by a small river that flows into the Danube.

From the Jurassic stone of the hills, water rises to quench the town and the brewery. The water is softened before meeting the wheat (representing a hearty 60 percent of the grist) and barley malt (pale, Vienna and dark are used in the brewery's principal product, Schneider Weisse). The mash is double-decoction. Hop extract and Hallertau-Hersbruck are employed, in two additions. The 1988 brewhouse is in stainless steel, with the vessels set into a marble floor.

A multistrain yeast is employed, and all fermentation is in open vessels, at 20°C/68°F. The brewery takes great care in the regime of fermentation and maturation to ensure that its products have the particular fruitiness and clove-like spiciness that characterize a traditional wheat beer, and monitors this constantly in its lab. In the bottle, the beer is primed with wort and the brewery's house yeast. It then has a week at 20°C/68°F, during which the typical flavour develops, and a fortnight at 8°C/46°F to stabilize the brew.

Schneider Weisse (12.85–13.5; 1050–4; 4.4; 5.5; 13 BU) is neither pale nor dark but has a distinctively tan colour (19 EBC). It has a big head; a fresh bouquet; a clean, restrained fruitiness, developing to the characteristic spiciness; a light but firm body, with plenty of carbonation; and a quenching tartness in the long finish.

The brewery is equally famous for its Weizen Doppelbock, called Aventinus. This beer was first made in 1907, when the Schneiders were brewing in Munich, and their bottling hall was on Aventine Strasse, but the name has grander allusions. The label bears a picture of Johannes Aventinus, the historian who first described Bavaria and its people. Rome's Aventine Hill, and the Bishop thereof, provide an ecclesiastical reference. Aventinus was the perfect response when more typical Doppelbock names aroused opposition from the brewers of bottom-fermenting examples such as Salvator.

Aventinus has a gravity of 18.5 Plato (1074; 6.1; 7.7), and is made from pale, crystal and dark malts. The crystal is of a type known as Caramalt, made in Bamberg. The beer has a very big head; a deep, tawny colour (43 EBC); malty notes in the nose; chocolate, fruit and spices in the palate; a medium to full body; and a clove-like finish.

I have seen this flavourful beer used to great effect to baste the skin on a roast knuckle of pork, but I think I prefer it with dessert, or as a bedtime drink on a summer's evening.

UPPER CANADA
The Upper Canada Brewing Company,
2 Atlantic Avenue, Toronto, Ontario
M6K 1X8, Canada
Tel: (416) 534-9281

Using the settlers' earlier name for Ontario, this sizable microbrewery opened in 1985, in an old warehouse, smartly renovated, in an industrial area near the Exhibition Stadium. The building has been softened with flower beds, a conservatory-style portico and a guest bar.

Upper Canada specializes in all-malt brews. It began with a Weihenstephan-trained brewer, but has since entrusted its kettles to two or three British successors. Its range includes lagers, a top-fermenting brew that began by resembling an Altbier or perhaps a Belgian ale but has since become more British-accented, and a wheat beer.

Upper Canada Wheat Beer, which is filtered, has a bright, full golden colour and a light body. It has a refreshing, slightly tart palate with a light fruitiness and only the faintest hint of spiciness. It is made with 35 percent of the defining grain and with pale barley malt (10.3 Plato; 1041; 3.4; 4.3). The hops are Northern Brewer, in one addition (18-20 BU).

Elsewhere in Toronto, the Growler's brewpub has a yeasty, spicy wheat beer in a more Bavarian style. In Victoria, British Columbia, Spinnakers brewpub has made a dark wheat beer with cherries, named Dunkel Krieken Weizen.

Belgian wheat beer

If a Muscat wine can taste of oranges, then so can a beer. It is the orange taste, and the sweet-and-dry spiciness, that distinguishes the 'white' wheat beers of Belgium and the products they have inspired in the Netherlands, France and the United States. The best of these are aromatized with Curaçao orange peel, coriander and other spices, in addition to hops. These flavours marry happily with the plum and apple characteristics that derive from the use of wheat.

In the Belgian tradition, the wheat is unmalted, which perhaps gives these beers more firmness of body, and graininess, than their German cousins. Nor do the Belgian-style brews (Hoegaarden, pronounced 'who garden', is the best-known example) generally have the intense lactic acidity of the Berlin wheat beers or the clove-like character of the south German examples. In a country that is fond of bottle-conditioned beers, it is hardly surprising that the Belgian 'whites' are sedimented. They typically have a full yellow-white colour, with a pale, dense head.

Just as 'white' beers have enjoyed a surge of youthful rediscovery in Germany, so have their Belgian counterparts. These movements have been independent of one another, although in both cases a new generation of drinkers has found a beer that not only has nostalgic appeal, but is also very refreshing.

Served fresh, Belgian wheat beers are fruitily quenching, but being bottle-conditioned, most can take two or three months' aging in a cool (but not cold), dark place, during which the hop will recede and the orange flavours perhaps be enhanced by some Madeira notes. At this stage, they offer the bonus of being a dessert beer, especially if the dessert has a bitter-orange or sweet apple flavour.

The Belgian style of 'white' beer has its origins in the stretch of Brabant east of Brussels and Leuven (in French, Louvain), a region of rich soil growing barley, oats and sugar beet – and more especially wheat. There has been malting and brewing here for at least six or seven centuries. In an area settled by the Celts, a monastery was established in the 15th century at what became the small town of Hoegaarden, near Tienen. Hoegaarden had its own Guild of Brewers in

Beers brewed from wheat are traditionally known as 'white' beers (*witbier* in Flemish, *bière blanche* in French) because of their very pale colour and a degree of cloudiness. The Belgian examples, spiced with coriander and Curaçao orange peel, are increasingly popular both as simple refreshers and, after a few months' bottle-ageing, dessert beers.

The monastic heritage of brewing in Hoegaarden is reflected in the cloistered design of the Kouterhof bar and restaurant.

The chunky tumbler designed to hold Hoegaarden.

**Behind Hoegaarden's cloisters, a courtyard
reminder of a château farm.**

the 1500s. It was natural that the brewers would use
the wheat, and perhaps the oats, of the region, but it is
not clear precisely when more exotic ingredients came
into play. It is not surprising, though, that this happened. Belgium was a part of the Netherlands when
many spice islands, including the orange-growing
territory of Curaçao, were colonized.

By the 1800s, Hoegaarden was the brewing centre
of a sizable region stretching toward Liège. It had 30
breweries, all making the 'white' beer.

By the mid-1950s, however, after two World Wars
and the decline of regional styles, 'white' beer was no
longer being made in Hoegaarden. Nor did it retain
much of a foothold elsewhere, although two other
breweries in Brabant continued to make the style until
the late 1970s to mid-1980s, and the De Kroon brewery of Neerijse, west of Hoegaarden, still has a very
cloudy, sweet and cidery Double White.

In the early 1960s, Pierre Celis, who had lived next
door to Hoegaarden's last 'white' beer brewery, was
lamenting the loss of the local brew with a few friends.
Celis had often helped out at the brewery, and had
learnt something of the production procedures. He
decided to revive the style. He bought equipment
from another defunct brewery and started production
of his 'white' beer in 1966. He called his brewery De
Kluis ('cloister'), as a tribute to the monastery that
had started Hoegaarden's brewing tradition.

By the mid-1980s, the revival of the style was gaining ground, and brewers elsewhere in Belgium began
to introduce 'white' beers. In West Flanders, Riva's
Dentergems Witbier has a sweet, apple-and-honey

character; and De Gouden Boom's cloudy Brugs Tar-
webier/Blanche de Bruges has a yeasty but soft palate
(*tarwe* means wheat). Later came the dry, herbal and
orangey Steendonks Witbier (from Palm, in Brabant);
the tangily fruity Blanch-ke (from Van Honsebrouck,
in West Flanders); the remarkably wheaty Haecht
Tarwebier (from Haacht, in Brabant); and the very
pale, lightly perfumy Oudenaards Wit Tarwebier
(from Clarysse, in East Flanders). Van Honsebrouck
later produced a lightly herbal example called Vlaam-
sch Wit/Blanche des Flandres. To the south, the
Brasserie du Bocq, in Purnode, makes the appetizingly dry, herbal Blanche de Namur; and in Hainaut,
the Brasserie de Silly calls its example Titje, an aromatically fruity beer with a tart, quenching palate.

In the mid- to late 1980s, several breweries in the
adjoining beer country of northern France started
making similar products, but generally without spices.

At the same time, one or two Dutch breweries
launched Belgian-style wheat beers; there are now a
dozen or 20 such brews made in the Netherlands.

The first was made at Heumen, near Nijmegen, in
Gelderland, at a farmhouse maltings and brewery dating from the 1700s, which had closed in the 1920s,
and reopened in 1984. The brewery was revived
under the name Raaf ('raven') by Herm Heggens and
his wife Rian. Raaf was later acquired, specifically for
its tart, spicy-tasting Witbier, by Allied Breweries'
Dutch subsidiary Breda/Oranjeboom.

Heineken, through its subsidiary brewery De Rid-
der, of Maastricht, has the well-balanced Wieckse
Witte. This has a very 'white' colour; a melony fruitiness and plenty of spicy, herbal coriander in the nose;
and a light, refreshing palate, drying in the finish.

This style is also in the repertoire of the Maximili-
aan brewpub, which opened in Amsterdam in 1992.
This brewery, at 6–8 Kloveniersburgwal, in the old
inner city, produces a wide range of unfiltered beers.

Meanwhile in Belgium, Pierre Celis was bought
out by Interbrew, the Artois company. Since then, the
beer has lost a little of its fruity roundness, although it
must still be regarded as the classic example of its
style in the Old World.

Having exported his beer to the United States,
Celis moved to Austin, Texas, where he had friends,
and in 1992 opened a brewery there.

Belgian wheat beer producers

Many brewers have added wheat beers to their ranges in recent years, but credit for the style's revival must go to one man – Pierre Celis. He is now making a world-classic example in the United States.

HOEGAARDEN

Brouwerij De Kluis, 46 Stoopkens Straat, 3320 Hoegaarden, Belgium Tel: (016) 76 76 76

The brewery, with one wall proudly standing since the 1500s, is on the site of a former farm; like many farms in northern Europe, the premises have in the past been used for malting, brewing and distilling. The equipment first used by Pierre Celis has long been consigned to the museum of agricultural life, at Bokrijk, in the Belgian province of Limburg. Today's smart, blue-tiled brewhouse has copper and stainless steel vessels.

The principal beer, usually known simply as Hoegaarden, is made from roughly equal parts of raw wheat and malted barley. A small proportion of oats was originally used, but this refinement was eventually considered unnecessary. I believe the oats imparted a smoothness that has since diminished. The original gravity is 12 Plato (1048), and the water is hard. Hoegaarden is not a hoppy beer (with just under 20 units of bitterness), but it does have some Kent Goldings for dryness and Saaz for aroma.

The spices (coriander seeds and dried Curaçao orange peel) are milled before being added, and there is some speculation about the inclusion of a third spice, possibly cumin seeds. The brewery is reluctant to discuss its 'trade secret'.

Fermentation takes a week, at 18–24°C/64–79°F. The beer is then warm-conditioned for three to four weeks at 12–15°C/53.6–59°F before being bottled with a dosage of glucose and a different yeast for the secondary fermentation of around ten days, at 25°C/77°F. It emerges with 3.8 percent alcohol by weight, 4.8 by volume.

The brewery also produces an outstanding beer which it describes as a Tripel, called Hoegaarden Grand Cru (18.4; 1073.5; 7; 8.7). This has a similar spicing but is not a wheat beer. It has a hazy, peachy colour; a fruity, complex palate, with suggestions of melon or mango; and a warming finish. It is very much a liqueur of the beer world, and it will evolve in the bottle for up to four years.

Yet a third celebrated brew is called Forbidden Fruit (De Verboden Vrucht or Le Fruit Défendu); it has 7.2 percent alcohol by weight, 9 by volume, and its label is based on Rubens' painting of Adam and Eve. Forbidden Fruit is well-balanced, dark, rich and sweet, hitting the palate with notes of chocolate and vanilla, and hinting at the coriander that is used in its production.

There is also a very fine, drier, sparkling beer called Julius, with some resemblances to Duvel (see page 128), and an abbey *dubbel* type named St Benedict.

The beers are highlighted as both accompaniments and ingredients in the restaurant adjoining the brewery, the Kouterhof, Tel: (016) 76 74 33.

CELIS

Celis Brewery, 2431 Forbes Drive, Austin, Texas 78754, USA Tel: (512) 835-0130

Bolo-tied Pierre at the new Celis brewery in Austin, Texas.

Pierre Celis's new brewery is a smart, modern building, set in the spacious, leafy Walnut Creek Business Park, around four miles northeast of Austin's downtown.

The 1930s' copper brewhouse formerly produced Pils and Whitbread Pale Ale (under licence) at a brewery near Geraardsbergen, in Belgium.

Limestone water emerges from what was once a deep inland sea, in an area where fossils of ichthyosauri and plesiosauri have been discovered. Hard, 'red', winter wheat is grown around the small Texas town of Luckenbach, known to fans of country music as the home of Waylon Jennings. Pale barley malt from Belgium is also used, and the hops are Willamettes and Cascades, from Oregon and Washington. As in Belgium, coriander seeds and Curaçao orange peel are employed.

The beer is fermented with a yeast very similar to that used in Belgium. After primary fermentation, the brew has one week of lactic, after which it is pasteurized, then repitched with the same yeast for a further fermentation in tank. The beer is bottled with a yeast sediment.

Celis White, as the beer is known, is very similar to the original Belgian product, though perhaps softer, slightly fruitier, and fuller in flavour.

The brewery also makes a creamy, perfumy and flowery ale called Golden. This uses a highly distinctive yeast once employed by Ginder Ale, of Belgium, but reputed to have originated from the Bohemian Forest. There is also a bronze ale, fruitier and drier (slightly woody?), made with another Belgian yeast. Although this has a gravity of little over 11 Plato (1044–5), it is called a Bock. This product is clearly intended to compete with the local Shiner Bock, a dark lager of standard gravity. Texas state law does not permit bock beers of an appropriate strength.

More styles are expected from Celis, a restless and always imaginative brewer.

ALES

I n modern usage, ale indicates a brew that has a warm fermentation, traditionally with strains of yeast that rise to the top of the vessel. These 'top-fermenting' yeasts distinguish ales from lagers, where the yeasts work at cool temperatures, at the bottom of the vessel.

What does this mean for the consumer? A brew made with a warm fermentation is likely to have a fruity aroma and palate, and often a complex flavour.

The term ale refers only to the method of fermentation, and has nothing to do with the types of malt or hops used, or the colour or strength of the brew. In archaic English usage, an ale used to mean a beer without hops; in some parts of North America until recently, brewers regarded it as a beer with more hops than a lager. Neither of these meanings applies today.

Some American states' laws insist that a brew with more than 4 percent alcohol by weight be called an ale, but such requirements were drafted by bureaucrats with no know-ledge of the matter. Some British drinkers have not encountered golden ales, and think that the colour must always be a reddish amber, but that is not the case. An ale can be in any hue the brewer fancies.

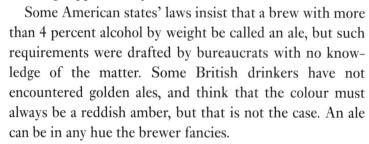

The expression is most associated with the British Isles. Ireland and Scotland have their own distinctive styles of ale. English variations include mild, bitter, pale ale, the hoppier India pale ale (IPA), brown ale, the stronger old ale and the very potent barley wine. The word 'ale' was some-times used to indicate mild rather than bitter, but that usage has been forgotten. Today, the lay drinker may use the term ale colloquially. If three people agree to 'go for an ale', one may be as good his word, but the others may equally well have a stout or a lager.

Being an English word, the term ale is principally used in regions where that is the first language, including North America and Australasia. Ale waned in popularity in North America for a time, but is now enjoying a revival. So are porters and stouts, which are also made with ale yeasts, although these roasty brews are regarded as a family in their own right.

Brews similar to pale ales are also made in Belgium. These are sometimes known by the English word ale – or, in the French-speaking part of the country, as *spéciales*. It is technically correct to regard most other Belgian speciality styles as broadly being in the ale family, even though they are not described as such in their own country. In Britain, the term ale has even been used to cover a spontaneously fermenting lambic from Belgium, but that is stretching a point.

The ale family might also be regarded as including certain German speciality beers, notably the Altbier of Düsseldorf and the Kölsch of Cologne. Wheat beers, although usually top-fermenting, form a style of their own.

Members of the ale family are typically fermented at 15–25°C/59–77°F. The classic styles of the British Isles are usually matured for short periods, often just a week, at natural cellar temperatures. If that procedure has been followed, they will most fully express their aroma and flavour if served at a similar temperature. Elsewhere in the world, ales are often given a cooler maturation, perhaps for a couple of weeks or more. Those products may be more susceptible to being served chilled.

The modern English language is fortunate to have the two words, beer and ale. Those who care can use beer as an overall term, and ale to identify the warm-fermenting types. In the 1400s and 1500s, the Germanic bier/beer was used in England to identify the new, hopped, brews, and ale the older type without the hops. Etymologically, ale has Old Saxon origins. Versions of the word are used to describe all types of beer in Norwegian and Danish (*øl*), Swedish (*öl*) and Finnish (*olut*).

The third European word for a fermented grain beverage, the Latin cerveza/cervoise, was also at one stage used only to indicate an unhopped version.

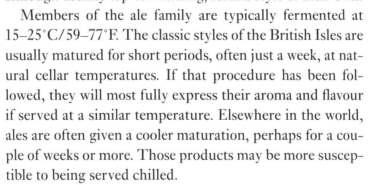

Mild

Today's tender sensibilities should favour a style called mild, and perhaps they will. The designation refers to mildness of hop character. A mild is gentle, sweetish, certainly not bitter. Some milds are pale in colour (lower 20s EBC), but more are tawny or dark (up to around 100). The darker milds are sometimes seen as a draught version of a brown ale, and the style may trace its lineage to the lesser porters.

Mild is an ale intended to be consumed in quantity, more as a restorative than a refresher. It was once a harvest-time drink, a reward for farm-workers. Mild has also been described, confusingly, by the designation 'hock'. The term 'hock cart' was once used to identify the last load of grain from the harvest. This may simply have derived from the German *hoch*: the 'high' cart. Among rural breweries in Britain today, Gale's of Horndean, Hampshire, has a dryish mild; Adnams of Southwold, Suffolk, a more chewy example; and Bateman of Wainfleet, Lincolnshire, a very smooth Dark Mild. Just north of London, the country town of Hertford, an old centre of the malting trade, has the McMullen brewery, which makes a subtle and beautifully balanced pale brew mysteriously called AK (see page 71). This is a mild, although the brewery no longer identifies it as such.

The style was also popular in areas of thirst-making industry, and has retained its strongest loyalties in the West Midlands towns of Birmingham, Walsall, Wolverhampton and Dudley, and to a lesser extent the Manchester area.

Mild came to be seen as an old-fashioned style, with a 'cloth cap' image. The darker examples also suffered from the mistaken belief that brews with a full colour are necessarily heavier in body or stronger in alcohol. Only when the style had become almost forgotten could a new generation of drinkers rediscover it. There are indications that it may now have gone full circle and be making a comeback.

In their own insouciant style, drinkers of mild enjoy a reverie at the Beacon Hotel. This sturdy pub holds its ground in a sliver of countryside between Wolverhampton and Dudley; the pub has been fastidiously restored. The 'recipe' for its ale was found in a cigar box lodged in a bank safe.

Mild refers to the hop character: these are not bitter beers, but can nevertheless be full of flavour, whether they are pale or dark. They are also generally low in alcohol, at around 3–3.8 percent by volume, and make good lunchtime drinks. Perhaps this explains their new-found popularity?

In the early 1990s, the London brewery Fuller's reintroduced its cask-conditioned mild, under the name Hock, and some of the best pubs in the capital began to offer Highgate Mild, from a long-established brewery in the West Midlands (see page 71).

Most milds are relatively light in body and very low in alcohol, but they can be full of flavour. The complex Highgate is probably the classic example. Other famous West Midlands milds include the malty, fruity, slightly winy Banks's (see page 70), the lightly chewy Holden's and the chocolaty Ansells. To the south of Manchester, Robinson's has a soft-tasting pale Best Mild; to the north, Thwaites a more intense, licorice-like dark example.

In the days when work was manual, readily available, and back-breaking, more powerful restoratives were required. Many styles of beer were stronger in those times, and that is the justification for the potency (4.8 percent alcohol by weight, 6 by volume) of the highly regarded Original Dark Ruby Mild

made at the Sarah Hughes Brewery, in the Beacon Hotel, at Sedgley, near Dudley. This is really a brewpub, around 125 years old, but it ceased production in 1957. Sarah Hughes was once the publican and brewer; her grandson and successor John revived the house beer in 1987. The Original Dark Ruby Mild has a magnificent colour, a clean fruitiness, and just the faintest hint of syrupiness.

In south Wales, a perhaps fuller-bodied variant is sometimes known simply as dark. A fine example in this interpretation is the toasty Dark made by Brains of Cardiff. In the shipbuilding towns of Newcastle-upon-Tyne and Sunderland in northeast England, a version with a faintly burnt-tasting malt character is confusingly called Scotch ale. In Scotland, similar beers, usually dark, are – again confusingly – identified as light ale or 60/- (sixty shilling ale). Maclay's malty example is a good one.

One or two American microbreweries have now introduced the style, and I was greatly impressed by the reddish-brown, light-bodied, smooth, fruity Mariners' Mild, which I tasted at the Pacific Coast brewpub in Oakland, California, in 1990. I was equally taken with a mahogany-coloured, soft, creamy mild, with notes of chocolate and coffee, from the Goose Island brewpub of Chicago. I would also deem to be a dark mild the malty, nutty brew curiously launched as a Cream Ale by the Shaftebury brewery in Vancouver, Canada. I have heard that a mild is being made by the Knysna microbrewery, of Cape Province, South Africa, but have not had the opportunity to taste it. No doubt there will be more.

Above the door of many an English pub is the name of the publican who has applied for a licence to sell ale and porter. Beneath the one on the far left, John Hughes has a pint of mild ale with brewer Lee Cox (right).

Highgate Mild can now be enjoyed in many pubs throughout Britain.

Mild producers

Many of Britain's rural breweries have kept the traditional harvest-workers' ale in their repertoire, but some of the best-known milds, such as Banks's and Highgate, come from the industrial West Midlands.

BANKS'S
Park Brewery, Lovatt Street,
Wolverhampton, West Midlands
WV1 4NY, England
Tel: (0902) 711811

Banks's and Hanson's were once a pair of West Midlands milds, from Wolverhampton and Dudley respectively. The owning company, which dates from 1890, is called Wolverhampton & Dudley Breweries, though only the first still operates. Tucked behind a row of Georgian cottages on the edge of the city centre, it is one of the biggest independent breweries in Britain. Its principal product is its mild, although it also makes a bitter. Managing director David Thompson is privately a farmer, with the odd field of barley, and professionally a maltster and brewer.

'The boss grew some Maris Otter barley, but it didn't make malt good enough for our beer,' I was once told at the brewery. 'He is very good at chewing malt. He can tell you straight

away whether it will make good beer.' The company favours Maris Otter for its 'rich, deep, round taste', and contracts individual farmers to grow this variety, which has become a rarity. Banks's has two maltings, both employing the floor system, and takes a pride in using no chemical aids.

The water rises from a borehole two miles away at the village of Tettenhall. It is somewhat hard, and is softened for the mild. The hops are predominantly Goldings (from East Kent) and Fuggles (preferably from the River Teme area of Worcester), with some Progress and Bramling Cross (25 BU). Eight growers contribute to each batch, and the hops are weighed out by hand. At the brewery, I have seen hop-pockets labelled by their growers in Parsonage Farm, Lulsley Court and Pipe-cum-Lyde. The names could be slipped into a Miss Marple story without anyone suspecting a thing.

Despite its being a large brewery, Banks's works in relatively small

batches. It has five mash tuns and the same number of kettles, and its brewing system is simple and traditional.

The attention to detail is remarkable. Like many British beers, the Banks's products are 'fined' (clarified) in the cask with isinglass, a gelatinous substance obtained from the swim bladders of tropical fish. The brewery insists that the isinglass be provided by the Pungas catfish of Southeast Asia, and that it be supplied in its whole dried 'leaf' as opposed to the shredded or ready-made jelly forms used by most other brewers. 'Very expensive, Saigon leaf,' the head brewer once told me, as though he were discussing something to smoke or snort. 'The Chinese want it for bird's-nest soup, and what with the troubles they've had in Vietnam...'

Banks's Mild (1036, 9 Plato, with 2.8 percent alcohol by weight, 3.5 by volume) has a full, reddish tawny colour (40 EBC); a palate that is very clean in both its maltiness and fruitiness, and a hint of sweet winyness. 'It is an extremely difficult beer to get right,' said the head brewer. 'When it is on song, you don't notice that you are drinking it – just that your glass is suddenly empty.'

To the products of rustic English counties, Banks's brewery adds Saigon leaf, obtained from Southeast Asian catfish. This mysterious-sounding element has even found its way into the brewery's advertising.

The company's chairman helps choose the hops that boil in Banks's 1950s' copper kettles.

HIGHGATE

*Highgate Brewery, Sandymount Road,
Walsall, West Midlands WS1 3AP,
England
Tel: (0922) 23168*

This delightful ale perfectly illustrates complexity of flavour in a brew
that is otherwise very light. Highgate
has a gravity of only 1035.5 (just
under 9 Plato, 2.6 percent alcohol by
weight, 3.2 by volume), but contains
six malts, grains and brewing sugars,
with pale ale, crystal and black malts
the key ingredients (it has the colour
of a dark wood: 63 EBC). By comparison, the hopping is very simple:
Goldings, added just once (22 BU).

The yeast character is complex.
The principal culture, which has four
strains, is believed to have been
passed on from one brew to the next
since Highgate was built in 1895.
Experimental attempts to separate the
strains and reculture them have not
produced the same toffeeish notes in
the beer. A second yeast, which ferments the beer slightly further, has
also been used for many years. The
two yeasts are blended, and pitched
together. The fermenters are open,
made of oak and in some cases lined

with copper. The end result is a
remarkably smooth ale, with a teasing
balance of maltiness and fruitiness,
and a hint of iron (from the water?).

Highgate, a listed building, is the
smallest brewery owned by the
national group Bass. For some years,
it produced only Mild – an unusual
specialization – but in the late 1980s
revived its seasonal old ale.

The malt for Highgate Mild is screened for any remaining stones from the
farmer's field in this grain riddle, known in the brewery as 'the coffin'. It has
been in use since the brewery was founded.

McMULLEN

*McMullen & Sons, The Hertford
Brewery, 26 Old Cross, Hertford
SG14 1RD, England
Tel: (0992) 584911*

A pargeted cottage dating from the
1600s provides the guest bar at this
classic country brewery. The
McMullen family, distantly from Ireland, founded the brewery in 1827,
and in about 1832 started making an
ale called AK which is today their
most widely known brew.

There were once more than a dozen
beers called AK in Hertfordshire, and
a good few in other parts of the country. The term always seems to have
indicated an ale of modest strength,
and there are many theories as to its
origin, but none decisive. In a
2,000-word investigation in *The Journal of the Brewery History Society*,
enthusiast Martyn Cornell guessed
that the 'a' indicated ale, and the 'k'
perhaps kyte, an Old Flemish word
meaning a small beer.

The site began as a farm, and a
seed warehouse now occupies the
former maltings, with their towered
oast. The brewery's main buildings
date from 1891, and the rooftop clock
installed at that time formerly graced
Wormwood Scrubs prison in London. Four members of the
McMullen family are in the company. The brewery's manager and
foreman, not McMullens, are father
and son.

AK is made from pale ale and
chocolate malts, and Goldings hops.
The yeast seems to unmask a malty
dryness, but there are also leafy hop
flavours and a refreshingly acidic
fruitiness. It has the characteristic
gentleness of a mild, and considerable
flavour development.

Being a very old-fashioned company, McMullen's finally caught up
with the unfashionability of mild as
the tide was turning. Although AK is
surely a pale mild, the company
dropped the designation just as it was
coming back into style.

Bitter

Sweetness, bitterness, sourness and saltiness are the salients among the several million aroma-and-flavour experiences available to humans. A bitter experience may be unpleasant in metaphor but can be arousing in reality. The sensuous Italians sharpen their appetite, and sometimes calm their digestion (or, the next day, their hangover), with bitter drinks made from quinine, herbs and spices. Those are known as bitters, always plural. The beer is called bitter, always singular.

Many traditional foods and drinks have intense characters. In the days when few of us knew flavours from beyond our own homelands, we acquired the taste of what was local or went without. The British novelist Graham Greene, who came from the brewing family that owns Greene King in Suffolk, recalled that he forced down his first pint of bitter to prove his manliness. Some days later, he continued, 'I drank bitter for the second time and enjoyed the taste with a pleasure that has never failed me since.'

No marketing man would ever have created a category called bitter, but to the beer-drinker the word is mouthwatering. Every British pub-goer can recognize bitter, and regards it as a drink in its own right, probably unaware that it is a type of ale. Although the word 'ale' is familiar enough, few Britons could define it. Nor could many, offhand, name other styles of ale in Britain, though the words mild, pale or brown might bring a glimmer of recognition.

'Pale and bitter ales' are grouped as one in a book on *The Defects of Beer* by the gothic-sounding James Death, in 1889, but the two terms did not seem to find separate lives for some decades. In 1948, *The Brewer's Art*, published by Whitbread, said that pale ale was sold both in the bottle and on draught, but parenthesized the second as 'bitter'. It seems to me that pale (or, in lower gravities, light) was seen as a refined term for the table or even the cocktail bar, while bitter sounded like a down-to-earth draught for the boys in

The fuller name of the brewery embraces Smith and Turner, although it is a long time since these beerwrights produced an 'entire' (a predecessor to porter). The nostalgic allusion is forgivable in a pub as rich in history as The Dove, Hammersmith, London. The pub overlooks the River Thames.

Bitter is the principal style of ale sold in Britain, ideally enjoyed freshly drawn from the cask, in a pub, with friends. If a sociable evening is planned, devotees prefer a bitter that is low in gravity and alcohol. A good hop character is of the first importance, but beyond that it is a very wide-ranging style.

the boozer. In those days, bottled beer was seen as being more sophisticated, though that perception would later be stood on its head.

In Australia, where the designations pale and sparkling ale had already appeared, bitter seems to have come into use around 1910, never altogether vanished, and enjoyed a revival in the early 1990s. In its early days in Australia, bitter referred to a true, top-fermenting ale. Today, it more often describes a lager with an ostensibly bitter palate. Only the odd microbrewed example is truly an ale.

Elsewhere in the world, the notion of calling a relatively hoppy lager a bitter has cropped up in Alsace, France, where the Fischer/Pêcheur brewery uses the term for its Fischer Bitter, a lager with a pleasantly dry hoppiness.

When I began to take an interest, as a teenager in the late 1950s, every pub's principal offerings were draught bitter and mild. How bitter? More bitter than the mild. Each term was defined by the other, like left and right in a political party. There seemed no more precise definition than that. The bitter was usually paler, although both styles occupied a wide range of shades. Bitter might range from straw to chestnut, mild extend to ruby or mahogany. Bitter was almost always more expensive and usually slightly stronger than mild, but it was taste that most clearly separated them. Bitter was the drier; mild the sweeter.

The dryness may come in part from a use of paler malts in bitter as against mild, and perhaps a greater attenuation, but the essential ingredient is the hearty smack of hops. Pale ale malts are the principal grist; if crystal is used at all, it is employed with great restraint. Bitter's ascendancy came at a time when Fuggles and Goldings were the dominant hop varieties, and they are still the classics for the style.

If the beer is to be bitter, the emphasis must be on kettle hops, though there is also a tradition of a handful in the cask. Examples of bitter with an outstanding dry-hop character include Adnams' Extra (notable for its Fuggles aroma), from Southwold, Suffolk; Ind Coope Burton Ale (Styrian Goldings); and Timothy Taylor's Landlord (Styrian Goldings again), from Keighley, West Yorkshire.

It seems natural enough that some emphatically dry bitter is made in the southeast of England, near the hop country of Kent. Not far from Canterbury, the small town of Faversham, set amid hop gardens, is said to have had breweries since monks made beer there in the 1100s. It once boasted 84, but now has just one, Shepherd Neame, founded in 1698, believed to be England's oldest. The front door is surrounded by decorative mouldings of hops, and inside the

Some drinkers find that metal tankards impart a metallic tinge, but others like the natural cool, and may keep their own tankard at their local pub.

This house, once home to the brewer at Fuller's, is now the company's offices. It was built around 1800, and the wisteria is said to have been growing since the turn of the century. Behind the house is the brewery itself. Just around the corner is Chiswick Square, featured in Thackeray's *Vanity Fair*. In the local churchyard lies Hogarth, whose bawdy engravings include *Beer Street*.

brewery are several unlined teak mash tuns (used, curiously, in the making of lager). Shepherd Neame's Masterbrew Bitter has a firm, dry malty start and a good, hoppy attack as it moves into its long, dry finish (35 units of bitterness). All the hops are locally grown, with Omega and Target for bitterness and Goldings for aroma.

The county of Kent is contiguous with London, where the hops were traditionally traded, and the capital has two world-class breweries, Young's (see page 78) and Fuller's (see page 76), both noted for their dry examples of bitter.

Some brewers have only one bitter, others boast two or three, in ascending gravity. Like packagers beginning with 'large' and moving up to 'giant', or newspapers that first print the 'final' edition, then move on to 'late extra', some brewers introduce themselves with 'Best Bitter' then progress to fancier designations. Where a higher-gravity bitter is named 'Special' by the brewery, the lower-gravity brew informally becomes 'ordinary'. There are no rules. Fuller's already had two bitters when a stronger dark ale metamorphosed into Winter Bitter in 1969 and was renamed ESB (Extra Special Bitter) in 1971. Although the term has no precise definition, some brewers elsewhere have taken it to indicate a 'super-premium' bitter with a gravity in the 1050s (Fuller's ESB has 1054, 13.5 Plato).

The Thames Valley has many other distinguished examples of bitter, among them a delightfully hoppy 'ordinary' from Brakspear of Henley-on-Thames, and so does the south of England as a whole. Even Southerners sometimes believe the popular wisdom that the best beer, especially bitter, comes from the North, but no such simplistic judgment can be made. Although a similar range of gravities has traditionally been made in most parts of the country, perhaps workers in the industrial North were once more likely to choose the heftier examples, and that may have begun the belief. At least one brewery in Yorkshire used to make a special strong bitter for the steel city of Middlesbrough, for example.

Every corner of the country has its own excellent examples, from around 200 nationals, regionals, locals, micros and brewpubs. Nor is there any style of beer so subject to the characteristics of its own brewery or region. The water may make a difference, or local custom, or techniques of fermentation.

Many West Country bitters seem typically fruity. Among them are: from Wiltshire, the bitters of Archers and Arkell's, both in Swindon, and of Mole's in Melksham; from Dorset, Hall & Woodhouse's Badger Best Bitter (the brewery is at Blandford Forum) and Palmer's Best Bitter (Bridport); from Somerset, the Ash Vine brewery's Bitter (Trudoxhill, near Frome); and from Devon, Blackawton's Bitter (Washbourne, near Totnes).

Relatively sweetish bitter is made in the West Midlands (Batham's Best is a good example), some very dry ones in Greater Manchester (where the austere

Holt's is the classic). In Lancaster, the term Extra Special Bitter recurs in a malty example from Mitchell's. This was launched in 1972, at a gravity of 1045 (11.3 Plato), as a premium bitter; in 1988, Mitchell's ESB went up to 1050, as a super-premium, a northern counterpart to Fuller's.

Wards of Sheffield has a distinctively malty Sheffield Best Bitter; Timothy Taylor makes its outstandingly aromatic Landlord; while their larger neighbour Tetley, of Leeds, produces the softer, creamier interpretation associated with the Yorkshire Square fermentation system; it does use the Yorkshire Square System, albeit in stainless steel, for all of its ale. Tetley is Britain's (and therefore the world's) biggest producer of cask-conditioned ales. Theakston's Best and XB both have the slight 'yeast bite' also associated with Yorkshire.

In the northeast of England the Hadrian microbrewery, founded in 1987, has brought back some of the assertive hoppiness once associated with bitter in Newcastle. Its Gladiator and Centurion Best hint at the famous Roman wall, built in the second century on the orders of the emperor Hadrian, of which substantial parts remain.

Across Britain's borders, the Welsh brew bitter but the Scots prefer maltier styles, with names like heavy and export, or designations in the old shilling system (see page 106).

Leapfrog Scotland to Norway and a bitter appears, along with a pale ale, a stout and various other styles, in the Oslo Mikro Bryggeri, which is actually a brew-pub. This 'Micro Brewery' opened in late 1989. When I tasted the bitter, in the summer of 1991, it was very tart. Since the microbrewery movement began, examples have popped up elsewhere, but nowhere as persistently as in the United States.

American bitter

What may be the first two beers to have called themselves bitter in the United States were both launched in the same year, 1984, and in the same state, Washington, by Hale's Ales and the Independent Ale Brewery, now known as Redhook (see page 77). In Canada, Wellington County, of Guelph, Ontario, pioneered British-style bitter (see page 78), while Conners (which has brewed on several sites) began with a sweeter interpretation.

In the late 1980s and early 1990s, the term bitter spread across North America, especially in brewpubs. In Denver, Colorado, the Wynkoop brewery makes a hoppy Extra Special Bitter and an even more assertive Special Old Bitter (check out the acronym), both

Of the two London independents, it is Young's that still uses horses to deliver its beer locally ... but its trucks are just as eye-catching. The brewery also has a live ram to embody its symbol.

East Kent Goldings, pictured here at Tony Redsell's China Farm, are the classic aroma hop in English bitter. The style owes more to bitterness than bouquet, but it gains from this aromatic addition.

The Redhook brewery makes a range that stretches from wheat beer to porter, but it is best known for its ales. Its pale Ballard Bitter is somewhat bland, but its ESB has much more character.

dry-hopped. In Minnetonka, Minneapolis, Sherlock's Home (see page 110) has Bishop's Bitter (hoppy, with the acidity of some British counterparts) and its own SOB, with a sustained hop character. In Portland, Maine, Gritty McDuff's has a well-balanced, soothing bitter that is again very much in a British vein.

Other examples I have tasted recently include the smooth, malty, rounded Big Time ESB, from Seattle; the grainy, hoppy Cole's Special Bitter, from Salt Lake City; the gentle, complex Oasis ESB, from Boulder, Colorado; the very hoppy Buffalo Bitter, from the Firehouse Brewery, in Rapid City, South Dakota; and the aromatic, dry, very drinkable Best Bitter of Goose Island, in Chicago.

Bitter producers

Almost every brewer in England, and some in Scotland and Wales, makes at least one bitter. Interpretations vary between regions and brewers. As the style spreads internationally, the London brewers Young's and Fuller's are becoming a significant influence.

A classic English bitter … in the classic British pint glass, here seen engraved with the brewer's name.

An accompanying classic English hand pump … from which the classic English pint is pulled.

FULLER'S
Fuller, Smith & Turner, Griffin Brewery, Chiswick Lane South, London W4 2QB, England
Tel: (081) 995 0230

Fuller's basic bitter is called Chiswick, after the neighbourhood that accommodates the brewery (visible on the road from London's Heathrow Airport to the city centre). This bitter is fruity, with a flowery hop character, and very light and refreshing. The floweriness derives not so much from the Northdown and Challenger in the kettle, but from a dry-hopping with Goldings.

After Chiswick (1034; 8.5; 2.8; 3.5) come London Pride (1040; 10; 3.3; 4.1) and ESB (Extra Special Bitter: 1054; 13.5; 4.4; 5.5). The London Pride perhaps best expresses the house character of Fuller's: a soft texture at the front of the mouth (a less bicarbonate, more chloride, water?); strong maltiness; and a honey-flower character from the house yeast. This beer is not dry-hopped. The persistently award-winning ESB is, and that results in a powerful combination of the characteristics displayed by its smaller brother brews.

Fuller's reckons there has been a brewery on its site for 300 years, but the present business dates from the 1820s. In the late 1980s, Fuller's introduced a new winter ale called Mr Harry, after an imaginary connoisseur of beer. Although this began as a light-hearted enterprise to illuminate the odd winter month, Mr Harry has become a seasonal fixture. This ale has a gravity of only 1048 (12 Plato), but is all-malt, with a crystal character.

HALE'S ALES

410 North Washington, Colville,
Washington 99114, USA
Tel: (509) 684-6503

109 Central Way, Kirkland,
Washington 98033, USA
Tel: (206) 827-4359

Mike Hale acquired a taste for ales on his travels in Britain in the early 1970s. In 1981, he found himself a position as an unofficial 'apprentice' at Gale's brewery, near Portsmouth in the south of England. Then, inspired by America's first microbrewery, New Albion, he decided to try his hand in his homeland. With Gale's' blessing, and a sample of its yeast, he began in 1983 to brew in converted dairy tanks in Colville, Washington.

Colville is a remote country town, near the borders with Idaho and Canada. Hale, who has a pilot's licence, flew me from Seattle, across the Cascade Mountains, so that I could sample his beers. He was trained as an electrician, but is a typically resourceful Westerner – he built his brewery himself. He had previously been a member of the local council in Colville. Later, he opened a second brewery, in the Seattle suburb of Kirkland.

The first product of the Colville brewery was an American pale ale, but a year later Hale's added a hearty Special Bitter, made from the local limestone water, pale ale and crystal malts, Cluster and Idaho Hallertau hops. This product has since been subtitled Tom Sheimo's Favourite, in memory of an early brewer at Hale's.

When I first tasted the Special Bitter at Colville, I noted its subtle amber colour; warm aroma; soft, round, malty body; and a depth of hop bitterness. When I sampled it five or six years later at the Kirkland brewery, I found it much the same, but also noted its hop aroma.

THE PUMPHOUSE

17 Little Pier Street, Darling Harbour,
Sydney, New South Wales, Australia
Tel: (02) 291 841

The Pumphouse, built in 1891, was originally concerned with water, rather than beer. It drove a hydraulic system that operated lifts throughout the city. The Pumphouse ceased to function in 1962, although some of its equipment remains. It became a tavern in 1988, and a brewery was added a year later. The founders commissioned a British-made, 80-hectolitre brewhouse, though they might have thought smaller had they known Australia was on the brink of a deep recession. The brewery serves not only the Pumphouse but also 20 or 30 other bars in the city.

Its early products included that rarity in Australia, a genuinely top-fermenting bitter, which is further distinguished by its use of British-grown Fuggles and Goldings hops. My first taste of this ale came when I was handed a glass in a Sydney pub. I was shocked by the freshness and assertiveness of its hop bitterness in a country where such robust characteristics are not usual. The product has a name borrowed from English pubs, Bull's Head; a gravity of 1040 (10 Plato), 3.6 percent alcohol by

weight, 4.5 by volume; a bronze-red colour; a light to medium body; and a fruity-hoppy character, with the bitterness coming through especially strongly in the finish.

REDHOOK

3400 Phinney Avenue North, Seattle,
Washington 98103, USA
Tel: (206) 548-8000

Entrepreneur Gordon Bowker, who had already helped launch the Seattle 'alternative' newspaper *The Weekly* and the coffee company Starbucks (precursor of the espresso boom), came to London in 1980 to visit the Great British Beer Festival, and told me about his plans to launch a microbrewery. In 1982, he and Paul Shipman, formerly of the Chateau Ste Michelle winery, launched the Independent Ale Brewery in the Ballard neighbourhood of Seattle . Their copper vessels were bought second-hand from the Wacker brewery, of Gröningen, Baden-Württemberg.

They began with the extremely fruity, sweetish Redhook Ale, and followed it in 1984 with the paler,

At the Redhook brewery tap, kettles have replaced trams in this former tramshed in Seattle.

nuttier, lightly malty Ballard Bitter. In 1987, a seasonal ale with a drier fruitiness, and more hop character, was launched as Winterhook. In 1988, this became a year-round product, under the name Redhook ESB. This ale has an amber colour, a Tettnang hop aroma and a good bitterness in the finish.

The same year, the brewery moved into an old trolley barn (tramshed) in the Fremont district, installing new vessels. It has become one of America's biggest microbreweries, with a pub attached. Redhook, devised as a catchy brand name with a maritime undertone, is now the corporate style.

WELLINGTON COUNTY

950 Woodlawn Road West, Guelph, Ontario N1K 1B8, Canada
Tel: (519) 837-2337

From Toronto, it is around 40 miles to Guelph, an historically important town that houses an agricultural university and was once a centre of brewing, in Wellington County. The town's tradition, originating from its artesian wells and hard water (ideally suited to ales), is now enjoying something of a revival. In 1985, the Wellington County Brewery was established, with a view to making English-style ales. At the end of the same decade, the larger Sleeman's brewery reopened (see page 165).

There is a reference to traditional brewery architecture in Wellington County's neat, purpose-built premises, and the same values inform its splendid ales. British malts, East Kent Goldings and Styrians (widely used in England) give an immediately recognizable character to the brews, although North American materials are also used. The ales can be found cask-conditioned in selected outlets.

A member of Britain's Arkell brewing family founded a community near Guelph, and the name has been adopted by Wellington County for one of its beers. Arkell Best Bitter,

especially in cask form, has an earthy Goldings aroma, a balance of maltiness and fruitiness, and a long, hoppy finish. Special Pale Ale is sweeter and fruitier, County Ale bigger-bodied. Iron Duke is a beautifully balanced strong ale (5.2 percent alcohol by weight, 6.5 by volume). The brewery also makes an imperial stout.

YOUNG'S

Young & Co, The Ram Brewery, Wandsworth, London SW18 4JD, England
Tel: (081) 870 0141

No marketing man would have created a product called 'ordinary', any more than he would have dreamed up the title 'bitter'. There is nothing ordinary about Young's Bitter (1036, 9 Plato, 3 percent alcohol by weight, 3.7 by volume), but that is how this brew is affectionately known by local drinkers, to distinguish it from the higher-gravity, slightly maltier Special Bitter (1046; 11.5; 3.9; 4.8). A counterpart to Special Bitter is sold in bottles as RamRod, and the brewery

also has a magnificently hoppy strong pale ale known in Britain as Export (and Special London Ale in the United States).

Young's 'ordinary' Bitter most straightforwardly expresses the house character of this fine brewery's ales: a much appreciated dryness that is almost astringent (the bicarbonate water?); a light, clean maltiness (the variety is Maris Otter); an aromatic, earthy bitterness (the hops are the classic Fuggles and Goldings); and a faintly tart, lemony fruitiness (from the very distinctive house yeast).

The brewery is set behind high walls in a busy part of south London; if you happen to be passing on a double-decker bus you may catch a glimpse of the geese that guard the brewery, or the ram that is its mascot. Despite the traffic, deliveries to local pubs are still made by magnificent, jingling horse-drawn drays. The brewery is full of antique equipment, some still in use, other items enjoying an untroubled retirement. There is a steam donkey-engine, a turn-of-the-century grist mill and copper-lined wooden fermenters.

Like most brewery horses, Young's shires are known for being remarkably placid in traffic, although a pair called Tom and Jim did once damage several cars and a motorcycle, and demolished a road sign, after an impatient and inconsiderate driver honked his horn at them. The brewery incurred a dozen insurance claims.

Pale ale

It sounds poetic, romantic and delicate, but this British designation should not be taken too literally. The pallor of some of its American namesakes is far removed from the original meaning of the term, which indicated pale (and clear) as opposed to dark brown or black. A true pale ale is not golden: it has a dash of colour in its cheeks. It is at least bronze, if not amber-red. In achieving this colour, British brewers use what they specifically term pale ale malt, and this imparts its own character to the flavour, too: a very light nuttiness.

Long before bright golden lager was developed in Continental Europe, British brewers had created a stir with translucent amber-red ales. These brews established a reputation in Europe, the Empire in India, and the Americas, during Britain's expansionist Victorian period. They are now having something of a second wave, albeit on a smaller scale.

A popular verse of the mid-1700s referred to the pale ale made by a brewer called Hodgson, in Bow, London. His brewery was obviously well known at the time, but it has long vanished. Pale ale was popularized in the mid-1800s by producers in Burton, the small town on the river Trent, in the Midlands, that is now England's brewing capital.

Burton was the site of an abbey from at least the beginning of this millennium. By the 1200s, the monks had established the town's brewing history. Wells in Burton and the Trent Valley produced plentiful water, the availability of which was appreciated long before its quality was understood. The first brewing family in Burton was that of Hugh de Allsopp, who fought in the Crusades under Richard I. A later Allsopp was brewer to King Charles II. An early

> If a bitter is usually a dry-tasting draught beer, is a pale ale its rounder brother in the bottle? The two terms overlap, though pale ale is perhaps more glamorous. In Britain, the term IPA, an abbreviation of India Pale Ale, is too casually used; it should indicate a stronger, hoppier interpretation.

England's classic ale-brewing regions

Pale ales are famously produced in Burton-upon-Trent and Tadcaster. Milds are the major style in the West Midlands, and brown ales in the northeast, especially Newcastle-upon-Tyne. Bitter is brewed throughout England and Wales; Scotland has its own styles of beer. The county of Norfolk is renowned for its barley; Kent, Worcester and Hereford for their hops.

Burton pale ale was produced experimentally in a teapot at the Allsopp brewery in 1822.

The company later merged with Ind Coope, and became the basis for Allied Breweries, which today produces Burton Ale, Double Diamond and many other famous names.

Is Ind Coope Burton Ale a pale or a bitter? These two terms overlap. Pale ale is the longer-established term, and it is not clear when bitter came to be used. Although bitter was mentioned in the 1850s, and is listed as an 'important' style in the anonymous 1934 work *A Book about Beer*, it was still being placed in quotation marks in 1948, in *The Brewer's Art*. In Britain today, the term bitter is far more widely used.

Traditionally, pale ale was more often applied to a bottled product, usually of premium gravity and quality. Perhaps the term seemed better to suit an ale that visibly sparkled in the bottle, while bitter had a more matter-of-fact sound, suiting a lower-gravity product pulled from a pump. Where a brewery uses both designations, its pale ale will have a higher gravity than its bitter. In Britain pale ales range in gravity from the lower 1040s to the lower 1050s.

Again, where a brewery produces ales under both designations, the pale may be less obviously hoppy than the bitter. It could be argued that pale ales are distinguished more by that light nuttiness of malt character, while bitter emphasizes the dryness of the hop in the finish. It is tempting to argue that pale ales, having been popularized by Burton, should be hopped with varieties from the nearby growing area in Worcestershire and Herefordshire, but that might be stretching a point. Given the size of the industry in Burton, hops have always been bought from both that region and Kent. Nor does the region have a famous hop variety, although it grows some good Fuggles that are well suited to the balance of a pale ale.

Worcestershire is perhaps more widely known for its sauce, and Herefordshire for its beef cattle. The two might be put together with a glass of pale ale. To my palate, the light, fresh character of some pale ales goes even better with lamb. Some British breweries used to bottle what they called a dinner ale, but this practice died as wine became more accessible. Perhaps Bass should make more use of Manet's 1882 painting *The Bar at the Folies-Bergères*, in which bottles of the company's Pale Ale have pride of place among the wines.

Manet found Bass Pale Ale, from Burton, sitting happily beside the champagne at the Folies-Bergères in Paris. Such premium ales had a slightly raffish sophistication well into the 1950s. By the 1980s, they were again beginning to appear on 'wine' lists in restaurants, mainly in the United States.

Burton's water

Burton certainly popularized pale ale, even though the term was subsequently used in every other British brewing town. On that basis, perhaps a pale ale should, in addition to its premium gravity and quality, have certain Burton characteristics.

Burton's water, which rises through sandstone with a high content of gypsum, makes a major contribution. It has a calcium sulphate character, and most Burton brews have to some degree a sulphury nose. This may sound unpleasant, but enthusiasts of Burton beers are disappointed if they do not find this characteristic. I am reminded of a Japanese company that was trying to produce a 'brewery-fresh' quality in its beer. This product seemed to me somewhat sulphury on the nose. 'Ah, yes,' said the brewer. 'That is our aim. We want the beer to smell as fresh as a bath-house.' I suppose the same could be said of some spa waters. In the case of the Burton pale ales, the calcium sulphate is only one component among a complex of aromas and flavours.

Some calcium is needed in all brewing waters because of the biochemical effects it has upon natural enzyme reactions in mashing and yeast development. The levels of calcium in Burton's water make for a firmness of body, and length, that seems to suit the balance of pale ale as a style. The sulphate encourages the extraction of bitter resins from the hops, making for a dryness that seems also to suit the style.

In the Trent Valley, brewers with the deepest boreholes, perhaps more than 1,000 feet, still use their own well water. Brewers with shallower wells worry about the intrusion of farmers' fertilizers. They may filter their water and add back the appropriate salts, or do the same with town water (Burton's town water comes in part from deep wells). Elsewhere in Britain, and wherever in the world people seek this character, 'Burton salts' are added to brewing water. This is especially true where pale ales are being produced. Brewers talk about 'Burtonizing' their water.

The Burton Union system

Another feature of Burton's brewing tradition is the 'union' system of fermentation. This probably derives from the simplest of all methods: fermentation in a wooden cask.

Draught Bass, as served in Britain, is quite distinct from export versions, mainly by virtue of the cask-conditioning. It is also more hoppy, and less strong.

In the days before yeast behaviour was understood, and when there was no means of controlling temperature, an especially lively cask or a warm day would have led to a foaming overflow. A way of dealing with this would have been to channel the overflow into a second vessel, let it settle, then add the liquid back to the cask. This circulatory arrangement is the basis for the Burton Union system.

It may have begun simply as a means of rescuing overflow, or of collecting yeast to pitch into the next brew. Because malty protein and hoppy residues would have been left behind in the cask, the yeast overflowing would have been relatively clean. Early brewers may have been using this system empirically to select and maintain a good yeast strain.

The system was not originally unique to Burton, but it assumed extraordinary proportions there with the growth of the town as a brewing centre. As the breweries of Burton became the biggest in the land, their arrangements of interlinked casks for fermentation grew to fill galleries and halls alive with the

The swan-neck tubes carry the self-propelled, bubbling, fermenting wort into these troughs, where it regains its composure before flowing back into the 'union' casks below.

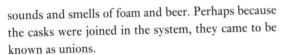

Each union cask is about four times the size of a standard British barrel, and they are all bolted into position in this curious Victorian machine.

Both fire and steam are used to bend the casks' staves into shape. The scale of the cooperage worker gives some idea of the size of these special vessels.

sounds and smells of foam and beer. Perhaps because the casks were joined in the system, they came to be known as unions.

During the Victorian period of expansion, so much money was invested in these great structures that they continued to be used long after their maintenance was proving a costly nightmare. Ind Coope was the first to abandon the system, followed in the early 1980s by Bass's Burton brewery. At least some of Bass's marketing people felt this was a mistake – surely a more limited union system could have been retained to make a premium product? The company did take the last of the union yeast as a basis for its future culture, in order to try and maintain the character of its products, including the famous bottle-conditioned Worthington White Shield and cask-conditioned Draught Bass (see page 86).

Soon afterward, a tiny Burton Union system was assembled at the Loaded Dog brewpub, in Melbourne, Australia, but never used with much success; the pub subsequently stopped brewing. Elsewhere, union casks from Bass were rescued and used as decoration, notably at the Commonwealth brewpub, in Boston, Massachusetts.

The third major brewer in Burton, Marston's (see page 87), took a different view. In the early 1990s, Marston's began to expand its Burton Union system – making a considerable investment in cumbersome equipment regarded everywhere else as being hopelessly outdated.

At the time, the brewery had eight sets, each comprising 20-24 union casks, divided between two halls. The casks at Marston's are around four times the size of a normal (36 gallon, 288 pint, 163.6 litre) British barrel. It was decided to add a further four sets, of 30 unions each, in a new hall.

Oak shipped from Memel (now Klaipeda), on the coast of Lithuania, was traditionally used for heavy cooperage in British breweries. After World War II, this supply diminished. A cooper told me he once found shrapnel in staves. Forest between Frankfurt and Heidelberg provided wood for Marston's new unions. The unions were made by a 200-year-old firm of coopers, with a dozen employees, near Manchester.

At Marston's brewery, fermentation begins in conventional open squares, some of copper, others stainless steel, clad with pine. These are arranged in galleries, with the Burton Union sets below. After two days, the fermenting wort is 'dropped' to the unions.

Each set is a two-deck ironwork gantry, about 12 yards long. Set transversely along the lower deck is a line of union casks. Along the upper deck is a long, shallow trough.

From the fermenters, the wort is decanted into the trough, from which pipes feed the casks. As the fermenting wort foams in the casks, it can escape through swan-neck tubes which flow back into the trough. This circulation continues for three to four days. The beer is then racked into conventional casks, and spends three or four days in the brewery's cellar before being primed, fined and dispatched.

During this circulation in the unions, much of the yeast is left behind in the trough. This provides a good supply for future fermentations, and means the beer is very bright.

As a living organism, yeast adapts to its habitat. Just as a circus lion leaping through a blazing hoop every night would develop even more powerful hind legs, so the yeast making the long journey through the Burton Unions since the early 1800s has evolved its own characteristics. Marston's yeast is a symbiosis of at least two strains, and possibly four. Traditional Burton yeasts are very powdery, remaining in suspension to create a thorough fermentation. This creates a characteristic dryness in a pale ale. At the same time, the cleansing effect of the union system provides for a bright beer. This is significant in cask-conditioned ales, which are not filtered. More importantly, these unusual yeasts make for distinctive, complex flavours. Marston's cannot produce all of its beer in the unions, but extended the system in order to create enough yeast to give every brew that same fingerprint.

A pint of hand-pulled, cask-conditioned Marston's – but is it a bitter or a pale ale? It is a brew of modest bitterness, but great complexity and sophistication.

Marston's premium pale ale is called Pedigree, and around 40 percent of this product passes through the unions. Pedigree is filtered and pasteurized for bottling, but the product is much better known as cask-conditioned draught. As beers made with a yeast that still lives in a Burton Union system, both versions must be regarded as classics. A carefully tended, cask-conditioned Pedigree is a remarkable pint.

India Pale Ale

Burton's growth as a brewing town came before it could distribute its beer by rail or by metalled roads. It was part of the canal era, benefiting from a waterway that linked the town through the rivers Trent and Humber to the North Sea. It shipped its beer to the Empire, especially to India.

Beers to be shipped across the world were made to high gravities (sometimes up in the 1070s) so that

The Alaskan Brewing Company's pale ale has a malty nose, a soft, refreshingly fruity palate, and a dry, hoppy finish; better with caribou than crab.

they could slowly ferment on their journey, reaching the peak of condition as they arrived.

They were also extremely heavily hopped, so that the magic flower could protect them against infection by wild yeasts. Hopping rates cited for those days would seem incredible to a brewer today: four or five pounds per barrel, with another one or two for dry-hopping. Today one pound per barrel would seem heavy. Some adjustments have to be taken into consideration: it is not clear whether the hops were always fresh, or perhaps aged to reduce bitterness, since part of their purpose was as an anti-infectant; the higher gravities required heavier hopping; the hops grown then were not as bitter as today's specially bred varieties; and beers were, anyway, much hoppier in those days.

India Pale Ale became a style in itself, often abbreviated to IPA. IPA became popular in Britain, too, and the term is still used, although few drinkers understand the Indian connection. (Nor do many users of Worcestershire sauce realize that the recipe was brought home from Bengal by Lord Sandys.) No British brewer today produces an IPA with the gravity or hoppiness of the Victorian specifications.

American IPA

At the height of the India Pale Ale trade, in 1830, a brewer named Peter Ballantine, from Ayr, Scotland, emigrated to the United States. (I have found no evidence that he was related to the whisky merchant of the same name, although that enterprise was established at around the same time.) Ballantine brewed in what was then America's ale capital, Albany, New York, and the company later moved to Newark, New Jersey. Ballantine's products were subsequently made at the Narragansett brewery, on Rhode Island, and at the former Berghoff (then Falstaff) brewery, in Fort Wayne, Indiana. They now emerge from the Pabst brewery, in Milwaukee, Wisconsin.

The name of Ballantine is most commonly associated with a golden ale featured in a series of painted bronzes by Jasper Johns. In its Newark days, the company also made a strong, amber-red, well-hopped Christmas brew called Burton, aged for years in coated wooden tanks that were topped up like a sherry *solera*. I sampled a 1950's edition of Ballantine Burton, still in good condition (albeit faintly hazy), more than 25 years later. It tasted like a very aromatic, hoppy barley wine.

Ballantine also produced what it called an India Pale Ale, matured in wood for as long as a year. This beer, also amber-red, carried a claim that it was 'aged in wood', and the sales material referred to the tradition of this style being matured in casks aboard ship.

In Newark, in the early 1960s, this was said to have a gravity of around 1070 (17.5 Plato) and 60 units of bitterness. At that time, the brewery used the slogan, 'with the flavour that chill can't kill.' I sampled a Ballantine IPA at the brewery on Rhode Island in the late 1970s; it had a gravity of 1078 (19.5 Plato) and 45 BU. It was said to be dry-hopped, and to have been held in wood for five months. The beer had a very hoppy nose; a firm, full body; a soft carbonation; and a lasting bitterness.

In the late 1980s, I tasted the beer again at the Fort Wayne brewery. By then it had a gravity of 1054 (13.5 Plato) and 35-40 BU. It was being fermented (still, I was told, with the original yeast) in coated wood, dry-hopped, and matured in metal tanks for four to six weeks. It still had a good hop character, especially in the finish, but I seem to have decided to quit while I was ahead. I have since tasted a moderately characterful Pabst version, but not at the brewery. Since then, Pabst has reintroduced its lightly fruity, toffeeish Old Tankard Ale.

Meanwhile, pale ales have been popping up all over America, from Boulevard's rounded, hoppy example in Kansas City, to the soft, smooth, malty pale ale of the Santa Fe Brewing Company, to the famously fruity, complex interpretation from Sierra Nevada of California (see page 88).

The revival of IPA as a distinct style can be credited to brewing scientist and hop expert Bert Grant, who started his microbrewery in the former Switzer opera house at Yakima, Washington, in the early 1980s. Yakima is the capital of the hop-growing region, and Bert rightly believes in using local materials. Soon after he opened the brewery, I visited him and tasted his range, which included an IPA. Albeit conventional in gravity (1048; 12 Plato) and golden in colour, it was the hoppiest IPA I had ever tasted. That early essay was said to have 60 units of bitterness, and that was not difficult to believe. It was full of both the resiny flavour and bitterness of the hops. I have sampled it many times since, and always found it very hoppy, but nothing could match the shock of that first encounter.

Since then, the Pacific Northwest has become quite a region for IPA, boasting examples that are assertively hoppy, with a good flavour development and a powerful finish. In 1990, I tasted a nicely hoppy new example at the Noggins brewpub in Seattle. In the same city, Ed Tringali, brewer at the Big Time pub, was working on an IPA aged over oak chips, but had none available when I called. In Seattle again in 1992, I sampled a new IPA at the Pike Place Brewery, already known for a creamy, nutty Pale Ale of 1052-4 (13-13.5 Plato). The IPA was called East India Pale Ale (1066; 16.5; 65 BU). After primary fermentation, this had been matured over oak chips. It had been in the tank ten or 12 days when I sampled it, and the grapefruity flavour of the Chinook hops was to the fore. It was an astonishingly refreshing beer.

Many drinkers are unaware of the origin of the term IPA; Grant's illustrates it. This brewery's labels bring life to all its designations.

Rival painter Willem De Kooning observed that Jasper Johns' agent 'could sell beer cans' as art. In 1964, Johns proved him right. This *Painted Bronze* now resides in a Swiss art gallery.

Duckstein

An amber, top-fermenting brew somewhere between an English pale ale and a Belgian ale has been a great success in Germany in recent years. This beer, called Duckstein, has a hint of fruit in the nose, some fruity maltiness in the start, and a distinct tartness, as well as some late hop character, in the finish.

The name Duckstein is said originally to have been a corruption of Tuffstein, a form of volcanic rock. A style of beer with this name was made in the 1700s and 1800s in the beech-clad Elm Mountains, at Königslutter, near Braunschweig (Brunswick). The beer, which took a calcium sulphate character from the local water, was thought of as a light refresher. It contained a proportion of wheat.

The modern version, made by the Feldschlosschen brewery in Braunschweig, is produced entirely from barley malt and lagered over beechwood chips.

Pale ale producers

The small town of Burton-upon-Trent in the Midlands of England is still home to the classic producers of pale ale, but flattering imitations are now being made across the United States.

BASS

Bass Brewers, 137 High Street, Burton-upon-Trent, Staffordshire DE14 1JZ, England Tel: (0283) 511000

Britain's biggest beer-maker has a wide variety of products, ranging from Tennent's lagers to Highgate Mild, plus several local ales from its regional breweries. Its famous pale ales are Worthington White Shield, which appears only in bottle, and Draught Bass.

Draught Bass is made at Burton. Water from the brewery's own deep wells is used, though it is subjected to some filtration and balancing. The beer is brewed to a gravity of 1043 (10.7 Plato), from pale ale malt. The brewery likes the malt for Draught Bass to be made from a single variety of barley, grown in an identifiable stretch of countryside. In recent times, it has been Halcyon barley, from north Norfolk.

Northdown and Challenger hops are strongly favoured by the company's brewers. Bass believes these varieties, which are similar, have a soft, flowery, nutty character. There is only one addition. The beer is not intended to be assertively aromatic or bitter, though it once had decidedly more hop character than it does today. The Bass two-strain yeast makes a very important contribution to the character of the beer. Some tasters have noted the aroma and flavour of hot lemon juice, others argue for a faint licorice note.

In Burton, the beer is often served very flat. One London pub has made a speciality of serving cellar-matured Draught Bass. This pub, The White Horse, at Parson's Green, Fulham, keeps the casks unbroached sometimes for several weeks, to allow a natural carbonation to develop in the

form of a very fine, sustained bead. The casks have to be kept under constant supervision so that excess carbonation can be gently released when necessary. This greatly accentuates the complexity of flavours in Draught Bass. Sometimes this pub also dry-hops the beer.

A canned version of 'Draught' Bass is injected with nitrogen to imitate the softness of beer from the tap. It is a pleasant enough beer, but lacks the life and subtlety of the real thing. The bottled Bass exported to the United States is made to a higher gravity and alcohol content, to meet laws in some states that require an ale to have more than 4 percent alcohol by weight, 5 by volume. It has a different hop specification, and is filtered and pasteurized.

Draught Bass's closest cousin in the bottle is Worthington White Shield. The Worthington brewery, which was also in Burton, was founded in the mid-1700s, acquired by Bass in 1927, and closed in the 1960s. Bass has continued to produce its most famous beer, White Shield.

Worthington White Shield is one of the few bottle-conditioned ales in Britain, and is customarily poured with great care so that the sediment is left behind. Bar staff, reluctant to risk doing the job less than perfectly, will often invite customers to pour their own. Some drinkers later swallow the yeasty sediment as a tonic. White Shield was favoured by devotees of naturally conditioned ales in the days when the cask versions seemed to be vanishing. It faded somewhat when cask-conditioned ale began to enjoy a revival in the mid-1970s.

White Shield was originally brewed at Burton, switched to a Bass brewery in Sheffield, and has since been posted for a move to Birmingham. The beer is made to a gravity of 1050.5 (12.7 Plato), from pale ale and

White Shield, 5.6 percent alcohol by volume, is a 'strong ale' in Britain.

crystal malts; hopped with Northdown and Challenger, in one addition; fermented with the Bass yeast; filtered; primed with sucrose; reyeasted with a different strain; and warm-conditioned for two to three weeks before being released.

Enthusiasts store it at a natural cellar temperature, and serve it after six to 18 months, during which time the aroma and flavour develop considerably. White Shield is a malty, fruity and complex ale. It has a slightly sharp, refreshing attack, and some smokiness, though the last characteristic has diminished in recent years. Its slight tartness perfectly cuts the richness of steak-and-kidney pie.

GEARY'S

D L Geary Brewing Company, 38 Evergreen Drive, Portland, Maine 04103, USA Tel: (207) 878-2337

This new-generation, English-accented pale ale brewery on the East Coast is worthy of a wider reputation. English micro-pioneers Peter Austin and Alan Pugsley helped David Geary establish the brewery in 1986.

Geary, who once sold medical equipment, learned beer-making in short stays at several breweries in Britain. His own premises are on the site of a former brewery, but in a modern industrial building, masked by maples.

The brewery uses pale ale, crystal and chocolate malts from Britain and American-grown hops. Geary Pale Ale (1047; 11.7; 3.6; 4.5) is dry and crisp, with lots of hop flavour (rather than bitterness) and a pronounced (but in-balance) fruitiness. The brewery also makes a stronger (1070; 17.5), very characterful bittersweet winter product called Hampshire Special Ale.

MARSTON'S

Marston, Thompson & Evershed, Shobnall Road, Burton-upon-Trent, Staffordshire DE14 2BW, England Tel: (0283) 31131

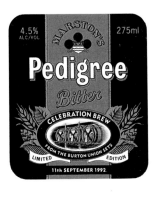

The renowned Marston's Pedigree has a hint of dessert apple in the aroma (Cox's Orange Pippin?); a light, clean, soft texture; a lightly nutty maltiness; and a flowery, hoppy elegance in the finish. When well kept, it is a very complex beer.

It is brewed from pale ale malt, around 80 percent of which is made by the floor method. Gravity is 1043 (10.7 Plato), and the beer has 3.6 percent alcohol by weight, 4.5 by volume; 18-19 EBC; and 26 BU. The hops are Fuggles and Goldings, from five growers.

The brewery's several other products include a hoppier Best Bitter; a caramelly, chocolaty, dark ale called Merrie Monk; and a creamy winter ale, Owd Roger. The chunky, red-brick brewery dates from the 1870s, and has been owned by Marston's since 1898.

SAMUEL SMITH

The Old Brewery, Tadcaster, Yorkshire LS24 9SB, England Tel: (0937) 832225

Fashionable in the United States, sighted from Tokyo to Tasmania, Samuel Smith's Pale Ale comes from a brewery with the deepest of regional roots in Yorkshire.

Its typically rounded, malty, faintly buttery-tasting palate is a regional characteristic, deriving from a yeast bred in the Yorkshire Square system of fermentation. This method employs double-decked square fermenters, linked by a porthole in the central floor. As the fermentation foams in the lower chamber it begins to rise into the upper one. There, it settles, leaving yeast residue behind, and sinks back into the lower one. Was this circulatory method developed to cope with stolid Yorkshire yeasts, or did it help develop them? That is not clear, but the yeasts that work in this system do not ferment especially thoroughly, creating a relatively full-bodied beer.

It has been suggested, but not proved, that the method was developed with the help of a 1772 paper delivered to the Royal Society (an association founded in 1660 to promote scientific research) by the Yorkshire-born chemist Joseph Priestley. The paper was on the absorption of gases in liquids. Priestley, who was also a clergyman, had a church in Leeds from 1767–72, and lived during that time in a house adjoining a brewery. He was also a political dissident, and in 1794 emigrated to the United States, where he was offered

The renowned Old Brewery Pale Ale leads the ranks of excellent beers exported from Samuel Smith's Yorkshire brewery.

(but declined) the Principalship of the University of Pennsylvania.

The first brewery to use the Yorkshire Square system is said to have been Bentley & Shaw, whose beers (under the later name Hammond's) were the first I sampled, as a teenager in the late 1950s. The Leeds brewery Tetley still ferments in squares, but these are now made of stainless steel; those at Samuel Smith's are made of stone. Yorkshire is built on sandstone, which was once quarried to make pavements in London, as well as fermenters for breweries and textile dyeworks, but Samuel Smith's seems to have found Welsh slate less permeable. The Yorkshire square system has over the years been used by several other breweries, all in Yorkshire or bordering counties.

Samuel Smith's is in Tadcaster, between Leeds and York. The brewery was founded in 1758 to serve an adjoining coaching inn, The White Horse, which is still open for business. The Smiths bought the establishment in 1847, and a member of the family later started a second brewery next door.

The original brewing company remains family-owned. The second brewery, John Smith's, is now owned by Courage, part of the Foster's group of Australia. There is a third sizable brewery, owned by Bass, in Tadcaster – a village with a population of no more than three or four thousand people.

Tadcaster, which sits on an underground lake of limestone water, began to gain a reputation for its pale ales in the 1880s and 1890s, and came to be regarded as the North's answer to Burton-upon-Trent.

Samuel Smith's Pale Ale (1048-52; 12-13 Plato; 4.1; 5.2; 35 EBC; 26 BU) is similar to a cask-conditioned draught beer available in Britain under the name Museum Ale. With this form of conditioning, it seems to develop more fruity-winy notes. The brewery also makes an excellent Nut Brown Ale and several outstanding styles of stout, notably an oatmeal and an imperial.

SIERRA NEVADA

Sierra Nevada Brewing Company, 1075 East 20th Street, Chico, California 95928, USA
Tel: (916) 893-3520
Taproom and restaurant:
(916) 345-2739

The best-known pale ale in the United States is that from the Sierra Nevada brewery, among the walnut groves of Chico, a college town north of Sacramento, California. This revered establishment was founded in 1981 by home-brewers Ken Grossman and Paul Camusi.

When I first visited them, not long after they opened, they were using vessels converted from the dairying industry. Later, before word had spread to Germany of the microbrewery movement, they were able to buy second-hand copper kettles there.

Their prudence and care, quality control and singleness of purpose made Sierra Nevada into a great little brewery. When I called in 1990, the kettles were at work, set into an immaculate tiled brewhouse, overlooked by a bar and restaurant.

Neither a malt nor a hop kiln, but Sierra Nevada's brewhouse.

When I sampled Sierra Nevada Pale Ale in 1981, my note said that it was 'bronze-red in colour, very well balanced, eminently drinkable, with a floral bouquet and a smooth, malty, fruity palate.' A decade later, with many tastings in the intervening years, I noted that it had 'a huge, fresh floweriness of Cascade hops...a tremendous hop taste...citric fruitiness...in beautifully complex harmony.'

The beer is made to a gravity of 1052 (13 Plato), with 4.2 percent alcohol by weight, 5.3 by volume, from pale and crystal malts, with hops added at several stages. It is bottle-conditioned. A companion Sierra Nevada Draught is fractionally darker, very dry, and very slightly lower in alcohol. Sierra Nevada also makes an outstanding porter and stout and a range of seasonal brews, including the renowned Big Foot barley wine (see page 105).

SUMMIT

Summit Brewing Company, 2264 University Avenue, St Paul, Minnesota 55114, USA
Tel: (612) 645-5029

Norwegian-American Mark Stutrud and his wife Margaret van Eckhout, who is of Dutch origin, were therapists to substance abusers before establishing their brewery in 1986. They had been keen home-brewers, but they surprised their erstwhile colleagues by turning professional.

One of their early consultants, Fred Thomasser, then aged 70, had begun as a cooper in New York, and remembered working for a brewery there that produced a top-fermenting, dry-hopped ale up to 1940.

Summit takes its name from a famous Victorian thoroughfare in St Paul, the state capital of Minnesota. The brewery's premises were formerly a showroom for pick-up trucks, and the smart copper brewhouse once saw service at Hirschbrau of Heimertingen, near Memmingen, in Baden-Württemberg.

The flagship product is Summit Extra Pale Ale. It is pale bronze in colour, and starts sweet with a touch of malt, then becomes perfumy, fruity and dry, with a nicely hoppy finish. It is made to a gravity of 1048 (12 Plato), from pale and crystal malts, with American hops added at three stages, and fermented with a yeast strain from the National Collection of Yeast Cultures in Norwich, England.

An American tasting ale, despite the symbolically English darts.

English brown ale

New generations of young beer-lovers seem to keep rediscovering Newcastle Brown Ale. It is Britain's biggest-selling bottled ale, and a popular import in cities as diverse as Paris and San Francisco. To the British, its image is reinforced by an inverted snobbery, an urban chic enjoyed by Newcastle, the northeastern city whose emblem is a series of steel bridges across the River Tyne, and whose memories are of shipbuilding, heavy engineering, armaments, coal, and great soccer teams (the last not necessarily all in the past). Do the Parisians and San Franciscans know this? Perhaps not. Maybe they just like the beer.

Newcastle lays vague claim to being the first city in England to have made beer, before Roman times, and its interest in brewing was probably encouraged by the incursions of its Viking neighbours. The city had a brewers' and bakers' guild in the 1300s. A merger of several local beer-makers in 1890 created Newcastle Breweries Limited.

In the days when most beers were notably darker, the biggest brewery in Newcastle introduced its translucent, reddish brown ale to rival the pale ales of Burton and the Midlands. This style of ale is malt-accented, but with a firm, nutty dryness and a gentle fruitiness. Like the spirit of Newcastle, the style has proved to be enduring.

A brewer with the not-quite-appropriate name of Colonel Porter developed Newcastle Brown Ale over a period of three years. It was launched in 1927, and took first prize for bottled beer at the Brewers' Exhibition in London the following year.

Newcastle is faced across the River Tyne by the town of Gateshead, which has its own brewery, originally established to provide beer to the federation of working men's clubs in the area. The Federation Brewery has a brown ale called High Level, after one of the bridges over the Tyne. This has a hint of butteriness, and is sweeter and fruitier.

In the same metropolitan area, but on the River Wear, is the town of Sunderland, once also known for shipbuilding and for marine diesel engines. Its local brewery, Vaux (probably a Norman name, but long

Newcastle Brown Ale and similar brews from northeastern England were launched as rivals to the pale ales of the Midlands. Strong, malty and deep amber, they are very different from the older brown ales from London and the south, which are lower in alcohol, darker and sweeter.

There are richer and more assertive brown ales, but none better known than Newcastle's. Its label shows the most famous of the Tyne bridges. In total six bridges cross the River Tyne in the centre of Newcastle; in the foreground is the 1876 Swing Bridge.

Today's singularly boastful label still features the blue star that is the brewery's logo, overlaid with Newcastle's skyline, including the Tyne bridge and the keep of the castle that gave the city its name.

The year after its creation, Newcastle Brown Ale won an award, and the word 'champion' found its way into this 1930 press advertisement. A glass might well be a restorative at the 18th hole, though it has other uses.

since Anglicized to rhyme with 'forks'), makes a brown ale called Double Maxim. The name derives from the Maxim gun (an early machine gun) used in the Boer War by Captain (later Colonel) Ernest Vaux, and was first used on a 'Single' Maxim (subsequently known as Light Brown Ale); the Double did not appear until 1938. This brew has a good crystal character, with a dash of chocolate malt, and is notably smooth.

Farther south is the River Tees, with towns traditionally known for heavy steelworks and bridge-building. Camerons of Hartlepool did for a time make a fruity, nutty Brown Ale.

Across the Tees and a little beyond the accepted boundaries of the northeast, Samuel Smith's, of Tadcaster, Yorkshire, has the richest, maltiest and nuttiest of the brown ales in this regional style. Its Old Brewery Brown Ale, known in some markets as Nut Brown, has a gravity of 1048 (12 Plato), with a colour of 65 EBC and 34 units of bitterness.

Elsewhere in England, brown ales are of the older, much darker and sweeter style, often with notes of caramel and black invert sugar, and usually lower in gravity and alcohol. This interpretation is especially associated with London's former tradition of very dark brews, born of a chloride water character. The best-known example is probably Mann's Brown Ale (1034–5, 8.5–9 Plato). This has its origins in Whitechapel, east London, in the 1808 Albion brewery, acquired by James Mann in 1819. The brewery became Mann, Crossman & Paulin, and was acquired by Watney in 1959. Production moved to Watney's brewery in Mortlake, London, and that plant is now owned by the Courage/Foster's group.

Once, every English brewery included a beer of this type in its range, and a good few still do, though the numbers are shrinking. Typically, these brown ales have a colour of around 125 EBC and a bitterness of around 20.

While the nuttier northern brown ales might well accompany local dishes such as cheesy salads or the local (savoury) leek pudding, the southern style is sweet enough to accompany desserts. In his 1956 *Book of Beer*, Andrew Campbell was hesitant about the serving of beer with 'acid fruit', but did allow that brown ale with apple pie was 'at least one exception'.

The combination arises in a traditional hot drink, a variation on the wassail bowl, called the Brown Betty. This is made from (ideally, brown) ale, sweetened with (brown) sugar, often spiced, sometimes laced with cognac (why not malt whisky?) and topped with baked apples. A similar drink is traditionally served on Shrove Tuesday in Oxford, at Brasenose College. Although the college has a brass nose as its emblem, its name is a corruption of the Old Flemish *brazenhuis* (brewhouse). The days when a college might have made beer for the university are long gone, but the city's brewery, Morrells, makes a range of beers with academic names, including the tawny Varsity Ale.

Elsewhere in the world

The English style of brown ale is finding some characterful producers in the United States. The Belgians make a quite different style, with a distinctively sweet-and-sour palate, as well as a very sweet type (see pages 118–120). Australia has top-fermenting dark brown ales that are usually given the stylistic designation 'old' (see page 99).

New Zealand hints at the flavours of the past by adding a dash of colour to some of its lagers. These 'browns' or 'draughts' (usually served from a cellar tank) are considered by the drinker, wrongly, to be something other than lager. Their colours are barely brown, but their flavours are slightly fuller and maltier than those of conventional lagers. Among the more characterful from the national producers are Monteith's, from Dominion's brewery in Greymouth, and the hoppier Waikato Draught, curiously described as a bitter beer, from Lion. The only brew I have tasted in New Zealand that really struck me as a brown ale was the bottom-fermenting Hog's Head Dark, toffeeish and fruity, at the Loaded Hog, a bar attached to the Plains Brewery in Christchurch. Other New Zealand micros make interesting dark products, but in styles closer to strong, old or Scottish ales.

The one and only? Yorkshire people yield to none in regional pride. Is any other English county worth mentioning? Samuel Smith tops its labels and glasses with the county's emblem, the white rose.

The colour of a brew changes during production. These samples were taken at various stages of the brewing of Newcastle Brown Ale.

Brown ale producers

Newcastle Brown is the classic of the style, but is a comparatively recent creation. Its North American emulators have each interpreted 'brown ale' in their own way, from Brooklyn's coffee-like brew to the vinous, chocolaty Pete's Wicked Ale from California.

BROOKLYN

The Brooklyn Brewery, 118 North 11th Street, Brooklyn, New York 11211, USA
Tel: (718) 486-7422

If Newcastle has a counterpart in the United States, might it be Brooklyn? Perhaps: there is a famous bridge, and there are some fine Victorian buildings, and there was a great team. Brooklyn also lends its name to an outstanding brown ale.

The Brooklyn Brewery was established in the late 1980s by journalist Steve Hindy and banker Tom Potter. While working for *Newsday*, Hindy had covered the Middle East, where he spent some of his leisure time home-brewing. Potter, a beer-lover, was keen to have his own business. They engaged as a consultant veteran brewer Bill Moeller, who had in earlier years made the famous old East Coast beer Rheingold, among many other American classics.

Moeller helped Brooklyn create a robust lager and an even more hearty brown ale, both of which have initially been contract-brewed at F X Matt, of Utica, New York. Brooklyn Brown, at 1054–6 (13.5–14 Plato), 4.8 percent alcohol by weight, 6 by volume, is higher in gravity and alcohol content than its British counterparts. With pale ale malt, crystal, chocolate and black, it is also fuller in colour and flavour. Its chocolaty and roast coffee notes are underpinned with the firm dryness of Northern Brewer hops, and given a refreshing splash of Cascade fruitiness. Unusually for a beer of this style, it is dry-hopped. A complex (after-dinner?) brew that is closer to Newcastle than London, but bigger than either.

ELM CITY

New Haven Brewing, 458 Grand Avenue, New Haven, Connecticut 06513, USA
Tel: (203) 772-2739

The Dutch disease has culled the once-famous elms, but Elm City Connecticut Ale sounded more distinctive than New Haven Brown when the local microbrewery named its first product in 1989.

New Haven is an industrial city, and in that role is somewhat depressed, like Newcastle. Also like Newcastle, it has a university – but rather more famous, in the neo-Gothic form of Yale. Sporting teams? Well, former president George Bush captained Yale's baseball team. A lesser-known alumnus, Blair Potts, studied American history, and was coached in rowing by Richter Elser, whose visits to the Henley Regatta had left him with an infectious enthusiasm for British ales. Today, Potts makes the ale at New Haven Brewing, in a building that has variously been a power station, trolley car barn (tramshed), and ferry terminal on the Mill River. Elser, among many other publicans in the area, serves the product in his tavern, Richter's, with its Moorish-looking pre-Prohibition interior, in the old Taft Hotel, on New Haven Green.

Brooklyn is better known for its lager, but its brown ale is equally capable of winning medals.

Elm City Connecticut Ale is not identified as a brown, but has the solid amber colour and maltiness to qualify. In the aroma, there is an appetizing reminder of barley-sugar candy, the palate is malty-fruity, and the finish is smooth and lightly dry. The ale has an original gravity of 1052 (13 Plato), and is produced from American two-row, crystal and chocolate malts, Northern Brewer and Willamette hops, and Whitbread yeast. The brewery also makes a golden ale and the dryish, coffee-accented Blackwell Stout.

NEWCASTLE

Scottish & Newcastle Breweries, Tyne Brewery, Gallowgate, Newcastle-upon-Tyne NE99 1RA, England Tel: (091) 232 5091

In 1960, Newcastle's main brewery merged with McEwan's and Younger's, of Scotland. The creation of this larger group gave a wider distribution to Newcastle Brown Ale, and created a confusion: the beer is sometimes wrongly described as being Scottish on beer-lists in the United States. The group still has a sizable brewery in Newcastle, and the brown ale is its biggest product there.

Pale ale and crystal malts are used – the latter, albeit in a small proportion, providing a defining characteristic. The crystal malt is relatively full in colour. A distinctive feature of production is that Newcastle Brown is a blend of two ales made for this purpose. One of these, a stronger dark ale, is not available in its own right. The brown ale, with an original gravity of 1044–6 (11–11.5 Plato) and an alcohol content of 3.8 percent by weight, 4.7 by volume, has a colour of 50 EBC and 24 units of bitterness. The lower-gravity beer in the blend is marketed as Newcastle Amber (1031; just under 8 Plato; 30 EBC; 19 BU). Basic English bittering hops are used, as the beer is not intended to be flowery in aroma.

Newcastle Brown Ale has just the nutty, winy character to wash down savoury dishes, such as this leek pudding, a regional speciality.

The brewers feel that the production of the strong ale creates fruity esters that would not occur if Newcastle Brown were made in a conventional way, without the blending procedure. There are very restrained notes of pear-drops and banana, balanced with a faintly roasty maltiness, a touch of residual sugar, and perhaps the gentlest yeast-bite in the mouth-drying, moreish finish.

PETE'S WICKED ALE

Pete's Brewing Company, 514 High Street, Palo Alto, California 94301, USA Tel: (415) 328-7383

Pete Slosberg, a marketing man in northern California's 'Silicon Valley', was a home-brewer until he decided to turn professional with several partners and a 'wicked' ale recipe. Despite its flippant name, Pete's Wicked Ale has won awards in some serious judgings, including the Gold Medal in the Great American Beer Festival's brown ale category.

The ale has a dark copper colour, a rich aroma, and a chocolaty, malty, winy palate. It has a gravity of 12.5 Plato (1050), and is brewed from two-row, crystal and black malts, with Cascade hops. It was originally

produced under contract in California by the Palo Alto Brewing Company. When that venture failed, Pete's moved to Schell's, in New Ulm, Minnesota. At Schell's, the ale was top-fermented.

More recently, it has been made by bottom-fermentation, at the Minnesota Brewing Company in St Paul. Like Schell's, this brewery was founded in the mid-1800s. It closed in 1990 and reopened in 1991, under the ownership of mainly local investors, headed by Bruce Hendry, a former chairman of Kaiser Steel. It proudly displays a photograph of its fleet of trucks in 1939, when the twin cities of St Paul and Minneapolis were bubbling with successful big breweries.

When I called soon after its reopening, veteran brewmaster Siegfried Plagens, from Berlin, was pleased to be back at work, trying his hand at an Anglo-American ale, and winning a medal for his troubles.

The brewery was also reviving Grain Belt Beer, an ordinary lager that was in living memory a local icon. Grain Belt was once produced in its own brewery, another turn-of-the-century building a few miles away. The old Grain Belt building is now a windowless hulk, silhouetted in looming reproach to all those drinkers who deserted their local brewery in favour of the national offerings of the television commercials.

Old ale

Throughout history, people have often felt that nothing is as good as it once was. 'Old ale' implies a style of the past, and the term already had that nostalgic meaning a century ago, according to John Bickerdyke, in *The Curiosities of Ale and Beer*, published in 1889. Old ale is primarily an English style, and most entrants suggest the intention of a Georgian heartiness. They are to varying extents dark, rich and sweet, typically with suggestions of soft, curranty fruit and black treacle. Neither fruit nor treacle are ingredients, although some specifications include, in small quantities, one or more types of sugar.

Old ales are sometimes, though not always, strong. Often, their gravity will suggest a higher alcohol content than actually emerges. The reason is that they are not very thoroughly fermented: the aim being to leave some of the sweetness, flavour and body of the malt sugars in the beer. In recent years, I have taken part in several tastings at a London pub – The White Horse, Parson's Green – that were arranged with a view to further defining the style. In sampling ales presented as being 'old', it became clear that there were more variations than I had previously categorized.

Some breweries with milds make a similar product, with a gravity in the 1040s (perhaps 11 Plato; and 3.4

> Whether they are aged, or merely traditional in style, old ales tend to be full in colour, rich in flavour, and often sweet. Brews like this are often regarded as winter warmers.

percent alcohol by weight, 4.2 by volume), but with a higher proportion of crystal and black malts, and possibly a longer maturation, under the designation old ale. Adnams of Suffolk and Harveys of East Sussex, both fine breweries, use the term old ale to describe examples in this modest interpretation, although both have more robust products under the designation barley wine. Adnams' Old Ale is lightly toffeeish, with some hop character; Harveys' is slightly medicinal.

Other breweries of long-established reputation use a bitter, at a similar or higher gravity and strength, as a base for their old ale, again with variations in malt content and maturation. Among them are Brakspear of Henley-on-Thames (perfumy, dry), Hook Norton of Banbury (clean, well-balanced), King & Barnes of Horsham, West Sussex (malty, dryish), and Timothy

Huge, upright, wooden tuns like these were once used in many breweries to store or mature beer. These rare survivors at Greene King are the 'secret ingredient' which contribute to the winy, oaky flavour of the brewery's old ale, Strong Suffolk.

The Cheval Blanc of the beer world? Strong Suffolk, with its iron-like taste, stands up to pickled herring.

Taylor of Keighley, Yorkshire (the sweetish Ram Tam). Of the newer generation, Cotleigh in Somerset (with Old Buzzard) and the Oak brewery of Greater Manchester (Wobbly Bob) take a similar approach.

Some brews with the typically dark and sweetish characteristics of an old ale do not specifically identify themselves as such. Young's smooth, toffeeish Winter Warmer (1055; 14 Plato; 4; 5) is a good example, and so are some other seasonal brews.

The popular classic
The most instantly recognizable old ales are in the range 1055–80 (16-20 Plato; 4.5–6.7 alcohol by weight, 5.8–8.5 by volume). Many of these are dedicated to mythical, or actual, characters, whose names are affectionately preceded with the adjective old.

Theakston's Old Peculier (see page 98) is arguably the definitive example of this interpretation. It is a classic that persistently beats more esoteric rivals in experts' tastings. Old Peculier is made at the town of Masham, in Yorkshire, the county historically most associated with strong ales. A long rhyme published in the 1600s has Bacchus dissatisfied with every imaginable drink, from 'Alicant', 'Frontineack' and 'Renish' wines, until he discovers the ales of Northallerton and Thirsk, both towns near Masham. (It is tempting to pronounce the name as Mash-am, but it is actually rendered as Mas'hm.)

Old Peculier has a gravity of 1057 (14–15 Plato; 4.2; 5.6), and a notable soft-fruit character. At the uppermost level of gravity (1080) are, for example, Owd ('old') Roger, from Marston's of Burton-upon-Trent, and Old Tom, from Robinson's of Stockport, Cheshire, both with more warming alcohol in the finish. American visitors have been astonished that a beer could be called Old Jock, but this strong and sweetish example from Broughton, Peeblesshire, sounds perfectly wholesome to a Scot. From the Robinwood brewery, in the down-to-earth Yorkshire town of Todmorden, emanates Old Fart, which needs excusing but can nonetheless be enjoyable.

Five years old
Some old ales may derive their designation from the tradition of making a strong brew to lay down as a provision for summer, when production was not possible, the term in this instance implying a product that was some months old, perhaps to be enlivened by blending with a younger brew.

One example is made by Greene King (see page

Yorkshire companions: the county's famous old ale and its parkin, a dense gingerbread made with treacle and oatmeal.

Adnams' brewery is right by the sea, at Southwold in Suffolk. Its characterful old ale welcomes fishermen to this day.

By the Midlands, the local accent has already elided 'old' into 'owd' – or is this a result of the potency of this brew?

Speciality malts such as crystal are still delivered in the sack, rather than being tipped into silos.

98). When the novelist Graham Greene celebrated his 80th birthday, he marked it by visiting his family's brewery in Bury St Edmunds, Suffolk. While there, he brewed a commemorative batch of St Edmund, the company's barley wine (1060; 15 Plato; 5.2; 6.5). As well as being bottled in its own right, this product is blended with two others that are not available to the consumer in their 'straight' forms. One is a tawny, malty ale of 1052 (13 Plato; 4.4; 5.5), the other a stronger brew of 1107 (27 Plato; 9.6; 12). The latter is a very old ale indeed: it is matured for between one and five years, in tuns of uncoated wood.

The blend of three is marketed as a draught Winter Ale (1060; 15 Plato; 4.8; 6), but a yet more interesting combination, of only the two 'secret' beers, is available as the bottled Strong Suffolk (1058; 14.5; 4.8; 6). While the Winter Ale is the more rounded and malty, the Strong Suffolk is the most distinctive, with its winy, oaky and iron-like character. This beer is filtered and pasteurized, and is not intended for laying down, although it may round out for a month or two. At brewers' dinners, Strong Suffolk has been served with the pickled herring of the region. I feel that its acidity and power work well in this combination. The beer is also used in Christmas puddings sold by a shop near the brewery. This very distinctive beer is not to be confused with Suffolk Strong, a bottled counterpart to the hoppy Extra made by the local rival Adnams of Southwold. Within Adnams' considerable range of characterful brews, the Suffolk Strong is really a bitter or pale ale. It is not particularly strong, at 3.6 percent alcohol by weight, 4.5 by volume.

Becoming old in the bottle

The highly regarded Gale's brewery (see page 98) makes a winter product (fruity and tart enough for spring) called 5X that is a blend of its bitter and its (usually bottled) Prize Old Ale. The latter (1094; 23.5 Plato; 7.2; 9) is surely an example of old indicating 'aged'. At the brewery, it is matured for six to 12 months in glass-lined cast-iron tanks. The beer is bottled with no additional sugar or yeast, and is neither filtered nor pasteurized.

The beer develops considerably with bottle-age. The last, slow work of the yeast in the bottle may increase the alcohol content to ten or 12 percent, or even more. Such increases can take place in any bottle-conditioned beer, depending upon its levels of viable yeast and residual sugar.

When it is young, the Prize Old Ale is spicy (cough drops?), with a sharp acidity. After five or six years' bottle-age, it gains a more complex, smoother palate, with a brandy- or Calvados-like character. A former brewer at Gale's argued that 20 years' bottle-aging was an optimum, not a maximum. No two batches, or bottles, will age in exactly the same way, but after 20 years the beer can begin to taste hard and brittle.

Perhaps it is the proximity of Normandy that suggests Calvados. I wonder whether Gale's Prize Old Ale could be drunk as *un trou Normand*? I could imagine the beer creating a space for the apple dumplings or soufflés of Normandy, or a pungent Camembert, Livarot or Pont l'Evêque cheese.

Among English ales that become 'old' in the bottle, the most famous is Thomas Hardy's Ale, from the Eldridge Pope brewery (see page 97). Perhaps not every consumer realizes that this is named after the writer Thomas Hardy (1840–1928), whose pastoral but dark novels reached a new audience through John Schlesinger's movie *Far From the Madding Crowd*, and Roman Polanski's *Tess*. Hardy lived in Dorchester, took tea with the great-grandfathers of the present Pope family, and alluded to their beer in his work. In 1968, a literary festival to commemorate Hardy was held in Dorchester, and Eldridge Pope made what was intended to be a one-off special brew to mark the occasion. The beer was so popular that the brewery began to produce it annually, and then quarterly, in numbered editions.

It was for many years the strongest ale produced in Britain, but has in recent times been exceeded by various brews created with the *Guinness Book of Records* in mind. Because of a law (now challenged) forbidding the mention of strength on labels, the legend 'England's rarest beer' has been used on batches exported to the United States, where it has a considerable following. Who is to say what is really England's rarest beer? Perhaps some commemorative edition from a defunct brewery – certainly not Thomas Hardy's, which is readily available, albeit in small quantities and a limited number of outlets.

Thomas Hardy's is brewed to an original gravity of 1125 (28+ Plato), and emerges with an alcohol content of 9.98 by weight, 12.48 by volume. Its label used to urge people not to consume it for five years, and still suggests that it will last 20. In the year of its brewing, it is very syrupy in texture, and excessively malty and yeasty in flavour. Even after one year, it may develop in aroma, roundness and balance; after five it begins to gain sherryish and Madeira-like notes.

I have enjoyed many vertical samplings of Thomas Hardy's 'vintages', in both Britain and the United States. At the brewery in 1986, I sampled two bottlings from the original, 1968, brew. A small, 'nip' bottle with a metal cap had matured further, and become lighter, drier and sharper than a pint with a drawn cork. The slower fermentation had suited the beer better. I found it extremely complex, with a faintly smoky aroma, reminiscent of a fire made from logs of fruit wood. The palate was profoundly fruity, soft and powerful. Like many breweries that also own pubs, Eldridge Pope buys wines and spirits to supply its outlets. The man responsible for this, Master of Wine Joe Naughalty, joined in the tasting. He found the 1968 pint 'creamy, elegant and superbly balanced.'

With its sherryish qualities, Thomas Hardy's is tempting as a mid-afternoon restorative, perhaps with the author's allegedly favourite snack, Dorset knobs, the local biscuit. Or with fruitcake, or petits fours after dinner? With its literary links, it is also the perfect beer with a book at bedtime.

Old ale producers

Some actually call their products old ales, others do not. The tradition may be simply to be darkish and top-fermenting (as in Australia). Or rich and medium-strong (like Old Peculier). Or there may be a long maturation in the tun (as with Strong Suffolk) or in the bottle (Prize Old Ale and Thomas Hardy's Ale).

ELDRIDGE POPE

Eldridge, Pope & Company,
Weymouth Avenue, Dorchester,
Dorset DT1 1QT, England
Tel: (0305) 251251

Sarah Eldridge started a brewery in Dorchester in the 1830s. In 1870, lawyer Alfred Pope and his brother Edwin became involved, and in 1880 a large brewery was built in red and honey-coloured brick. This was largely destroyed by fire in 1922, but was rebuilt in its original style. The brewery is neatly set alongside Dorchester railway station, and originally provided beer to pubs along the line; this made for a curiously elongated estate (most breweries serve a radius, rather than a line).

The brewery has its own well, providing very hard, chalky water, which has to be softened slightly. The beers are characteristically very soft-tasting, although this may derive also from the choice of malts. The hops are Worcester Fuggles and East Kent Goldings, with Styrian for dry-hopping. The house yeast, a very robust mixed strain, no doubt also contributes to the softness of beers such as the fruity Royal Oak pale ale, the outstandingly hoppy Goldie barley wine and the famous Thomas Hardy's Ale.

Thomas Hardy's is made entirely from pale ale malt, and gains its colour both from its density and from caramelization in the boil. It is pitched with yeast several times during fermentation and the three months of maturation in glass-lined mild-steel tanks. At least half of this maturation is at ambient temperatures, after which the beer

is chilled to precipitate the yeast. It is not filtered or pasteurized, nor primed or reyeasted, at the bottling stage. Thomas Hardy's Ale should always be stored, and served, at a natural cellar temperature.

GALE'S
George Gale & Company, Horndean, Portsmouth, Hampshire PO8 0DA, England
Tel: (0705) 571212

The mansarded tower of Gale's brewery, in Hampshire.

From seafaring Portsmouth, it is ten miles inland to The Ship and Bell, a coaching inn at the village of Horndean, on the road to London. The inn seems once to have been a brewpub, and the Gale's family connection is believed to go back more than 250 years. A freestanding brewery building, made of wood, burned down before the present brick structure arose in 1847. The brewery tower, dating from 1869, dominates the village.

Water, with some bicarbonate content, is from the brewery's own well. A cast-iron mash tun and a copper kettle dating from 1926 are kept in use for the small batches of Prize Old Ale. A larger, stainless steel kettle produces other ales, including the malty, faintly smoky Horndean Special Bitter, known as HSB. East Anglian Maris Otter floor malt is used (pale ale and black in the Prize Old Ale, which has a longer boil), with Hereford and Worcester Fuggles and East Kent Goldings. Prize Old Ale and the cask draughts are dry-hopped with Styrian Goldings.

The house yeast – which seems to produce very dry, fruity ales – was selected down from three strains to the dominant one in recent years, although it very easily reverts. Fermenters include some in uncoated New Zealand pine, others lined with copper, and some oak lined with stainless steel. Between the two World Wars, a brewer took the unusual measure of climbing into a fermenter to commit suicide.

A less excitable Yorkshire brewer who came to work at Gale's created Prize Old Ale in the early part of this century. It won its first award in the 1920s, and has been winning hearts and minds ever since.

Gale's, which can make 60,000 barrels of beer a year, is probably the largest brewery in which I have seen bottling and corking carried out by hand. Such special treatment is reserved for the Prize Old Ale.

GREENE KING
Westgate Brewery, Bury St Edmunds, Suffolk IP33 1QT, England
Tel: (0284) 763222

The mysterious marl at Greene King, in Suffolk.

Today, it is very much a rural region, whose claims to fame include its barley-growing and malting, but once East Anglia was a kingdom. Edmund was a king, murdered by the Danes in AD 870 and buried at the site of what became a powerful abbey. With a monastic history, it is no surprise that Bury St Edmunds became a centre of brewing; there are still three maltings in the town. The abbey gates, and parts of its walls, survive, and tunnels

that may have been used as hiding places during the dissolution link with the cellars of the last remaining brewery, Greene King.

The brewery dates from at least the 1700s. After training with Whitbread in London, Benjamin Greene came to Bury in 1799 or 1800, acquired the brewery with a partner, and merged it with a rival on the same street.

The Greene King maltings and brewery occupy buildings in a variety of periods, from the timbered and flint-clad to the modern, most of them ranged along one street, behind which lie water meadows sloping to the River Linnet. The company makes its own pale ale malt, but buys in crystal and Carapils, and has its own wells. Several hop varieties have been used in recent years, including Target and Yeoman. The house yeast, which has two strains, seems to produce beers with a clean, firm fruitiness, with hints of apple or pear.

The most interesting vessels in the brewery, in a tucked-away gallery, are the two ceiling-high oak tuns, each of 60 barrels, in which the strongest old ale is matured before blending. These Victorian vessels are kept in shape by a resident cooper, who spends most of his time in the company's wine-and-spirit department. The tuns are topped with what looks like sand and gravel but is, I was firmly told, Suffolk marl ('soil consisting of clay and lime': *Oxford English Dictionary*). This mysterious material is meant to filter out any wild yeasts or other microflora in the air before the wood can breathe them into the beer.

THEAKSTON
T & R Theakston, Wellgarth, Masham, Ripon, Yorkshire HG4 4DX, England
Tel: (0765) 689544

England's modest mountains, the Pennines, give rise to the Yorkshire Dales. Wensleydale is still remembered for a cheese originally made in an abbey, and monks may well have introduced brewing to the region. With sheep grazing on its hills, the little town of Masham also became a centre of the medieval wool trade in 'the golden prebend of York'. As a powerful town, it gained a degree of independence from the local archdeacon, and was allowed to establish its own 'peculier' ecclesiastical court. The court, of 'four-and-twenty men' still sits to propose churchwardens and dispose grants to apprentices.

A long-established brewpub in Masham was acquired by the Theakston family in 1827. Half a century later, the Theakstons built their own maltings and brewery.

The oak-clad, cast-iron mash tun may have been bought second-hand when the brewery was founded. The copper brew-kettle, with its oddly pyramid-shaped flue, was acquired second-hand in the 1950s. There is a cast-iron hop-back, an open cool-ship (still in use) and some slate vessels (though not in the Yorkshire Square system) among the open fermenters. The brewery is very smartly kept, and has 20,000 visitors a year. Its guests are entertained in the former stables.

Among the brewery's several products, its best known is its Old Peculier. It is said that this old ale has been made since the early days of the brewery, and that it has been called Old Peculier since the 1890s.

Old Peculier is made from pale ale and crystal malts, torrefied (highly heated) wheat, brewers' caramel, and three sugars. It has a colour of 90–95 EBC and a bitterness of 28–29. Several hop varieties, including Northern Brewer, are used, but Fuggles are the keynote. The beer is also dry-hopped with Fuggles. The brewery's yeast, which has been in use at least 30 or 40 years, is a mixed strain. It imparts a typically fruity character, and makes for relatively full-bodied ales. This soft fruitiness sometimes resembles blackcurrant in the Old Peculier.

Old Peculier, both the product and its name, captured the imagination of

beer-lovers during the real ale renaissance of the 1970s. Rather than expanding its delightful little brewery, Theakston's continued to make Old Peculier there, but acquired another plant, in Carlisle, Cumbria, in which to produce its bitter. The financing of this ultimately led to Theakston's takeover by Scottish & Newcastle. The Carlisle brewery has since been closed. All of the Theakston's products are still made in Masham for the North Yorkshire market, but are also produced in Newcastle for wider distribution.

TOOHEYS
29 Nyrang Street, Lidcombe,
New South Wales 2141, Australia
Tel: (02) 648 8611

The sons of Irish immigrants, James and John Toohey bought a brewery in Sydney in the mid-1800s. In 1973, Tooheys moved out of the city centre, leaving its brewery opposite the Central Station to be demolished. Now its concrete water-tower is an ugly landmark on the western edge of the city.

In their large product portfolios, both Tooheys and Tooth (see below) still have what they term an 'old', which in Australia suggests a true ale as opposed to a lager.

Tooheys Old was for a time renamed after the company's Hunter brewery (now in mothballs), farther north at Newcastle, New South Wales. The style was traditionally popular with coal miners there, and was the mainstay of the brewery.

After a period as Hunter Old, the ale has had yet another change. It is now known as Tooheys Old Black. It actually has a tawny to dark brown colour (60 EBC); is made from pale and roasted malt to a gravity of 1040–2 (10.4 Plato; 3.3; 4.4); and hopped to 15 units of bitterness with the ubiquitous Australian variety Pride of Ringwood. The multistrain ale yeast produces a fruity, estery character. The beer has some acidity,

becoming lightly chocolaty toward the finish.

This style perhaps owes less to an English old ale than to a mild or a Welsh miner's 'dark'. Australian miners have been known to order it as 'ordinary', but it can nonetheless be served with élan. In a classic Australian 'hotel' dining room, the Keighley, I was served consommé with a dash of Tooheys Old Black.

TOOTH
Carlton & United Breweries,
26 Broadway, Sydney, New South
Wales 2000, Australia
Tel: (02) 282 0941

John Tooth, from Cranbrook, Kent, founded his brewery in Sydney in 1835. He called his premises the Kent Brewery, and his insignia was the white horse of the Anglo-Saxon conquerors of his native county, Hengist and Horsa, with the motto 'Invicta'. 'Unconquerable'? Up to a point. Foster's, during their Carlton period, slapped their bold sanserif logo all over the elegant 1930s-style gateway to the brewery.

Inside, the brewery offices have a wood-panelled sumptuousness from the epoch of 'beer barons'. The brewery has that extra scale that the space and pride of the New World brought to Victorian architecture.

Surprisingly, the brewhouse is cramped and ugly. During a boom period in the mid-1970s, it was refitted with space-saving rectangular vessels, recessed into the floor, with motors above the mash tuns to drive the stirring forks. The impression is of being in a ship's engine room.

Kent Old is also known as Brown. It has a reddish, amber-brown colour (30 EBC), and is brewed from pale and crystal malts (1042–4; 10.5–11; 3.3; 4.4), with Pride of Ringwood hops (just over 20 BU) and a bottom-cropping ale yeast. It is lightly fruity (bananas?), smooth and sweetish, with a faintly earthy back-taste.

Barley wine

If it is made from barley malt, it is – of course – beer, not wine. The romantic term 'barley wine', which originates in England, may have been coined by rural home-brewers to describe their most impressively potent efforts. It probably found its way onto labels when mechanization made bottling more widespread, in the late 1800s, but the earliest printed reference I have seen was a label from 1903 for Bass No 1 Barley Wine, which is still made. When the style became popular among revivalist brewers in the United States in the 1980s, the various authorities governing labelling were uncomfortable about a beer being described as a wine. This led to the cumbersome description 'barley wine-style ale' on some labels.

I have never found any evidence to support the occasional suggestion that the designation for this style came from the use of wine yeasts, or that this was ever practised in the past by commercial brewers. In recent times, however, the Dock Street brewery of Philadelphia has used wine yeasts to great effect (see page 104).

The term is customarily used to describe a top-fermenting ale with an alcohol content approaching that of a wine, perhaps in the range of 6–12 percent by volume, and occasionally more (unfortified grape wines range from around 8 to 15 percent alcohol). These products are usually, but not always, bottled rather than draught. Traditionally, small 'nip' bottles containing only one third of a pint are used.

Barley wine is a term frequently used by ale-producers in England to describe their strongest brew. Colours vary from bronze to mahogany, but these beers are always heavy and malty, with lots of the fruitiness imparted by an ale yeast. Often, they have a hint of the appropriate winyness and they may be enjoyed as dessert beers or as nightcaps. Traditionally, they were matured in the cask, which was rolled round the brewery yard from time to time to rouse the yeast in its secondary fermentation.

In their depth of flavour, and richness, some of these beers can match a hefty red, or even a fortified wine, and others are more reminiscent of a brandy or whisky. Some devotees may regard them as an extension of the winter warmer, but there are examples that would perform well as a dessert beer, others as a digestif, and some make the perfect beer with a book at bedtime.

The style is far older than its name. Beers like this were once known simply as 'first sort', or branded on the cask with the highest number of crosses, or whatever symbol was used. Where an English brewery has

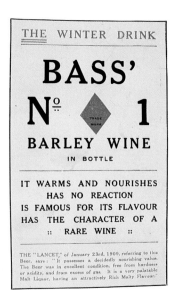

THE WINTER DRINK

BASS'
Nº ◆ 1
TRADE MARK
BARLEY WINE
IN BOTTLE

IT WARMS AND NOURISHES
HAS NO REACTION
IS FAMOUS FOR ITS FLAVOUR
HAS THE CHARACTER OF A
:: RARE WINE ::

THE "LANCET," of January 23rd, 1909, referring to this Beer, says: "It possesses a decidedly nourishing value. The Beer was in excellent condition, free from hardness or acidity, and from excess of gas. It is a very palatable Malt Liquor, having an attractively Rich Malty Flavour."

Bass No 1 barley wine may have been the first, but no one is sure. The number was originally an internal code in the brewery. Bass's red triangle (used on pale ales) and diamond (on stronger brews) became Britain's first and second registered trademarks in 1875. The 1909 testimonial from the respected medical journal *The Lancet* suggests that barley wine was recognized for its benefits to health long before French reds became a fashionable defence against heart attacks. The excessively devoted risk an encounter with Young's devil.

several potent products, with designations such as 'strong', 'old', 'winter', or names linked to seasonal events such as college terms, courthouse sessions or even annual audits, the most powerful of all is likely to be called 'barley wine'. A notable exception is the Eldridge Pope brewery of Dorset (see page 97), which has a hoppy barley wine named Goldie (at around 8.5 percent alcohol by volume) as well as the stronger, sherry-like Thomas Hardy's Ale (12.48 percent).

The earlier, and descriptive, term 'stingo' (originating in Yorkshire) has been used by a couple of English breweries as a brand name linked with the designation 'barley wine'. The Scots term 'wee heavy' is also descriptive, and versions north of the border do tend to be especially rich, malty and dark.

The effect of extremely high gravities on a top-fermenting yeast can make for a very estery, winy-tasting brew. The allusion to wine is rounded out by the tradition that barley wine was kept in wooden casks to mature for up to 18 months. The casks were rolled in the cellars or the brewery yard once a week to rouse the yeast to continue its work. Sometimes further hops were added to the cask from time to time, and perhaps priming sugar and yeast.

A barley wine called Domesday II, brewed in Redruth, Cornwall, in December 1986, was pitched with three strains of yeast, on a total of eight occasions, before being bottled a year later. From an original gravity of 1143–7 (around 36 Plato), it produced 15.86 percent alcohol by volume. The Cornish Brewery Company thus secured their objective of a place in the *Guinness Book of Records* for the strongest beer ever made. I found the beer intensely malty, syrupy and sweet, but with some cherry-like fruitiness, and with suggestions of both port and oloroso sherry. Brewer Tony Wharmby told me that the port character seemed to fade, and the suggestion of sherry to grow, as the beer was stored in the bottle.

Traditionally, barley wines were dark in colour, perhaps mahogany. Bass No 1, originally called simply a strong ale and later labelled as a barley wine, is the most widely available example of this style in Britain, though Young's Old Nick (see page 105) has become better known internationally.

The Exchange Brewery, in Sheffield, Yorkshire, launched a pale (amber-coloured) counterpart, called

The magical cask that transforms the appetizing Golden Pride into an even winier vintage in the cellars at Fuller's. The cask formerly stored a famous old ale in a Hampshire brewery.

Gold Label, in 1951, and there are now several other examples of this style.

In 1961, the Exchange Brewery was taken over by the national brewing company Whitbread, who in 1992 celebrated their 250th anniversary. As part of their celebrations, they asked Exchange to make an even stronger ale. The fruity, spicy (apricot, aniseed) Gold Label has 10.9 percent alcohol by volume, but the darker, reddish Celebration Ale had 11.5. It took ten weeks to ferment and mature, during which time yeast and protein were taken off, but the beer was not filtered or pasteurized before being bottled. Nor was any priming sugar or fresh yeast added. Fresh from the maturation tank, it was almost still, reminiscent of a hefty Pinot Noir or perhaps a port. A true barley wine, surely. It had a velvety texture, a fruity (cherry), smoky palate and a hint of acidity in its warming, alcoholic finish. Head Brewer Jim Burrows reckoned it would eventually resemble one of those *pétillant* wines with a malolactic fermentation. Burrows said he intended to fill some into a sherry cask and lay it down to see how it fared. Where the beer

In addition to their names, many breweries have a symbol that originally identified their premises. Fuller's has the griffin. This practice probably derives from the time when all beer was made in brewpubs. In the days before widespread literacy, pubs and inns could be recognized by symbols. Heraldic devices such as griffins, unicorns and lions became popular after the Reformation, replacing religious images.

will reach maturity is uncertain. Shortly after the celebrations, Whitbread announced that the brewery was to be a victim of 'rationalization'.

A similar private enterprise is carried on at Fuller's brewery in London (see page 76). This brewery had once used a two-barrel fermenter to make a tiny quantity of a dark, strong ale for the directors at Christmas. When the brewery grew too big for two-barrel batches, an alternative plan was devised for the private seasonal beer. In September, a small quantity of the brewery's Golden Pride barley wine would be decanted after fermentation and filled into an un-coated wooden hogshead (a 54-gallon cask), where it would spend three months' maturation. Golden Pride is already dry-hopped, but in this special version it gets a second dose in the hogshead, which is rolled once a week. In December the beer is racked from the hogshead into pins (smaller casks, holding four and a half gallons each), and takes a further four days to drop bright.

Golden Pride, which has a production time of five to seven weeks, has an appetizing, creamy-fruity aroma; a honeyed palate; and a very smooth, firm body; finishing with a dry back-taste. The version with the extra three months has a teasing, winy, medicinal quality. This may be because Fuller's acquired their hogshead from Gale's of Hampshire, who had previously used it for their Prize Old Ale (see page

98). No doubt when Fuller's yeast enters the hogshead, it meets a whole party of resident micro-organisms transplanted from Hampshire. No wonder brewer Reg Drury keeps it well isolated.

Brewers often have fun working on their barley wines, even if these products are not marketed with much vigour. It takes skill to coax yeast to make very strong beers, and to produce examples that are not excessively rich and cloying. A working brewer can enjoy the challenge, and his company may feel that it should have an extra-strong product for anyone who may fancy such a beer. The style was never a huge seller, even in the days when it might have restored the energies of an exhausted farm-worker, or seemed to warm hearts in a cold house before the days of central heating. Today, it remains in the portfolio of many a brewer, but is rarely promoted.

Whitbread for a time advertised a glass of Gold Label as being 'twice as strong as a double Scotch, and half the price.' This made sense only because measures of Scotch were so small in England, and not much bigger in Scotland. Nor would it be permitted to advertise beer in this way today, which is perhaps just as well.

The notion that a barley wine is a warming drink makes a lot of sense in Jack London's misty San Francisco Bay, and perhaps prompted Anchor (see page 104) to extend its maritime theme with the name Old

With its chapel-like private entrance on the left, and its central courtyard, Dubuisson has the marks of a classic Belgian château-farm brewery. Another Belgian regional brewer, Van Honsebrouck in West Flanders, bottle-conditions a strong, yeasty, malty 'castle beer' (Kasteelbier) in its 1736 mansion at Ingelmunster. In an English-speaking country, these would be called either barley wines or old ales.

Foghorn when it first made an essay into the style in 1975. From that year, small batches were brewed sporadically, and in 1985 it became a regular product.

This was the first revivalist barley wine in the United States, and it has inspired many others. They are made all over the United States, but especially in northern California and the Pacific Northwest, the great new ale-brewing regions.

From California, I have also greatly enjoyed Beacon Barley Wine, rich but hoppy, made by the Front Street brewpub in Santa Cruz; and the legendary Big Foot, from the Sierra Nevada Brewing Company in Chico (see page 105).

In Oregon, I have encountered the malty, fruity, alcoholic-tasting Old Knucklehead, from the Bridge-Port Brewery of Portland; and the hoppy barley wine of the Hood River Brewing Company.

Across the state line in Kalama, Washington, Hart makes the beautifully balanced Snow Cap, an allusion to a peak in the nearby Cascade Mountains. Hart's better-known peak is its Pyramid Wheaten Ale (see page 61). In Seattle, the Big Time brewpub makes the extremely malty Old Woolly, and Pike Place produces the subtly peaty, malty, creamy Old Bawdy (the brewery's premises are on a site that was formerly a 'house of ill repute'). Whether barley wines are an aphrodisiac is open to discussion. In the mood of Henry Fielding's *Tom Jones*, perhaps they are.

Does barley wine sound merely quaint, or hopelessly old-fashioned? In some markets, it is frowned upon for being confusing. Where, though, is the romance in 'super strength ale'? That sounds like rocket fuel.

Barley wine producers

While barley wine is a minor speciality in Britain, the style is growing in popularity elsewhere. Not all producers identify their strong ales in this way, but some make outstanding examples.

ANCHOR
Anchor Brewing Company,
1705 Mariposa Street, San Francisco,
California 94107, USA
Tel: (415) 863-8350

This brewery's Old Foghorn is without question one of the world's great barley wines. With its lively balance of malty sweetness, estery fruitiness and slightly citric dryness of hop character, rounded into a soothing warmth, it is the beer world's answer to a cognac.

It is made from an original gravity of 1100 (25 Plato), comprising pale and crystal malt, and only the first runnings from the mash tun are used. The hops are Cascades, and there are 65 BU. Fermentation is with an ale yeast, in deep vessels, with frequent rousing. The beer has between nine and 18 months' cold conditioning on dry hops, and is flash pasteurized. It emerges with around 7 percent alcohol by weight, 8.7 by volume.

It was originally presented in nip bottles, but the handling of these became a problem as the company's flagship Anchor Steam Beer (see page 233) grew in popularity. Recently, Old Foghorn has been available only on draught. It is much sought after.

BUSH BEER
Brasserie Dubuisson, 28 Chaussée de
Mons, 7904 Pipaix, Belgium
Tel: (069) 66 20 85

The Belgians do not customarily use the term barley wine, but this product has very much the character of the style. It is also notable as the strongest beer in Belgium, subject to whatever challenges may arise. Over the years, its potency seems to have increased, and it declared 12 percent alcohol by volume when strengths started to be printed on labels in European Community countries.

Dubuisson, founded in 1769, is the largest of three small breweries in the community of Leuze, between Mons, in the Belgian province of Hainaut, and the French city of Lille. Parts of the building are original, and it is very smartly kept, with pantiled roof and green-painted shutters. The brewery is owned by a family called Dubuisson ('bush' in English). Bush Beer, with its English name but no designation of style, was introduced in 1933, at a time when British brews were very popular in Belgium. Today, the brewery's only other product is a similar Christmas beer.

In the 1980s, the company began to export its beer to the United States. Because the USA already had a beer called Busch (though it is hard to see the two products being confused), the Belgians adopted the name Scaldis, from the Latin for the Scheldt, Belgium's biggest river.

This renowned beer has a gravity of 1096 (24 Plato), and is brewed from three specifications of malt. It is hopped three times, with German aroma varieties and Kent Goldings. A Belgian ale yeast is used. The beer has ten weeks' maturation at 7°C/44.6°F. It is filtered, but not pasteurized. The longish maturation at the brewery, and the filtration, give it a quite different character from the many strong ales in Belgium that are yeastily conditioned in the bottle.

For a beer of this strength, it is not at all cloying. It has a chewy but nutty maltiness and a superb balance of clean, dry, aromatic hoppiness in the finish, with Goldings' influence very evident. After an autumnal walk in the Ardennes, it would make a superb restorative, but the brewery promotes it as an apéritif. It is just about dry enough to do the job.

DOCK STREET
Dock Street Brewery and Restaurant,
2 Logan Square, Philadelphia,
Pennsylvania 19103, USA
Tel: (215) 496-0413

This smart brewpub, in an elegant part of Philadelphia, makes a wide variety of styles, with a great deal of attention to detail. In October 1991, it produced its first Dock Street Barley Wine, to an original gravity of 1106–7 (26.6 Plato).

The beer had Perle, Tettnang and Fuggles hops in the kettle, to 60 BU, and was dry-hopped with Northern Brewer and Fuggles. It was fermented with an English ale strain, but given three further dosages of champagne yeast. The barley wine was released after four months. It emerged with 9.5 percent alcohol by weight, 11.8 by volume.

The resulting product had a reddish-brown colour, verging on black; a herbal aroma, with hints of licorice; a creamy palate; and a surprisingly dry, light, spritzy finish. It is expected that this will remain in the repertoire, as a winter brew.

On a snowy day in Philadelphia, Dock Street makes a warm bolthole, with its cinema-like interior.

GRAND RIDGE

The Grand Ridge Brewing Company,
Main Street, Mirbo North, Victoria
3871, Australia
Tel: (056) 681647

This microbrewery, bar and restaurant is about 100 miles east of Melbourne, at Mirbo North, in the Strzlecki hills of the Gippsland region. The area is known for peaches, berry fruits, venison and a blue cheese; the latter makes a good partner for the brewery's Moonshine Extra Strong, a barley wine of 1080 (20 Plato) and 6.8 percent alcohol by weight, 8.5 percent alcohol by volume.

This warming, complex product has some Scottish, faintly whisky-like, malt notes; hints of vanilla; and a dash of Seville orange in the finish. It is dry-hopped with Goldings. In the bar and restaurant, it is served in a liqueur glass.

Moonshine Extra Strong, a malty heavyweight, was originally made by a Scottish brewer at Grand Ridge as a special for New Year's Eve in the early 1990s. (The brewer wanted to call the beer 1080, after the gravity. Being a recent immigrant, he was unaware that, in Australia, 1080 is the name of a rabbit poison.) Neither barley wines nor Scottish-style wee heavies are commonly found in Australia, so this product was noteworthy. It is to be hoped that it will remain in the brewery's repertoire.

SIERRA NEVADA

Sierra Nevada Brewing Company,
1075 East 20th Street, Chico,
California 95928, USA
Tel: (916) 345-2739

A famous microbrewery and tavern with a renowned barley wine: its name, Big Foot, captures the imagination, and its character is as big as the name implies, with a huge hoppiness in its earthy aroma, a chewy palate, and a great depth of flavour. It is also bottle-conditioned.

Big Foot has a gravity of 1096 (24 Plato) and 8.48 percent alcohol by weight, 11.06 by volume. For some years, it was the strongest beer in America, but other micros now occasionally brew more potent products.

Sierra's entrant has four weeks' bottle-conditioning at the brewery, and begins to become winier if it is kept for a further three months. The beer remains in good condition for a maximum of one to two years.

Big Foot is made available in late winter and early spring, and is followed by other styles at different times of the year. Visitors who want a rich softer drink can enjoy a novel treat made from Sierra Nevada's malt: the brewery tap serves its own malted milk. Or, if they prefer to eat their 'beer', they can enjoy pancakes with malt syrup instead of the more usual maple.

WHITBREAD

Porter Tun House, Capability Green,
Luton, Bedfordshire LU1 3LS,
England
Tel: (0582) 391166

Whitbread's 250th anniversary ale was presented in style. Beneath the wrapping, the bottle looked as though it had emerged from Oporto in about 1800. The beer was sold at the price of a good wine, and Whitbread encouraged buyers to lay it down for at least three years, hinting that 20 might be a more suitable period.

YOUNG'S

Young & Co, The Ram Brewery,
Wandsworth, London SW18 4JD,
England
Tel: (081) 870 0141

Old Nick Barley Wine was a minor speciality at Young's, as in many other English breweries, until the company began to export. Since then, to the astonishment of the brewery, Old Nick's popularity has soared; and its label – with a lively depiction of the devil – has caused some heartache in the Bible belt of the USA (at least, in those states where a beer of this strength is permitted to be sold).

It is an excellent example of a dark barley wine. Old Nick has a reddish-brown colour (75–80 EBC); with a gravity of 1084 (21 Plato) and 5.8 percent alcohol by weight, 7.25 by volume. The beer has a considerable character of relatively dark crystal malt, and is hopped with Fuggles and Goldings, especially the latter (50-55 BU). It has four weeks' warm conditioning.

The result is a liqueur-like product, with a warm aroma, notes of banana, and a teasing balance of sweetness and dryness.

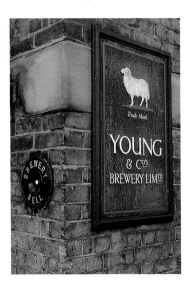

Young's keep a live ram as a company mascot, as well as the dray horses that deliver its beers.

Scottish ale

Perhaps because it can be a cold, gusty, snowy country, Scotland has traditionally produced ales that are enwrappingly full-bodied and malty. Some of the best-known examples are also tawny or dark brown.

In order to accentuate maltiness and body, the Scots sometimes ferment their beers less fully than brewers elsewhere. Therefore, alcohol content can seem low in relation to gravity.

Scotland grows a great deal of barley for malting, although the beer-brewers have to share this with the world's largest whisky-distilling industry. Most of the breweries are in the south, while the greater number of distilleries is in the yet-colder north. The beer and spirit belts divide the country, though neither activity is wholly confined to its own side.

Beyond the northern mainland, on the biggest island of Orkney, the local microbrewer (see page 109) occasionally brews an ale from a grain called bere, a less developed forebear of barley, which is ground in an 1873 mill powered by a waterwheel. It would be satisfying to report that the bere beer was sustainingly hearty, but it is thinnish and cidery. That is why bere is more often blended with buttermilk and salt or sugar, then cooked on a griddle to make bannocks, cousins of the oatcake.

The Scots make not only beer and whisky but also broth out of barley, and they have another typical grain, oats. Crusts found on Neolithic pots uncovered

The Scottie dog and the name MacAndrew's are a trademark for a malty strong ale from Caledonian.

on the island of Rhum in 1985 suggested that a brew had been made from barley and oats, honey or heather, meadowsweet and royal fern. This conclusion was based on an analysis by a botanist specializing in archaeological deposits. Heather ales were made in several parts of the British Isles, and the idea has never entirely died. I have a 1978 cookbook from Orkney with a recipe in which the mash is made from fully bloomed heather and spiced with ginger.

Scotland's brewers

In Edinburgh, a rock formation called Arthur's Seat, a local landmark, is said to have provided water for an abbey brewery in the 12th century. There are still abbey ruins, and the area – Holyrood and Canongate – became the city's brewery quarter. At the height of the British Empire, 'Scotch ale' was a massive export and Edinburgh one of Europe's greatest brewing cities. As recently as 1960, there were 16 breweries in Edinburgh, and Scotch ale still haunts odd corners of the world, near and far. Low-gravity 'Scotch' ales are made in the northeast of England, and strong ones in Belgium and the Caribbean.

There was a terrible cull of breweries in the 1960s. The postwar urge to put the past behind was still evident, and neither the conservationist movement nor the Campaign for Real Ale had arrived. Some of the lost beers linger as ghosts. Campbell, Hope & King is gone, but its first name is continued in a strong, malty but dryish Scotch ale made by Artois in Belgium. The name of the extinct Deuchars brewery has been resurrected for a hoppy ale made by Caledonian.

The only brewing companies that remain in Edinburgh are Scottish & Newcastle (with its headquarters in the former Abbey Brewery of Younger's, but its production on the McEwan's site at the opposite

Scottish ales are often known simply as 60/-, 70/-, 80/- or 90/- (ask for a 'sixty shilling' etc), a reference to a long-gone unit of currency in Britain. The number of shillings indicated the price of a barrel of the beer. This terminology, using the prices of the late 1800s, has in recent years enjoyed a revival, in parallel with the designations Light (indicating body and alcohol, not colour, and an ale of 1030–4 original gravity), Heavy (1034–8) and Export (1040–3). The 90/- ales are individualistic brews, with gravities ranging from 1050–80.

end of the city – see page 109), Caledonian (see page 108), and the Rose Street brewpub, in the centre. The brewpub, owned by Allied, uses extract but produces commendably malty ale.

The Caledonian brewery was founded in 1869, scheduled for closure in 1987, but rescued by a management buy-out. The manager who led the buy-out, and still runs the brewery, Russell Sharp, had previously worked for the producers of Chivas Regal whisky. Hardly surprisingly, the Caledonian ales have an outstanding malt character. This has become one of Britain's finest breweries.

A 14th-century monastery near Dunbar, on the coast between Edinburgh and the border with England, gave rise to the Belhaven brewery, which traces its commercial origins to 1719. Belhaven still has a reputation for good, traditional Scottish ales, with a malty-toasty character (some devotees also detect a fruity hint of gooseberry jam). Belhaven's products include a rich winter ale called 90/- (1070; 17.5 Plato; 5.8 percent alcohol by weight, 7.2 by volume) and a bottled counterpart called Fowler's Wee Heavy.

The Fowler's brewery, of Prestonpans, just outside Edinburgh, closed during the 1960s. Its famous Wee Heavy passed as a brand to Bass, but is produced under contract by Belhaven. 'Wee' means small. A 'wee heavy' is a strong, dark brown (typically 50–100 EBC), malty Scottish ale intended to be served in a modest measure, traditionally one third of a pint.

The oldest inhabited house in Scotland, Traquair, near the town of Peebles, south of Edinburgh, may have been brewing at the beginning of this millenium, and certainly was in 1739, as it is again now. Its oaky Traquair House Ale is a classic representation of the dark, strong style (see page 110).

Also near Peebles, the Broughton microbrewery makes somewhat English-accented ales under the name Greenmantle. The village of Broughton was the birthplace of novelist John Buchan, who wrote *Greenmantle* and *The Thirty-Nine Steps*. The brewery was founded in 1980 by James Collins, of the famous Scottish publishing family, and David Younger, of the brewing dynasty. Its Old Jock (1070; 17.5; 5.2; 6.5) is something between an English barley wine and a Scottish wee heavy. In recent years, the brewery has also launched a characteristically silky Oatmeal Stout.

After Edinburgh, the town of Alloa, in Central Scotland, is the country's other brewing centre. Maclay, founded in 1830 and still privately owned, makes soft, malty-fruity (a hint of sweet apple?) brews, including a rather pale, dryish product with the simple name Scotch Ale (1050; 12.5; 4; 5). The Alloa Brewery Company, owned by Allied, produces a malty but dryish ale called Arrol's 80/-. Nearby, at the oddly named village of Dollar (derived from dolour, though it is not such a bad place), the

Traquair House (left) has had its own brewery on the premises since at least 1738, probably much longer. Belhaven has been selling its ales since 1719.

Harviestoun micro was established in 1985 in a 200-year-old stone cowshed. This brewery produces malty-fruity ales with a hint of vanilla. Scotland traditionally celebrates New Year more than Christmas, so Harviestoun's winter brew is called Nouveau. The brew has a gravity corresponding with the year. During the 1990s, these have been in the 1090s; a new century will pose its problems.

Englishman Dick Saunders was on holiday with his Scottish wife Karen in 1989 when they alighted from the train at Taynuilt, near the West Highland resort and harbour of Oban. Saunders, a carpenter, was greatly taken by the 100-year-old woodwork in Taynuilt station. Today, he has a brewpub in the station buildings. His beers, including one neatly named Station Porter, are by Scottish standards on the hoppy side. This is not surprising, as he grows his own hops, trained up the signal box. He obtained cuttings from vines cultivated by home-brewers a century or two earlier and left to grow wild.

Licorice has been used as a seasoning in an occasional porter from the Borve microbrewery, which began life on the isle of Lewis but is now in a former school at Ruthven, near Huntly, in the Grampian mountains. The brew is called Borve Cairm Porter, after the Gaelic word for licorice, *car meal*. The porter, at 1048 (12 Plato) has an unusual slate colour, a relatively light body, and a complex of sweetish flavours in the middle.

The brewery also makes Borve Extra Strong (1085; 21; 8; 10). This dark ale has part of its primary fermentation and all of its secondary, over a period of four months, in American oak casks that have first been used to mature Bourbon and then Scotch whiskies. The beer seems to pick up hints of a Bourbon-like vanilla character and some of the smokiness of Scotch. A classic wee heavy.

In recent years, I have tasted some outstanding Scottish-style ales in North America. My particular favourite is the Piper's Pride at Sherlock's Home, a lovingly recreated '1890s' pub in Minnesota (see page 110). I have also enjoyed a malt-accented 90/- Ale at the Odell Brewing Company, in a former grain elevator in Fort Collins, Colorado. Doug Odell, an American of Welsh extraction, was inspired to brew after a vacation in Scotland. He obtains his malt from Hugh Baird, of Scotland and England.

In Auckland, New Zealand, the Shakespeare brewpub makes a flavourful, lightly malty Scottish ale called Macbeth's Red. The name matches the colour.

Scottish ale producers

Some Scottish home-brewers still make the heather ales of Neolithic times, but malt is more likely to provide the accent in commercial Scottish ales today. They have been almost as inspirational internationally as the distilled product of barley malt.

CALEDONIAN
The Caledonian Brewing Company, Slateford Road, Edinburgh EH11 1PH, Scotland
Tel: (031) 337 1286

Seen from the road, the office buildings could belong to a minor railway. Behind, down a hill, are the former maltings and the working brewhouse and cellars; there is a bowling green built for the staff; and, yes, a railway in the valley once fetched the barley and took away the beer.

As a student, Russell Sharp shovelled malt here before graduating and working in the whisky industry. After his return, he made the beers all-malt. The favoured barley varieties are Golden Promise and Pipkin. Seven or eight malts are used.

A deep-bed mash tun makes a gentle extraction of the malt's sugars. Sharp remembers also shovelling coal until blazing fires boiled the kettles, 'as though it were Hell's kitchen.' The kettles are still direct-fired, though with gas flames, and this is the only full-sized brewery in Britain with direct-fired kettles. The kettles are open, too, one with a detached wooden hood and the others with copper. 'We are boiling, not stewing,' argues Sharp. 'This gives flavours that you cannot achieve with stainless steel and steam heat.' The principal

Determinedly Scottish Bert Grant, in his brewery's Yakima pub.

hops are Fuggles and Goldings, in the form of blossoms.

The classic draught version of a Scottish ale is probably the 80/-, and Caledonian's interpretation has a tawny colour; a sweetish, malty start; a soft hop flavour; and a deep, restrained fruitiness. It is made from pale ale, amber, crystal, black and wheat malts to a gravity of 1043 (11 Plato), with 3.4 percent alcohol by weight, 4.2 by volume, and has a colour of 30-32 EBC and 36 units of bitterness. I am especially fond of a richer, sweeter, maltier, reddish-bronze ale called Merman (1050; 12.5; 4; 5). In the American market, the brewery has the peach-coloured MacAndrew's, with a clean, malty fruitiness (1062; 15.5; 5.3; 6.5). A similar but slightly more potent brew in the Scottish market is the Edinburgh Strong Ale (1078; 19.5; 6.4; 8). The brewery also makes several organic ales.

Caledonian additionally distributes other small brewers' beers in Scotland, and holds a festival on the first or second weekend in June.

GRANT'S
Yakima Brewing and Malting Company, 1803 Presson Place, Yakima, Washington 98902, USA
Tel: (509) 575-1900

When he started his brewery, Bert Grant began with what he called a Scottish Ale. Pressed on his justification for the designation, he pointed out that he himself was born in Dundee, Scotland, although he

admitted to having left when he was two years old.

Grant's Scottish Ale, amber in colour with a dense head and big bouquet, does have the clean, soft, malty-fruity character of his homeland, although its floral hoppiness owes much more to his adopted Yakima Valley. The keynote malt is crystal, and the gravity is 13–13.5 Plato (1052–5), with just under 4.5 percent alcohol by weight, 5.6 by volume.

McEWAN
Fountain Brewery,
159 Fountainbridge, Edinburgh
EH3 9YY, Scotland
Tel: (031) 229 9377

Internationally, the name McEwan's (sometimes rendered for ease of reading as MacEwan's in export markets) is much better known than Younger's, although the two are inextricably tied. William Younger was founded in 1749, William McEwan in 1856, and the two merged to form Scottish Brewers in 1931. In a further, cross-border, merger, Scottish & Newcastle came into being in 1960.

The McEwan's brewery buildings, ranging from the handsomely Victorian to the anonymously modern, straddle a busy road just west of the city centre. The flagship ales are characteristically Scottish, with some maltiness, and a hint of roasted barley that is reminiscent of peat – but the

use of a high proportion of corn (in the form of maize grits) makes for an undue sweetness and lightness. McEwan's Export, the biggest-selling canned ale in Britain (1042.2; 10.5; 3.6; 4.4), has a Scottish accent, despite being designated an India Pale Ale. There is more character to the cask-conditioned 80/- (1042; 10.5; 3.6; 4.5; 25 EBC; 30 BU). A darker adaptation of this ale now serves as Younger's No. 3.

There is a more aromatic malt character, greater richness and creaminess, a complexity of flavours, and a warming belt of alcohol, in some of the stronger dark ales produced for overseas markets. McEwan's Scotch Ale is made for export at 1085 (21; 6.8; 8.5). The brewery also produces Gordon Highland Scotch Ale (1090; 22.5; 7.2; 9) and a similar Christmas beer for Belgium; in French markets, these products are sold under the name Douglas.

ORKNEY
The Orkney Brewery, Quoyloo,
Sandwick, Orkney KW16 3LT,
Scotland
Tel: (0856) 84802

From the northernmost tip of the Scottish mainland, it is a short hop to the main island of the Orkney group. From the islands' capital, Kirkwall, it is a further 45 minutes' drive west to the Atlantic shore and the hamlet of Quoyloo. In a derelict 1878 schoolhouse, former publican Roger White in 1988 established a brewery.

His malty-fruity brews include the

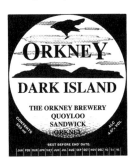

well-balanced Raven, amber-red rather than black, and modest in strength (1038; 9.5; 2.9; 3.8); the chocolate-tinged Dark Island (1045; 11.3; 3.7; 4.6); and the slightly sweeter but threatening Skullsplitter (1080; 20; 6.8; 8.5), complex and winy, with a notably long finish.

SHERLOCK'S HOME

*11000 Red Circle Drive
(Crosstown and Shady Oak),
Minnetonka, Minnesota 55343,
USA
Tel: (612) 931-0203*

Distantly Scottish Bill Burdick, in his brewpub in Minnetonka.

Sherlock Holmes' creator, Sir Arthur Conan Doyle, was a Scot. If he could have forgiven the Sherlock's Home pun, perhaps he would have appreciated Piper's Pride, the outstanding Scottish-style ale produced by this British-accented brewpub in a suburb of Minneapolis.

Its Scottish-American creator Bill Burdick is distantly related to the Maxwell Stuarts of Traquair. He and his wife Carol were married at Traquair House. They both worked for a restaurant group before establishing the pub and brewery in 1989.

The first time I tasted Piper's Pride, in 1990, I thought it was a good example of a malty but well-balanced Scottish ale. In several tastings since, I have come to feel that it is an outstanding manifestation of the style. It

has a tawny-to-dark colour; a lightly malty palate, with a hint of butterscotch in the middle; and a gently herbal, hoppy dryness in the finish. Piper's Pride is made to a gravity of 1046-8 (11.5–12 Plato), from pale ale, amber, crystal and oat malts, with Fuggles, East Kent Goldings and quassia (a bitter extract from a Caribbean and South American tree). Burdick malts the oats himself, and buys the quassia from a pharmacist.

Quassia is referred to, albeit disparagingly, as an ingredient in strong ales in Sir Walter Scott's novel *The Antiquary* (1816). Burdick's specification for the ale is derived from the William Younger's brewhouse journal of 1843.

Burdick also produces a deliciously oily, liqueurish, hoppy Winter Warmer derived from the Belhaven 90/- specification, and the most English-tasting bitter I have come across outside the British Isles (with 48 units of bitterness). These brews are offered cask-conditioned.

TRAQUAIR

*Traquair House Brewery, Innerleithen, Peeblesshire, The Borders EH44 6PW, Scotland
Tel: (0896) 830323*

The Quair is a burn (stream) that flows into the Tweed, an historic border between Scotland and England (and a river famous for salmon). Where the burn meets the river, Traquair House was built. Parts of the present house date from 1107 and its beer is first mentioned in an account of a visit by Mary Stuart (Queen of Scots, and briefly of France) in 1566. Much of the house was built in the 1600s, and the brewkettle is believed to date from 1738 (there is a receipt for its purchase).

In 1965, soon after succeeding to the house, and while still exploring its 40 or 50 rooms, the 20th Laird of Traquair, Peter Maxwell Stuart, came upon its disused brewery.

Without replacing any of the equipment, he had soon put it back to work. The batch size is four barrels, which makes it one of the smallest breweries in the world. In 1985, Maxwell Stuart released a brew called Catherine's Ale, to celebrate his daughter's 21st birthday. Lady Catherine took over the brewery after his death in 1990.

A spruce-covered hill that forms one side of the Tweed Valley has a spring that supplies water. Pale ale malt and roasted barley are used, and the mash takes place in an oak tun (today lined with plastic), to a gravity of 1085 (21; 5.6; 7). The brew-kettle, shaped like an open cooking pot, was once fired with wood, but gas is now used. Exclusively East Kent Goldings hops are bought from the renowned grower Tony Redsell. Fermentation is in unlined oak vessels, followed by two to three months' maturation in metal casks at the Belhaven brewery in Dunbar, where the ale is bottled. It is sold in Britain and exported to some other European countries, the United States and Japan.

Traquair House Ale has a tawny to dark brown colour; an earthy oakiness in the aroma and palate, with dryish notes of walnut, bitter chocolate and malt; and a long, warming finish. The brewery produces occasional commemorative specials and, at a more conventional gravity and strength, Bear Ale. This is named after heraldic figures of bears on the main gates. The house has 50,000 visitors a year, and holds a weekend beer festival at the end of May.

At Traquair, the open brew-kettle, set into a stone surround, is believed to date from 1738.

Irish ale

The gentle rain, cool breezes and fertile soil of Ireland have raised barley for around 5,000 years, and brewing of some description seems to have taken place among Celts in Ireland since the Bronze and early Iron Ages. Saint Patrick is said to have had his own brewer, and Ireland's medieval monasteries continued the custom. By the 1600s, brewing was a cottage industry, usually run by women – alewives. Later in that century, a trade guild was established in Dublin.

Some brewers were said still to be using herbs, notably gentian, rather than hops, in the 1600s and early 1700s. If the use of hops in brewing began in Bohemia or southern Germany, and spread by way of northern France and Flanders across the North Sea to England, it is reasonable to believe that the practice crossed the Irish Sea, to the western edge of Europe, at a late stage. The breweries of the time made ale – although porter was introduced during the 18th century. Fragments of evidence suggest that the native Irish interpretations of ale have always leaned more to the malt than the hop, although they have also grown markedly sweeter in the second half of this century.

Why Irish maltsters and brewers have tended toward specifications that produce characteristically reddish ales is less clear, although each major brewing nation does have slightly different approaches to malting. In recent decades, the ale breweries have been owned by Guinness, whose influence possibly led to the current use of roasted barley.

A brewery which may date from a 15th-century friary – G H Lett, of Enniscorthy, County Wexford – had a product called Ruby Ale at the time of its closure in 1956. A member of the family, George Killian Lett, has licensed the name to Pelforth in France, and Coors in the United States. Both make reddish brews under the George Killian name. The version from Pelforth is malty, strong (5.2 percent alcohol by weight, 6.5 by volume), and top-fermenting. The Coors' version is lighter in body, but still with a malt accent, and is fermented with a lager yeast, at temperatures warm enough to give a hint of ale character. It has 4.4 percent alcohol by weight, 5.5 by volume.

All of Ireland's ales are malt-accented, often with a buttery note, rounded, and with a soft but notable fruitiness and reddish tinge. This profile must have origins in Irish brewing tradition, although it was undoubtedly also influenced by the success of some malty, but tawnier, Scottish brews.

Barley farmer Dave Snyder is neighbour to brewer Ed McNally in Canada. The breeze off the Rockies is cooler than that from the Wicklow Mountains, but the beer is as Irish as McNally.

A barley fillup – Smithwick's barley wine topped up with its ale – will keep out cold and damp.

Although Ireland had a number of independent brewers well into this century, the ale tradition has long played second fiddle, initially to porter, then to stout, largely represented by the mighty Guinness. More recently, lager has also become a force in the land. In the 1960s, the last independent ale brewery in Ireland, Perry's, of Rathdowney, County Laois, closed. Today, there are three specialist ale breweries in the Republic – Cherry's of Waterford, Smithwick's of Kilkenny and Macardle of Dundalk – all owned by Guinness. (The six counties of the Northeast have Bass and the Hilden microbrewery, but producing a less obviously Irish style.)

The first ale from the Guinness group that I ever tasted, in the early 1960s, was called Time. It was a reddish, malty-tasting product, but it did not survive its terminal name. Around the same time, I sampled the reddish, but drier, Phoenix, then brewed at Cherry's, now at Macardle. Phoenix today is very similar to Macardle. Smithwick's ales (see page 113) have in my view the most typically Irish ale character, with just a hint of butteriness.

It may seem fanciful to suggest that the sweet, buttery notes and the ale fruitiness make a good accompaniment to traditional Irish dishes featuring pork, cabbage (or kale) and potatoes, but it is true. A good example is the classic hotpot called colcannon, made from potatoes, kale, leeks or green onions and cream, and often served on Hallowe'en.

In the late 1980s, inspired by the Campaign for Real Ale, a microbrewery called Dempsey's operated for a time in Dublin, making an interestingly Irish-accented cask-conditioned ale. With no recent tradition of cask-conditioning, the Irish were not ready for this and the brewery closed. The beer had been exported in bottle to the United States and a blander, bottom-fermenting imitation of it has since been produced by the old-established Huber brewery, in Monroe, Wisconsin. Some older breweries imagine that the American-Irish may be taken by such ales, but that is unlikely. Those who do not drink mainstream American lagers are likely to go for stout.

Several new-generation brewpubs and microbreweries in North America have taken up the theme, with a better sense of the market: Irish-style ales may well be appreciated by more adventurous drinkers who enjoy sampling a repertoire of classic styles.

Among the older breweries, Genesee, of Rochester, New York, has Michael Shea's Irish Amber, rather light-bodied but with some malty sweetness. Among the new, McGuire's brewpub, in Pensacola, Florida, has a malty, buttery, vanilla-scented Irish Red on draught. A bottled counterpart, McGuire's Irish Ale, is brewed elsewhere under contract. This is slightly bready, and fruitier. The Goose Island brewpub, in Chicago, has a fruity, buttery, Irish-accented Honker's Ale. The Marin Brewing Company, at Larkspur Landing, on San Francisco Bay, makes the buttery, full-bodied, smooth St Brendan's Irish Ale. A very Irish-looking cross appears on the Celtic Ale made by Scottish-Canadian brewer Bert Grant in Yakima, Washington, but the product is less obviously malty than roasty and hoppy, and very dark. Like several of Grant's brews, it is a law unto itself.

The most characterful Irish-style ale I have tasted is made at the Big Rock Brewery, owned by Ed

Phoenix Beer, once national, now has pockets of local support.

George Killian's has ceased to be a native Irish beer. It emigrated.

Smithwick's is Ireland's principal ale, and is widely exported.

Kilkenny is easy to pronounce in the Irish-Gallic bars of Paris.

McNally, in Calgary, Canada. McNally's Extra has a rich, amber-red colour; a buttery-malty aroma and palate, with lots of complexity and depth; a rounded, slightly syrupy body; and a long, warming finish, with a dash of hop. It is a very strong interpretation of the style, at 16.2 Plato (1064–5), 5.6 percent alcohol by weight, 7 by volume. The malts are Canadian pale and British crystal and black, and the key hop is Eroica.

McNally, whose family left Ireland at the time of the potato famine, was a well-connected lawyer in Calgary before 'retiring' to a farm that raised cattle and grew barley for malting. He soon became restless.

Inspired by a friend who had been a brewer, he decided to try his hand. Not long before his 60th birthday, McNally acquired an industrial unit on the edge of Calgary, in the foothills of the Rockies. A second-hand brewhouse from Franconia produced the first beers, in 1985. An early consultant was Charles McElevey, who had helped create Redhook Ale in Seattle, Washington. Head brewer Bernd Pieper was born in Germany and has made beer in Switzerland and Africa. At Big Rock, he produces a wide range of flavourful lagers, ales and porters, each all-malt and unpasteurized but microfiltered.

Classic producer

SMITHWICK'S

E Smithwick & Sons, Saint Francis Abbey Brewery, Kilkenny, Republic of Ireland
Tel: (056) 21014

It is a spectacular sight. Look down from Saint Canice's cathedral and there, in the valley of the River Nore, are the tower and nave, intact but for its roof, of the 13th-century abbey church of Saint Francis – standing in the brewery yard of Smithwick's.

Kilkenny has been a prosperous agricultural market town, and in the 1640s and '50s was the home of an Irish Assembly. Parliament Street is lined with merchants' houses, and behind it stand the abbey ruins, and the brewery founded in 1710 by John Smithwick. The brewery has gradually grown to encircle the abbey. The business was privately owned until Guinness acquired an interest in the 1950s, and took control in the 1960s.

The basic Smithwick's Draught has a creamy head, a palate that is very soft at first but develops in sweetness, and a hint of treacle-toffee dryness in the finish. It seems bigger than might be expected from a gravity of 1036 (9 Plato), comprising a highly

modified pale ale malt, three percent roasted barley and 20 percent corn syrup. The hops used, in three additions, are Challenger, Northern Brewer, Northdown and Target for bitterness; Fuggles and Goldings for aroma. There are 20 units of bitterness and 29 EBC. The brewery has been using the same yeast for as long as anyone can remember. Smithwick's Draught is also made at Cherry's in Waterford. Bottled and canned Smithwick's, subtitled No 1, have a gravity one point higher and ten percent corn syrup.

A brew called Smithwick's Export in Canada and Kilkenny Irish Beer in some European countries has a gravity of 1048 (12 Plato) and is all-malt, with bitterness and colour both in the lower 30s. This has a definite malt character, a redder colour, and more butteriness – the taste of lightly buttered toast comes to mind. Italy has a yet rounder, maltier version at 1052 (13 Plato), and a 1059 (15 Plato) adaptation called Kilkenny Strong.

Smithwick's also makes a barley wine, brewed from pale ale malt, roast barley, caramel and flaked maize, to a gravity of 1062–4 (15.5–16). This is a very distinctive brew, with a

The angled line of the abbey is mimicked by the modern malt-barn.

coffee-coloured head and notes of pear-drop fruitiness, treacle toffee, roastiness, earthy hops and a very full body. In winter, Irish drinkers sometimes have a bottle of the barley wine poured into a pint glass, then topped up with Smithwick's ale. This very creamy, malty drink is known as a 'barley fillup'.

The Barley Wine is produced at the Macardle brewery but with Smithwick's yeast. Macardle's brews – a draught and its own bottled No 1 – again use pale ale malt and roasted barley, but their adjunct is flaked maize. Compared with their parallel brews at Smithwick's, those at Macardle are slightly hoppier (around 25 BU) and darker (mid-30s). The Macardle's yeast creates a slightly bready, cracker-like dryness.

Belgian ale

In some English-speaking countries the term 'ale' is applied to all Belgian speciality beers. As these are usually top-fermenting, it is not unreasonable to group them under this heading in an Anglophone market. Most of these brews are not, though, labelled with this English term in Belgium, and form separate styles, described in the next five chapters.

English and Scottish products, which became popular during the two World Wars, have nonetheless helped establish the term 'ale' in Belgium. There are English and Scottish imports, counterparts produced under licence, and local imitations. There is also one style of Belgian brew that is, in its own country, known by the English name 'ale'.

It is a style similar to an English pale ale, but more aromatic and spicy in both malt and yeast character. These Belgian ales have gravities around the standard 12 Plato (1048) and 4 percent alcohol by weight, 5 by volume; they are intended for everyday drinking, perhaps with a typical beer snack.

You may often encounter these beers as *spéciales belges*, or just *belges*, particularly in the French-speaking regions of Belgium.

They were traditionally popular in the area of Mons and – especially – Charleroi, but the only well-known example in Francophone Belgium today is the all-malt Vieux Temps. This ale has a strong, yeasty, fruit character (a hint of sweet plums) and a sherbety finish. It is hopped with Target and Pride of Ringwood. Vieux Temps is made at the St Guibert brewery of Mont-St-Guibert, between Namur and Brussels.

This is one of three ales produced in breweries owned by Interbrew. In Mechelen, south of Antwerp, Interbrew's Lamot brewery makes Horse Ale, which has a notably aromatic hop character (Styrian Goldings are added at a very late stage) and is spiced, possibly with licorice or grains of paradise. Since Interbrew has closed the once-renowned Martinas brewery in Merchtem, Lamot has taken over production of the complex, faintly syrupy Ginder Ale,

In Antwerp's golden era, the late 1500s, these hoists lifted cloth, spices – or beer.

Breweries large and small can be found in each of Belgium's nine provinces. Flemish is the language of the four northern provinces, French of the south, with Brabant divided.

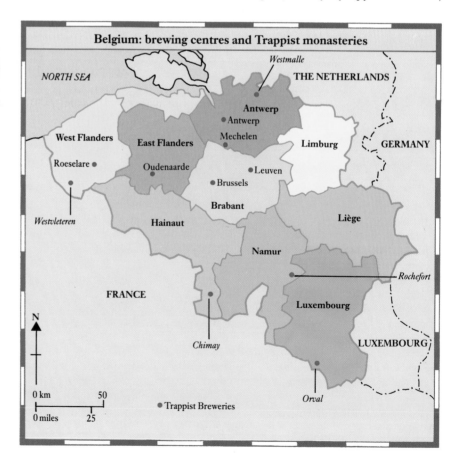

Belgium: brewing centres and Trappist monasteries

hopped with Styrian and Kent Goldings and Lublins from Poland, the latter perhaps imparting a distinctive tang. There is no ginger. The odd-sounding brand name derives from Van Ginderachter, the surname of a former brewer at Martinas.

The northwestern corner of Brabant is a present-day stronghold of the style, with both Op-Ale and Palm.

The first of these ales takes its name from the small town of Opwijk. It is made by the old-established De Smedt brewery, using three malts and a yeast brought from Britain just after World War II. The yeast makes a major contribution to Op-Ale's dry, lightly fruity character, and English Challenger hops, along with Styrian Goldings, give it its clean finishing bitterness.

Palm outsells all other Belgian ales. It comes from a brewery that goes back to 1747, in the village of Steenhuffel, but the name Palm was coined to symbolize the victory that liberated Belgium in 1918. The company brews by relatively traditional methods (double decoction, for example), but is very proud of its ultra-modern quality control.

Speciale Palm is made to a gravity of 13.2 Plato (1053), and has 4.1 percent alcohol by weight, 5.2 by volume. Its style is exceptionally fresh, clean and well-rounded, with aromas of toasty malt, a

Yeast tonic and De Koninck for principal Modeste van den Bogaert (centre) at the Pelgrim café, opposite the brewery.
Brabant is famous for its horses, as well as for its ales, or *spéciales*.

In both character and geography, Belgian ales stand between the classics of Burton and Düsseldorf. When the Belgians label their own brews with the English word 'ale', they mean something copper-coloured, fruity, spicy and soft. Inside Belgium, the term 'ale' is not usually employed to describe the country's many darker, stronger and more esoteric top-fermenting specialities. In export markets, it may be.

In Flemish, De Koninck means 'the king'. Beer and the king are unifying factors in Belgium, divided as it is between the Fleming and Walloon nations.

bitter-orange palate and a tartly refreshing finish. For the Christmas season the brewery produces a stronger version called Dobbel Palm (13.9; 1056; 4.4; 5.5).

Stronger still is Aerts 1900, a dry-hopped and bottle-conditioned ale of some character which, as its name suggests, sets out to capture a traditional turn-of-the-century style of beer. The gravity is 17.5 Plato (1070), the alcohol content 5.9 percent by weight, 7.4 by volume. It is one of two beers produced by Palm that carry the family name of the Aerts, who owned a well-known former Brussels brewery. Speciale Aerts is the least heavy of the Palm beers, with a gravity of 12.3 Plato (1049), and 3.9 percent alcohol by weight, 4.8 by volume – slightly lower in both gravity and alcohol than Speciale Palm.

Besides Mechelen's Horse Ale, the province of Antwerp has a tasty, malty, dryish Ster Ale from the old-established Sterkens brewery, at Meer, near the border with the Netherlands. This province also has, in its capital city, De Koninck, perhaps the best-loved ale in Belgium.

Flemish is a down-to-earth language. *Lek* is related to 'leak' and *bak* to 'bucket'. This is not a bucket with a hole in it, but the tapping system that runs the wort from the mash tun at the De Koninck brewery.

Brabo the 'hand-thrower' (*hand-werper*) is said to have given Antwerp its name.

Classic producer

DE KONINCK
291 Mechelse Steenweg,
2018 Antwerpen, Belgium
Tel: (03) 218 40 48

De Koninck began in 1833 as a brew-pub and beer garden. Its site, on the edge of the downtown area of Antwerp, was once just outside the city walls. The facade to the street is a whitewashed brick building that looks like a former maltings, and the brewery is set around a courtyard. The kettle is brick-clad, in a traditional Flemish style, with a hop sieve that is removed by a pulley system.

It makes only one product, called simply De Koninck. This brew is not identified as an ale, but that is what it is. It is an all-malt brew of 11.8 Plato (1047), 4 percent alcohol by weight, 5 by volume, made from Pilsner and Vienna malts, with exclusively Saaz hops (mainly imported from the Czech Republic, although some are grown in Belgium). It has a warm fermentation, but a (relatively short) cool conditioning.

The beer is at its best on draught, in which form (filtered, but not pasteurized) it pours with a rocky head, leaving a dense lacework. It has a russet-brown colour of 22–23 EBC. The beer is soft and perilously drinkable, with a lightly toasty malt character and a delicate hop balance (23.5 BU), but its defining characteristic is a gently fruity spiciness that has reminded some tasters of cinnamon. This is the product of the house yeast strain, about which the brewery's principal, Modeste van den Bogaert, is amiably vague.

The brewery supplies the odd bucket of surplus yeast to the café Pelgrim, just across the street, where it is served by the shot-glass to drinkers who ask for an extra dosage with their beer. Some drink the shot of yeast and wash it down with beer; others dump the yeast into the glass with the beer. Connoisseurs of De Koninck insist it be served by the goblet, described in Flemish as a *bolleke* (pronounced boll-uh-kuh). The alternative, flute, glass is thought suitable only for women, with male winks at the phallic subtext of the Flemish word *fluitje* (pronounced flout-yuh).

The pub-like Pelgrim is the perfect place in which to drink De Koninck, but there are other splendid spots. On the Grote Markt, one of the city's main squares, Café Den Engel, with its mirrors and marble-topped tables, has a studenty ambience. At Moriaan Straat and Hoofdkerk, Quinten Matsijs, dating from 1565, is Antwerp's oldest café. It offers De Koninck with *gezonden wurst* (Antwerp's local pork sausage) and *beuling* (black or white puddings). Regulars at the café enjoy a disc-throwing game called *ton*.

The best De Koninck I ever tasted was at a tiny, tiled, corner café somewhere in Antwerp. I lost a day there once and have been trying to find it ever since.

Bottling De Koninck.

Belgian cafés can be very basic, but nonetheless offer great pleasure and a wide selection of beers. Wiel's is a standard Pilsner-type lager made by Interbrew. This café also offers the Leffe abbey beers and the complex Ginder Ale from the same group.

Flemish brown ale

Escoffier took the trouble to specify which beers should be used in the classic beef and onion stew known as *carbonade flamande* but, in proposing either an old lambic or a stout, he suggested brews with family ties more distant than those of a crisp, dry fino sherry and a strong, sweet Pedro Ximénez.

The perfect beer, not just in squarely Flemish provenance but also in character, lies between the two: the sweet-and-sour 'provision beer' or 'old brown' typically made in East Flanders and especially around the historic town of Oudenaarde (in French, Audenarde), on the river Scheldt.

Whether this type of beer translates into English as an old ale or a brown ale is arguable; that it is one of the world's classic styles cannot be denied. Complex combinations of malts; a water high in sodium bicarbonate; in some instances a long boiling time, creating a hint of caramelization; multistrain, top-fermenting yeasts, sometimes with a lactic character; and the blending of 'young' and 'old' beers, make for a truly teasing style.

I would happily accept it as an apéritif (its raisiny sweetness in complex harmony with the rich, olive-like bitterness of a Montilla wine) and as an ingredient (the acidity of the beer tenderizes the beef, and the aforementioned flavours give a wonderful depth and piquancy to the finished dish). I am not sure I would drink it as a digestif, though that sodium bicarbonate in the water does make for a fluffy, soothing character. Belgian brewers know how to give a beer dimension.

The 11th-century Benedictine monk Arnold of Oudenaarde was himself a brewer before becoming a contender as the beer-makers' patron saint. (Another Saint Arnold, Bishop of Soissons, was born in Kortrijk, 20 miles away, in the same period. He is said to have ended a plague by immersing his crucifix into a brew-kettle and persuading the people to drink only beer.) Oudenaarde, which was once briefly the capital of Flanders, has some impressive architecture in the Flamboyant Gothic style, and the town hall's collection of tapestries is a reminder of the epoch when Flanders and its textiles were a dominant economic force in Europe. One of Oudenaarde's citizens was the tapestry designer Jean Gobelin, whose Paris workshop became world famous.

Did the bourgeoisie of those days dine off *carbonade flamande*? It is surely typical of *cuisine bourgeoise*, and Belgium's best-known contribution to that style of cooking. The name *carbonade* is said to derive from its being originally cooked over embers, perhaps of charcoal (a stipple of woodlands, and very slight hills, have given the area around Oudenaarde the soubriquet the Flemish Ardennes). The *carbonade* has long been made in a casserole, either on top of the

The truly Flemish carbonade is prepared at 'The Maltings' in Oudenaarde.

Oudenaarde, in the heart of Flanders, is on the waterway from the old industrial south to Ghent and the port of Antwerp in the north. Despite the ravages of several wars, the town is still rich in Flemish architecture.

Pale and dark malts, roasted barley and hops go into Liefmans' Goudenband, which is also a base for cherry kriek. The Belgians like to present their favourite bottles in a tissue wrapping – a token of esteem.

oven or inside (on a very slow heat), and is the classic example of a beer stew.

A hearty *carbonade flamande* is offered at the café De Mouterij ('The Maltings'), on Oudenaarde's market place. De Mouterij is run by Madame Rose Blancquaert, and it is her recipe I have given on page 265. The café serves a wide variety of beers but, if there is an emphasis on Liefmans, this is hardly surprising.

Oudenaarde's most widely known brewery, Liefmans, was already in existence in 1679 (I have seen tax documents from that year to prove it). When I first visited the brewery, several centuries later, in 1976, the owner had not long died, and Madame Rose, formerly the brewery's secretary, found herself in charge of Liefmans. From a theatrical background (she had once been a ballet dancer), Madame Rose became very much a 'hands on' manager.

Madame Rose startled me on one visit by slipping on a pair of sturdy clogs and vaulting into one of the vintage copper vessels that are a proud feature of the brewery. She wanted to demonstrate the formidable task of cleaning presented by these huge and beautiful vessels, which are still used for both fermenting and blending, although no longer for brewing.

Madame Rose remained the key figure at Liefmans during several changes of ownership, even running production while her son Olav studied the techniques of brewing at another company. At the beginning of the 1990s, she retired from the brewery, to re-emerge soon afterward as manager of De Mouterij.

In the intervening decade, Madame Rose's great energy and charm had done much to spread the popularity of the brewery's basic Oud Bruin ('old brown'), its classic Goudenband 'provision beer', and its kriek and frambozen.

Liefmans' Goudenband, with its Montilla palate and champagne spritziness, is the most sophisticated

Belgium's brown ales have a particularly sour-and-sweet character. The classics are very complex, with flavours sometimes reminiscent of olives, raisins and spices. Served at a cool cellar temperature, they are both refreshing and appetite-arousing. They are also very useful in the kitchen. Others are much sweeter, and better suited to being served with toffee pudding or a chocolate dessert.

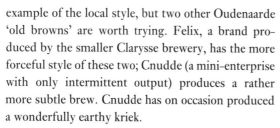

Ladies who lunch have an apéritif first...Bruegel's people emerge once more, unafraid of the pleasures of Flanders' table.

Mother Rose was a legend in Belgian beer. Now son Olav Blancquaert guards the cellars and tirelessly promotes the brew.

example of the local style, but two other Oudenaarde 'old browns' are worth trying. Felix, a brand produced by the smaller Clarysse brewery, has the more forceful style of these two; Cnudde (a mini-enterprise with only intermittent output) produces a rather more subtle brew. Cnudde has on occasion produced a wonderfully earthy kriek.

Within the community of Oudenaarde, but in the village of Mater, is the Roman brewery, which traces its history to 1545 (not quite to the Belgae). Roman is a sizable local brewery, with three donkey engines preserved as museum pieces. Hoppy aromas are characteristic of Roman's well-made range, which includes a Dobbelen Bruinen of concentrated flavour and a drier brown, Oudenaards, with notes of chocolate.

To the east of Oudenaarde, in the small town of Zottegem, the Crombé establishment is a typical example of a Belgian small brewery: café to one side of the yard, family home (with Art Nouveau balcony, and an iron Flemish oven in the kitchen) to the other, brewhouse and cellars behind. The family has brewed sporadically in recent years, but its tart brown beers are a delight. Not far away in St Lievens-Esse, the small Van Den Bossche (like a miniature industrial building, with an iron staircase as its flash of Art Nouveau) produces a grainier-tasting brown.

Farther east at Mechelen, the Het Anker brewery makes a smooth, toffeeish but dry Bruynen, and the stronger, aromatic, immensely complex, sour-and-sweet Gouden Carolus (19 Plato; 1076; 5.6–6.2 percent alcohol by weight, 7–7.8 by volume), with a distinctively raisiny palate, aromatized with orange peel and coriander. Gouden Carolus benefits from at least a few months' bottle-age. I once tasted a 22-year-old that had not only the aroma but also the palate of an oloroso sherry. Het Anker, part of a *béguinage* dating from the 1400s, until recently used a canopied open cooler that covered the whole roof.

There are many brown speciality beers in Belgium, most technically ales in that they are top-fermenting. There are also around 30 brown table beers.

In Brussels, the Vandenstock brewery (a subsidiary of Interbrew) blends brown ale with lambic and sells it under the name Jack-Op. On the eastern side of the city, the town of Aarschot used to produce a similar 'district beer', and this tradition has now been taken up again in the Aarschotse Bruine from the nearby Biertoren brewery, of Kampenhout.

A brown ale of quite different character is Gildenbier. Its style was developed originally in Diest, to the east of Brussels, and it has become a speciality of Haacht, a brewery near the village of the same name. It is an ale of noticeable sweetness with a soft, caramel flavour that belies its strength: its gravity is 17 Plato (1068), and its alcohol content 5.1 percent by weight, 6.3 by volume. Three malts are used, with candy sugar added at both the brew-kettle and the maturation stages. There is more to this beer than the initial impression of ultra-sweetness. After all those apéritif beers, and the brews with which to prepare and accompany the main course, here is one to accompany a dessert of finest Belgian chocolate.

Liefmans' beers are laid down in cellars for their final maturation. Then they are wrapped by hand.

Anyone with a feeling for beers loves its graphics, typography, enamels and memorabilia. Speciality beer cafés in Belgium often make a feature of such items.

Classic producer

LIEFMANS
Brouwerij Liefmans, 200 Aalst Straat,
9700 Oudenaarde, Belgium
Tel: (055) 31 13 92

The Riva group, of Dentergem, West Flanders, acquired Liefmans at the beginning of the 1990s. Today, Riva makes the infusion of malts, and boils them with the hops, before sending the resultant wort for fermentation, maturation, blending and bottle-conditioning at Oudenaarde.

Gatinais and Triumph barley are the sources for the Pilsner malts used at Liefmans. Munich and Vienna malts and roasted barley are also employed. The water is treated to create the special Oudenaarde character, which is low in calcium but high in sodium bicarbonate. Whitbread Goldings are the principal bittering hop, along with two or three German and Czech aroma varieties. In recent years, Tettnang and Saaz have been the predominant aroma hops.

The brewery's basic Oud Bruin is brewed from a gravity of 12 Plato (1048) to 4 percent alcohol by weight, 5 by volume. It has seven days' primary fermentation in open copper vessels with the house yeast (which has for decades been cultured at the brewery, although its origins can be traced back to the famous West Flanders brewery of Rodenbach). There follow four months' maturation in metal tanks.

A beer of 13.2 Plato (1053) is brewed to have an additional maturation of six to eight months. During maturation, the brews are fined, and afterward they are centrifuged. The two brews are then blended, given a new dosage of yeast and priming sugar, and bottled as Goudenband. The bottles are matured for at least three months in the brewery cellars before being released. The finished product has 4.8 percent alcohol by weight, 6 by volume, a colour of 60 EBC and 20 units of bitterness.

Many devotees then keep the beer for several years in their own cellars. Brewer Olav Blancquaert feels it develops its greatest balance of fresh and winy characteristics at between three and five years, but some drinkers like to keep it for ten or 15.

Once a year, the brewery adds cherries to a proportion of its stronger beer after four to six months, and lets it enjoy a further fermentation for an additional six to eight weeks. This increases in strength to 5.7 percent alcohol by weight, 7.1 by volume, and has a good depth of flavour. Consumed fresh, it is on the sweet side, but the tartness develops for around 18 months. After that, the cherry character may diminish. A raspberry version, Liefmans Frambozen, is lower in alcohol (4.1 percent by weight, 5.1 by volume), with a huge bouquet, more sweetness and less fresh-fruit character.

The Liefmans beers are filled into wine bottles, and the magnum is a popular size.

Belgian red ale

'It's wine,' exclaimed an old advertisement for Rodenbach, the classic dark ale from the Belgian province of West Flanders. This product and the several others in a similar vein are almost Burgundian in their dark, red-brown colour, but the analogy does not stretch to their palate: they are thin but firm in body, sweet-and-sour, sharply thirst-quenching, and in my view the most refreshing beers in the world.

These are brews of great character: love 'em or hate 'em. It delights me to see how many drinkers, having never before tasted anything comparable, take to the red ales of Flanders like a duck to orange sauce. Having introduced a wary friend to the style, I have had difficulty in persuading him to explore any other of Belgium's beery treasures.

The sweet-and-sour character is common to the brown ales of East Flanders and the 'red' of the West, and the two are brother brews, but there are differences between them. One is obviously that the brewers of West Flanders seem traditionally to have used malts that provided a redder colour. Much more significantly, the classics among the redder brews, while having their primary fermentation in metal, are aged in uncoated wood (not in casks, but in ceiling-high vertical tuns), and this makes for a teasing blend of caramels, tannins and acidity. As the brew matures, lactic acid begins to build up, and there is some interaction with acetobacters in the wood itself. Some of the lesser producers use metal tanks, but add lactic cultures. Unlike the most famous browns, the classic reds are stabilized by pasteurization.

Their combination of distinctively reddish colour, wood-aging and acidity have led me always to consider the West Flanders specialities as a style in their own right. There is no acknowledged appellation to identify the style, although its Flemish tradition is clearly similar to that of the old ale called Strong Suffolk made just across the water in England by Greene King, of Bury St Edmunds (see page 98). Both interpretations have their origins in the storing of beers in wood at ambient temperatures, before either stainless steel or refrigeration became available. Each is geographically in a corner of its country, and they have somehow survived.

Once, such storage and blending was common, certainly in regions that stayed with the tradition of top-fermentation. In living memory, blended old ales were made in at least two other British breweries. Like Greene King, both were in the southeastern corner of England: Ridley's of Chelmsford (which still operates) and Truman's of London (which does not).

The classic Rodenbach is a blend of two beers: one at 13 Plato (1052), aged for at least 18 months and sometimes more than two years, the other a younger

Rodenbach variations: Alexander is the most approachable, Grand ' Cru the more challenging.

Rodenbach has more of these rare ceiling-high tuns than any other brewery, and is the only one to rely on them to impart the defining character to its principal beer.

brew of five to six weeks, at 11.5 Plato (1046). This blend has suggestions of Madeira, passion fruit, oak and hints of iron, and an alcohol content of 3.7 percent by weight, 4.6 by volume.

The aged beer alone is bottled as Rodenbach Grand Cru. It is a more assertive beer, darker, and slightly bigger in body. It has 4.1 percent alcohol by weight, 5.2 by volume.

A third version, called Alexander Rodenbach, is sweetened with cherry essence. The acidity of the classic red beers led some drinkers to lace them with grenadine: this is the beer for them.

In the United States, I once tasted a beer made with Rodenbach's yeast, aged for several years in oak casks, then primed with red and purple raspberries. This beer, called Dirty Rose, was made by a legendary home-brewer, Michael Matucheski, of Antigo, Wisconsin. It had a wonderfully subtle, cherry-tawny colour; a pronounced Rodenbach aroma; a dry, earthy palate (almost the 'old books' character of quinine apéritifs) and a long, warming finish.

In Rodenbach's home town, Roeselare (in French, Roulers), the restaurant Den Haselt specializes in local products. One memorable meal there began with an aperitif of Grand Cru laced with a dash each of Amer Picon and crème de cassis. This preceded prawn soup made with Rodenbach; rabbit pâté with a

> With their deep Burgundy colour and intense sharpness of palate, Belgian red ales are among the world's most distinctive beers. The key to their particular character lies in their aging in vast wooden tuns. Some drinkers seem to find the taste rather hard to acquire, and may take the edge off them by adding a dash or two of grenadine syrup; others find their tartness incomparably refreshing.

cherry confiture flavoured with Alexander; goose liver with apple served with Rodenbach; and a passion fruit meringue flavoured with Alexander.

The three Rodenbach beers have clearly different roles to play in a menu. The light acidity of the classic Rodenbach nicely suits shellfish dishes and salads; the relative weight of Grand Cru can be deployed effectively with liver, rabbit or game birds such as quail; Rodenbach Alexander is essentially a dessert beer.

Other notable red ales that help to define this particular West Flanders style include Petrus, made in wooden tuns by the Bavik-De Brabandere brewery in

The malting kiln is no longer used, and is one of only a handful preserved worldwide.

Den Haselt offers outstanding *cuisine à la bière*, emphasizing the Rodenbach brews.

'Old Triple'. A Belgian *tripel* is usually a golden ale in the abbey style, but this one is in West Flanders' redder mode.

'Running off' at Rodenbach. A well-made mash should flow evenly through each tap.

Bavikhove; Paulus, from Leroy, of Boezinge; Bacchus, from Van Honsebrouck, of Ingelmunster; Vander Ghinste's Ouden Tripel, from the Bockor brewery in Bellegem (which has some wooden tuns); Ichtegems Bruin, from Strubbe, in the small town of Ichtegem; and several variations, including the rather sweet Pandoer and the even more candy-like La Duchesse de Bourgogne, from Verhaeghe, of Vichte.

The East Flanders brewery of Bios has a dryish example called Vlaamse Bourgogne. Confusingly, a beer called Bourgogne des Flandres, a sweet hybrid between this style and a lambic, is produced by Timmermans in the Payottenland region of Brabant.

Classic producer

RODENBACH
Brouwerij Rodenbach, 133-141 Spanje Straat, 8800 Roeselare, Belgium
Tel: (051) 22 34 00

The Rodenbach family are of West German ancestry, from Andernach, near Koblenz. In the 1700s, during the period of Austrian rule, Ferdinand Rodenbach came to Roeselare as a military surgeon, and later became a local physician. The family went on to produce distinguished inventors, politicians and writers, in German, Flemish and French. In 1820, Alexander Rodenbach bought a local brewery, and in the 1870s another member of the family studied beer-making in England.

Every influence on Belgian history seems to have been absorbed in the Rodenbach brewery. It is even on Spanje Straat ('Spain Street'), no doubt a relic of that colonial period.

On one side of the street, masked by pines, horse chestnuts and weeping willows, is a grand house, almost a

château, built as a residence for the director of the brewery. The house has a spacious garden that slopes down to a lake, fed from a series of springs. The water also feeds the brewery.

A maltings with a conical tower, built in the late 1830s, is now a museum, and the centrepiece of the brewery. The brewhouse, with brass-railed stairways linking its various levels, remains faithful to the style of its original construction and fitting out in the 1920s and 1930s. The most impressive feature of the brewery is, of course, its maturation halls, with the largest tuns holding 600 hectolitres, and even the smallest containing 120 hectolitres. One hall contains nearly 100 oak tuns, arranged in five lines, with narrow paths between them, and there are ten smaller rooms. Four coopers, with a battery of numbered staves, hoops, reeds and beeswax, are needed to maintain the tuns, many of which have been in place since the early 1900s. One vessel still in use dates back to 1868.

Rodenbach's beers are based on four malts: a pale malt made from

summer barley; malts made from two- and six-row varieties of winter barley; and a Vienna malt. These make up around 80 percent of the grist, the balance coming from corn grits. A double-decoction method is used.

The hops are mainly the spicy Brewers' Gold, with some Kent Goldings. These are not especially bitter hops, and much of that characteristic vanishes during the maturation of the beer. The Grand Cru, for example, has a bitterness of 14–18 (and a colour of 60 EBC).

Analysis of the yeast, which is top-fermenting, has revealed an increasing complexity on closer examination. Only three strains had been identified at the time of my first visit to the brewery; later, this had risen to five strains. More recently, researchers at the University of Leuven have concluded that at least 20 cultures are present.

Roeselare, an inland port on an important canal across Flanders, has some interesting industrial archaeology. Rodenbach's brewery, with its maturation halls, should be regarded as a national treasure.

Saison

French Flanders and parts of southern Belgium were once primarily genever gin-making country, and their adherence to spirits may have led them to consider all beers to be light, refreshing drinks for the summer season. The typical rustic beers of these regions were once identified as saisons, and that term is still widely used on labels in Belgium to describe a particular style of beer made in artisan breweries in Wallonia, especially the province of Hainaut, and most notably its westerly stretch.

Originally, these beers were produced to a variety of gravities from 'children's strength' and 'family' to the regular, 'double' and 'royal' versions, the latter at a relatively modest 11.25–12.5 Plato (1045–50). Clearly, these were beers to be served at family meals. The batch specifically brewed in spring to be laid down as a provision for the summer was known as *la saison de mars* (March). It had to be sturdy enough to last for some months, but not too strong to be a summer and harvest thirst-quencher. It had a gravity of 13.75–15 Plato (1055–60), according to a 1907 treatise on the style.

These are top-fermenting beers. Traditionally, they have been made to have a reasonable amount of body and crispness, and to deliver a robust flavour.

In some instances, local hard water may have helped provide the body, mouth-feel and extraction of flavours from the grains, but the brewers also worked to produce mashes that were only partly fermentable. One technique was to take the first extraction of 'juices' from the malt at cold temperatures, producing a milky turbid wort that was heated, then added back to the mash. Sometimes the brewers used a small proportion of spelt (a variety of wheat that gives a very fine flour), or oats or rice (both raw).

The flavour was heightened by a generous dose of hops, and perhaps spices, and the fermentation further restrained by (multistrain) yeasts that worked quickly but not very exhaustively. Traditionally, these beers were at least partly fermented in the cask,

Refreshingly crisp, tart beers, saisons are typical of the French-speaking southern part of Belgium. The name is another reminder that, before refrigeration, it was difficult to brew in warm weather – these beers were made to be kept and drunk in the summer season. These spicy brews conspire to be at the same time thirst-quenching, sustaining and excellent with food. Try them with spicy sausages, duck, or lamb with juniper berries.

Star anise and dried orange peels at the saison brewery in Pipaix.

Pipaix's Jean-Louis Dits is a keen exponent of brewing with spices.

The Flemish spelling has been adopted as a brand name, and the Martens brewery's two versions of Sezoens are arguably styles in their own right.

The French '*caves*' implies a store from which beer can be fetched. This café is opposite the brewery.

and served in a very lively condition, with lots of fresh, resiny, bitter hop flavours.

British brewer George Maw Johnson, of Canterbury, described them at length in a paper he wrote during World War I. (Johnson founded *Le Petit Journal du Brasseur* in Belgium.)

Today, saisons are brewed predominantly with pale malts, perhaps gaining some colour in a long boil, and are still heavily hopped, usually with Belgian or English varieties. Either Franco-Belgian or English yeast strains, usually hybrid, are used, but fermentation is no longer in wood. The beers often have a warm conditioning in metal tanks at the brewery, and always a secondary fermentation in the bottle. Some are dry-hopped.

Most of these beers have a distinctive orange colour; a dense, rocky head; that refreshing crispness and carbonation; and hoppy, fruity flavours, often with citric notes. Their tartness and fruitiness make

them a good accompaniment to duck and to hearty stews and peppery sausages.

Despite the robustness of the beers, they are not especially well known outside their immediate region of production. The province of Hainaut has at least three or four saison breweries. Dupont (see page 127) is a classic example, but there are others.

A saison is made by the Brasserie de Silly, dating from 1854, in the village of the same name (the French pronunciation renders it less foolish). The beer is sold in Belgium at a gravity of 13.75 Plato (1055), and is full-bodied with an initial touch of sharpness and a smoother, sweeter finish. The version exported to the United States is less tart on the palate and stronger, at 20 Plato (1080). Silly also makes a more assertive beer in this general style, named for the nearby town of Enghien.

Saison de Pipaix is a fresh-tasting, fruity, tart beer seasoned with six spices, including anis, black pepper and a medicinal lichen. It is made in the village of Pipaix, in the Brasserie à Vapeur, a steam-powered brewery that is a fine example of Belgian industrial archaeology. The establishment dates from 1785, and equipment from 1919 is still used. The brewery was known as Biset-Cuvelier until 1984, when the owner retired. It was in some disrepair when it was reopened by two local schoolteachers, Jean-Louis Dits and his wife Anne-Marie Lemaire, both of whom were keenly interested in their region's history and traditions. Anne-Marie was killed in an accident at the brewery in 1990, but Jean-Louis continues to make a wide range of beers, many of them special editions to commemorate local events.

Across the Brabant border, at Quenast, is the Lefèbvre brewery, which has the sweetish Saison 1900 in its range. It is also the last brewery in Belgium to have a coal-fired kettle. The light but firm, aromatic, fruity, hoppy Saison Regal (recalling the old 'royal' category) is produced by Du Bocq, at Purnode, in the province of Namur. A welcome newcomer is the Fantôme microbrewery, in Belgian Luxembourg. Its saisons are spiced with locally grown herbs, which vary according to the season in which each brew is made.

Flanders does not produce a style under the name saison, but the Flemish translation, *sezoens*, is a registered brand name of the Martens brewery, at Bocholt, in Belgian Limburg, not far from the border with Germany. Sezoens is a magnificent, bright gold, top-fermenting beer of 12.5–13.5 Plato (1050–54) and 4.8 percent alcohol by weight, 6 by volume, full of the flowery, lingering taste of fresh hops. Classic German and Czech varieties have been used over the years, and the beer is dry-hopped twice, first at the beginning of maturation (two to three months at 0°C/32°F) and again two or three weeks before the end of this period. The beer is filtered. An amber-brown version called Sezoens Quattro has a malty, coffeeish tinge of sweetness and, again, a great deal of flavour development. Martens is a family-owned modern brewery which also has a remarkably comprehensive museum of beer-making.

Classic producer

DUPONT

Brasserie Dupont, 5 Rue Basse,
7904 Tourpes-Leuze, Belgium
Tel: (069) 66 22 01

A classic agricultural brewery, dating from 1850, set around a farmyard. The cast-iron brewing vessels appear to be original, and even the statue of Saint Arnold has a weathered appearance. The brewery has been in the Dupont family since 1920. A third-generation Dupont, Marc Rosier, now runs it as part-owner with his two sisters. Across the way, Caves Dupont offers agreeably straightforward local food.

The beers are similarly direct in style, with a solid, creamy head and typically brisk refreshing attack. Kent Goldings lead the hoppy aromas; fruit is restrained; and the finish is long and dry. They are complex examples of true artisan brewing.

The principal products are Saison Dupont, variously subtitled Vieille Réserve and Vieille Provision; an organic (*biologique*) counterpart; and the stronger Moinette beers in pale and dark versions. (*Moine* is the French word for monk, and an abbey is thought to have predated the farm on this site.)

The brewery has also made, between the two Moinettes in style, a beer dedicated to nearby Beloeil, which once had a beer called Saison Roland. It has also produced a saison type called Vieille des Estinnes for a former brewer in the area.

Many Belgian and French brewers have a figure of Saint Arnold. This one is in the brewery yard.

Belgian golden ale

One of the world's classic beers, much imitated in its own country, Belgium, is the deceptively strong (6.8 percent by weight, 8.5 by volume), golden, top-fermenting brew called Duvel. Strong golden ale is a prosaic description for such a beguiling brew, but Duvel and the beers it inspires have no formal appellation of style. They are nonetheless stylish brews.

There is nothing to say that a golden brew cannot be an ale, or is forbidden to be strong, but the unwary never expect what they get from Duvel. Even the first taste seems much too slender for the power within. The name means Devil. It is a corruption of Flemish, not French, and the pronunciation emphasizes the first syllable (DOO-vl), not the second.

Duvel is a creation of the Moortgat brewery in the village of Breendonk, north of Brussels. It appeared in its present incarnation only in 1970. The beers launched as rivals to Duvel have all had names implying roguishness but, predictably, none has usurped the original. These have included the darker, fruity (a note of cherries) Sloeber ('Joker'), from the Roman brewery in East Flanders; the firmer, rounder, fuller Deugniet ('Rascal'), from Du Bocq in Namur; and the assertive Judas, from Alken-Maes in Hainaut.

Despite its being a top-fermented true ale, the Belgians often drink this style very cold, and even refrigerate the Burgundy sampler glass in which it is typically served. In Belgium I have seen this treatment applied only to a few specific brews. Such icy punishment merely arouses the Devil, while it is an act of barbarism when applied to most other beers, as it is in some parts of the world.

Presented cold, Duvel serves as a potent apéritif. At a natural cellar temperature, it is a fruity digestif. The notion that it might be chilled, and its 'Poire Williams' bouquet, remind me of the *alcools blancs*, or colourless eaux-de-vie, of Alsace.

Its ability to be happily served 'warm' or cold derives from aspects of its production process, which is unusually elaborate.

Two-row summer barley is malted in France and Belgium to a colour of between 2.5 and 5.5 EBC (the finished beer has 7–9). After an infusion mash, hops are added to the boil three times. The varieties used (Saaz and a type of Styrian Golding) produce a beer with 29–31 units of bitterness. These two classic hops make a very important contribution to the bouquet and flavour of Duvel.

The original gravity of 14 Plato (1056) is effectively upgraded to 17 Plato (1068) by adding a measure of dextrose before the primary fermentation. This increases the brew's alcohol content and attenuation.

The original symbiosis of yeasts has over the years been narrowed down to just two strains, and both are used in primary fermentation. The brew is divided into two unequal batches, one for each yeast. At the

'Shush … Duvel ripening', says a slogan on the right of the building. When it is finally coaxed from its slumbers, the Belgians like to see it foam.

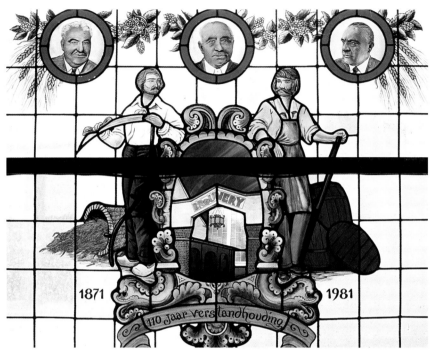

Moutery means maltings, but the Moortgat brewery no longer has a maltings on the site.

Scythe the grain, shovel the malt, brew the beer. Three generations of the owning family celebrate a century of Moortgat; in a spirit of understanding, according to the scroll.

primary fermentation stage, the brew spends five or six days in the vessels, at temperatures between 16 and 28°C/60–82.4°F.

This is followed by a secondary fermentation of three days in cold vessels, during which the temperature is gradually lowered to -1°C/30.2°F. The process of cold maturation is then continued for three to four weeks before the temperature is dropped to -3°C/26.6°F to achieve final precipitation and compaction of the yeast.

The next step is to filter the brew and add to it a dosage of one of the two original yeasts, together with a dextrose priming that lifts the original gravity to the equivalent of 18.3 or 18.4 Plato (1073). The brew is then bottled and left for ten to 14 days during its third fermentation. For this final stage, the temperature is 22°C/71.6°F.

The beer will not be released from the brewery until it has been stabilized for five to six weeks in cold storage at 4-5°C/39–41°F. Many Duvel addicts like to keep the beer in their own cellars for at least three more months before opening it.

The colour might suggest a light lager, but brews like Duvel are neither. They are strong, golden ales, full of fruity, hoppy, alcoholic complexity. Duvel's character develops in an elaborate triple fermentation. It is the original, and by far the best known example of the style, but Belgium has others. Will one eventually usurp the Devil?

Like other prized brews in Belgium, Duvel is served with a flourish. The beer is poured gently into its chilled glass, to be presented bright (though the yeast is well compacted at the bottom of the bottle). It emerges with a huge, rocky, very white head; a small, sustained bead; a satin-smooth body; its Poire Williams nose and slightly spirity palate; and a lingering dryness and perfuminess of the hops in the finish.

Classic producer

DUVEL

Brouwerij Moortgat, 58 Breendonk
Dorp, 2659 Puurs, Belgium
Tel: (03) 886 71 21

Duvel is made by the family-run Moortgat brewery, set among fields of cabbage, in the village of Breendonk, near the historically important city of Mechelen (Malines in French). The brewery was built in 1871, in the classic design of the period, but has been regularly modernized, with stylish touches of functional architecture. 'We have always financed ourselves,' Leon Moortgat told me in 1981 when he was running the brewery. 'We are prudent peasants.'

Moortgat originally made dark top-fermenting brews, and between the two World Wars sought to emulate the Scotch ales that were then fashionable in Belgium. The great brewing scientist Jean De Clerck, who was a consultant to Moortgat, removed the yeast sediment from a bottle-conditioned McEwan's and established that it contained between ten and 20 strains. Initially, a selection of these cultures was used to produce a dark beer. Upon tasting a test batch, so the story goes, a brewery worker hit upon the ideal brand name when he exclaimed: 'This is the Devil of a beer!'

Moortgat responded to the postwar fashion for Pilsner and other golden beers by launching a second phase of experimentation, again calling on De Clerck's expertise. This led to the present golden version replacing the dark Duvel in 1970.

The golden malt was originally kilned to its unusually pale colour at Moortgat. Eventually, the brewery persuaded freestanding maltings to work to its specification. Its own maltings was demolished to create space for more maturation warehouses, to meet its increased output.

The complex McEwan's yeast has over the years been selected down to two strains. Emile Moortgat, brewmaster at the time, told me: 'We isolated the strain that precipitated well in the bottle…and consumers wrote to complain that our beer was not as natural as it used to be. Still, those

A stylish, modern vessel at Moortgat.

complaints are important. It proves that customers are interested.' I hope the younger generation of the family will share this perfectionism.

People are always telling me that Duvel is not what it was. It is hard to be sure, since one cannot compare equally fresh bottles of different 'vintages'. It is like trying to determine whether Rocky Marciano was as good a boxer as Mike Tyson.

A full-flavoured rival to Duvel.

Trappist beer

While the other monastic breweries, in Austria and Germany, make beers in the typical styles of their countries, the abbeys of Belgium and the Netherlands have evolved a range of highly distinctive products with at least some shared characteristics.

Five Belgian abbeys (Chimay, Orval, Rochefort, Westmalle and Sint Sixtus at Westvleteren) and one in the Netherlands (Schaapskooi at Koningshoeven) make beer. All are of the Trappist order. These abbeys may be classified as monasteries in the strictest sense that they are enclosed communities; abbeys of some other orders pursue pastoral work in their villages, in which case the brothers may consider themselves not to be monks.

These six are the only Trappist breweries in the world. No other brewery is entitled to use the word Trappist on its labels. The term is in law an appellation of origin, not style, but it is impossible to overlook the contribution that these breweries, and their family of beers, make to the pantheon of styles. Between them, the monks of the six Trappist abbeys

Only a brew made at a Trappist monastery can use this appellation. These brews have a number of shared characteristics. All are top-fermenting and bottle-conditioned. Some are dry, but more are sweet. All are strong. They represent a family of styles in Belgium and the Netherlands; elsewhere, monasteries make more conventional styles.

in Belgium and the Netherlands produce around 20 beers. All are top-fermenting ales; all relatively strong; all bottle-conditioned, with plenty of yeast sediment; all very fruity and aromatic. Several have some of the rummy flavour that can come from the use of candy sugar in the kettle.

In the 11th century, Benedictines from the home of monasticism, southern Italy, founded an abbey on the

Orval's brewery buildings look more like chapels, but the monastery beyond blends Romanesque and Burgundian references with 1920s' boldness.

Orval makes not only beer but also bread, and two cheeses: a mild Cheddar and a Trappist type like that first made by monks at Port Salut in France.

Rochefort abbey was restored in 1887, and the brewery a dozen years later.

One of today's brewers keeps an eye on Chimay's distinctive yeast, originally isolated by the monastery's renowned Father Théodore. The yeast is used in both primary fermentation and bottle-conditioning.

site that became known as Orval. This is the oldest-established monastery among those that now brew, though its history has been interrupted for lengthy periods. Over those centuries, the monks of Saint Benedict, being judged by some brothers to have become too liberal, experienced a breakaway, known as the Cistercians (named after their founding abbey at Cîteaux, in Burgundy). They in turn saw a defection to a yet stricter order begun by the abbey at La Trappe, Normandy.

Avoiding contact with the ungodly world outside, the Trappists remained true to the rule of living off their own land, labour and resources. Such principles gave a strong foundation to their tradition of brewing, while other orders allowed the art to be lost.

After the interruption to monasticism caused by the French Revolution and the Napoleonic period, Trappists began to leave France and head for Belgium and the Netherlands, to restore old communities or form new ones. Rochefort, founded in 1230, began to brew again in 1899. Westmalle, founded in 1794, began to brew for the brothers in 1836, started to sell the beer in the village in the 1870s, and became a commercial brewer around 1920. Its most famous beer, the immensely complex Tripel, was developed after World War II.

Brothers from Westvleteren, founded in 1831,

went on to establish Chimay, in 1850. Between the two World Wars, Chimay popularized the term Trappist beer. After World War II, Chimay's then brewer Father Théodore worked on yeast strains and other questions with the great Belgian brewing scientist Jean De Clerck, and helped shape Trappist beers as we know them today. When Jean De Clerck died, in 1978, he was buried at the abbey, an honour to both him and the brewery.

The Schaapskooi brewery was founded in 1884–5 to finance the building of Koningshoeven monastery. Orval restarted brewing in 1931, to provide funds for its restoration, and successfully petitioned in the 1960s for Trappist beer to be made a legal appellation of origin.

In each case, the abbey owns the brewery, and a monk is assigned to its overall management. Some have monks as head brewers, others recruit from the secular world. Secular employees and monks work alongside one another, but the brothers must obey half a dozen calls to prayer during the day. The monks are permitted to have a table beer with their meals, and the amount taken is at their discretion. Stronger beers may be enjoyed on religious holidays. A novice monk once told me he rarely drank his monastery's strongest beer 'because it gives me a red head.' I think he meant it made him feel muzzy.

The dry Chimay White is served locally (and harmoniously) with vinegary, peppery *escavèche*, a fish dish the Belgians gained during Spanish rule.

The trout that rescued the golden ring for the princess avoided being turned into *escavèche*, and was immortalized instead in Orval's stylish graphics.

Chimay and Orval have their own inns nearby, where their beer (and the cheese they make) can be sampled. Visits to the breweries may be made only by appointment. Because the breweries are within the cloister, the monks are not allowed to admit women.

Abbey beers

While only the Trappists still have their own breweries, other orders in Belgium made beer in the past. The Benedictine monastery of Affligem (dating from 1074), northeast of Brussels, seems to have been the last to cease production, during World War II. Its monks are also credited with the introduction of hops to Belgium (perhaps from Picardy) in the 11th century. Hops are still grown next to the abbey. When I visited Affligem in the mid-1980s, I found a brother making cherry wine in the cellars. Affligem now earns a royalty from a range of fruity, dryish beers made

under licence by the nearby De Smedt brewery.

A Bavarian community of Benedictines at Maredsous, south of the town of Namur, became an abbey in 1878, and now has flowery beers made on its behalf by the Moortgat brewery, better known for its satanic Duvel (see page 130).

Several other abbeys now licence brewers to make beers bearing their names. These brews cannot be labelled Trappist, though they may use the word abbey (*abbaye* in French, *abdij* in Flemish or Dutch). They do not represent a distinct style, but their methods of production, aroma and palate make clear their inspiration. Sometimes there is no business relationship with a monastery, and a commercial brewery simply produces 'abbey-style' beers named after an ecclesiastical ruin, shrine, church or local saint. Some of the abbey beers are excellent, characterful brews, but none is a classic.

Cherry trees bless the abbey of Grimbergen, which licenses Maes to make its beer.

The abbey of Leffe (founded in 1152) was the first to enter a licensing agreement, in the early 1950s. The contract arose from the abbot telling a local brewer that the community was having financial difficulties. The very rounded, firm Leffe beers are now made by the Artois company Interbrew. The abbey itself, on the river Meuse, near Dinant in the province of Namur, produces tisanes from locally grown herbs.

Just north of Brussels, the monastery of Grimbergen, with its magnificent Flemish Baroque church, has a range of rather sweet beers made by Alken-Maes, the Kronenbourg subsidiary.

Corsendonk, near Turnhout, was a renowned Augustinian priory in the 15th century. It has been restored as a venue for high-level conferences, and offers Corsendonk beers to the heads of state and captains of industry who attend. The dark, chocolaty Pater Noster is made by Bios, of Ertvelde in East Flanders. The golden, perfumy Agnus is produced by Du Bocq, of Purnode, in the province of Namur.

The ecclesiastical allusion also has some currency in Belgium's neighbouring countries. The fruity Abbaye de Crespin Saint Landelin beers made by Enfants de Gayant, in Douai, south of Lille, have their origins in the defunct Rimaux abbey brewery on the borders of France and Belgium.

In the Netherlands, the Budels brewery launched, in the mid-1980s, a fruity, smoky, strong brew called Capucijn, the name being a reference to a monk's cowl. The Raaf brewery, near Nijmegen, has a rounded Dubbel and Tripel. In Amsterdam, t'IJ has four dryish, assertive examples, and there are others.

It was a greater leap of faith when 'abbey' beers began to be brewed in the United States.

The first was in Cambridge, a suburb of Boston, Massachusetts. The Cambridge Brewing Company, in a conservatory-like bar and restaurant, opened in 1989, initially making American-style ales and a porter. It was soon so successful that proprietor-brewer Phil Bannatyne needed some help at the kettle. He hired Darryl Goss, who happened to be a fan of Belgian styles. In 1991, Goss started work on a *tripel*, and this has since reappeared as a seasonal beer. It is brewed to a gravity of 1080–8 (20–22 Plato) from pale malt, with some dextrose in the kettle, and is spiced with whole oranges and coriander, as well as American bittering hops and Liberty (an aroma variety grown in Washington but derived from Hallertau Mittelfrüh). It emerges with a complex fruitiness; an aromatic character in which the coriander just overtakes the hops; and a frisson of alcohol (7 percent by weight, 8.75 by volume). Its name is Tripel Threat.

In 1992, Jeff Lebesch, with his wife Kim Jordan, started the New Belgium Brewing Company in Fort Collins, Colorado. Lebesch, an electrical engineer (of distantly Bohemian origin) had developed a passion for Belgian brews on business trips to Europe. He had spent 16 months brewing commercially in the basement of his home in Fort Collins, and had now established himself in a building previously used as an unloading shed on the railroad.

New Belgium's products include the soft, malty, fruity Fat Tire Amber Ale; a tart fruit beer made with Montmorency sour pie cherries, widely grown in Colorado; and two brews sinfully subtitled 'Trappist Style Ale': one called simply Abbey, the other Trippel. The tawny, darkish Abbey, made with five malts and demerara sugar, to a gravity of 1066 (16.5 Plato, 5.2 percent alcohol by weight, 6.5 by volume), with American Hallertau and Willamette hops, has a creamy palate and a fruitiness reminiscent of figs. The golden-amber Trippel (1074; 18.5; 6.4; 8), dry-hopped with American Hallertaus and Bohemian Saaz, has a huge, earthy floweriness. It is hard to imagine anything less congruous in Colorado, even in eccentric Fort Collins, which has no fewer than five breweries before the Wild West of Wyoming.

Trappist breweries

The six Trappist breweries are in quite different parts of Belgium, with one, Schaapskooi, just across the Belgian border with the Netherlands. Their beers are nonetheless linked, both by style, and by appellation.

CHIMAY
Abbaye de Notre-Dame de Scourmont,
6483 Forges, Belgium
Tel: (060) 21 03 11

When I first visited this brewery in the 1970s, tasting the beer to the accompaniment of an insistent cuckoo amid the birdsong, and Gregorian chants from the monastery church, I could not have imagined that I would one day drink Chimay to new-wave rock music in a club in San Francisco, or see it on sale in Tokyo's smartest department store. Chimay has become by far the best known internationally of the Trappist brews.

The name is pronounced 'she may' – which, as wags like to point out, is a little unfair on the monks. This monastery, in the Ardennes, stands on a small hill overlooking its own dairy pastures and shielded by woodlands, right on the French border, near the hamlet of Forges and the small town of Chimay, in the province of Hainaut. Chimay is now a centre for visitors to the moorlands of La Fagne and the Ardennes, but it once smelted glass, using charcoal from the forest. The early monasteries in the forest forged iron, among many other activities.

Chimay has its own artesian wells (this term is derived from nearby Artois, where this type of bore was first sunk). They offer a soft water with some acidity, both features clearly contributing to the 'house character' of the beers. The acidity perhaps enhances the fruity, blackcurrant sweetness.

Like several ale breweries, Chimay prefers winter barley. This is grown in Champagne and Gembloux, Belgium, and malted to two principal specifications. The hops are German and American, the latter imparting a faintly geranial note.

The most important influence of all is no doubt the multistrain yeast used in both primary and secondary fermentation. The yeast used before World War II had been passed from one batch to the next and perhaps originated in another brewery. The strains selected by Father Théodore work at unusually high temperatures, and quickly, and impart a powerful but rounded spiciness. Some tasters have detected a note of juniper, although this is not used, and others find nutmeg.

The monastery has three regular beers, each of which is identified in its standard-size (33cl) bottle by the colour of the metal crown cap. The three can also be found in larger (75cl), Bordeaux-style bottles with drawn corks.

The original, with a red cap, is often identified by the French description Capsule Rouge (it also has a reddish-brown colour). In the Bordeaux bottle, it is labelled as Première. It has a gravity of 15.75 Plato (1063) and an alcohol content of 5.5 percent by weight, 7 by volume. It has the typical house character, and will round out for about six months if it is stored at a natural cellar temperature, but does not require great bottle-age. The beer is best served at 15–18°C/59–64°F. It is bigger-bodied than any Bordeaux or Burgundy wine, and is the perfect accompaniment to the game of the Ardennes – rabbit, hare, wild boar – whether made into pâtés, roasted or casseroled.

The middle beer in the range has a markedly different character, with a paler, peachy colour and a much drier, firmer, hoppier aroma and palate. This was introduced in 1968, with a white crown cap (Capsule Blanche), and was made available in a Bordeaux bottle, as Cinq Cents, to mark the 500th anniversary of the town of Chimay in 1986. This has 17.75 Plato (1071) and 6.3 percent alcohol by weight, 8 by volume. It will become even drier, though perhaps lose some of its hop, if it is stored for a year or 18 months at a natural cellar temperature. It is usually served lightly cooled. I have enjoyed this drier version as an apéritif.

Chimay was restored in 1875, and is kept in pristine condition. Visits to the monastery can be made only by prior arrangement.

There is a peppery note to the vintage-dated Capsule Bleue or Grande Réserve, Chimay's strongest beer (19.62; 1081; 7.1; 9). This beer is very spicy indeed, and gains port-like notes after around five years. Beyond eight or nine, these begin to dry. It is a natural accompaniment to cheese. The monastery makes a velvety, mild Trappist cheese and has also in recent years produced other styles, including a 'beer cheese' containing Grande Réserve. I have enjoyed that, but still feel the beer is best with Roquefort, or even Stilton.

People taking a weekend drive in the nearby countryside like to stop for lunch at the busy inn on the abbey's estate, and it is possible to stay the night there, although the visitor is unlikely to meet any of the monks.

Like all Trappist abbeys, Chimay values its privacy, but the Roman Catholic worshipper may be able to take part in a service at the church.

ORVAL

Abbaye de Notre-Dame d'Orval,
6823 Villers-devant-Orval, Belgium
Tel: (061) 31 10 60

The name refers in French to a 'golden valley'. The hamlet of Villers-devant-Orval, near Florenville, in the Belgian province of Luxembourg, is in a valley in the Ardennes, between two rivers that form the border with France. Local legend has it that a countess, or princess, from Tuscany lost a golden ring in a lake in the valley and pledged that, if it were ever restored to her, she would thank God by building an abbey. The ring was brought to the surface of the lake by a trout, as depicted on Orval's label. Nothing is left of the first abbey, but there are ruins from the 17th and 18th centuries, alongside the present magnificent monastery.

The clarity of line in the buildings,

Surviving ruins of the original Orval.

the reflecting lake, even the topiary, seem to be mirrored in the single-mindedness of producing only one beer, available in only one bottle.

Orval is a beer of uncompromising character, too. Three malts, produced in Belgium to the brewery's own specification, and white candy sugar in the kettle, produce a distinctive pale orange colour. The hops are German and English, with the earthy Goldings playing a very important part. After its primary fermentation, the beer has a secondary of six to seven weeks at around 15°C/59°F, on dry hops (again, Goldings). Belgian brewers do not generally dry-hop, and this contributes greatly to Orval's individual character.

So do the yeasts. That used in the primary fermentation is a pure-culture yeast, but the secondary has a symbiosis of four or five. This mixed culture is added, with priming sugar, just before the beer is bottled. It then has two months in the bottle at around 17°C/63°F. The brewery considers this a third fermentation, rather than a maturation.

The beer has an alcohol content of 4–4.6 percent by weight, 5.2–5.7 by volume. It has an earthy, leathery, oily aroma, in which some tasters detect sage, and an intensely dry,

acidic palate. Orval will gain in roundness and depth of flavour if it is cellared for between one and two years, but it should not be laid on its side, as it does not come in a corked bottle. Because of its dryness, it is unmatched as an apéritif, and that is how I have most often seen it served in Belgium.

Orval has a shop selling the beer, along with bread and cheeses made by the monks.

The beer also adds its curiously sage-like aroma to sauces. The Belgian chef and devotee of beer Michel David once cooked for me a mouth-watering confection of beer-flavoured Ardennes game sausages, wrapped en croûte with goat cheese, with a tomato coulis laced with Orval. It gave a new dimension to toad-in-the-hole.

ROCHEFORT

Abbaye de Notre-Dame de
Saint-Rémy, 5430 Rochefort, Belgium
Tel: (084) 21 31 81

From the spectacular valley of the Meuse at pleasant little cities like Namur or Dinant, it is an easy drive southwest to Rochefort, which seems to me a classic Ardennes town — bulging with charcuteries, bakers, chocolatiers and restaurants. Although beer-lovers and gastronomes greatly appreciate the small hotel La Malle Poste, there is no special outlet for the brews of the monastery.

Like most of the abbeys, it is tucked away, in this instance a few miles up a country road, with typical Ardennes scenery on both sides: rolling vistas to one flank, woods to the other.

Its reserve, and at one point an abbot who was reputed to be the strictest in Belgium, led to Rochefort being perhaps the least widely known of the Trappist breweries. In recent years, many more beer-lovers have discovered its products.

The site was originally a convent. In 1595, it began to brew, using barley and hops grown in the grounds. Sad to say, their cultivation has long ceased, but Rochefort is still the most rustic of the Trappist breweries, in parts looking quite medieval.

Today's barley is grown in France, Belgium and the Netherlands and is malted in the Pilsner and caramelized Munich styles. Dark candy sugar is added in the kettle. Despite the malty, sweet accent of the beers, a relatively aromatic blend of hops is used, from Germany and Slovenia. Two strains of yeast are employed, in the same combination during primary fermentation and bottle-conditioning. White crystal sugar is used in the bottle.

The head brewer, Brother Antoine, told me that he liked to keep things simple. That philosophy works for him – he makes delicious beer. He took me for a tasting in his office, where the customary crucifix watches over a collection of several hundred drinking vessels.

Rochefort has three beers, with red, green and black crown caps respectively, identified as six, eight and ten in the old system of Belgian degrees. This is a measure of original gravity, now falling out of use in favour of degrees Plato.

Rochefort 6 (6 percent alcohol by weight, 7.5 by volume) has a pinkish-brown colour; a very soft body; and a perfumed, sweetish, fruity palate (some tasters have detected basil or bay leaves – I have wondered about sweet tea).

Rochefort 8 (7.3 percent alcohol by weight, 9.2 by volume) has a more brownish colour. Its character is similar, but more assertive, both drier and richer, with that aromatic fruitiness developing fig-like notes.

Rochefort 10 (9 percent alcohol by weight, 11.3 by volume) has a dense head; a deep claret colour; an enveloping body; and a spicy, earthy aroma and palate, with suggestions of chestnuts, candied fruits and bitter chocolate. Perhaps Rochefort 10 is the beer to go with the richest of Ardennes mousselines, as the great

dessert wines of France are paired with the pâtés of that country. As a dessert beer, Rochefort 10 is also the natural choice with the darkest of Belgian chocolate.

The Belgian chef Michel David uses Rochefort 6 as an ingredient in a leek sauce for sea bream, the eight with a bone-marrow brioche, and the ten in a sauce with shallots to dress a hot goat cheese salad.

SCHAAPSKOOI

Abdij Koningshoeven, 3 Eindhovense Weg, 5056 RP Berkel-Enschot, The Netherlands
Tel: (013) 358147

The old duchy of Brabant straddles the Belgian-Dutch frontier, and this monastery is on the northern side, near the city of Tilburg. The name means 'sheep's pen', and the brewery is at the 'King's Gardens' (in Dutch, Koningshoeven) monastery, on land that once belonged to royalty. Monks were often beneficiaries of nobility, who were, perhaps, anxious to book their place in heaven.

Like several breweries (and distilleries) of the late 19th century, this one has the rustic-industrial look of a country railway station. The abbey is in imposing neo-Gothic style. The production director is a secular brewer, but he is helped by three novice monks.

The beers are labelled La Trappe, with the Schaapskooi name in smaller type. (Beers bearing the name Koningshoeven are produced at the monastery for the cafés of Breda/Oranjeboom, the Dutch subsidiary of Allied Breweries.)

La Trappe Dubbel, at 16.5 Plato (1066; 5.2 percent alcohol by weight, 6.5 by volume), has a deep ruby colour, a yeasty fruitiness in the nose, great complexity of flavour (chocolate, sherry or Madeira, prunes, licorice?), and a firm body. Its specification includes pale malt, Munich and colour malts; and Northern

Brewer hops grown in the Hallertau region. A similar beer is produced under the Koningshoeven name.

Because of the popularity of Westmalle Tripel, it is generally assumed that this designation indicates a golden beer, but this is not necessarily so. La Trappe Tripel (17.5; 1070; 6.4; 8) has a full bronze colour. It has a good Goldings hop character, with suggestions of coriander. A Tripel under the Koningshoeven label has a dry, clean maltiness.

La Trappe Quadrupel (21–22; 1084–88; 8; 10) was launched in 1992. It is brewed as a yearly vintage and released in autumn. It has an autumnal, russet colour, a smooth, almost syrupy texture, a fruity, spicy palate, and lots of flavour development toward a lingering, somewhat tart dryness in the finish.

WESTMALLE

Abdij der Trappisten, 2140 Malle, Belgium
Tel: (03) 312 05 35

Few breweries produce a beer called 'single', although the terms 'double' and 'triple' are more often found, especially in Belgium. Westmalle has all three, but it is especially known for its triple, one of the world's great beers.

These terms are not intended to indicate a multiplication of the gravity or strength of the beer, but just an ascending order of potency, like the 'x' symbols dating from the days before widespread literacy. Nor is there any rule to say that each should represent a particular variation of style, although the Belgians very often take a *dubbel* to mean a dark, sweetish Trappist or abbey brew and a *tripel* to be pale and drier. This convention has been popularized by the range at Westmalle.

It is a very neat monastery, peeping through a curtain of elms onto a main road in flat, Flemish countryside to the northeast of Antwerp. Much of the building dates from the early 1900s, but the brewhouse exterior is clearly 1930s. The water is quite hard, which suits its paler products.

The brewery favours summer barley, from the French Gatinais region (between Paris and Orleans) and Franconia. It uses a wide range of hops, with the emphasis on Tettnang, Saaz and Styrian Goldings.

Westmalle's products, in common with their brothers, have an elaborate regime of maturation. They have a secondary fermentation (three weeks for the Dubbel, five for the Tripel), followed by a priming, reyeasting and a warm conditioning (two weeks and three, in this instance).

Some of the Trappist abbeys make a beer of modest potency for the monks to have at lunch and dinner, and this was the origin of Westmalle's golden, delicate, aromatic, salty 'single', known as Extra. The first time I tasted Westmalle Extra (4 percent alcohol by weight, 5 by volume), it was available only to the monks. Since then, various experimental versions have gone on general release.

Westmalle Dubbel (15.7; 1063; 5.2; 6) is made with pale and dark malts and candy sugar. It has a red-tinged dark brown colour; a soft, faintly syrupy body; and a sweetish, malty-chocolaty palate, with notes of raisins, bananas and passion fruit.

The famous Westmalle Tripel (20; 1080 7.2; 9) has a dense white head, leaving very full lacework; a strongly herbal aroma (coriander, thyme, rosemary?); and a clean, flowery-fruity (orange skins?) palate. All of those notes form a complex with a delicately dry hop character and a very clean, firm maltiness.

Why does it go so well with asparagus? It might be argued that lagers, with their hint of sulphur, are a better match, but perhaps the citric note in Westmalle Tripel finds an affinity with that lemon-grassy flavour that also lurks in the plant.

Guarded by saints, Westvleteren closes its doors to the outside world. Inside, its buildings vary from the charmingly rustic to a breathtakingly modern church.

WESTVLETEREN
Abdij Sint Sixtus, 8983 Westvleteren, Belgium
Tel: (057) 40 03 76

Close to the Channel ports, the war graves of Ypres (in Flemish, Ieper) and hop gardens of Poperinge, in the province of West Flanders, this is the smallest of the Trappist breweries.

When I first visited, it had a tiny brewhouse in a style that is classically found among artisan beer-makers in northern France and Belgium, with bricked-in vessels with copper lids that look as though they belong to giant saucepans. This has now been replaced by a modern brewhouse.

During the years when its capacity was really tiny, Westvleteren made its beers available only from a sales window at the door and in the nearby Café De Vrede. It seems to be finding it hard to break this habit. While some monasteries have been quite aggressively commercial, Westvleteren has taken the view that it should brew just enough to support itself.

Westvleteren does not brew every day, and the arrival of a new batch can attract a queue at the sales hatch. The

proprietor of a specialist beer shop in the Netherlands told me that he drove across Belgium to pick up a stock of the monastery's strongest beer, arrived at five in the morning, and found that there was already a line of cars and bicycles down the lane.

Westvleteren's beers are very much malt-accented, although the monastery overlooks a hop garden. The brewery looks for richness and sweetness in its malts, and just a restrained balancing dryness in its hops.

Again, the old Belgian degrees are used, with coloured crown caps. This time, the brewery starts off with a green-topped Westmalle 4 Dubbel (3.2 percent alcohol by weight, 4 by volume) for its own table. The red 6 Special (5; 6.2) already begins to weigh in with spicy notes of vanilla, licorice and ginger. The blue 8 Extra (6.4; 8.4) adds more fruitiness, reminiscent of melon, both acidity and sweetness, and some liqueurish notes of alcohol. The famous yellow 12 Abbot (8.8; 11) is yet bigger and very creamy and soothing. It is the perfect accompaniment to the local tarte Mazarine, a very sweet, cinnamon-flavoured cake similar to a rum baba.

Bière de garde

Devotees have long regarded this style as a minor classic, and in recent years it has become more widely recognized, especially in Britain and the United States. It is one of those styles of beer that are often presented in champagne bottles, and it has an incidental claim to such dress: malting barley grown in the Champagne region of France is sometimes used in the bières de garde, which are produced some 50 or 60 miles to the north.

Bières de garde were originally beers made in February and March to be laid down as a provision for the summer, when the weather did not permit brewing. Dutch-speaking Flemings had a '*provisie bier*' and the British a 'keeping beer', though neither had quite the same style as today's bières de garde.

The style belongs close to the Belgian border, in the northern part of France: the French lowlands. This area – embracing the Channel ports, French Flanders, Artois and Picardy – has about 20 breweries and its own distinct beer culture, as well as artisan-made genever gins (such as Houlle, Loos and Wambrechies), and gastronomic delights that are too often overlooked (as are its very varied scenery and often Flemish-accented architecture).

Sometimes the barley and hops are grown in the region itself, in which case the local appellation Pas-de-Calais/Région du Nord may appear on the label. Inland from Calais and Dunkerque, this small but old-established region of hop-growing straddles the border between Belgian and French Flanders, flanked by the towns of Ypres and Hazebrouck.

One of the earliest hints of hops' use in brewing is a reference to their being required (for unspecified purposes, but very possibly the making of beer) by monks in Picardy prior to AD 822. Over the centuries, hops (*houblons* in French) have clearly been central to the region's folk culture.

The bière de garde style developed in farmhouse breweries, and several examples are still produced on a very small scale. The farmhouse brewery is typically housed in buildings roofed with terracotta pantiles, set around a courtyard. Some of these produce only three or four thousand hectolitres a year, some perhaps nine or ten. Others come close to a hundred thousand. The bigger breweries, making bières de garde alongside more conventional brews, range from 250,000 to two million hectolitres a year.

Breweries attached to farms did not have bottling lines. Customers would either buy the product by the

The name means 'beer to keep', implying that it was laid down as a provision to be drawn upon during the summer. The style belongs to northern France, and bières de garde often appear in champagne bottles. Traditionally, they were top-fermenting, and some still are. They have a malt accent and an ale-like fruitiness, often with spicy notes, and are medium to strong in alcohol.

The windmill reveals the Flemish flavour of this region, and in the flatlands the tiniest hill counts as a 'mountain'.

A Flemish touch again in the gables and the flat land. The architecture, the landscape and many names are Flemish, from the Belgian frontier to an imaginary line between Calais and Cambrai, which was the border in Burgundian days. Flanders had originally been carved out in the ninth century, as a northern territory of the French King Charles the Bald.

cask or bring empty gin crocks or cognac or wine bottles to be filled with beer. They would add their own sugar to the bottle as a priming.

Bières de garde were originally top-fermenting, and some still are. Others seek an ale character by employing a bottom yeast at warm temperatures. The style predates the introduction of bottom fermentation, which came late to the region, arriving with industrial-scale brewing after World War I.

The beers were also unfiltered, and two or three are still bottled on their lees (*sur lie*). They were originally high in density and alcohol – and most still are. Typically, they have 15–19 Plato (1060–76) and 5.6–6.4 percent alcohol by weight, 6.5–8.5 by volume.

Bières de garde have an ale-like fruitiness, though this is sometimes very restrained. Their accent is most often toward malt, usually of a spicy, aromatic specification. The signature malt may be kilned in the Vienna style, perhaps to 60 EBC, and mashed for body. Some brewers in the area use a long, vigorous boil, with a view to creating a malty caramelization in both flavour and colour; some chaptalize with malt syrup, glucose or sugar. The finished beers vary in colour from full gold to a dark reddish-brown, but many are somewhere in between, perhaps with 30–35 EBC. For the gravity, the bitterness is often modest, perhaps in the mid- or upper 20s. Most bières de garde use spicy but soft, restrained hop varieties such

as Brewers' Gold. Even the water may be softened, as in some lager breweries.

Bières de garde sometimes have a dash of cellar character, with suggestions of oak or cork, even though all are today matured in metal tanks. Critics might regard this as a defect, but I feel it can add complexity and charm. Some have a month or more of cold (0–2°C/32–35°F) maturation. Several bières de garde also have a degree of alcohol taste among their complex of characteristics.

These big, spicy aromas and flavours make bières de garde a perfect accompaniment to the hearty foods of the region – which include tripe sausages (*andouillettes*), lamb and rabbit dishes (often served with leeks, which also feature, sometimes with onions and squashes, in the local *flamiche*, a vegetable tart) and cheeses such as the soft, strong-smelling Maroilles. The odd bière de garde is even rich and toffeeish enough to go with the region's sinful sugar pie, *tarte à la cassonade* (see page 269).

In the region, allusions to the lore of brewing often appear in the names of restaurants, brasseries and cafés, many of which prepare the odd dish with beer. The word brasserie translates as 'brewery', and originally indicated an establishment that produced beer and served it with food. This tradition has been revived by the café Les Brasseurs in Lille (22 Place de la Gare, Tel: 20 06 46 25) and the Bailleux brewery at

Gussignies (see page 142). They are true brasseries. Les Brasseurs does not make a bière de garde, but its other styles are worth sampling.

The tradition of bières de garde began to retreat between the two World Wars and all but vanished after the second, but it has enjoyed a revival since the 1970s with the growing interest in speciality food and drink. Now once again there are breweries which specialize in this style, while to others it is a minor product. The brewery Enfants de Gayant in Douai, for example, promotes its strong lagers but also produces the malty bière de garde Lutèce. The dryish, fruity bière de garde Pot Flamand turns out to come from Picardy, where it is made by the Brasserie Clerck (a noble Flemish surname in brewing), and that is about the farthest-flung example. Bières de garde have cropped up elsewhere occasionally, but not memorably.

With bières de garde now being brewed year-round, some producers also make a seasonal special in March, under the name bière de mars. This is usually very malty. Christmas beers are also widely made, and these are usually stronger and darker than the principal product. Similar seasonal beers are made by the lager-brewers of Alsace.

The region once had a tradition of 'white' wheat beer (especially in and around the Flemish town of Cambrai), and this is enjoying a small revival. Another style produced in the region is porter, a vestige of the British military presence during the two World Wars. This is particularly associated with the Pelforth brewery, which is owned by Heineken. Pelforth Porter is aromatically malty, with a slightly burnt taste, top-fermenting, and relatively strong, with 4.8 percent alcohol by weight, 6 by volume. The brewery Jeanne d'Arc in Ronchin, near Lille, has a Scotch ale in its portfolio. The Steinbeer brewery, of Evin Malmaison in Artois, makes a pleasant Vienna-style lager called Spéciale 1883.

Many breweries in the north typically make a *blonde* (pale), an *ambrée* (deep gold) and a *brune* (dark). These are usually lagers, though the odd *brune* is top-fermenting. For seemingly everyday beers, these may be quite strong: typically in the range of 4.4–5.2 percent alcohol by weight, 5.5–6.5 by volume.

Serge Ricour in the brewhouse of St Sylvestre, in hop country between Steenvoorde and Hazebrouck, in French Flanders. The family's beers include 3 Monts.

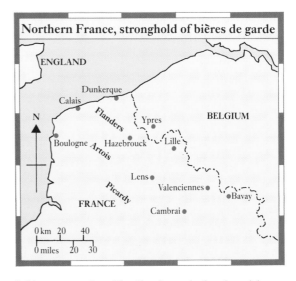

Seldom more than 20 miles from the border with Belgium, the traditional French brewing region nevertheless produces its own distinctive style.

Bière de garde producers

Outside France, there have been only sporadic essays into this style. In the traditional region, the producers range from the odd brewpub and a domestically operated commercial brewery to three or four classic farmhouse operations and others working on a more industrial scale.

ANNOEULLIN

Brasserie d'Annoeullin, 4 Grand'
Place, 59112 Annoeullin, France
Tel: 20 85 78 57

Annoeullin's bière de garde has the confusing name Pastor Ale. Neither an ecclesiastical brew nor an English-accented ale, a second glance reveals the name to be a Euro-pun at the expense of Beethoven: 'C'est une symphonie,' sings the beer's advertising slogan.

Pastor Ale is a pale bière de garde, well rounded and spicy, with hints of honey and cherry in its fruitiness. It is made entirely from pale malt, at 15 Plato (1060); Flemish hops are used for bittering, with Saaz for aroma; the yeast is bottom-fermenting; the beer emerges with 5.2 percent alcohol by weight, 6.5 by volume.

The brewery also makes a wheat beer, L'Angelus Bière de Froment. This contains 30 percent wheat, has 18 Plato (1072) and 5.6 percent alcohol by weight, 7 by volume. It has a bouquet suggesting spices (though none are used) and a perfumy, fruity palate, with some syrupiness. These beers are filtered, but not pasteurized.

The small brewery is in the little town of Annoeullin, between Lille and Lens. It was founded in 1905, and has very old equipment, including a traditional mash tun and copper-domed kettle. Since the mid-1970s it has been operated by Bertrand Lepers, the fifth generation of a family that has brewed and grown hops in the region for more than 100 years. Monsieur Lepers and his wife Yolande run the brewery, and promote their products, with great vigour and charm. Like several of the small northern breweries, Anno-euillin also makes beers under private labels for supermarkets.

BAILLEUX

Brasserie Bailleux, Café Restaurant
Au Baron, Place du Fond des Rocs,
59570 Gussignies, France
Tel: 27 66 88 61

A revivalist brewery hidden in the hills of French Hainault in the village of Gussignies, north of Bavay and Bellignies, right on the Belgian border, an area rich in Gallo-Roman history. The brewery, named after its owners, the Bailleux family, opened in 1989, in the café-restaurant Au Baron. Roger Bailleux, who formerly made less interesting products for a national brewer, fires the kettle for a range of top-fermenting bières de garde *sur lie*. His son and daughter-in-law run the restaurant.

The three principal beers all have 15.5–16 Plato (1062–4) and 5.6 percent alcohol by weight, 7 by volume. Three or four malts are used, and Flemish Brewers' Gold hops as well as Hallertau, Spalt and Hersbruck.

Cuvée des Jonquilles has a very attractive, full gold colour; a dense head; a faintly oily body; a fruity, dry palate; and an appetizingly hoppy, bitter finish. Saison Saint Médard, with a darkish russet hue, is softer and maltier, with a balancing tartness in a long finish. Of the three, it is the truest bière de garde, despite the designation saison (a nod to Belgium). Cuvée de Noël, originally made just for the Christmas season but now

available year-round, is dark brown, with notes of bitter chocolate and a decided spiciness.

These beers are available to be consumed on the premises or taken away, in which case they can be laid down for three to 18 months at a natural cellar temperature. The restaurant (open only at weekends) cooks with beer, has a *flamiche au Maroilles* (a rich tart made with the strong local cheese) among its specialities, and features a wood-fired grill under an old brew-kettle hood.

CASTELAIN

Brasserie Castelain, 13 Rue Pasteur,
Bénifontaine, 62410 Wingles, France
Tel: 21 40 38 38

Owned and operated by the enterprising Yves Castelain, 'artisan brasseur', this brewery is known especially for its bières de garde under the name Ch'ti, which is local patois for a Northerner. The labels show a coal miner, in tribute to the now-vanished industry of the area. The brewery is in the former mining village of Béni-fontaine, near Wingles, just north of Lens, on the borders of Flanders and Artois. The building, dating from 1926 but utilitarian in architecture, has been well maintained, and its gleaming copper kettles are visible from the street. It has its own shop on the premises, and there is a small hop garden at the rear.

Gatinais and local barley are used, with Flemish and Hallertau or Tettnang hops. The bières de garde are fruity, malty and sweetish; they are chaptalized, bottom-fermented and very thoroughly filtered, but not pasteurized. The Ch'ti range appears in a *blonde* and a *brune*, both 15 Plato (1060) and 5.2 percent alcohol by weight, 6.5 by volume; and an *ambrée* of 14 Plato (1056) and 4.9 percent alcohol by weight, 6.1 by volume. The *blonde* has a cookie-like maltiness; the *ambrée* has more complexity of malt character and depth of flavour; the *brune* is beautifully balanced, with some port-like notes.

Castelain also makes a very fruity-tasting stronger speciality called Sint Arnoldus (18; 1072; 6; 7.5), which is filtered, then reyeasted and bottled *sur lie*. There are, additionally, seasonal beers; a remarkably pale, refreshing, organic brew called Jade (12; 1048; 3.5; 4.6); and a number of private labels.

LA CHOULETTE
Brasserie La Choulette, 16 Rue des Ecoles, 59111 Hordain, France
Tel: 27 35 72 44

A delightful farmhouse-style brewery, founded in 1885, and very antiquated. It takes its name from a French game, an antecedent of lacrosse. The brewery is at Hordain, near Bouchain, south of Denain and Valenciennes.

La Choulette specializes in bières de garde *sur lie*, using a blend of top-fermenting yeast with a bottom culture that works at warm temperatures. 'Evolution is constant...I am always searching,' explains Alain Dhaussy, who runs the brewery with his wife Martine. His grandfather had been a brewer but Alain had studied pharmacy before resuming the family tradition with the purchase of La Choulette.

A family friend had owned the brewery, which made a 'farmhouse' top-fermenting style until the mid-1950s, then switched to lager production. Alain and Martine revived it as a

specialist brewery in the late 1970s.

The products have a distinct delicacy and complexity. The golden Bière des Sans Culottes (a reference to the 'trouserless' poor of the French Revolution) has 17 Plato (1068) and 5.2 percent alcohol by weight, 6.5 by volume. It has an outstanding bouquet, with an intentional yeasty note (like the toastiness of a champagne); a soft, pear-like fruitiness, balanced with maltiness; and a warming, slightly alcoholic finish. The amber La Choulette (18; 1072; 5.6–6; 7–7.5) has a subtle and attractive colour; an even softer fruit character; and a notably clean maltiness. The Brassin Robespierre, stronger still at 19-20 Plato (1076-80) and 6–6.4 alcohol by weight, 7.5–8 by volume, reverts to gold, with a smooth, soothing palate.

Local malts and both Flemish and Hallertau hops are used. These beers are given a rough filtration, leaving some yeast in the bottle. A beautifully balanced Framboise, made with natural raspberry extract, is filtered bright, but not pasteurized.

DUYCK
Brasserie Duyck, 113 Route Nationale, 59144 Jenlain, France
Tel: 27 49 70 03

This is the name, clearly Flemish, of the family who gave a wider popularity to bière de garde by offering it ready-bottled. Their pioneering brew is called Jenlain, after the hamlet in which their brewery stands, southeast of Valenciennes. In Flemish tradition, the Duycks have a handsome house overlooking the brewery. Theirs dates

from 1840, and bears the family crest over the door.

The family had been making beer even before Félix Duyck founded the brewery at Jenlain in 1922. It is today run by his son Robert and grandson Raymond. It still produces the more conventional Duyck Bière, but in the postwar period it has promoted its bière de garde Jenlain, which is available on draught as well as in the bottle.

Although production has increased from 20,000 hectolitres a year to 90,000, the exterior of the brewery still has the appearance of farm buildings. The copper kettles are crammed in tightly. In true Northern fashion, the Duycks take a pride in having acquired much of their equipment second-hand. Just as the English are being mildly disapproving when they talk of Scottish thrift, so the rest of France takes this view of its Northerners. They, for their part, regard it as admirably sound sense. Waste not, when your inherited memory is of a living clawed from the sea and the marshy flatlands.

A blend of barleys from Flanders, Champagne and Burgundy is used, with the emphasis on the variety Plaisant. The hops are from Flanders, Alsace, Germany and Slovenia. The beer has a full maltiness, with a notably spicy character, reminiscent of anise and vanilla. Jenlain has 17 Plato (1068) and 5.2 percent alcohol by weight, 6.5 by volume.

When I first encountered this beer, the brewers said they were using a top-fermenting yeast. More recently, a bottom culture has been used, at warm temperatures, but there have been experiments with a return to a top yeast. When I sampled both together, the top-fermented version had more complexity and fruitiness, with orange notes and hints of smokiness. The beer is filtered, but not pasteurized.

Duyck uses different yeasts in a paler, slightly less strong, Printemps (springtime) beer and a darker, hoppier, Christmas brew.

GRANDE BRASSERIE MODERNE DE TERKEN

3 Quai d'Anvers, 59100 Roubaix, France
Tel: 20 26 92 26

Perhaps it was a 'big, modern brewery' when beer was first made on the site in 1896. Undoubtedly it earned the soubriquet when the present company was created by a merger in 1920. There are hints of Art Nouveau and a stylish 'Saint Arnold's Chapel' in which the wort was once cooled. The canalside brewery makes its own contribution to an area noted for industrial archaeology. It is north of Lille, at Roubaix, on the Belgian border.

Grande Brasserie Moderne is a cooperative, specializing in the home delivery of beer. Its bière de garde is Septante 5 ('75'), with an alcohol content of 7.5 percent by volume. This beer is made with a blend of winter and spring malts from Champagne, and a little from Flanders. The styles of malt include Munich, crystal and roasted. Gravity is 20 Plato (1080).

The hop grist is quite complex, beginning with Northern Brewer as extract for bitterness, then moving to several varieties as pellets for aroma. These include two French growths: Brewers' Gold, from Flanders, and Strissel Spalt, from Alsace. The latter has some characteristics of Saaz, and is the principal aroma variety in the small hop-growing region of Alsace. German Hallertau-Hersbruck and Tettnang are also used. The Strissel Spalt and German hops seem to make an important contribution to the character of the product. Its very soft, liqueur-like palate develops perfumy, fruity, estery alcohol notes.

Septante 5 is labelled ambiguously as a beer of 'Haute Tradition'. It is, in fact, made by bottom fermentation, and is claimed to have a maturation of ten weeks to three months at 0°C/32°F. I feel that some cellar character is an essential part of its personality. It is flash pasteurized. The brewery makes a wide variety of other styles.

MONCEAU ST WAAST

Brasserie de Monceau St Waast, 59620 Aulnoye-Aymeries, France
Tel: 27 67 39 02

The Franco-Flemish name identifies the brewery's home village, in the green, rolling countryside of the Avenois, between Cambrai and the Belgian border.

The building began life as a cheese dairy in the 1870s, and in 1891 became a brewery. It is best known by its location, although some labels identify it as Brasserie Descamps. It escaped closure in recent years when it was acquired by the municipality as a working museum of artisan brewing. The splendid grist mill and cast-iron mash tun are probably original, and the two bricked-in coppers, with saucer-style lids, were once fired with coal and now with gas flame. An upright open cooler is still used.

This antique collection has been stirred into life by a former home-brewer, Patrick Duquesne, who ferments his beers with a Belgian top yeast, then filters them.

A wide variety of brews is made, all with a sweet-and-sour character reminiscent of some beers from Belgian Flanders. The beers are not pasteurized. They include an everyday beer called L'Avenoise and a fresh-tasting Pêche. The house bière de garde, with 13 Plato (1052) and 4.4 percent alcohol by weight, 5.5 by volume, combines this tartness with a relatively malty character. It appears under two labels: in French, Vieille Garde; and in English, the jokey Old Garde.

ST ARNOULD

Groupe St Arnould, Brasseries Semeuse, 234 Rue Roger Salengro, Hellemmes, 59260 Lille, France
Tel: 20 56 93 33

Named after the French and Belgian saint of brewing, Groupe St Arnould makes its mainstream beers in St Omer and its specialities, including a bière de garde called Réserve du Brasseur, at the Semeuse brewery, in Hellemmes, an industrial suburb of Lille. There was also for a time a bière de garde called St Leonard, from the Facon brewery at Pont de Briques, Boulogne, but this was discontinued in the late 1980s.

Réserve du Brasseur is made from Munich, crystal and Vienna malts, to 15 Plato (1060) and 5.2 percent alcohol by weight, 6.5 by volume. It has a clean, lightly malty palate, developing into a harmonious orchestration of flavours. It is filtered and flash pasteurized. The brewery also has a flowery, aromatic, soft wheat beer called L'épi de Facon.

ST SYLVESTRE

Brasserie de St Sylvestre, St Sylvestre-Cappel, 59114 Steenvoorde, France
Tel: 28 40 15 49

Classic artisan farmhouse brewery, making top-fermenting bières de garde in hop country, at St Sylvestre-Cappel (Flemish for chapel), between Steenvoorde and Hazebrouck. The former parish hall serves as the quality-control laboratory of the brewery, and the buildings stand behind, sloping down to a hop garden.

It has been variously claimed that the first brewery on the site was founded in the early 1500s, or during the French Revolution, but the documented history begins in the mid-1800s, and some of the buildings probably date from the turn of this century. The Ricour family have owned the brewery since 1920. Pierre Ricour runs the business with his wife and two sons.

English and French malts are used, with Flemish Brewers' Gold and German Tettnang hops. Monsieur Ricour likes to mention that the coal used to fire the boiler for the kettle comes from Lorraine. Three yeasts are used, each for different beers. I have never met a brewer who laid such a strong emphasis on yeast's contribution to aroma and flavour.

The principal product is a bière de garde called 3 Monts, named after three small hills in the immediate area, the Monts des Cats, Cassel and Recollets. In the flatlands, a hill is a cause for celebration. 3 Monts is made exclusively with Pilsner-type malt, and some sugar adjunct, to 19 Plato (1076) and 6.8 percent alcohol by weight, 8.5 by volume. It is filtered, but not pasteurized. It has a full gold colour; a slightly sour aroma (some cellar character?); a dry palate, with some yeast-bite; a rounded winyness; and a hint of alcohol.

The brewery also makes an 'abbey type' Bière des Templiers, again with 19 Plato, this time *sur lie*. This is an all-malt beer, with a very attractive rich amber colour; a fruity (apricot), creamy palate; great depth of flavour; and a sappy, almost oaky, finish. From mid-February until the end of March there is also a hoppier, unfiltered Bière de Mars (the brewery pioneered the revival of this style); and at Christmas a maltier, chocolaty Bière de Noël.

My tasting of St Sylvestre's products took place en famille. Afterward, we headed down the road for lunch at a cottagey restaurant called Au Petit Bruxelles. For a first course, mushrooms and shallots had been poached in local gin. Then came rabbit cooked in 3 Monts – accompanied, of course, by the same beer. We switched to the ecclesiastical Templiers with a cheese from a nearby abbey.

St Sylvestre is a hamlet in French Flanders. Its everyday brew is called Hop Country Beer. Flemings use the word hop or hommel. The French say houblon.

THEILLIER

11 Rue de la Chaussée, Louvignies,
59570 Bavay, France
Tel: 27 63 10 18

This remarkable brewery, which deserves to be better known, is in the Gallo-Roman town of Bavay. Roman foundations support the cellars, and the brewery is beneath the owners' house, which was built in 1670. It is a classic example of a domestically operated commercial brewery. Items of equipment 150 years old are still in use, though a set of kettles was stolen during the Franco-Prussian war.

When his father was imprisoned during World War II, 15-year-old Armand Theillier found himself operating the family brewery. He has run it ever since, helped by his wife Janine, but with no other staff.

They brew 70 hectolitres three times a month, making only one product: a bière de garde called La Bavaisienne. It is an all-malt beer of 16.5–17 Plato (1066–8). Monsieur Theillier claims to use only pale malt, in which case he must boil very vigorously indeed. It is only lightly hopped, with Brewers' Gold. The beer has a rich amber colour; a dense head, leaving thick lacework down the sides of the glass; a malty aroma; and a rich, sweet flavour. Bring on the *tarte à la cassonade…*

Altbier

Some German beers use the adjective *alt* ('old') in their names merely to imply a vague traditionalism, but the connoisseur is looking for a more specific style of brew.

When the 'new' technique of lager-brewing spread west from its central European birthplace, it did not find acceptance everywhere. The 'old' tradition of top-fermentation retained a hold in some brewing cities of the west and north. Here, especially in Düsseldorf and its neighbouring towns, the term Alt is used as a noun (or compounded as Altbier) to indicate a local style of top-fermenting beer. Although a style with its own distinctive character, Alt is Germany's counterpart to the ales of Belgium and Britain.

Within Germany, Altbier is very much a local style; it has remained a tradition, though in a smaller way than in Düsseldorf, in Münster and Hanover. In recent years it has begun to be brewed elsewhere, notably in the United States and, experimentally, in Japan. Some of these distant examples are faithful to the German original, but others have been deemed Altbiers in competitions simply because they combine warm fermentation with cold maturation.

The examples made in the Düsseldorf area are the classics of the style. They have a colour somewhere between bronze and copper-brown (30–40 EBC); a distinctively clean, rounded maltiness that is nonetheless not overpowering; combined with a hoppy bitterness (lower 30s to, occasionally, 50 BU), especially in the finish. The hop, too, is pronounced without being overwhelming. They are beautifully balanced beers. The fruitiness of top-fermentation is very restrained, and these brews very definitely manifest the smooth palate that comes from a relatively cold maturation.

The Düsseldorf Altbiers have gravities of around 12 Plato (1048), and are made with two or more malts (predominantly Pilsner-type, with one or two variations of Munich, and perhaps the tiniest dash of black). Some Düsseldorf brewers favour an infusion mash, but the decoction system is also widely used.

Two or three hop varieties may be used: the Düsseldorf brewers have traditionally favoured Spalt. Open fermenters are sometimes employed, especially in the brewpubs. The warmer temperatures of top-fermentation (in this instance, perhaps reaching

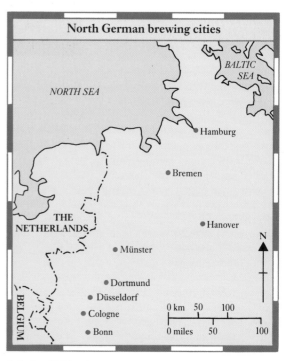

Zum Uerige's butcher makes juicy Cracow sausages (with a hint of coriander?). Try the brawn, too.

North German brewing cities

BALTIC SEA

NORTH SEA

THE NETHERLANDS

BELGIUM

• Hamburg

• Bremen

• Hanover

• Münster

• Dortmund
• Düsseldorf
• Cologne

• Bonn

N

0 km   50   100

0 miles   50   100

Ask for Altbier in Düsseldorf, Münster and Hanover; Kölsch in Cologne.

Altbiers are the copper-coloured, dryish ales of northern Germany – sociable brews in Düsseldorf's taverns. Their all-malt smoothness and German hop character is rounded by a period of cold maturation.

18–22°C/ 66–72°F) may be reflected in less intense cold conditioning, at 0–8°C/32–47°F, for anything from three to eight weeks. Alcohol content is typically 3.6–3.8 percent by weight, 4.5–4.7 by volume.

Any beer-lover planning a trip to Germany should include Düsseldorf on his or her itinerary. This elegant city on the Rhine is a bustling business centre, with fine shops and a superb gallery of modern art. In contrast, the Old Town – despite tourism – retains its own charm.

In many taverns in Düsseldorf, Altbier is the everyday brew. Four of these taverns brew their own: three are in the Old Town (*Altstadt*), and the fourth,

Ferdinand Schumacher, is not far away. At Zum Schlüssel ('The Key'), 43-47 Bolker Strasse, near the birthplace of the poet Heinrich Heine, and Zum Uerige, 1 Berger Strasse, the brewhouses are visible from the bar area. Im Füchschen ('The Little Fox'), 28 Ratinger Strasse, and Schumacher, 123 Ost Strasse, have charming breweries adjoining the taverns. A visitor who could call into only one of these brewpubs should choose Zum Uerige (see page 152), but anyone who loves beer would sample all four.

Of the three brewpubs in the Old Town, Zum Uerige has the hoppiest Altbier, followed by Im Füchschen; Zum Schlüssel's is lighter and fruitier (Zum Schlüssel is under the same ownership as the freestanding brewery Gatzweiler, which makes a similar Alt). Ferdinand Schumacher's is softer and maltier. An elderly gentleman in Schumacher once told me that his doctor had prescribed the beer as a cure for kidney stones; he certainly looked well on it.

Several times a year, each of the brewpubs makes a single batch of a special beer, perhaps slightly stronger, possibly dry-hopped, or with a longer lagering period. Each batch will probably be consumed

The gilded sign reveals a rambling tavern that is an institution in Düsseldorf. An '*Uerige*' translates as a

cranky fellow, but the private owners are happy publicans, often in evidence.

within 24 hours. Designed as a bonus for loyal regulars, these are sold at the same price as the normal beer. They are announced only by discreet signs at the pubs. They are not made at busy times or holidays, but at least one of the four Altbier-brewing taverns will be having a special beer day every other month. The three in the *Altstadt* call their special beers Sticke (local slang for 'secret'). Zum Uerige has been known to announce its Sticke with a handbill showing a blindfold drinker. Ferdinand Schumacher refers to its sweetish special as Latzenbier (beer from the wood).

In the brewpubs and taverns, especially in the Old Town, Altbier is often dispensed from a barrel by gravity, with no carbon dioxide pressure, blanket or otherwise. The beer pours with a good, but not huge, head. It is traditionally served in stubby cylindrical glasses. As one is drained, another will be brought by the waiter; the only way to stop this happening is to place a beer mat over the top of the empty glass. Only the reckless combine Altbier with north German corn or caraway schnapps; the remedy next day is a local bitters called Killepitsch.

On its home ground, Altbier tends to be treated as a sociable drink or consumed with typical local foods, which lean heavily toward pork, liver and offal. For Saturday lunch in winter, Zum Uerige famously offers pea soup with a salted pig's trotter. The tavern has its own butcher and sausage-maker on the premises, even though its meals are regarded only as

snacks. Im Füchschen is renowned for its *Eisbein*, a huge, pickled knuckle of pork. One speciality every beer-lover should experience is Zum Uerige's malodorous Mainzer cheese marinated for six hours in Altbier. Much as I enjoy these German 'beer foods', I think the rounded, smooth, tasty, Düsseldorf style of Altbier goes especially well with red meat in a pot-roast, such as the Viennese speciality, *Tafelspitz*.

Among the other Altbiers made in Düsseldorf or nearby towns, I have over the years found Frankenheim hoppy and light-bodied; Schlösser malty but dry; Düssel the fruitiest; Diebels (from Issum) firm-bodied; Hannen (Willich and Mönchengladbach) softer and rounded; and Rhenania (Krefeld) slightly thicker-tasting.

In the university city of Münster, capital of Westphalia, the Pinkus Müller brewpub produces a somewhat eccentric interpretation of Altbier (see page 151). This is a golden beer, containing 40 percent wheat, made by top-fermentation. A house speciality is the lacing of this Altbier with diced fruits that have been steeped for 24 hours in sugar syrup. The syrup is made at a ratio of one kilo of sugar per litre of water. A large spoonful of the mixture is put into each glass, and the beer poured on top. The flavour of the fruit suffuses the beer and marries with the acidity of the wheat. The fruits used change with the seasons, so the 'Altbier Bowl' – as this drink is known – may be redolent of summer fruits or deliver a citrus kick. There is tradition behind this whimsy: spring and harvest

Im Füchschen is the best of the brewpubs for a full hot meal. It is one of those typical German taverns where customers are happy to share tables, and to move up to accommodate a stranger. The tables are long and scrubbed, and groan under the weight of the helpings.

Widmer's brewhouse in Portland, Oregon, is a gleaming, modern affair far from the early improvisations. The inspiration was Düsseldorf's best. Widmer Altbier can be enjoyed with food at the Heathman Hotel, or B Moloch's bakery and brewery.

festivals produce similar punches across Europe.

Hanover has a considerable history of brewing, and the region is also known for corn schnapps and German gins. The town's Lindener Gilde brewery makes Broyhan Alt, named after the great Hanover brewer Cord Broyhan. It is similar to the Düsseldorf Altbiers, but slightly higher in gravity, darker in colour and lighter in hop character.

The Feldschlosschen brewery of Braunschweig, in addition to its recently introduced Duckstein (see page 85), also makes an Alt. While the Duckstein is available only on draught, or in flagons, the Brunswiek Alt (using this archaic spelling) can be found in the bottle. The Duckstein is intended as a lighter, more refreshing beer, the Brunswiek Alt is perhaps a more contemplative glass.

The two are made with different top-fermenting yeasts and the Alt is more assertive all round in its flavours. It has a dense, creamy head; a very good malt character in both aroma and palate; a rounded fruitiness; and an appetizing hop dryness in the finish.

Several brewers in other German cities produce Altbiers of a character broadly similar to those of Düsseldorf, and in the mid-1980s the style spread to some neighbouring countries.

In the Netherlands, Arcense produces a dryish, slightly thin example named Altforster, and the Budels brewery a slightly stronger one called simply Alt. De Leeuw, of Venlo, makes a Venloosch Alt, which I have not tasted. Grolsch's smooth Amber (see page 150) is clearly a member of the Altbier family.

In Switzerland, I have tasted a fruity, dry Altbier, with lots of hop in the finish, from the Warteck brewery, of Basel. Austria also has the odd Altbier, and I have enjoyed the malty example called St Thomas from the Nussdorf brewery, in Vienna (see page 151).

The greater spread of the style has been in North America, and it has even manifested itself in Japan.

Altbier producers

The best-known producers are certainly those in the Düsseldorf area, from the sizable Diebels and Hannen to the brewpubs such as Zum Uerige, but this German style can boast an interesting blend of emulators elsewhere in the world, from Austria to Japan. Some describe themselves as Altbier, others simply as Amber.

ALASKAN

Alaskan Brewing Company,
PO Box 241053, Douglas,
Juneau, Alaska 99824, USA
Tel: (907) 780-5866

Unlikely though it may seem, the Alaskan Brewing Company's principal product is an Altbier. This beer, called Alaskan Amber, has been a regular award-winner at the Great American Beer Festival.

It is the product of a remarkable revival. There were about 50 breweries in Alaska during the Gold Rush, but they all eventually closed (Prohibition saw off the last of them). An attempt by the German group Oetker to revive the industry in the 1970s soon failed. In the early 1980s, Geoff Larson, then a chemical engineer in a gold mine, but also a home-brewer, decided that he would like to make beer professionally. When he and his wife Marcy were planning their business in the Alaskan capital, Juneau, they discovered that a German immigrant brewer there had made what sounded like an Altbier around the turn of the century. (He had also advertised in a local newspaper that he used Saaz hops.)

Close to the site where the German had brewed, the Larsons went into business in an industrial building next to a couple of fish smokeries and a coffee-roasting company, in a place called Lemon Creek. Geoff and Marcy are enthusiastic about the local foods of Alaska.

Geoff had previously worked with alcohol in pharmaceuticals and perfumes, and has an earnest interest in yeast. He told me that he worked with 15 strains before selecting one to ferment his Altbier.

'I wanted a yeast that would convert all the simple sugars into alcohol but leave all the complex ones to contribute to the aroma and flavour.' He succeeded. There is an appetizing malt bouquet and palate in the remarkably smooth Alaskan Amber. It is made to a gravity of 14.25 Plato (1057); uses pale and crystal malt, Cascade and Saaz hops; and emerges with 4.2 percent alcohol by weight, 5.25 by volume. At beer dinners in Alaska, this brew has been used in a caribou stew: a counterpart to Scottish ale with venison.

The Larsons have added further beers to their portfolio, including a smoked porter, and a couple more microbreweries have opened in Alaska.

GROLSCH

Grolsche Bierbrouwerij, 1 Brouwerij
Straat, 7523 EA Enschede,
The Netherlands
Tel: (053) 833 333

Not the well-known product of Grolsch, of course: that is a popular Pilsner-type lager. The Altbier in the brewery's portfolio is called Grolsch Amber (the English word is used). This product has been advertised in the Netherlands with the slogan: 'The secret love of the true beer-drinker.'

Grolsch does not call its Amber an Altbier, but the product is very much in that style. Indeed, the company's breweries, at Groenlo and Enschede, in the east of the Netherlands, are not far from Altbier country.

Grolsch Amber is an all-malt beer. A proportion of wheat malt is used, for improved head retention. It is top-fermented, but has a late pitching of a second yeast culture, on which it has a cold maturation. It has a full amber colour (32 EBC) and 40 units of bitterness. In palate, the beer starts lightly malty; it has a smooth body; and it finishes with a hearty hop bitterness.

KIRIN

Kirin Brewery Company, 26-1
Jingumae 6-chome, Shibuya-ku,
Tokyo, 150 Japan
Tel: (03) 5485-6170

As Japanese breweries begin to experiment with distant styles, it is interesting that Kirin, Sapporo and Suntory have all made limited releases of Altbier on the same lines as those made in Düsseldorf. This is, after all, a relatively minor and localized style, albeit less challenging to the novice than some. Could it be that Japanese executives have enjoyed this style in Düsseldorf? That city just happens to be the European headquarters for many Japanese companies.

Kirin's Alt is made at the company's experimental microbrewery in Kyoto. It has excellent lacework; a good bronze-copper colour (35 EBC); and a strongly malty accent, with a hint of toffeeish dryness. The beer has a gravity of 11.5 Plato (1046) and 4.08 percent alcohol by weight, 5.1 by volume; it has 33 units of bitterness.

I found it on tap in the Spring Valley brewpub. This establishment is in the Kirin Beer Village, something of a theme park set around the company's

1991 brewery in Yokohama (near Namamugi railway station). The pub is loosely modelled on the 1905 brewery in Yokohama to which Kirin traces its origins. The brewpub itself produces a firm, hop-accented, golden lager.

NUSSDORF
Brauhaus Nussdorf, 1 Freihof Gasse, Nussdorf, Vienna, Austria 1190
Tel: (0222) 37 26 52

The name means 'nut village', and is a reference not to the populace but to the walnut trees there, on the edge of the Vienna Woods. The local aristocratic family Bachofen von Echt ran a sizable brewery in Nussdorf for five generations, but this closed in the 1950s. In 1984, the current Baron Henrik Bachofen von Echt restored the tradition.

The Baron lives in an 1805 castle set into the steep hill where the woods slope down to the Danube. At river level, there is a separate entry to the wine cellars, which are in the foundations of a Roman fortification. Some of these cellars are rented out for the bottle-aging of sparkling wine, but Baron Henrik converted the rest into a brewpub, decorated with memorabilia from his family's original business.

His initial products were a dry stout and an Altbier, the latter called St Thomas Brau after the local saint. This is a copper-coloured brew of 12.25 Plato (1048–50) with a complex malt character and a hearty hop dryness coming through in the finish. It has 4.4 percent alcohol by weight, 5.5 by volume.

I once joked with the Baron about the word Echt (which in German means 'real') in his title. He explained that it was taken from a village on the borders of Belgium and the Netherlands. 'Is there a Hapsburg connection?' I was prompted to ask. 'No,' replied the Baron. 'Our family is older than that.'

PINKUS MÜLLER
Brauerei Pinkus Müller, 4-10 Kreuz Strasse, 4400 Münster, Nordrhein-Westfalen, Germany
Tel: (0251) 45151-52

Pinkus Müller began as a chocolatier, bakery and brewery, and has been on the same site since 1816, and through six generations. Today, it is a brewery and tavern. I once visited the family and was introduced to a very friendly confusion of sisters, daughters and cousins, all modestly proud of the pub and tavern. The youngest daughter, 19 at the time, was studying brewing at Weihenstephan, the institute attached to the world's oldest brewery, near Munich.

Pinkus Müller has four dining rooms; in the main one the centre-piece is a Westphalian oven, set among Dutch tiles. The fireplace is hung with Westphalian hams. Pancakes are another speciality. Homilies on drinking and sociability are painted in gilt on the beams.

This brewery's Alt must be regarded as a one-off. With its golden colour and its 40 percent wheat malt, it is not in the style widely recognized as Altbier. It is, though, a delightful and distinctive beer in its own right, which can be regarded as an 'old' speciality of Münster.

It has a gravity of 11.3 Plato (1045–6), is top-fermented, and has a remarkably long (six months) maturation at natural cellar temperatures, in conventional lagering tanks with some resident lactic culture. It emerges with 4 percent alcohol by weight, 5 by volume. The beer is very crisp indeed, with a faint, quenching acidity in the finish.

The brewery also makes a light, fruity Weizen (60 percent wheat); a firm, dry Pilsner-style lager; and a malty but dry organic lager called Spezial. Finding barley grown without fertilizers is less difficult than tracking down hops unprotected by pesticides, but one or two growers have begun to oblige.

ST STAN'S
Stanislaus Brewing Company, 821 L Street, Modesto, California 95354, USA
Tel: (209) 524-2337

A German speciality comes to the heart of California.

Members of the Old German Baptist sect that lives in Stanislaus County, around the town of Modesto, in hot, almond-growing country in the Central Valley of California, are probably too abstemious to enjoy the Altbiers made in the local brewery, but many other Americans do. The brewery, which specializes in the style, was founded in 1984 by an American, Garith Helm, and his wife Romy Graf, who is German (but not a Düsseldorfer; she is from the Bavarian town of Würzburg).

Helm, working as an engineering manager in the armaments industry, said he had decided he preferred beer to bombs. He first brewed in a converted cheese-dairying vessel on his cattle and horse farm. The spent grains fed the cattle. Later, a purpose-built brewery, taproom and restaurant were established.

Stanislaus is unusual in that it makes several Altbiers. Its principal products are St Stan's Amber, at 12 Plato (1048) and 4.5 percent alcohol by weight, 5.6 by volume, malty and fruity (a hint of figs), and St Stan's Dark (14; 1056; 4.8; 6), which is reddish-brown, and even maltier, with some chocolaty and roasty notes. This rather sweet brew has found a novel use as a sauce on chocolate mousse at the renowned Lyon's pub (7294 San Ramon Road, Dublin, California), on the east side of San Francisco Bay.

In the second week of June, Modesto celebrates its favourite son George Lucas with an 'American Graffiti' week. For the occasion, the brewery makes a hoppier Graffiti Alt. It also has a winter barley wine and other specialities.

SAPPORO

Sapporo Breweries, 7-10-1 Ginza, Chuo-ku, Tokyo, 104 Japan
Tel: (03) 3572-6111

Sapporo Alt has a dense head, a bronze colour (24 EBC), a light body, starting with a hint of malt and moving to a fruity, dryish finish. It has an original gravity of 11 Plato (1044) and 3.8 percent alcohol by weight, 4.7 by volume. The malt is pale and crystal and the hops all European aroma varieties; it has 23–24 BU. I found this beer in the Lion Brasserie near Sapporo's head office, under the Komatsu Building, in the Ginza district of Tokyo.

SUNTORY

Suntory Brewery, 1-2-3 Motoakasaka, Minato-ku, Tokyo, 107 Japan
Tel: (03) 3470-1104

An Altbier has been produced on occasion at Suntory's experimental Musashino microbrewery, in the horse-racing town of Fuchu City, west of Tokyo. This beer has had limited availability in Suntory outlets, and through orders placed by individual consumers at wine merchants or liquor stores.

I tasted it at the brewery. It is a darkish and very malty interpretation, almost rummy, soothingly smooth, with the fruitiness of cherry pie or orange marmalade in the finish (12.2; 1048–50; 4.2; 5.3). It was made from Pilsner, crystal and wheat malts, and hopped three times, initially with extract, then with Hallertau-Hersbrucks from Germany.

WIDMER

Widmer Brewing Company, 929 N Russell Street, Portland, Oregon 97227-1733, USA
Tel: (503) 281-2437

With a grandfather from Düsseldorf (though their other antecedents are from Berlin and Switzerland), Kurt and Rob Widmer chose an Altbier as their flagship when they opened their first brewery, in 1985, in Portland, Oregon. They cite Zum Uerige as their inspiration. Brewer Kurt had previously worked in the pharmaceutical industry.

The Widmers' early brews of Altbier, using three malts and a tiny dash of roasted barley, and hopped with American Perle and Tettnang, were extremely bitter. Since then, the beer seems to have been toned down a little, but it still has a fine malt and hop character, with an excellent bitterness in the finish (11.5; 1046; 4.1; 5.2).

The company has gone on to make a wide range of German styles and to open a second brewery in the town. It has a further, very small, brewery at the B Moloch bakery and snack restaurant in Portland (901 SW Salmon Street). B Moloch (named – in reverse – after the French caricaturist H Colomb) has links of ownership with the stylish Heathman Hotel opposite. Both hold beer dinners from time to time.

ZUM UERIGE

Obergarige Hausbrauerei, 1 Berger Strasse, Düsseldorf 1, Germany
Tel: (0211) 84455

The classic Düsseldorf Altbier brewery, surrounded by its own tavern. The building dates from the 1830s and was restored after World War II. The copper overlooks a bar called The Brewhouse, and among the tavern's other rooms is surely one to suit every mood. One is decorated with a Hogarthian relief of old Düsseldorf, another with cartoons in graffiti, a

Cautionary tale from the walls of Zum Uerige.

In Germany, Altbier comes in a small cylindrical glass.

third with fading photographs of local actors and writers; one room has snugs and vaulted ceilings, two more have stained-glass windows. The customers vary as widely: wild youths and dignified matrons each have their own corner.

Zum Uerige is run with great pride and energy by Josef Schnitzler, a member of a local brewing family, and his wife Christa. The house brew is the driest of the Düsseldorf Altbiers, made to a gravity of 12 Plato (1048), with three malts and Spalt hops, and emerging with around 3.8 percent alcohol by weight, 4.6 by volume, and bitterness in the upper 40s to lower 50s. It is aromatic, tawny in colour, with a rounded maltiness and a slowly unrolling hop character.

Kölsch

The best-protected *appellation contrôlée* in the world of beer is that of Kölsch, the golden ale that takes its name from the city of Cologne (Köln in German).

Kölsch is noted for its delicacy rather than for any more robust distinctiveness, but the legally protected denomination has helped ensure that Cologne and designated adjoining towns and counties support around 20 breweries, all making this style. No metropolitan area anywhere in the world can match that.

The name Cologne derives from the colonial importance of the city to the Roman Empire, and there is some evidence of the brewing of mead or beer in the Rhineland during that period. In the early Middle Ages, there were half a dozen monastery breweries in the city, and far more when beer-making and tavern-keeping became a trade. The area also has historical links with brewing across the border in what is now Belgium, from the time of Duke Jan Primus ('Gambrinus') of Brabant. Cologne's Guild of Brewers dates from 1396, and is the oldest trade organization in the city. As the historical capital of the Rhineland, Cologne has continued to have a distinct regional brewing tradition.

Cologne is one of those cities that are made up of neighbourhoods. Its people were traditionally said to be quietly proud, and resistant to outside authority or influence. Before World War I, almost all of its beer was produced in brewpubs. These breweries all made top-fermenting beers, sometimes known as Wiess (the Cologne rendition of 'white'), indicating top-fermentation rather than the use of wheat, although that grain was (and still is) sometimes employed. Faced with competition from larger companies introducing Pilsner-style lagers from elsewhere in Germany, especially between the two World Wars and after 1945, the Cologne brewers gradually refined their own beers. Their well-established cooperation,

> **As pale as a Pilsner, but with the fruitiness of an ale, Cologne's beer has its own teasing delicacy. Can any other beer be both an apéritif and a digestif?**

The distinctive Kölsch glasses and the typical serving tray for the beer in a poster from an early cooperative campaign by Cologne brewpubs.

which continues today in the Cologne Association of Brewers, seems to have helped them maintain a united front.

There are fewer brewpubs today, but still a couple of famous examples, and several brewery taps. Top-fermentation has continued. What changed was the introduction of paler malts, cold maturation and filtration. The local brewing tradition was saved, at some expense to its distinctiveness.

In the 1960s, a consensus developed in the Association as to what constituted the Kölsch style of beer. In the 1960s and 1970s there were court cases to prevent the use of the term Kölsch by brewers from outside the region.

In 1985, the definition of Kölsch, the terms by which it may be described (no one may claim to have the 'original' or 'premium', for example), the shape of the glass (no extraneous decorations) and the beer's region of production were enshrined in a Convention agreed between the Association and the German Government department that deals with fair trading, monopolies and anti-trust law. The Convention restricts the use of the term Kölsch to Cologne and already-established producers from Dormagen in the north to Bonn in the south, and Bedburg in the west to Bielstein in the east. The Kölsch Convention, set out on parchment, and bearing the signature and seal of each member of the Association, is a matter of great pride to the producers.

Today's Kölschbier

Kölsch has a conventional gravity and strength (11–12 Plato, 1044–8, just under 4 percent alcohol by weight, 5 by volume), is very pale, with a fine bead, and is clean-tasting (all-malt), remarkably light-bodied (very well attenuated), soft and drinkable, only faintly fruity (often in the aroma and the beginning of the palate), with a slight acidity and a restrained but definite hoppy dryness (with units of bitterness typically in the upper 20s), often slightly herbal-tasting in the finish. If wheat is used, it is generally to the extent of less than 15 percent, perhaps to give added complexity to the fruitiness, more likely to provide paleness of colour, and to enhance head-retention and lacework. The all-malt grist, the level of hopping, the degree of attenuation, the extent of maturation (two to six weeks, at 0–4°C/32–39°F) and the absence of sugar priming distinguish it from everyday golden ales in North America.

As the Kölsch style developed, so did the custom of serving it in small (20cl) glasses. These are taller and

St Peter seems to hold the key to this tavern in Cologne, a heavenly city for the beer-lover.

narrower than those used for Altbier in Düsseldorf and elsewhere. The attenuation of the beer, and the shape of the glasses, suggest to consumers that this is something light, not filling, and appetizing. I have on more than one occasion seen a waiter help himself to a glass in one swallow.

Kölsch seems to have the capacity to settle the stomach in advance, like those apéritifs based on white wine that the French favour. A brewer was once telling me that his Kölsch was good for the digestion, and I mentioned that I could see no reason why it should perform this task better than many other beers. 'I don't know why, either,' he replied, 'but you can feel it.' He was right.

In Cologne's brewpubs during the early evening, small casks are raised from the cellar by dumb-waiter, tapped, and exhausted within minutes. To the visitor, in the jostled space of the standing area (known to locals as the *Schwemme*, or 'swimming bath'), it is an impressive sight. The waiters, whose uniform jackets or shirts are traditionally blue, over leather aprons, carry specially designed circular trays that hold the glasses like cartridges in a revolver. The waiters are known as Kobes, on the presumption that they are called Jakob (as all Glaswegians are christened Jimmy, Irishmen Paddy, and Americans in B-movies answered to the name of Mack). Kölsch is often served with a snack of *Mettwurst* (a lightly smoked sausage) or the local blood sausage (referred to as Kölsch caviar).

This being a delicate style, there are not dramatic differences, but each brewery has its own house character. Over the years, I have found Dom Kölsch sweet at the front, with a drier finish; Garde perhaps the most fruity and acidic, and a favourite of mine; Gereons fruity, with a dry finish; Gilden heavier in texture; Kürfursten again starting sweet and finishing dry; Reissdorf light, soft, hoppy, and another favourite; Sester fruity and dry; Sion flowery and hoppy; Zunft creamy, with a dry finish; and there are others I have not tasted, in addition to those listed on pages 155–6.

The Association says it has protected the term Kölsch worldwide, but in the United States, several brewpubs have begun to use the term. Perhaps these should be identified as Cologne-style golden ales.

From the Boulder Creek Brewing Company, founded in 1990 in the town of the same name south of San Jose in California, I have enjoyed the fresh, fruity, quite hoppy and bitter St Severin's Kölsch (Cologne has a similar brand name, without the saint). The Broad Ripple Brewing Company, founded in 1991 in Indianapolis, has a big-bodied Kölsch, with some fruit and lots of malt and hop. The Coyote Spring Brewing Company, founded as Barley's Brewpub in 1990, in Phoenix, Arizona, has a very good example of the style: it has a dense head, and is very pale, perfumy, soft and light. The brewery gives it the alliterative brand name Koyote Kölsch.

In 1992, at Suntory's experimental Musashino brewery in Fuchu City, Japan, I tasted a Kölsch made with 15 percent wheat and both German and American hops. It was soft and spritzy, with a fruitiness reminiscent of vanilla, and a lightly hoppy dryness in the finish. I found it a very good example of the style, albeit far from home.

Kölsch producers

Upholding the local style proudly, Cologne's brewers – from Früh, at the city's most well-known tavern, to Hubert Heller's crypt-like brewpub – are all worth a visit.

P J FRÜH
Cölner Hofbräu, 12-14 Am Hof,
5000 Köln, Germany
Tel: (0221) 236618

Probably the most famous place in which to drink Kölsch is the turn-of-the-century tavern-restaurant of Peter Josef Früh, near the cathedral, on the street called Am Hof. When I first visited this establishment, the brewery was upstairs, but production has now shifted out of the city centre, though the offices remain.

The tavern at Am Hof becomes very busy in the early evening, but to stand in the *Schwemme* while the beers whistle by like golden bullets is to know that you have been in Cologne. When your legs tire, explore its cavernous rooms for a table, and sample some of Cologne's folk-foods.

Früh has a couple more taverns, and its beer is well known in Cologne. It is a soft, very drinkable Kölsch, delicate in both its fruity start and its gently hoppy, dryish finish (Hallertau and Tettnang are used, as pellets).

GAFFEL
Privat Brauerei Gaffel-Becker,
41 Eigelstein, 5000 Köln, Germany
Tel: (0221) 160060

The name Gaffel indicates the political wing of a trade guild. The Gaffel site, today tucked into a narrow street of shops and restaurants in the heart of Cologne, near the railway station, is known to have accommodated a brewery since 1302.

The present owners, the Becker family, have been there since 1908. The incumbent, Heinrich Becker, is a devoted collector of drinking vessels and advertising material, with a particular passion for *Jugendstil*, and has established a private museum in the

The taverns of Cologne serve endless variations on the smoked leg of pork, but there may also be game, such as boar and pheasant, from the rural Rhineland.

brewery. The establishment was once a brewpub, but now has an elaborately pubby 'tap' at 20–22 Alter Markt, in the Old Town.

The Gaffel Kölsch is one of the driest, with a very light start, developing to dryness, then a quick, spritzy finish. The brewery has its own well, though the water is softened, and makes a point that its hops are whole (pellets), not extract. The dryness, almost nutty, seems to derive especially from the yeast, which is a mixed culture, and which ferments with extreme vigour, creating a huge head in the vessels. Some of these are open, and remarkably long.

HELLER
Brauhaus Heller, 33 Roon Strasse, 5000 Köln, Germany
Tel: (0221) 242545

Hubert Heller qualified as an engineer but was seduced by the student beer-bars of Berlin in the 1960s. Twenty years later he opened a speciality beer café in his native Cologne, in premises that formerly housed a distillery making a liqueur bitters. In 1991, he turned this into a brewpub. Brauhaus Heller does not open for lunch. Its hours are from 4 in the afternoon until 1 in the morning.

Entrance is through an arch and down stairs into a high-ceilinged, vaulted, brick cellar, the chambers separated by stained-glass windows and decorated with gargoyles commissioned by Heller and carved from basalt quarried in the Eifel lakeland region of the Rhineland Palatinate. The coppers visible behind the bar date from 1924, and belonged to a defunct brewery.

Heller produces one brew, which is available sedimented as Ur-Wiess and filtered as Kölsch. The barley malt (grown in the Rhineland Palatinate) and blossom hops (from Hersbruck, Bavaria) are organically cultivated.

In the Ur-Wiess, the yeast seems to add a little texture, but no bite, and the typical fruitiness eventually emerges, followed by a dash of late hop bitterness. With the yeast removed, the Kölsch tastes maltier, creamier and sweeter.

KÜPPERS
Küppers Kölsch Brauerei, 145-155 Alteburger Strasse, 5000 Köln, Germany
Tel: (0221) 37790

It is a pleasant tram-ride along the banks of the Rhine, heading south on route 6, 15 or 16, to Schonhauser Strasse and the Küppers brewery, the only really large producer of Kölsch, and one of the youngest.

In a smart, pine-trimmed hall, the block brewhouse performs a single-decoction mash, with a small proportion of wheat, and uses hop extract. The tall, ridged, outdoor tanks used for fermentation and lagering give the place the look of a fortress.

The soft, sweetish beer can be sampled within the building at the brewery tap (Brauerei Ausschank, 157 Alteburger, Tel: 373242). Better still, it can also be enjoyed there as a rather yeasty Wies. A full menu is served. The brewery tap, built in the mid-1980s but with *Jugendstil* references, adjoins a very impressive museum.

MALZMÜHLE
Brauerei Schwartz, 6 Heumarkt, 5000 Köln, Germany
Tel: (0221) 210118

The 'Malt Mill' brewpub is in the heart of the Old Town, on the Haymarket. The beer it produces is, indeed, malty: sweetish, almost reminiscent of marshmallow.

The brewery, founded in 1858, was rebuilt in 1935, damaged during World War II, and subsequently restored. It has its own well, providing water from the Eifel, uses a proportion of wheat in its mash, and makes three additions of Hallertau hops, as blossoms. Open fermenters are used.

The brewery is upstairs, and the café-restaurant downstairs. I have found it the quietest and most restful of the Kölsch houses.

PÄFFGEN
Gebrüder Päffgen, Obergarige Hausbrauerei, 64-6 Friesen Strasse, 5000 Köln, Germany
Tel: (0221) 135461

Cologne has its wet and windy evenings, but Päffgen's branch on the Haymarket is an inviting beacon of warmth. The beer will be cool, but not ice-cold.

The 'top-fermenting house-brewery' belonging to the brothers Päffgen is to the north of the city centre, in a wood-panelled, late 19th-century building; there is also a handsome tavern-restaurant of an earlier style in the Old Town, at the upper end of the Haymarket. The Friesen Strasse house is generally smokier and pubbier, while the Heumarkt address can look pristine and scrubbed early in the day, but becomes bustling and convivial later.

The beer has a slightly grainy character, with a good hoppy dryness in the finish.

American ale

Ale was the first great brewing tradition of the United States, and may be so again. The country's ale-brewing tradition fell into the sleep of Rip Van Winkle, but has now awakened and is kicking up a storm across the nation. Volumes may be small, but there are far more ales produced in the United States than any other style, most of them from about 300 new-generation microbreweries or brewpubs. Among them are several interpretations, old and new, that are unique to North America.

In Washington Irving's tale, Rip Van Winkle was a Dutch colonist who fell asleep in the Catskill Mountains after having sipped from a mysterious keg. When he awoke, America had become independent. The Dutch West India company opened the country's first commercial brewery, in Lower Manhattan, New York, in 1632. The early Dutch, British and Irish settlers in New York and on the eastern seaboard produced ales, porters and other top-fermenting beers. Buffalo, Albany, Brooklyn and Philadelphia were early brewing capitals.

Coinciding with the coming of railroads and refrigeration, a later wave of immigrants, from Bohemia and Germany to Pennsylvania and the Midwest (notably the cities of Cincinnati, St Louis and Milwaukee), spread their newer lager tradition nationally, from the mid-1800s to the second half of the 1900s.

For a long time the two styles were rivals in both

The most fashionable brews in some parts of the United States, especially the West Coast, are a new generation of ales. These are often distinguished by an intensely floral hop character, featuring the varieties grown in Oregon and Washington states, and a fresh, assertive palate. Such ales are ideal partners to the new American cuisine.

the East and Midwest. New York's oldest tavern, McSorley's, on 7th Street in the East Village, has continued to serve only ale, though an unexciting example. The choice of ale, as opposed to lager, once indicated a thoughtful drinker, and arguably does once more. When the present-day essayist Verlyn Klinkenborg wrote *The Last Fine Time*, described by *Newsday* as 'a landmark in national self-examination', he set his story around a family's bar in Buffalo. In one vignette, just after World War II, a customer went into the bar and ordered Ballantine's Ale. The bartender mentally noted him as a person 'of such meticulousness…a Ballantine's man'. (Ballantine's, then produced in the East, in New Jersey, is today made in the Midwest.)

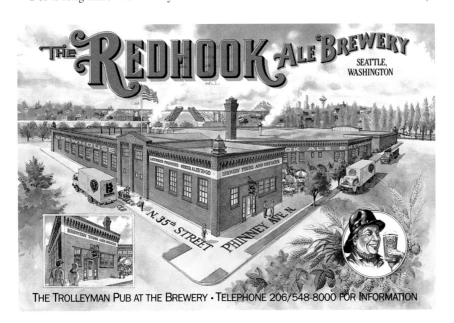

THE TROLLEYMAN PUB AT THE BREWERY · TELEPHONE 206/548-8000 FOR INFORMATION

Redhook is one of the biggest among the new generation of American ale brewers, and it is in the heartland of the style, the Pacific Northwest. This postcard, with its hint of nostalgia, emphasizes the traditionalism of ale. The brewery is in a former tramshed … as are the Hoster brewery in Columbus, Ohio; Free State, in Lawrence, Kansas; and New Haven Brewing, Connecticut.

As the lager brewers' greatest volumes of production moved, with shifts of population, to the Rockies (Colorado is currently the biggest brewing state by volume) and the West Coast, those same regions began to see the emergence of small new ale brewers in the late 1970s and 1980s (Denver, San Francisco and – especially – Portland and Seattle are the new ale capitals of the United States). Then the pendulum began to swing back East. There is a slight difference in the accent of ale-brewing in the West and East. The West Coast brewers, with scarcely any ale tradition, have developed their own variants; some of those in the East have tried to restore the region's traditions.

Today's counterpart to the Ballantine's man might be ordering a Catamount Amber. Or visiting the old-established literary bar Chumley's (down an alley at 86 Bedford and Barrow, Greenwich Village), in search of New York Harbor Ale, Thomas Point Golden Ale or Harpoon Ale. If Rip Van Winkle were awakening in the Catskills today, he might head for the Woodstock brewery in Kingston, New York state (established in 1992, making both lagers and ales).

Old-generation survivors

The original American ales were produced at a time when all beers were relatively dark. Lagers arrived during the period when brewers in Pilsen and Budweis had popularized golden styles. In response to this competition, the established ale-brewers started to use paler malts.

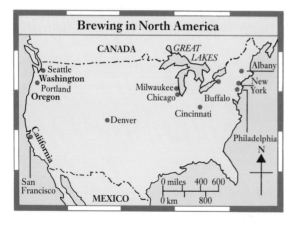

Early brewing traditions came with the immigrants, first to the East Coast, then to the Midwest. Ales now challenge the wines of the West Coast.

As an older style, the ales were well hopped for bitterness, while the lagers were accented more toward aroma. Once again, ale-brewers responded to the competition by gradually reducing the hop character of their products.

Pressure to make products that were even paler in colour, lighter in body, and cheaper, led both lager and ale-brewers to use the native grain, corn (maize), as an adjunct. Brewers on the East Coast also used sugar, brought in by sea. Perhaps because the East Coast brewers often specialized in ales, this style came to be associated with the use of sugar. Some of these sugars, notably invert, were said to leave a particular flavour and mouth-feel.

The darkest and most hoppy style to have survived, albeit in diminished form, is represented by Ballantine's India Pale Ale, discussed in this book under pale ales (see page 84). This style originally assumed the hop character and high gravity of a beer meant to be shipped across the ocean. A similar style dating from the days when it was impossible to brew in the warm months, and made to be cellared during the summer, was known as stock ale, a term that was also used in Britain. The term has only recently vanished in Britain, and has been revived in the United States by the Boston Beer Company (see page 164).

The American IPAs and stock ales were winy-tasting brews, often made with water heavily treated with calcium sulphate to resemble that of Burton. They were seen as autumn and winter drinks, and were often served at room temperature, sometimes 'still', from casks behind the bar.

Ale, with no further designation, was still a little fuller in colour and hop character than a Pilsner lager. Finally, there was cream ale, mildly hopped and sweetish, as pale and sparkling as a Pilsner, but produced more quickly. The distinction between ale and cream ale (the latter a purely American creation) has become a very fine line in recent decades.

Among the older generation of American ales, only a few have retained much colour. Apart from Ballantine's IPA (as opposed to the regular Ale of the same marque), there is the revived Old Tankard from Pabst of Milwaukee, and Rainier Ale, from Seattle. Rainier Ale was one of the most satisfying products on the West Coast before the microbrewery movement

The BridgePort brewery was started by an Italian-American family of wine-makers, yet its ale has an almost Scottish maltiness.

Beer-lovers flock to Portland, Oregon, to enjoy local brews at places like BridgePort. The city is one of the new beer capitals of the United States.

started. It has since both lost character and been over-taken by many new ales.

More often, old-generation survivors among American ales are golden. They are no longer espe-cially hoppy, though different varieties may be used to create a mildly distinctive palate. These ales are usu-ally as light-bodied as a mainstream American beer, though perhaps sweetened with sugar (primed and then pasteurized). Some are still fermented with ale yeasts, while others use a lager yeast, though fermen-tation may be at warmer temperatures. The resultant product should have at least a touch of fruitiness.

Over the decades, the alcohol content of many drinks has reduced. Frontiersmen needed stronger refreshment than lawyers and stockbrokers. As an older style, perhaps ales tended to be stronger than lagers. After Prohibition, legislators in some states wrote this into laws concerning permitted levels of alcohol. This has left those states with the notion that anything with more than 4 percent alcohol by weight, 5 by volume, is an ale (or a malt liquor, whatever that may mean). Equally, those states insist that all ales must be over 4 percent by weight. Most are therefore brewed to nudge just beyond this minimum. (Some British ales have to be produced to higher gravities for the American market.)

If there is a classic in such a contrived style as the old-generation, golden American ale, it must be 12-Horse, from the Genesee brewery (after the river of the same name), in Rochester, New York. This important industrial centre (Kodak, Xerox, Bausch &

Lomb) is in the west of the state, about 370 miles from New York City, and on Lake Ontario.

Genesee's products have a substantial body of very loyal supporters, but the brewery is by no means a household name even on the East Coast, and little known elsewhere. Despite this, it is by far the largest regional brewer in the United States, capable of mak-ing four million barrels (4,692,000 hectolitres) a year, and would be regarded as a giant if it were in Europe. It traces its history to the 1850s, and has some fine buildings from the 1870s.

Genesee 12-Horse Ale, launched in 1934, has a hint of sweet, soft fruitiness in the aroma; a light, perfumy, sweetish palate; and just a hint of (faintly winy?) dry-ness in the finish. The same brewery makes a cream ale which is paler in colour, and even sweeter and lighter. I believe this is made by blending 12-Horse Ale and the brewery's regular lager beer. The cream ale became very popular in the 1950s.

Along with Genesee, America's other best-known cream ale is Little Kings, made by the Schoenling brewery. Schoenling was established in 1934, after Prohibition, in Cincinnati; the brewery is still housed in a striking 1930s' building.

In 1986, the company merged with its last local rival, the much older Hudepohl, at whose site, on the Ohio river, brewing then ceased. Little Kings is light in body, but with a distinctly sugary creaminess, and a slightly sweet, sulphury note. On a couple of occa-sions over the years, the brewery has told me that it believes the product's character owes much to the use of Belgian-grown Hallertau hops. Canadian Haller-taus are also used. The yeast is bottom-fermenting.

New-generation ales

Even in such a reticent style as cream ale, the new generation of brewers produce the more interesting beers. In 1992, the Dock Street brewpub, in Philadelphia, introduced a cream ale of great delicacy and complexity. It began slightly sweet; had a firm but crisp body; and developed to a sugary, lemon-sorbet tartness and spritziness in the finish, with a late flowery tinge of hops. It was made from two-row and Munich malt, with 25 percent dextrose. Northern Brewer hops were used in the kettle, and Yakima Fuggles for aroma and dry-hopping. The ale was warm-conditioned, *kräusened* and lagered. Dock Street's head brewer at the time, Lou Farrell, worked with consultant Bill Moeller, who made the famous Neuweiler's Cream Ale in the postwar heyday of the Ortlieb Brewery of Philadelphia. Turn-of-the-century texts were also consulted.

As to a golden brew called simply an ale, with no further qualification, the first revivalist is the fine example made by the Catamount microbrewery since its launch in 1987.

Catamount is in White River Junction, Vermont. This is a one-street town where the White River meets the Connecticut River, across the state line from Lebanon, New Hampshire. It is also a minor rail junction and the home of Dartmouth College. The brewery takes its name from the mountain lion that is the emblem of Vermont ('The Green Mountain State'). One of the partners in Catamount was a home-brewer, who had also worked in a micro in Britain. The well-designed, neatly fitted brewery is in a 1911 meat-packing plant.

Catamount Gold is an all-malt, American-hopped (Willamette), top-fermenting ale. It has a grassy, fresh hop bouquet; a soft, smooth, lightly malty palate; and some fruitiness toward the finish. Catamount additionally makes an Amber (which is also an ale). This has a good, aromatic, dryish, malty character (pale, Carapils, crystal) and again good hop notes (Galena and Willamette), with the fruity finish. The brewery also produces its own superbly creamy porter and a number of contract brews, including the East Coast batches of the wonderfully malty Pike Place Pale Ale. Catamount is one of the outstanding microbreweries of the East Coast.

While Catamount's Gold, Amber and (dark brown to black) Porter are each very individualistic products, less distinctive entrants in these three colours have become a lazy range for many brewpubs and micros. This is especially true in the sun-belt states, where warm-weather thirsts and trend-driven audiences often make for a less discriminating clientele. 'We have our gold, our amber and our dark,' can be a discouragingly vague introduction to a brewery's range. 'Gold' can just mean a light-bodied ale of no particular character. The term 'amber' has in recent years come to be used very widely in the United States, but it has no agreed meaning. In colour, brews

The Pacific Coast brewpub in Oakland produces not only a classic mild but also a range of more hoppily American-tasting ales.

Brewer Bert Grant's Oldsmobile. Real ale really means cask-conditioned, and it can be found in America, especially in the Northwest.

Pike Place brewery, in Seattle, is one of the tiniest in America. It adjoins the city's famous Pike Place food market.

At its Philadelphia brewpub, Dock Street makes a wide range, but its Amber is made in Utica, New York.

The Boston Beer Company's original brewhouse; after the infusion, the spent grains were emptied by hand.

described as amber range from a deep gold or bronze to a copper-red. Some are lagers, others ales, and the odd one a hybrid.

The term was popularized by Matthew Reich, an energetic and charming young New Yorker, who had worked for a bank and a magazine publisher before becoming a wine-buff and then a lover of fine beers. At the beginning of the 1980s, Reich engaged brewing consultant Joe Owades to help him create a new beer. They had it produced under contract at F X Matt, in Utica, New York, until Reich had raised the money to start a small brewery and taproom in Chelsea, close to the roots of American beer in Lower Manhattan. Reich was far ahead of his time in New York, a city more conservative than it would ever concede, and his brewery location, perhaps hastily chosen, was less than ideal. Chelsea did not survive, but the beer is still made, back at F X Matt (see page 164). The beer, which is bottom-fermenting, is called New Amsterdam Amber, and is something of a hybrid between a Vienna-style lager and an ale. At an early stage, Matt added a robustly dry-hopped product (still bottom-fermenting) called New Amsterdam Ale. This tasty product also survives, though the New Amsterdam Brewing Company is now under different ownership.

Along the way, Reich had also helped popularize contract-brewing.

Reich's original inspiration was the Steam Beer of the Anchor Brewing Company, in San Francisco (see page 233). While Anchor is best known for its Steam Beer, it also makes an outstanding ale that represents a completely new American style.

In the early 1970s, Anchor's owner, Fritz Maytag, had made a pilgrimage to visit great British breweries such as Young's of London, Marston's of Burton-upon-Trent, and Timothy Taylor of Keighley, Yorkshire. Inspired by the individuality of their products, he began work on a truly robust ale that would be emphatically American. The ale he created was first produced in the spring of 1975, to commemorate Paul Revere's ride of 200 years earlier. (Revere rode from Boston to Lexington to warn the American revolutionaries that the British were coming to arrest them. The ride signalled the start of the War of Independence.)

Anchor is justifiably proud to have introduced this product as early as 1975, because that places it first among the new generation of American ales, ahead of the microbrewery movement. Liberty proved so popular that a version was later released as a Christmas brew, and finally it entered the company's permanent range as Liberty Ale in 1983.

Unlike most British ales (which tend to have a small proportion of invert sugar), Anchor Liberty is an all-malt brew. Nor does it have the reddish colour and light nuttiness of pale ale malt. A more conventional American pale malt sets the tone for a straw-like colour and drier texture. Over the years, it seems to have become slightly drier. While a 'premium' ale in Britain might have a gravity of 1048–55 (12–13.5 Plato), and a roundness of residual sugar, Anchor Liberty weighs in at 1057 (14.25), and is well attenuated, with an alcohol content of just under 5 percent by weight, just over 6 by volume.

The most important difference, though, is hop character. While the classic ale-brewers in Britain firmly believe in Fuggles and Goldings, and are often dismissive of American varieties ('they have too much flowering-currant aroma'), Anchor has no such inhibitions. Quite right, too. Britain and the United States are different countries, and the hops from each have their own virtues, which deserve to be understood and appreciated. Anchor Liberty positively blossoms with American hops (the Cascade variety), and is full of their perfumy, floral, lemony, pine flavours. While traditionalist British brewers like to dry-hop their draught beers in the cask, Anchor adapted this procedure to the maturation tank in the production of Liberty. It is very heavily dry-hopped, and has a huge, very aromatic bouquet.

British influence and American pride have in the years since continued to mingle on the West Coast, especially in the San Francisco Bay area, the rest of northern California, and beyond in Oregon and Washington states. These elements have been the parents of a whole generation of new American ales, many characterized by a relatively pale, dry malt character and especially by a hearty hopping with very floral (sometimes slightly citric) varieties from Oregon and Washington.

The Pacific Coast brewpub, opposite the Oakland Convention Centre, is not to be missed by any visitor to the San Francisco Bay area. No state has more breweries than California, and most are in the north. From the Bay, many beer-hunters head up to the micros and brewpubs of wine country.

Sierra Nevada lines up its styles, from left: Summerfest, Porter, Celebration Ale, Pale Ale, Big Foot Barley Wine, Stout. Each is quite different in character. Microbrewers do not deal in Light, Dry and Premium.

British ales inspired Jack McAuliffe during his military service in Scotland. When he returned to his native country, he established America's first microbrewery, in Sonoma, northern California, in 1976, releasing his first product the following year. His brew-kettle could make a barrel and a half of beer per batch. His New Albion Ale was, as its name suggests, somewhat English in style, but its successors at the Mendocino Brewing Company (see page 165) have a more American accent.

Sierra Nevada Pale Ale (see page 88) is another example of the Anglo-American marriage. It affects the English description pale ale, but is very new American in style.

Just as Italian and French wine-makers inspired the distinctively American, and world-class, products of northern California (and, increasingly, Oregon and Washington), so the grape has been followed by the grain. In these three states, which together have well over a hundred new breweries, some of the world's great ales are now made. Arguably, there is also a parallel in flavours. Just as the depth and complexity of European wines contrasts with the clean, fresh, fruity, spicy character of some West Coast products, so the same comparison can be made between British ales and those from the United States. Those piney, flowery, fruity American hops seem just the match for the peppers, squashes and chilies that feature so vigorously in the new American style of cooking. Many of the brewpubs have eclectic kitchens, providing food to match the beers (Willett's, in Napa, California, for example).

While California has the most breweries as a state (and Colorado more per head of population), Portland (with a great many brewpubs) and Seattle are the best-lubricated cities. Seattle has many establishments that identify themselves simply as 'ale-houses'; there are a number of these in the university district and adjoining neighbourhoods. In Seattle, a popular bumper sticker says 'Save the Ales'. As though they were threatened.

Sierra Nevada began as an improvised brewery, with minimal capital expenditure. In a dozen years, it has become one of America's biggest microbreweries, and positively glistens with pride. It has copper kettles in a traditional-looking brewhouse, but does not jib at modern steel tanks.

American ale producers

From revivals of very old styles, such as the stock ale made by the Boston Beer Company, to new classics such as Red Tail ale from California, North America is now home to hundreds of brews.

F.X. MATT'S TRADITIONAL
SEASON'S BEST
HOLIDAY AMBER BEER
FROM AMERICA'S AWARD WINNING BREWERY

BOSTON BEER COMPANY
The Brewery, 30 Germania Street, Boston, Massachusetts 02130, USA
Tel: (617) 522-3400

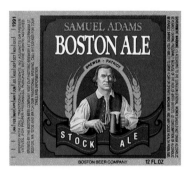

The decline and revival of American craft brewing is perfectly illustrated in the fortunes of the German-American family Koch. Five generations were brewers until the last of them laid down his malt shovel in Ohio during one of the industry's bouts of mergers, in 1956. His son, Jim Koch, went to Harvard and became a management consultant. When we got together in 1984 so that he could tell me about his plans to become a brewer, we spent an evening visiting bars in the course of research, but could not decide what style of beer he should make.

In 1985, Koch's Boston Beer Company began with Samuel Adams Boston Lager, produced under contract at Pittsburgh Brewing. The lager was a great success, but Koch still did not have a brewery of his own, and his aggressive marketing style led his detractors to make a point of this.

In 1988, he moved into a part of the sturdy Victorian premises of the former Haffenreffer brewery, which had closed in 1965. He installed, and considerably upgraded, a tiny mash tun and kettle originally designed by the British microbrewer Peter Austin for

Bill and Marie Newman, in Albany, New York. At his brewery, in Jamaica Plain, on the edge of Boston, he has also installed a pre-Civil War bar, where visitors can sample his wide range of specialities.

Koch primarily uses the brewery to make his draught Samuel Adams Boston Ale. This characterful and welcome revival has a distinctively brassy (pale amber?) colour; a firm, slightly oily, malty body; and an earthy, perfumed hop flavour, especially in the finish. It is produced from a gravity of 1052 (13 Plato), hopped three times in the kettle (with Fuggles and Saaz) and once, heavily, during maturation (Kent Goldings), *kräusened* and cold-conditioned. For bottling, the beer is contract-brewed at F X Matt.

F X MATT
The F X Matt Brewing Company, 811 Edward Street, Utica, New York 13503, USA
Tel: (315) 732-3181

Not every old-generation brewer understands the new, but most are willing quietly to offer counsel and practical help. His grandfather, from the Black Forest, founded the brewery; Francis Xavier Matt II devoted a working life to ensuring its survival as an independent before himself becoming (in the best sense of the word) a godfather to many new ale-makers on the East Coast. This sealed his status as a brewing legend.

The F X Matt brewery is in the heart of what was once ale-brewing country, in Utica, an old cotton textile town on the Mohawk river in central New York state. (In the establishment of towns in the region, the ancient Carthaginian name Utica, along with Rome, Syracuse, Troy and

others, was conferred by an enthusiast for the classics.)

The brewery buildings date in part from the 1850s, and one has an elegant cupola. The brewhouse block itself, perhaps dating from the 1930s or '40s, has a neon sign announcing Utica Club Ale. When I first visited the brewery, in 1981, this was its only ale: a golden, top-fermenting brew in the American tradition, with a pleasantly estery fruitiness. When I called a decade later, the legendary F X conducted me to a tasting room set out with a dozen brews he was making under contract.

New Amsterdam, Samuel Adams Boston Ale and Brooklyn Brown were among them. For some entrepreneurs, he was making lagers, like Erin (sweetish start, dryish finish) or Olde Heurich (hoppy start and finish, malty middle). For Mass Bay, which has its own micro producing draught ale, he was contributing a bottled Golden Lager (hoppy bouquet, malty palate). For Dock Street, he was producing the original Amber Beer (malty, with a perfumy, ale-style fruitiness). So it went on.

Whatever the Matt brewery's contribution to house character, each product had its own malt and hop specification, and a healthy handful of different yeasts was being used. It was an impressive range, and one of my favourites was Matt's own newly launched draught porter, with a lightly toffeeish, fruity palate and a characteristically smooth texture.

Visitors to the brewery can sample its own products at its 1888 tavern.

MENDOCINO BREWING COMPANY

Brewery and Tavern, 13351 Highway 101, Hopland, California 95449, USA
Tel: (707) 744-1015

The first microbrewery in the United States, New Albion, was ahead of its time in 1976–7, and closed in 1982–3, but a couple of people who worked there were able, using the same equipment and yeast strain, to help found Mendocino Brewing, in the tiny town of Hopland, in 1983. Since then, Mendocino has expanded its brewhouse considerably, but the beer is still made in a reproduction hop kiln behind a turn-of-the-century, tin-ceilinged saloon on Highway 101, California's main north–south route.

Hopland is an appropriate location for one of America's first brewpubs. Hops were grown in the town until 1953; cultivation ˌgradually moved north through California until it had concentrated itself across the state lines in Oregon and Washington. Since the mid- to late 1970s, wine grapes have been grown, and pears. It is thus that the pioneering micro-brewers moved from one wine-growing region, the Sonoma Valley, to another, the Russian River and Sanel Valley of Mendocino County.

The brewery has a wide range of excellent ales, but its emblem Red Tail (1054; 13.5 Plato; 4.4; 5.5), cop-per in colour, made with pale and crystal malts, Cluster and Cascade hops, is an American classic: remark-ably round, smooth and flavoursome, with a superb balance of malt, hop and fruit. Nor should visitors miss the seasonal strong ale, Eye of the Hawk.

PORTLAND BREWING COMPANY

1339 Northwest Flanders Street, Portland, Oregon 97209, USA
Tel: (503) 222-7150

The greatest profusion of new-generation ales in America is to be found in the cities of Portland, Ore-gon, and Seattle, Washington.

While many of these have to vary-ing degrees a British heritage, the flagship products of Portland Brew-ing typify the American approach.

Portland Ale (1048; 12 Plato; around 4 percent alcohol by weight, 5 by volume), bronze in colour, has lots of American hop aroma (the variety is Cascade); a light, crisp, dryish palate, and a good bitterness (32 BU), espe-cially in the finish (Cascade and Nugget). A more robust, amber ale, named McTarnahan's – after a stock-holder – has a creamier character but the same dryness and fruitiness. This has 1042 (13 Plato) around 4 percent alcohol by weight, 5 by volume, and is hopped entirely with Cascade (40 BU).

This brewpub and micro was estab-lished in 1986, in a former creamery building, by three high-school bud-dies, one a Porsche service represen-tative, another in real estate and a third a pianist, who still plays on the premises. In 1992 a 140-barrel (164-hectolitre) brewhouse was acquired second-hand from the Sixen brewery, of Nördlingen, north of Augsburg, Bavaria. Production at the pub will continue, but there will also be a larger brewery on the edge of town.

SLEEMAN'S

Silver Creek Brewery, 551 Clair Road West, Guelph, Ontario N1H 6H9, Canada
Tel: (519) 822-1834

Having brewed in Truro, Cornwall, and then in St Catherine's and Guelph, Ontario, the Sleeman family lapsed from the industry in 1933 and belatedly returned in the late 1980s, inspired by the micro movement.

Micros can be relatively large in Canada, and this one is, with a capac-ity of 100,000 hectolitres.

In its earlier heyday, Sleeman's principal product was a Cream Ale, and that style has been restored, ostensibly based on an 1898 family recipe. It is made from a gravity of 1052 (13 Plato), with 70 percent bar-ley malt and 30 percent corn grits; is brewed by direct flame, in traditional copper vessels; has a warm fermen-tation with a bottom-cropping ale yeast; then a relatively warm matura-tion for two or three weeks. It emerges with 4 percent alcohol by weight, 5 by volume, and 22 BU. It has a perfumy, sweetish bouquet, and a slightly tart, fruity flavour development.

Other products include the dryish Silver Creek Lager.

The Portland Brewing Company makes distinctively American-tasting ales, and its pub fits the style. Will the cosiness survive expansion?

Adelaide sparkling ale

Australia, having been settled first by people from the British Isles, began its commercial brewing industry in the early and mid-1800s with ales and stouts. Given the initial difficulties of obtaining barley and hops, or cultivating them in an unfamiliar and often harsh environment, and with a climate that can be extreme, the early brews must have been very rough-and-ready. Bottle-conditioning was widely used, because 'bush' hotels did not have cellars. Perhaps because of the dosage needed to start the secondary fermentation, these were sometimes known as 'sugar' beers. The least cosmopolitan of the old cities on the mainland of Australia is Adelaide, and that is the only place where this style of brewing has survived.

I felt that I was drinking history – an early breed of British pale ale, adapted to colonial conditions, then trapped in amber – when I first sampled Adelaide's classic, Coopers Sparkling Ale, in the 1970s. The name seemed ironic. If served with the gentle hand of a seducer, the ale might just sparkle, but any more clumsy technique results in a cloud of haze. The beer is heavily sedimented and cloudy, and the lively secondary fermentation in the bottle gives it an almost aggressively rough carbonation and fruitiness. It is sharp, sherbety, and exploding with flavours.

At the time, Coopers was seen in Adelaide as being old-fashioned, but was already known by repute to a handful of serious beer-lovers elsewhere. Since then, this style of ale has been revived by two other companies, and begun to be celebrated as a speciality.

Thomas Cooper, from Carlton, near Skipton, Yorkshire, was 26 when he and his wife, the daughter of a retired innkeeper, emigrated to South Australia in 1852. He worked as a shoemaker and then a dairyman, and is believed to have brewed his first ale as a tonic for his wife, using her recipe. He then began to supply his neighbours. He started to brew commercially in 1862, supplying only private customers. Cooper's wife died young and he remarried, eventually fathering 16 children. Six Coopers, of the fourth and fifth brewing generations, are now working within the company.

Cooper was a lay preacher, a Methodist. Cooper's religious convictions led him to see pubs as dens of iniquity, but he probably regarded beer as a nutritious beverage to be taken at home. Methodism's founder, the evangelist John Wesley, had praised beer, while condemning wine and spirits.

Widely available in Australia, the beer has a complex flavour hidden beneath the haze.

Most breweries based in major cities produce standard, gulpable lagers; Adelaide is a pocket of ale-brewing tradition.

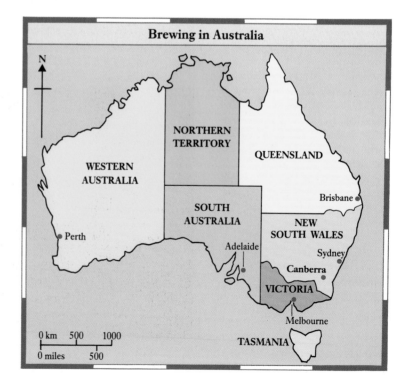

Brewing in Australia

N

WESTERN AUSTRALIA

NORTHERN TERRITORY

QUEENSLAND

SOUTH AUSTRALIA

NEW SOUTH WALES

Brisbane

Perth

Adelaide

Sydney

Canberra

VICTORIA

Melbourne

TASMANIA

0 km 500 1000

0 miles 500

When the generations of the Cooper family get together for a beer, their bar-table is one of the mighty 'puncheons' (hogsheads) in which the beer once began its secondary fermentation.

Timothy Cooper, cardiologist and brewer, monitors a batch during its bottle-conditioning.

Perhaps because he did not supply pubs, Cooper's business experienced great difficulties for some years, but in 1881 he moved to the site where the brewery still stands. He chose a site on the edge of Adelaide, in the bush, where land was cheaper than in town. The brewery now sits incongruously in a street of villas in a residential suburb around four miles east of the city centre. The brewery comprises a cluster of small brick buildings, painted in cream with green trim. In the brewery yard is a bricked-in kettle, with its own tall chimney, which was retired 30-odd years ago. The present brewhouse, in zinc-clad stainless steel, has an agricultural look.

Because Thomas Cooper never acquired an estate of pubs, his company was not an especially attractive prey to bigger brewers on the takeover trail. That is probably why it survived through the decades when it was an anomaly in the Australian brewing industry and emerged with the benefit of its own mystique.

'Sparkling ale' seems to have been a well-known designation in Australia by the late 1800s. The word 'sparkling' may have been a response to the brighter lager beers that began to appear in the 1880s and '90s. The production and serving of good ale was difficult in the very hot weather, and the advent of refrigeration and pure-culture yeasts made it possible for brewers to switch to more stable lager styles. Since at

Australia may be famous for standard lager, but there is more tingling refreshment in a glass of supposedly sparkling ale, the country's own contribution to the world of beer styles.

least World War II, lager brewing has been dominant in Australia.

Coopers' conservatism in this matter was extreme. Not only did the company continue to produce true ale and stout, the brewery did not even begin to make lager until 1969. Coopers Stout is outstanding: dry, coffeeish, oily and robust (14.5 Plato; 1058; 5.4; 6.8).

In 1991, Coopers Dark was launched. This is a dark brown ale made with pale, crystal and roasted malts and offering a complex of fruity and chocolate notes, at a gravity of 9.3 Plato (1036–8), with 3.6 percent alcohol by weight, 4.5 by volume.

The name, albeit an obvious one, was suggested by the brewery's technical manager, Timothy Cooper, who enjoyed a famous Welsh mild called Brains Dark while studying cardiology in Cardiff. (Brains is the name of the brewery, and has no physiological or mental connotation.) In the days when Coopers' ales were less well appreciated, members of the family were trained in alternative professions. Dr Cooper continues occasionally to help out in a local hospital at weekends.

In a Celtic confusion, something very similar to Coopers Dark has also appeared under the name Scotch Ale. This version was created in an experiment in which Coopers did the brewing, then fermented the ale in vessels installed as a showpiece at an Adelaide pub, the Earl of Aberdeen.

When I first tasted Coopers Sparkling Ale, it had an amber-red colour. Soon afterward, it became golden, losing some of its character in the process. When I taxed a member of the Cooper family about this, he at first said there had been problems in the maltings. Then he conceded that the earlier version had been made by producing a golden beer and blending in some stout. I had found the blend interesting,

and the brewery was trying to blandify its ale just at the moment when it was gaining a cult following – a less beneficial instance of being behind the times.

At the time, Coopers was fermenting its ale in tuns made from the Australian hardwood jarrah (similar to mahogany). These are still in working order, but no longer used. Nor does the brewery any longer drop the beer into oak hogsheads as a means of leaving behind the yeast, though it retains some of these 'puncheons' in its guest bar. And it still produces highly distinctive brews, including its famous Sparkling Ale.

Much as the Australian brewing industry has laughed at Coopers over the decades, its far larger local rival has in recent years tried to establish a competing product. So has a revivalist microbrewery, though it has had its ups and downs. Outside Australia, there is nothing quite like the robust sparkling ales of Adelaide, although there are many more elaborately produced bottle-conditioned brews.

The ears of barley, and the promise of prime malt, truck their way from Dry Creek to the agricultural-looking brewery. Such bold statements of the origins of beer could usefully be studied by many breweries elsewhere, whose beers seem less honestly earthy than Coopers'.

Sparkling ale producers

Genuine ales are a rare phenomenon in Australia. One city has clung to them, and in recent years seems to have been making them a civic style. (A brewpub, the Port Dock, in Port Adelaide, makes draught ales with a more British accent.)

COOPERS

Coopers Brewery, 9 Statenborough Street, Leabrook, Adelaide, South Australia 5068, Australia
Tel: (08) 332 5088

At Dry Creek, 12 miles north of Adelaide, Coopers has its own maltings, built in 1985. Local varieties of two-row barley, grown close to the sea, are turned into pale, crystal and roasted malts. Devotees of maritime malt's 'sea breeze' character can no doubt find it in Coopers. The company's classic ales and stout are brewed from 82 percent malt, the remainder of the grist being liquid cane-sugar, which is now widely used in all Australian beers.

As in many Australian breweries, all the hops are Pride of Ringwood, grown in Victoria and Tasmania, and used in the form of pellets.

The company's ales and stout are made with a top-fermenting yeast. Fermentation is now in cylindro-conical vessels, after which the brew is centrifuged. A controlled proportion of fermenting beer that has not been centrifuged is added, along with sugar, prior to bottling or kegging, to promote the secondary fermentation. The brewery claims to warm-condition its bottles and kegs for six weeks before releasing them. Some consumers then like to cellar the ale for up to two years.

An old product which had been known as Light Dinner Ale was resurrected in 1989 as Original Pale Ale: it is very fruity (apples, pears, bananas?), with a nice dash of hoppy acidity and dryness in the finish (9.2–3 Plato; 1036–8; 3.6; 4.5). The classic Coopers Sparkling Ale has the same characteristics but in greater intensity, with lots of banana notes and acidity (11.5; 1044–6; 4.7; 5.8), a colour of 10–11 EBC, and 25–26 units of bitterness.

KENT TOWN

Kent Town Brewery, 2 Rundle Street, Kent Town, South Australia 5067, Australia
Tel: (08) 362 9100

Kent Town was once the brewery quarter of Adelaide. As the Adelaide Grand Prix circuit skirts the city centre, it passes a landmark, a building constructed in 1876 from the slatey blue stone quarried locally. This building began as a brewery, with an ornamental fountain that poured beer. It later became a maltings, and today has elements of both. Its principal role is to supply malt to its parent, the South Australian Brewing Company, but some of this comes back in the form of an ale to be fermented at Kent Town.

The notion of reviving a beer with a Kent Town identity came from the master maltster at the time, Gordon Welsh – a voluble Scot, from Renfrew, near Glasgow. Kent Town Real Ale was launched in 1989, as a competitor to Coopers, with the slogan 'A new cloud on the horizon'.

The draught version is not pasteurized, although the bottles are (therefore not meeting the British definition of a real ale). Both are very hazy, more so than Coopers, though they have a less yeasty texture. Kent Town Real Ale (12.2–4 Plato; 1048–50; 4.4; 5.5) pours with a smooth, solid head. It has a full gold colour, with a green tinge. It is very soft and fruity, on the sweet side (pears, plums, gooseberries with sugar?), and most refreshing.

LION

Lion Brewing, 31–39 Jerningham Street, North Adelaide, South Australia 5006, Australia
Tel: (08) 267 1922

This handsome little stone-built brewery, with a three-storey tower, dates from 1850. It closed in 1914, was restored and reopened in 1986, closed again in late 1991, and reopened in early 1992. In its modern incarnation, it has been a project of microbrew consultants Graham Howard and David Paul. The Old Lion Hotel, in the brewery cellars, is under separate ownership.

Like its competitors, Lion's Sparkling Bitter Ale is actually meant to be cloudy, but it is less so than Coopers and Kent Town. It also has more malt and hop character, especially the latter. In addition to Pride of Ringwood, English Goldings are used, and the hops are added three times. It has 4 percent alcohol by weight, 5 by volume. The brewery's other products so far include a light, soft, faintly burnt-tasting, smoky porter that is a very good example of the style.

PORTERS AND STOUTS

Porters and stouts are very dark brews, almost black, with a highly toasted or roasted taste. The malts used, and sometimes raw barleys, are kilned to a darkness resembling that of almost-burnt toast, or roasted like cocoa beans or coffee. These were originally London styles, and later came to be strongly associated with Ireland. The classic examples are made with top-fermenting yeasts of the type used in ales. To the roasty flavours, an ale yeast will add fruitiness.

Porter was originally the dominant term, although the description stout was also used colloquially from the earliest days. In the heyday of porter, a single brewer would make several gravities and strengths, and the fuller-bodied, 'stouter' examples seem gradually to have become a style in their own right.

Today, if a brewery uses both designations, to describe different beers, its porter will always be lighter in body (though not necessarily lower in strength) than its stout. Insofar as this happens, it is usually in English-speaking countries. Elsewhere in the world, the term porter is more widely used, and the designation stout seen less often.

These very dark brews arose in part from advances in malting techniques. While malts dried by the wind or fire had in earlier days made for murky brown beers, industrial refinements in kilning gradually gave the brewer a more solid colour and flavour.

Amber and brown malts were used in early porters, before a high-temperature roasting process was patented in 1817. In this system, the grains were roasted in a rotating drum, so that they could be exposed to higher temperatures without being burned. The method is much the same as that used to roast coffee. In his book on porter, beerwriter Terry Foster suggests that this 'patent' malt may have initially been used in products identified as stouts, and may have helped popularize that term.

As malting became even more sophisticated, attention moved in the opposite direction, to the creation of the sparkling pale ales that were the next great style in Britain and Pilsner lagers in Bohemia. (Porter and stouts may have lingered in London and Dublin because these cities' waters, high in carbonates, were not ideal for the production of paler styles in the days before brewers knew how to make the necessary adjustments.)

Porter was the style being produced when the industrial revolution began, earlier in Britain than elsewhere in Europe, and thus it swept all before it as the breweries mechanized and the cities teemed with thirsty workers.

The big industrial brewers stored huge quantities of porter, often for long periods, in wooden tuns. During this period, there would be some growth of microflora such as *Brettanomyces*, imparting its characteristic 'horse blanket' aroma, and that came to be associated with the style. Because porter was made when its home country was at its height as an international power, it reached some distant parts of the world, and still lingers in unlikely corners.

From the toffeeish porters of Estonia to the malty examples of northern France, to the sweet version made by Tsingtao in China, many of these vestigial examples might in today's parlance be better regarded as stouts. In some distant lands, it is still considered necessary to have a *Brettanomyces* character in a true porter or stout.

The motherland was less universal in its influence by the time stout took its present forms. It has fragmented into the English type (sweet – also made in Scotland), the Irish style (dry) and the 'Imperial Russian' type (very strong) originally made for export to the Baltic. At the sweeter end, there is also oatmeal stout, and at the drier oyster stout, both recent revivals.

Porter

When things go wrong and will not come right,
Though you do the best you can,
When life looks black as the hour of night –
A pint of plain is your only man.
Flann O'Brien, 1939

A pint of plain? What Flann O'Brien meant, and had no need to explain to his fellow Dubliners, was plain porter. The term was commonly used in Ireland to distinguish the basic stuff from the fuller-bodied dry stout. The dominant Irish brewer, Guinness, continued to make a porter until 1974.

Plain porter is a useful term, and one that could be

> In the British Isles, porter came to mean a roasty, black, top-fermented brew that was a lighter-bodied counterpart to stout. It need not necessarily also be lower in alcohol. Porter went through a period of decline, vanished altogether from its native islands, then returned to become a style newly fashionable among lovers of flavourful beers. New-generation porters are also being widely produced in North America.

revived. Today, it would help distinguish the new-generation porters of the English-speaking world (which generally follow the rule of being less full-bodied than stout) from those vestigial examples elsewhere that are often much stronger.

For four or five years after the demise of Guinness's version, there was no porter anywhere in the British Isles. Then, with the growth of interest in traditional brews brought about by the Campaign for Real Ale, two British breweries decided in 1978 to revive the style. One, the Penrhos microbrewery set up on the Welsh border with the help of *Monty Python* actor Terry Jones, closed before the brew had time to establish itself. The other, the renowned Timothy Taylor brewery, in Keighley, Yorkshire, used its Black Bess Sweet Stout as the basis for a porter, which it still produces as an occasional winter speciality to a gravity of 1043 (10.5 Plato), with 3 percent alcohol by weight, 3.7 by volume. Predictably, this is a somewhat sweet brew. It has a good fruitiness, with hints of apple, but lacks hoppiness, perhaps roastiness, and certainly complexity. However, porter is a sideline to the brewery that produces the wonderful Landlord bitter.

Many British breweries launched porters during the 1980s. I have enjoyed examples ranging from the dry, roasty, coffeeish Pickwick's Porter, made by the Malton Brewery in Yorkshire; by way of the syrupy

Harveys of Lewes, East Sussex, launched a bottle-conditioned porter in 1993. Brown malt, of the type employed in the 1700s before roasting techniques were perfected, was used.

interpretation from Oak of Heywood, near Manchester; to the aromatic style from Woodforde's of Woodbastwick, Norfolk; and the slightly medicinal Essex Porter from Crouch Vale of Chelmsford, Essex.

An early entrant was the Burton Bridge microbrewery, whose well-balanced Burton Porter seems to me to fit the style very well. It has a mahogany colour, not quite opaque; a light body; and a fruity palate, developing coffeeish and roasty notes before a dash of hoppiness in the finish (1045; 11.25 Plato; 3.6; 4.5). This brewery is in the beer-making town of Burton-upon-Trent, in the middle of England.

Every student of brewing history knows that porter is supposed to have been first made at the Bell brewhouse in Shoreditch, London, in 1722. It is said that at that time it was called 'entire' (a word that still lingers in the stonework of some pubs) because it was intended to combine in one brew the characteristics of several contemporary beers. The new type of beer became popular with porters in nearby produce markets, and that is one theory as to how it acquired its better-known name. The name porter does not begin to be mentioned until the 1740s. I have often wondered whether it simply derived from a change of circumstance. Before this period, most beer was produced in brewpubs, to be consumed on the premises; the rise of porter coincided with the birth of industrial capitalism and freestanding (also known as 'common',

Burton Bridge's example has a light, fruity dryness that typifies a modern porter, and helps distinguish it from a fuller, more textured, stout. In the brewery's pub it is served with Staffordshire oatcakes.

The London district of Pimlico inspired an alliterative porter, at the Orange brewpub. The mysterious name Pimlico is said to derive either from a long-forgotten local drink or from the Pamlico tribe of native Americans.

or 'shipping') breweries. They had to deliver their beer, and the men who brought it may have announced themselves with the word, 'Porter!'

Porter returned to its birthplace, London, in 1984. It was introduced on the west side of central London, in Pimlico, at the Orange brewpub. Pimlico Porter is very dark, with burgundy highlights, and an assertive fruity-chocolaty palate, the two principal components in a good balance. It is made from pale ale, crystal and chocolate malts, to a gravity of 1045 (11.25 Plato), and has 3.2 percent alcohol by weight, 4.3 by volume.

Several bottles of porter newly recovered from an 1825 shipwreck in the English Channel found their way into the hands of brewing scientist Keith Thomas in 1988. He opened one at a gathering of beer-lovers, and we each anxiously took a sip, only to discover that the contents were largely sea-water. A further bottle had survived better, and yielded enough yeasty sediment for Thomas to culture up and use. He made a brew based on a Whitbread porter recipe of the period, giving it a primary fermentation with a modern top-fermenting yeast and a secondary with his English Channel culture. The porter was made to a gravity of 1055–60 (14–15 Plato), from pale, crystal, brown and chocolate malts and Goldings hops. It was very aromatic, with a slightly leathery, sooty aroma and some pepperiness; lots of rounded fruitiness and maltiness; and a very long finish. A cooperative called Flag produced the beer at the Pitfield microbrewery, in Hoxton, east London. As this neighbourhood merges into Shoreditch, it could be argued that porter had come home.

The Pitfield microbrewery also produced a cleaner-tasting, maltier London Porter under its own name, and made the award-winning old ale called Dark Star, but could never finance a move from its unsatisfactory premises, a former stable. The brewery closed soon afterward, and the two porters and Dark Star have since been made under contract elsewhere. For a time, Flag Porter was made at the Falcon and Firkin brewpub, in Victoria Park Road, Hackney, just to the other side of Shoreditch.

In the early 1990s, there was a further surge of new porters. Most came from larger regional brewers, including a soft, licorice-tasting example from Young's of London. More remarkably, porter was revived by Whitbread, the national brewer most strongly associated with the style (see page 175).

The licorice-tasting, bottom-fermenting porter made by the United States' oldest brewer, Yuengling (established in 1829), in Pottsville, Pennsylvania, is a vestige of British colonial tradition (even though the founder came from the Stuttgart area of Germany). So is the similar, but maltier, Stegmaier Porter, from Wilkes-Barre, Pennsylvania.

There are at least 60 or 70 new-generation porters now being produced in the United States, with established classics ranging from the creamy Catamount, from Vermont, to the gently coffeeish example from Sierra Nevada of California.

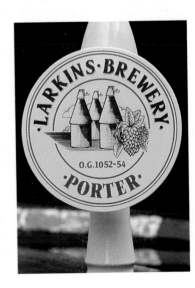

Having closed its London brewery in 1976, Whitbread produces its revivalist porter at the opposite end of the country. Nearer to London, at Chiddingstone, near Edenbridge, in Kent hop country, the Larkins microbrewery, founded in 1986, produces an outstandingly complex example of porter.

Porter producers

The company which began as one of London's early porter brewers, Whitbread, has recently re-introduced the beer it originally made famous 250 years ago, but the style had already been gaining popularity with a new generation of brewers, both in Britain and North America.

BOULDER

Rockies Brewing Company,
2880 Wilderness Place, Boulder,
Colorado 80301, USA
Tel: (303) 444-8448

'Nobody makes real porter any more. What do you think it was really like?' David Hummer asked me one day in the late 1970s. I answered him as best I could. Hummer, a physicist, was doing some research work at a university in Britain when he developed a taste for the local beers. Not long after the first microbreweries were established in California, Hummer and a couple of friends went into production in a former goatshed, at Longmont, near Boulder, Colorado. Later, they moved into a purpose-built brewery (looking more like a modern church) in Boulder itself. The earlier microbreweries closed and Boulder, established in 1979–80 and the veteran of several corporate restructurings since, is now the oldest in the United States.

The Boulder beers were originally bottle-conditioned, but that is no longer the case. The Boulder Porter brewed in the goatshed, in home-made equipment, was well-balanced, with a gentle but definite roastiness, and some fruity, yeasty dryness. At the new brewery, with equipment that was less improvised, the porter at first seemed little changed, but then gained some earthier, rooty, licorice notes. In recent years, it has become cleaner and smoother, with more restrained roastiness and a fruitiness that is less dry. The malts are pale, two versions of crystal, and black, and the beer is brewed to a gravity of 1052–6 (13–14 Plato), with American Hallertau as the signature hop.

WHITBREAD

The Whitbread Beer Company, Porter
Tun House, Capability Green, Luton,
Bedfordshire LU1 3LS, England
Tel: (0582) 391166

The best-known of the porter brewers had made none for 60-odd years when it was decided to revive the style, in 1992, as part of the company's 250th birthday celebrations. The beer was made available on a trial basis, and its popularity encouraged the brewery to introduce it as a regular product the following year.

Initially, three breweries in the Whitbread group were asked to produce porters adapted from the company's 1859 brewhouse journals. The breweries had to be specialists in top-fermenting styles, capable of producing small runs. Without a brewery in London, Whitbread selected Cheltenham, Sheffield and Castle Eden, County Durham.

The brewhouse journals indicated the number of pounds of malt per barrel, rather than the gravity, but the principal Whitbread porter seemed to have had 1066 (16.5 Plato). The 1992 brewers were asked to work in a gravity from the mid-1040s to the lower 1050s (11–13 Plato). The intention was to produce a porter that could be consumed as a regular drink and, bearing in mind that tax in Britain was on gravity, to make the product affordable in this role. The basic malts were pale, brown and black, and the hops Fuggles and/or Goldings. In order to adjust to the lower gravity of the beer, greater bitterness of today's varieties, and drinkers' more timorous tongues, only a fraction of the volume of hops in the original 'recipe' was used (something between a quarter and a sixth).

Each of the three breweries made several test batches before choosing one to place before a tasting panel, of which I was a member. Cheltenham produced the palest porter, looking for the brown malt 'woodiness' that the brewer felt would have characterized early examples of this style. I found it chocolaty, well balanced and drinkable, but lacking excitement.

Sheffield added licorice to one test brew and oak chips to another (the latter to mimic aging in wooden tuns). Like a boxer leaving his best punch in the gym, Sheffield held back the batch the brewers thought best. They felt it would be too assertive for the consumer. The one submitted, which included enzymic and chocolate malts and wheat, was very fruity but seemed lacking in other elements.

The winner, Castle Eden's entry, had a solid black colour, with ruby highlights; lots of malt-loaf, burnt currant and figgy notes in the bouquet; and more of these characteristics in the palate; with a faintly oily, smooth but light body; and a long, slightly smoky, finish. This porter is brewed to 1052 (13 Plato; 3.7; 4.6), with some chocolate malt. Only Goldings hops are used, both in the brew-kettle and for dry-hopping. The colour is 290 EBC and there are 40 units of bitterness.

The Castle Eden brewery began in 1826, in an inn on a coaching route. The owning family was called Nimmo, and I remember drinking a dry, fruity ale under that name in about 1961. Nimmo's, by then a sizable local brewery, was acquired by Whitbread in 1963.

Dry stout

A true dry stout lives up to its name. It is uncompromisingly roasty, with plenty of hop bitterness. The best are top-fermenting, with the fruity acidity and complexity that brings. It could be a challenging combination, yet a dry stout is one of the world's most popular beers: Guinness, born in Dublin, Ireland.

Two more brewers of dry stouts, Murphy and Beamish, are also Irish, both in the city of Cork, and their products are becoming much more internationally available. Around half of all beer consumed in Ireland is dry stout. There are also dryish stouts in the ranges of some brewers in Belgium and the Netherlands, the Indian subcontinent, Singapore, Australia, Japan and North America. Some of these are bottom-fermenting and several are so strong as to be more in the style of 'Russian' imperial stouts. Despite these many fine products, dry stout is synonymous with Guinness, and that name is a symbol of Ireland.

The first brewing Guinness was probably Richard, born around 1690, who was land agent to the rector of Celbridge, in County Kildare. Richard brewed beer for the rector's table. The rector left £100 to Richard's son Arthur, who used it to buy a brewery in nearby Leixlip (a Viking name meaning 'salmon leap'). Arthur Guinness subsequently sold this business and bought a disused brewery in Dublin in 1759. This was to be the birthplace of a dynasty, a colourful, titled family that has retained a significant stake in the company (though not in its management since 1992), and has featured in almost every aspect of Irish and British public life.

Within ten years, Arthur Guinness was brewer to Dublin Castle. Irish brewers were making ale at the time, and that was Guinness's original product. He continued to make ale even after he had launched his first porter, in the 1770s.

Guinness best expresses its complexity of flavours when served at a natural cellar temperature, but survives a gentle cooling.

The son of a country land agent, Arthur Guinness founded Ireland's dynasty of brewers, politicians, literati and socialites.

The great dry stouts are brewed in Ireland, and are instantly recognizable in their black creaminess. They are famously sociable brews, lubricating wit, music and literary tribute. They also have the stinging intensity of an amontillado sherry. By no means every glass of dry stout is served with oysters or lobster, but that is a marriage made in heaven.

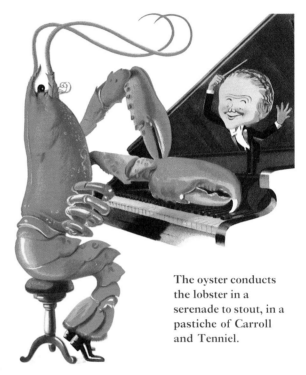

The oyster conducts the lobster in a serenade to stout, in a pastiche of Carroll and Tenniel.

In 1799, the brewery decided to produce only porter. For a time, there were two gravities of porter, marked with a single and a double 'x', and already a stronger third version for export to the Caribbean. In 1820, the double was renamed Guinness Extra Stout Porter, and at some point the export version became known as Foreign Extra Stout. The porter was overtaken in sales by the stout after World War I. In 1974, the porter was dropped, but the stouts flourish.

When porter declined in Britain, stout remained, but as a speciality. Why did a beer of this family, in the form of dry stout, remain dominant in Ireland, and become an acknowledged style?

One reason may be that restrictions on the use of energy during World War I made it difficult for British maltsters to roast their grains, thus reducing the availability of these styles. These restrictions were not imposed in Ireland, where the Home Rule movement was very active as a prelude to rebellion and independence. Guinness managed to continue firing its kilns, though during the troubles it did sometimes use peat to heat its kettles.

The powerful presence of Guinness must also have been a factor in sustaining porter and stout as national styles. The company always placed an emphasis on quality; it dominated the Dublin market when the city was still the second largest in the British Isles; when other brewers distributed only locally, Guinness used the canal system to market its products nationwide; it took as its trademark the harp, a national symbol. All Irish writers seem to have dipped their pens in Guinness, but British authors from Dickens and Trollope to Graham Greene also alluded to the black stuff. As early as 1860, it was the dominant stout in Britain.

Emigrants after the potato famine of the 1840s, and Irish soldiers, took the beer all over the globe. An Enniskillen Dragoon allegedly wrote home to say that he had sustained himself on Guinness after being wounded at Waterloo. Bismarck was said to have a private supply, as was Robert Louis Stevenson during his years in Samoa.

In the 1920s, the British advertising agency S H Benson polled drinkers as to why they favoured Guinness. 'It does me good,' was the reply, and this became the basis of advertising for many decades. Guinness is not notably high in calories, but its assertive flavours make even one glass a very satisfying sensuous experience. Not satiating, though – because of its dryness, it arouses the appetite. Without being strong, it has enough alcohol to be a mild relaxant. The bottle-conditioned version, containing live yeast, might also act as a mild laxative. For those reasons, it is sometimes given to patients in hospitals in Britain and Ireland. Sweden's only porter was available only on doctor's prescription until the 1960s. In some countries, stout is seen as an aphrodisiac, or as a beneficial bath for newborn babies.

One of Dublin's famous Georgian doors on the house at the brewery.

The stainless-steel fermenters are designed with that same solidity that characterizes all hardware at Guinness. They are the latest addition to a brewery that has been moving with the times for more than 200 years.

Having been so successful for so long, Guinness has had the confidence to maintain traditions. I suspect its heavy hopping – a key factor in dry stout as a style – has its origins in the days when porters were kept for very long periods, sometimes a year or more. In the 18th and 19th centuries, these were high-gravity beers, and they would have required a substantial period of secondary fermentation. The formative years of porters and stouts were before the introduction of refrigeration, so large stocks were vatted in advance for summer. The *Brettanomyces* acidity that developed was enjoyed by many drinkers. The only means of protecting these beers from less welcome microbiological intrusion would have been to hop them heavily. Sometimes, these 'stock' porters were blended with freshly made 'running' brews. This method is still used to make Guinness Foreign Extra Stout. Having been such a large exporter at such an early stage, before the development of pasteurization, Guinness would also have hopped very heavily to preserve its beers on their long journeys.

Stout and oysters

The lore of dry stout is rich in references to oysters, and the union of the two at table is a happy one.

Like most marriages, this resulted from a chance encounter. When porter was the everyday drink of London, oysters were one of its more readily available and inexpensive foods. Where London's river, the Thames, opens to the sea, the nearby coast has towns like Whitstable and Colchester that are famous for their oysters. Any reader of Dickens knows that a working man could eat and drink cheaply if he stayed with oysters and porter. By the mid-1800s, the growth of London, over-dredging of the oyster beds, and perhaps industrial pollution, had rendered the bivalve the luxury that it has been in Britain ever since. The custom of drinking porter or stout with oysters on the half-shell survived in the chophouses that retained Georgian traditions after Britain's hearty gastronomy began to yield to French grandeur.

In the City of London today, the fish restaurant Sweetings offers black velvet (stout and champagne, half and half) in a silver tankard as an accompaniment to oysters.

Ireland has similar restaurants, and in the city of Cork a fine bar and restaurant called The Oyster Tavern. On my occasional visits, I have observed that it is a favourite dining place for priests, so it seems that the marriage of stout and oysters has been sanctified.

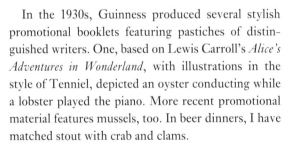

Like all the best country pubs in Ireland, Morrissey's, in Abbeyleix, County Laois, doubles as a grocer's store and tobacconist.

Ireland's oyster capital is Galway, which grows the European flat, similar to the Belon of Brittany. Galway hosts an oyster festival each September.

In the 1930s, Guinness produced several stylish promotional booklets featuring pastiches of distinguished writers. One, based on Lewis Carroll's *Alice's Adventures in Wonderland*, with illustrations in the style of Tenniel, depicted an oyster conducting while a lobster played the piano. More recent promotional material features mussels, too. In beer dinners, I have matched stout with crab and clams.

At first thought, it might seem that the assertive flavours of stout would overpower the delicacy of shellfish, but they do not. That very intensity and acidity seems to awaken the salty-sweet, gamey flavours that can lurk in the meat of these primitive creatures. The same observation could perhaps be made about the serving in Spain of dry sherries with squid *tapas*.

At the end of August and beginning of September, Murphy's Stout sponsors an oyster festival in the village of Claren Bridge, in Galway, Ireland. In the last week of September, Guinness has a similar festival in the town of Galway. In the early 1900s, the long-defunct Colchester Brewing Company made a product called Oyster Feast Stout. This was probably a conventional stout, and was produced to celebrate the oyster harvest.

Oyster stout

There have also been stouts in which the oyster was an ingredient. As stout and oysters go together so well, the idea was that they might share a bottle, however disgusting fishy beer might sound (there is a cocktail made with aquavit and clam juice). These products were made at the time when it was fashionable to emphasize nutritious elements in beer.

The oysters may have first actually entered the stout when the shells were ground and used as a finings to help precipitate unwanted solids. Being very alkaline, they counteracted sourness in beer. I doubt this method has been used this century, though who can be sure? If Budweiser can add beechwood chips...

Another material used in finings is Irish moss (a seaweed, also known as carrageen), and I have heard at second-hand of this having been added simultaneously with whole oysters, although it seems that the shellfish were intended to enrich the beer. The earliest account I have heard from someone who has himself made an oyster stout came from a brewer who had worked for the defunct Hammerton brewery in London. In 1938, this company added oyster concentrate to its oatmeal stout before bottling (and pasteurizing). The brewers and directors enjoyed two test batches, but the oyster concentrate went bad before a third could be made.

After World War II, at least three British breweries made oyster stout, and the product lingered until the 1950s or early 1960s. The best-known, and probably last, example of that period was made by the Castletown Brewery on the Isle of Man, now closed. Peter Shardlow, who today acts as a microbrewery consultant, remembers having made this beer. He recalls that a granulated extract of oysters was added to the kettle, and says that the finished beer did not have a pronounced fishy character.

This variation has in recent years begun to appear once more. In the United States in 1992, the Pike Place microbrewery, in Seattle, obtained from an oyster packer a supply of the liquid that is found when the shells are opened. The variety was Totten Inlet 'European flat', on the briny side and similar to the famous Belon of Brittany. The liquid was used in the kettle as a generous one-sixth of the brewing 'liquor' to produce an oyster stout. The initial batch was considered by the brewery to have too overwhelming an oyster flavour, and was blended with a 'straight' stout. I found the blended version only lightly oystery, with a hint of salt and a very creamy mouth-feel. This was a special brew for an oyster festival in a local restaurant, The Brooklyn. This restaurant offers shot glasses of beers from local microbreweries, each paired with a different variety of oyster. At the height of the new oyster season each November it carries 45 varieties, and almost as many beers. The Seattle area is rich in oysters, and no doubt more of the local brewers will experiment with oyster stouts. Redhook has talked of it, and Pike Place has considered a brew made with whole oysters.

Later in 1992, the brewer from the Marin Brewing Company of Larkspur Landing, California, made a test batch of oyster stout at home. I found this very firm and smooth, with a distinct iron taste, and perhaps a dash of fennel. I was not sure that I could recognize oysters. The Front Street brewpub, in Santa Cruz, California, faced the challenge by placing an oyster in a glass of stout and serving it as a shooter.

Asahi's little-known brew is a lingeringly dry delight, but notably higher in alcohol than the Irish classics. Is it a dry stout, or a Japanese Imperial?

Many believe that Guinness does them good, although health claims are now discouraged.

This romantic depiction of hop-pickers is in the museum at the Guinness brewery in Dublin. A dry stout should have plenty of hop bitterness, as well as its characteristic roastiness and fruitiness.

Dry stout producers

Guinness, the classic dry stout from Ireland, is known and loved in far-flung corners of the globe. Beamish and Murphy, also from Ireland, have a smaller circle of loyal adherents. North American drinkers are discovering a whole new range of dry stouts from microbreweries.

BEAMISH

Beamish & Crawford, South Main Street, Cork, Republic of Ireland
Tel: (021) 276841

The city of Cork is divided by two channels of the River Lee. In a bend of the southern channel, by a fierce weir and an old fort, is a site that is said to have accommodated a brewery since the mid-1600s. It was an ale brewery until Messrs Beamish and Crawford established their company there in 1792, with a view to producing porter. The principals, both originally Scottish-Irish Protestant landowners from the north, were exporters of butter and beef from Cork. They called their new business The Cork Porter Brewery. In the distant past, Beamish was thought of as the Protestants' brewery, Murphy the Catholics'.

A step-gabled tower and a half-timbered facade (built in the 1920s but worthy of a Tudor mansion) signal the brewery. The entrance hall is galleried like an Elizabethan theatre. After such flourishes, the beer is made in a modern block brewhouse.

A porter was produced until the 1960s, though the term was no longer used at that time; the brewery simply identified its products with a single, double and triple 'x'. Today's flagship product is a dry stout.

Beamish Stout has a gravity of around 1039 (9.75 Plato), and an alcohol content of 3.4 percent by weight, 4.2 by volume. While definitely a dry stout, it does have a distinctly chocolaty note, some silkiness of body, and a very delicate hop character. Chocolate malt, rather than roast, provides the keynote, and some wheat is used to help the creaminess of texture, lacework and head. The wheat was once raw, but is now malted, to improve fermentability and therefore lightness of body. The hops include Challenger, Goldings and – unusually – the German Hersbruck. It has 38–42 units of bitterness.

In 1962 Beamish & Crawford was acquired by Carling O'Keefe, of Canada (coincidentally, the original O'Keefe came from Cork), and that group has since been taken over by Foster's of Australia, better known for its lager.

GUINNESS

Arthur Guinness & Son, St James's Gate, Dublin 8, Republic of Ireland
Tel: (01) 536700

The Wicklow Mountains' soft water, by way of the delightfully named Rivers Dodder and Poddle, was brought in the 13th century to a cistern at the abbey of Saint Thomas, and later became the supply not only for Arthur Guinness's brewery but also for the city of Dublin. The abbey stood outside the city walls, near Saint James's Gate. Around the abbey, there grew up a neighbourhood of millers, brewers and distillers, all working outside the jurisdiction of the city. The district is still called The Liberties, and is now a famous old corner of Dublin.

In the 1760s, Arthur Guinness built a gate of his own, its keystone decorated with a relief of Ceres, the Roman goddess of grain. Next to the gate is a row of Georgian houses, in one of which Guinness lived. The present brewing director has his office in one of the houses.

No other brewery uses as much roasted barley as Guinness, which prepares its own. The air is heavy with a delicious aroma that suggests a giant coffee-roaster. A hop store built in the 1870s and '80s has been turned into an elaborate museum for visitors. Tracks remain from an eight-mile narrow-gauge railway that once carried materials around the site. The brewery has its own 1930s' power station, a miniature of the one at Battersea, London.

The Victorian brewhouse, laced with decorative railings, vertical iron ladders, catwalks and gantries, has massive mash tuns and kettles, their hatches and hoods raised by chains slung over pulleys. Its vessels saw Guinness become the biggest brewery in the world until its American sales were stalled by Prohibition. The brewhouse worked until the 1980s, and has gathered dust since.

The new brewhouse has stainless-steel vessels in the traditional shapes and, outside, a tree of the variety brewer's spruce (*Picea brewerana*), from the Pacific Northwest. A 90-year-old fermentation block, the first steel-framed multi-storey building in the British Isles, has the look of an early industrial building in Chicago. Today, fermentation is in outdoor cylindro-conicals.

Dublin's upward-step infusion mash is geared to leave sufficient unfermentable sugars to provide some body. The brewery looks for hop flavour, as well as bitterness, and uses several varieties, among which Goldings are perhaps the most influential, in one addition. The brewery claims still to use its original yeast, though this has over the years been selected down from several strains to one, which was arrived at in about 1960. It works at high temperatures (around 25°C/77°F), and is very dispersed, having neither risen to the top nor sunk to the bottom, when it is removed by centrifuge. The Guinness yeast seems to make for some fullness, a freshness, an aromatic character and a moderate fruitiness.

Dublin makes five or six principal versions of Guinness, in a total of 19 variations, and exports around 40 percent of its output. Guinness is available in more than 120 countries. It has sister breweries in Britain, Malaysia and Africa, and nearly 30 licensing agreements.

Guinness for Ireland and several other markets is made from pale malt, flaked barley (about 25 percent) and roasted barley (around ten percent), with no other grains or sugars. All of the grain is grown in Ireland. In line with the German Purity Law, the barley is replaced with pale and roasted malt in Continental Europe. To my palate, this makes for a smoother and richer Guinness, but without quite the complexity or mouth-feel of the traditional version.

The Dublin procedures are followed in some countries, such as Britain; others use a proportion of local grains like maize and sorghum, and some blend into their own basic beer an essence or powdered extract derived from Dublin's production. Inevitably, the last method produces a less complex stout.

Draught Guinness for the Irish and American markets, soft and creamy, with a tang of hoppy acidity in the finish, has an original gravity of 1039 (9.75 Plato), 3.4 percent alcohol by weight, 4.2 by volume, 130 EBC and 45 BU. This beer is flash-pasteurized. The version brewed in Britain is much the same.

Bottled Guinness made for Ireland is not pasteurized. This has a similar specification but, being bottle-conditioned, has a spicier, fruitier, drier, more complex and lively, fresh character. Bottle-conditioned Guinness is produced only for the Irish market, although it is bootlegged elsewhere. The bottled version sold in Britain is pasteurized.

The all-malt version, both draught and bottled, for Continental Europe has a little more than 4 percent alcohol by weight, 5 by volume, and a more coffeeish character.

Bottled Guinness for the United States is not all-malt, but is stronger (4.8 percent alcohol by weight, 6 by volume), with a high bitterness (50+) and lots of flavour.

The strong bottled version sold in some European countries, notably Belgium (1073; 18; 6; 7.5, 50+ BU), combines richness, creaminess, fruitiness and sweetness.

The famous bottled version known as Foreign Extra Stout, and produced for tropical countries, has a similar strength but with a more complex palate, featuring lactic, winy and 'horse-blanket' (*Brettanomyces*) notes. This is a blend of beers, one of which has been matured for up to three months in wooden tuns that are at least 100 years old (bitterness is in the mid-60s).

In Ireland, Guinness was originally supplied to publicans in casks, from which they did their own bottling, leaving the beer to condition for a couple of weeks before selling it. Because the beer in the cask could become excessively lively, some publicans began in the 1950s to release the natural carbonation and dispense the beer as draught, pumping it with air. This produced a very creamy pint. The creaminess derived in part from the small bubbles caused by the nitrogen within the air. Guinness eventually devised a system using nitrogen and carbon dioxide.

Some countries have 'Draught' Guinness in a can, which contains a capsule of nitrogen that releases itself when the vessel is opened. A bar-mounted nitrogen-injector is used in Japan. For a time, American bars were fitted with an ultrasonic vibrator to nucleate the formation of fine bubbles. This system did not last. Perhaps it was felt to lack the romance of the 'slow pour' that produces the creamiest draught in Ireland, and in some of the best bars in cities like Boston and New York.

MURPHY
Lady's Well Brewery, Leitrim Street, Cork, Republic of Ireland
Tel: (021) 503371

A well consecrated to Our Lady was the original source of water for this brewery, though the town supply is now used. Murphy's is on the north side of town, in a building that was once an orphanage, though its facade is vaguely reminiscent of an Edwardian railway station. The vents of the former maltings bear witness to the existence of a brewery on the site since the 1850s. When I first visited, in 1983, Murphy's was still using most of its original equipment, including a coal-fired kettle, its hatches held down by huge counterweights shaped like shamrocks.

That year, the brewery, which has had several owners, was acquired by Heineken. In 1985, I was invited back to see a new block brewhouse blessed by two priests in the presence of the Prime Minister of Ireland. There has been further expansion since then.

Less assertive than Guinness, but drier than Beamish, the stout from Murphy's has a suggestion of well-done toast, a light roastiness, and a firm but relatively light, smooth body. Its gravity is 1037.8 (9.5 Plato) and it has 3.4 percent alcohol by weight, 4.2 by volume. It is brewed from pale malt, a small proportion of chocolate malt and roasted barley. The hops are all Target, and the beer has 35–36 units of bitterness.

NORTH COAST

North Coast Brewing, 444 North Main Street, Fort Bragg, California 95437, USA
Tel: (707) 964-2739

On the coast of northern California, just outside Mendocino, is a spot called Brewery Gulch. There is no longer a brewery there, but the promise is fulfilled a few miles up the road at Fort Bragg. This little town was a fort in the mid-1800s, then became a whaling port. Springs from the Coast Ranges feed the River Noyo, the town's water supply and the North Coast brewery, founded in 1987 in a former Presbyterian church and mortuary.

Principal Mark Ruedrich trained as a biologist, married an English-woman, and developed a taste for top-fermenting ales when he lived near the Blackawton brewery in Devon, in the southwest of England. His products include an aromatic, creamy, chocolaty, fruity stout called Old No 38. Despite those characteristics, its flavour development and finish leave it firmly in the dry stout category. It is brewed from a gravity of 1057 (14.25; 4.6; 5.7) from pale, crystal and black malts and roasted barley, and hopped twice, with

Clusters and American Hallertaus (around 50 BU). A top-fermenting yeast is used. The name Old No 38 derives from a locomotive on the diesel-smelling 'Skunk Train' railroad through the redwoods from Fort Bragg to the main Highway 101.

This dry stout is just one good example from many being produced by American microbrewers. Not far away, the Mendocino Brewing Company makes the medium-dry, fruity, chocolaty Black Hawk Stout; Sierra Nevada has a beautifully roasty Stout; the Butterfield Brewery, in Fresno, has a malty, chewy example; outside California, the Hubcap Brewery and Kitchen, of Vail, Colorado, has the very creamy-tasting, faintly whisky-ish Rainbow Trout Stout.

TOOTH

Carlton & United Breweries, 26 Broadway, Sydney, New South Wales 2000, Australia
Tel: (02) 282 0941

Tooths Sheaf Stout was a mouthful in its sibilance; the name has now lost its teeth, although the stout retains its bite. After Tooth's brewery was taken over by Carlton/Foster's, the name became simply Sheaf Stout. This excellent stout should be more widely available – its occasional appearances in the United States market, for example, have brought it a keen following there.

It has a solid black colour; a dark head; an almost woody aroma; a coffeeish palate; a tar-like oiliness of body; and a good hop bitterness, especially in the finish. Sheaf Stout is brewed from pale and crystal malts and roasted barley. It has a gravity of 14.1 Plato (1056.5; 4.6; 5.7). The colour is 200 EBC, and the bitterness drinks more assertively than its 35 units would suggest. This dry stout is made with a top-fermenting yeast.

The parent company's more strongly coffeeish Abbots Double Stout and lighter Invalid Stout, both brewed in Melbourne, are bottom-fermenting. So is the nicely roasty, dry Carbine Stout produced by Castlemaine in Brisbane.

As a hangover, so to speak, from colonial times, most Australian breweries still have a dry stout. I found a newer one in the wool-gathering town of Goulburn, between Sydney and Canberra. The Goulburn Brewery, built in the 1830s, had produced ale and stout for a century, then closed. The site embraced a former maltings, brewery, cooperage and tobacco-curing kiln. A priest, Father Michael O'Halloran, saw its potential as a working museum of industrial archaeology. He began to restore it in the late 1980s, as part of a project for disabled people. He installed a brewhouse, and in 1992 I tasted his firm, roasty, dry Extra Brown Stout.

Sweet stout

Just as some of the more acidic styles of beer in Germany and Belgium are sweetened by the drinker with fruit essences, so the British have used additions like lime juice (unnecessarily, in lager) or sugar (to fortify already-rich dark ales, porters and stouts). A beer that gains tartness from winy fermentations, and is then sweetened, has its own complex of flavours.

The great actor Charles Macklin, principal rival to David Garrick, 'was accustomed to drink considerable quantities of stout sweetened with sugar, at The Antelope, in White Hart Yard, Covent Garden,' according to John Bickerdyke's *The Curiosities of Ale and Beer* (1889). Macklin survived a charge of having murdered a fellow actor (in an argument over a wig), and lived to be 100 (1697–1797). The sweetened stout must have been powerful stuff, and it is still sometimes seen as a restorative or even a health drink.

Simonds, in Berkshire, was a famous brewery, and clearly enamoured of milk stout. When Simonds sold Mackeson to Jude, Hanbury, it did not realize that brewery was partly owned by its rival Whitbread.

Brewers eventually launched, and still make, stouts that pour sweetly from the bottle. These are no longer matured for long periods, and are therefore not winy, but they are sweetened with sugar before being bottled. Most bottled beers are pasteurized, but this is essential in a sugar-primed product, to prevent further fermentation. In line with their vestigial identity as a health drink, most of these sweet stouts are low in alcohol, typically around 2.4–2.7 percent by weight, 3–3.5 by volume. A classic example is Sweetheart Stout, from the Tennent's brewery of Glasgow, Scotland. In keeping with the theatrical tradition, the 'sweetheart' on the label is 1950s' Hollywood starlet Venetia Stevenson, former wife of Don Everly, of the musical Everly Brothers.

Milk stout

Products in this style were once colloquially known as milk, or cream, stouts, and many had such allusions in their brand names. Some consumers may have imagined these references to be metaphorical; others took a more literal view. Surprisingly, the latter were right.

Milk stout had its beginnings in the London of Sherlock Holmes, the fog of time parting to reveal emigrés, inventors and entrepreneurs.

In 1875, John Henry Johnson, of Lincoln's Inn Fields (described in his application as 'gentleman', though he was presumably a lawyer), sought a patent in London for the invention of a milk beer. He received provisional protection for the invention, which envisaged beer being made from whey, milk sugar (lactose) and hops. The inventors were a doctor of medicine and two chemists, Edouard and Pawel Landowksi, and Edouard Kosinski, 'all of Paris, in the Republic of France.' They also proposed a milk liqueur, somewhat ahead of Bailey's Irish Cream.

In 1895–6, the Patent Office accepted a specification from a manager of the Condensed Peptonised Milk Company, of Buckingham, for a similar invention. His application explained peptonizing as the separation of the components of milk by the use of a digestive enzyme that was a pancreatic extract. He proposed that the liquid could be used alone or with water in mashing for a brew.

Some years later, a lecturer in dietetics submitted a specification using lactose to produce a beer that

Sweet stouts, and their 'milk' and 'cream' variations, are often thought of as pick-me-ups, or even tonics for invalids. Many of them still contain milk sugars (lactose), and are relatively low in alcohol, but they need not be reserved for medicinal purposes: they are an excellent dessert drink, especially with fruit cakes.

Mackeson was once persuaded to remove the churn from its label, on the grounds that it misleadingly implied a health benefit. It has now been restored.

Guernsey may be famous for dairy cattle, but there is no longer any milk in its stout. For tradition's sake, the word remains on the label.

would have an improved food value, be lower in alcohol and less gassy. While the food value is a matter of judgment, the latter two factors are inarguable: they derive from the fact that lactose is unfermentable. It could also have been submitted that lactose would add a tinge of its own soft sweetness to the brew.

The dietician subsequently made several agreements with the Mackeson brewery, in the historic little port town of Hythe, Kent. This brewery made a test batch in 1907, put the product on the market, and by 1910 was already seeking a legal opinion over a rival product called Finn's Cream Stout. In 1920, Mackeson sold a controlling interest to Simonds of Reading, Berkshire (which later merged with Courage). Nine years later, the Mackeson brewery was sold off to Jude, Hanbury of Wateringbury, Kent, in which a controlling interest was held by Whitbread. By 1936, Mackeson's Milk Stout was available nationally, and the style began to be included in the range of most breweries.

When the health benefits were examined at an early stage, it was conceded that milk's fats and proteins were not used in brewing, but the lactose does leave carbohydrates and calories in the finished product. What the dairy industry provides as lactose, a by-product of cheese-making, comprises at least 95 percent milk sugars, though it could contain traces of other elements. The original Mackeson label bore the promise: 'Each pint contains the energising carbohydrates of ten ounces of pure dairy milk.' This text was later removed, although the company's position was that, in terms of calories, the beer had a nutritive value equal to good milk, while being lower in alcohol

than other stouts. It was thus thought a suitable, and easily digestible, nutritious beverage for the debilitated or invalid.

Some people drink stout in the belief that it contains iron. To a degree, all beers do. In the authoritative work *The Composition of Foods* (McCance and Widdowson), one unnamed stout is shown to have 0.05 milligrams of iron per 100 millilitres, another 0.02, while paler beers sampled had 0.01 or less. It has been suggested that it is the roasted barley in stouts

Cisk was originally a separate lager brewery, which made what it described as a Münchener stout. The Farsons label above predates the merger of the companies in 1946.

that provides the extra iron. The grains used in beer do contain traces of inorganic materials such as iron and calcium, and I have heard it suggested that roasting might bring about molecular change that binds in such elements, but have seen no scientific evidence to support this.

At a time when the British diet was lower in calories than it is today, and a majority of the populace was engaged in manual work, a sweet, energizing beer was no doubt welcome. After World War II, a debilitated nation faced food shortages. The Ministry of Food, which was trying to put things right by distributing malt extract and powdered milk, exercised its muscle to persuade brewers to remove the lactic language from their labels.

Several brewers found ways of maintaining the allusion. Watney, for example, continued to use their brand name Cream Label Stout, presumably on the

basis that no one could argue with the colour of the paper. Although this product is no longer seen in Britain, an adaptation called simply Watneys Cream Stout, brewed under contract at Ushers of Trowbridge, Wiltshire, is exported to the United States. It is a sweetish, somewhat toffee-like stout, with 26 units of bitterness, a colour of 275 EBC, 3.4 percent alcohol by weight, 4.2 by volume; 1048 (12 Plato).

Outside the jurisdiction of a British government department, the Guernsey Brewery, in the Channel Islands, still makes a product labelled Milk Stout, although it no longer contains lactose.

Consumers for a time still referred to sweet stouts in general as milk stouts, and chose them as a reward after a hard day's work. In the early days of television advertising in Britain, a distinguished actor, Bernard Miles, made a famous commercial with the sales pitch: 'Mackeson looks good, tastes good – and by golly it does you good.' In some markets, the label features a human pyramid, perhaps intended to imply that the beer imparts energy and strength.

As Whitbread grew to become a national giant, acquiring some brewing companies and entering into shareholdings or trading arrangements with others from the 1960s onward, Mackeson Stout replaced many local brands, though several remain.

On the once-British island of Malta, Farsons brewery (see page 188) produces a milk stout, containing lactose. This is served to nursing mothers, and its sales increase greatly in November as an ingredient in Christmas puddings.

In the more distantly British city of Boston, Massachusetts, the Boston Beer Company launched a rich, chocolaty cream stout in 1992. This is made without lactose, from pale, crystal and chocolate malts, along with malted wheat and roast barley, and hopped with Fuggles and Goldings (1056; 14 Plato; 3.5; 4.4). Despite its relative sweetness, Samuel Adams Cream Stout is popular with the Boston Irish on Saint Patrick's Day.

An advertising agency once asked me how I thought this type of stout should be promoted. I suggested that it could be the beer world's answer to Bailey's Irish Cream, but the idea was not pursued. If the notion of a creamy, sweetish, coffee-chocolate drink with a modest amount of alcohol seems quaint in a beer, why has the same combination been so success-ful in a liqueur?

Stout is often suggested as an accompaniment to, or ingredient in, fruit cake, and the sweet style does this job best. For those with a lifestyle sufficiently leisurely, or eclectic, to permit a mid-afternoon or early evening restorative, a glass of sweet stout and a piece of cake is an innocent pleasure.

Oatmeal stout

During the fashion for 'nutritious' stouts, several British brewers began to add oatmeal, an ingredient that has popped up in brewing over the years. From that period, the last oatmeal stout I have been able to trace was made by Eldridge Pope in 1975. In a book in 1977, I casually mentioned that the style had once existed, and around 1980 Samuel Smith of Tadcaster, Yorkshire, was persuaded to produce an oatmeal stout, originally for its importer in the United States: Merchant du Vin of Seattle. Since then, other British brewers have introduced oatmeal stouts, and the style has begun to be produced in the United States.

Brewers with vague recollections of having made the style in the 1950s maintain that they used up to 15 percent oats, though I wonder whether their memories are cheating them. Because oats gelatinize, they can make mashing difficult, and this is no doubt one reason why they are not a major grain in the brewing industry. Even a tiny percentage of oats, in the lower single figures, does seem to have an influence on flavour, unless this is a case of the taster being suggestible. Oatmeal stouts seem to have a distinctly firm, smooth, silky body, and a hint of nuttiness in their complex of coffee, chocolate and roast flavours.

The pioneering Samuel Smith brewery uses a low proportion of the grain, but its oatmeal stout is a good example of the style, deliciously silky, tasty, and delicately poised between the dulcet and the dry. In the end, it decides to be sweet. It has a gravity of 1048 (12 Plato), 3.6 percent alcohol by weight, 4.5 by volume, with 28–32 units of bitterness and a colour of 150–160 EBC.

The first American revivalist, in the late 1980s, was the Buffalo Brewpub, of Williamsville, New York. This pub, in a suburb of Buffalo, produced a light-bodied, smooth, dry oatmeal stout, originally for Saint Patrick's Day. Among the many other examples produced in the United States, I have enjoyed an almost oily, smooth example from the Goose Island brewpub, in Chicago; a smooth, sweetish interpretation from Oasis, in Boulder, Colorado; a soft, cof-feeish, fairly dry entrant from the Humboldt brewery (founded by former Oakland Raiders footballer Mario Celotto) in Arcata, northern California; and, from the same state, a light creamy candidate from Boulder Creek and a smooth, faintly winy one from Seabright in nearby Santa Cruz.

My American favourite is the beautifully silky Barney Flats Oatmeal Stout, from the Anderson Valley brewery at Boonville, California (see page 188).

Young's Oatmeal Stout is slightly oily, with notes of toffee, coffee and bitter chocolate, but is drier and less full in texture than the example from Samuel Smith, the first brewery to revive the style. Samuel Smiths Oatmeal Stout is a natural partner to Atholl brose, a creamy concoction of oatmeal, honey and whisky.

Sweet stout producers

Mackeson is perhaps the best-known sweet stout, while the island of Malta, with historic links with Britain, produces its own version. Both are often used to make the traditional British Christmas pudding.

FARSONS
Simonds, Farsons, Cisk, The Brewery, Mriehel, Malta   Tel: 440331

Simonds of Reading, Berkshire, exported ale and stout to Malta in the late 1800s, then helped a local company, Farrugia and Sons, to set up in 1927. The name was telescoped into Farsons. Around the same time, a rival company set up a lager brewery, the products of which included a bottom-fermenting stout. The breweries merged in 1946, and the Lacto Milk Stout, which uses an ale fermentation, was a product of that union.

Farsons brewery, fringed with palm trees, is a splendid example of 1950s' architecture. It also has a notable hidden feature. Throughout the building and its extensive grounds are ducts that guide all rainwater to a subterranean reservoir. This is Farsons' answer to a permanent shortage of water on the island. The brewhouse, with marble steps, brass rails and copper vessels, produces an interesting range of ales, the stout, and a lager called Cisk (a contraction of the name of the family Scicluna, who have a share in the brewery).

Lacto Stout has a coffee-coloured head and is virtually opaque. It is medium-bodied and slightly oily. The palate starts with a slightly sugary sweetness, then becomes fruitier and drier, with a hint of burnt currants and dark chocolate, and has a creamy finish. The brew is made to a gravity of 1046 (11.5 Plato), with 2.6 percent alcohol by weight, 3.4 by volume, from pale ale, mild ale and crystal malts (the latter accounting for a lot of flavour and colour) and brewer's caramel. It has 30 BU and a colour of 450 EBC. After fermentation, lactose is added in the form of powder. The brew also has added vitamin B.

MACKESON
The Whitbread Beer Company, Porter Tun House, Capability Green, Luton, Bedfordshire LU1 3LS, England Tel: (0582) 391166

The original brewery in Hythe is thought to have been established in 1669. Despite the takeovers in the 1920s, it continued to operate until 1968. Since then, Mackeson Stout has been moved around the Whitbread group, and is currently produced at the company's large, modern brewery at Samlesbury, Lancashire. Although the stout is a small speciality, it is still widely available.

It has a dark head and an almost black colour (225 EBC), with claret highlights. The mouth-feel is big and lightly viscous, though the beer is not satiating. The palate is reminiscent of sweetened espresso without the

grounds, perhaps with a dash of a liqueur thrown in (sambuca?).

Mackeson Stout is brewed from pale ale and chocolate malts, brewer's caramel and lactose, the latter representing at least nine percent of the grist (1042: 10.5; 2.4; 3). The lactose is added as powder to the kettle. It is hopped with Targets, in one addition (26 BU). The export version is made in the same way, but from a gravity of 1059 (around 15.3 Plato; 4; 5), with a colour of 300 EBC and 34 BU. The latter specification makes for a better-balanced character. In order to maintain their fullness of mouth-feel, neither version is centrifuged or filtered, though both are fined and then pasteurized. The lack of filtration means that inorganic elements and proteins will survive to a greater extent than in most other beers. There will also be a proportion of yeast, which contains vitamins, notably B.

OATMEAL STOUT PRODUCER

Anderson Valley, *Buckhorn Saloon, 14081 Highway 128, Boonville, Mendocino County, California 95415, USA Tel: (707) 895-1337*

An outstanding example of an oatmeal stout is made at this Boonville brewpub. The Anderson Valley grows wine-grapes and apples, once cultivated hops, and is said to produce a considerable amount of marijuana. The brewpub was built in a sympathetic style on the site of the early 1900s' Buckhorn Saloon.

Anderson Valley Oatmeal Stout (subtitled Barney Flats – a local allusion) has a flowery aroma, a balance of chocolaty sweetness and roasty dryness, and a silky smoothness all the way to its long finish. This brewery's products are quite widely available. Other products have included an excellent wheat beer, a wild black-

Imperial stout

There are few beers bigger in flavour than the very strong roasty brews once exported by the British, especially to the Baltic, and now often made locally. The export porters and stouts were brewed strong to travel, but their potency also suited Baltic weather and Slavic tastes. In the English-speaking world, these are often described as imperial stouts, the allusion being to their popularity in the Tsarist Empire. Where they are produced locally, the term porter is more widely used.

When a high gravity, roasted grains, and often a warm fermentation, perhaps with an ale yeast, are combined, the result is a brew of extraordinary power and complexity. Its intensity calls to mind the tarry sweetness of a Pedro Ximénez sherry. The roastiness melds with smoky, tar-like, burnt, fruity, estery notes and alcohol flavours. There is a suggestion of cocoa, or strong coffee, on a winter's night. The fruitiness is reminiscent of the burnt currants on the edge of a cake that has just been removed from the oven, or the Christmas pudding traditional in Britain, heavy with dried and candied fruits. The alcohol suggests that the cocoa or coffee, pudding or cake, has been laced with spirit.

Surely this was the style of brew envisaged by the Parisian 'decadent' writer J K Huysmans when, in his 1884 novel *Against Nature*, describing a quest for the rare and perverse in sensation, he imagined an all-black meal, involving Russian rye bread, caviar, game 'in sauces the colour of boot-polish', plum puddings, kvass, porter and stout.

At least ten London breweries made this style in the great days of porters and stouts. A famous area of production was the Thamesside district of Southwark, where Flemish immigrants originally established several breweries.

The brewery that came to be most associated with the style was founded in the 1600s and later owned by a family called Thrale, who were benefactors of the English essayist and lexicographer Dr Samuel Johnson. According to the then Lord Lucan, the aphoristic doctor described the brewery as 'not a parcel of boilers and vats, but the potentiality of growing rich beyond the dreams of avarice.'

From at least 1781, the brewery, through agents, shipped this style of beer to Bremen, probably the Nordic ports and certainly Stettin (Szczecin), Königsberg (Kaliningrad) and other Baltic ports.

The brewery was acquired at that time by a Scottish-American Quaker called Barclay, and later by Courage, founded in 1787 by a Scot of French

The strong porters that the British made for export have left their mark in other lands. In the English-speaking world, this style survives as imperial stout. These stouts combine tar-like notes with 'burnt' fruitiness and alcoholic warmth.

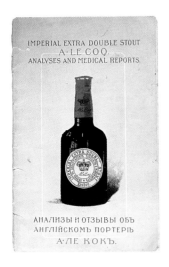

A booklet on the health benefits of imperial stout (brewed for him by Barclay's), shown far left, was produced by the Belgian exporter in Russian.

The label design on the near left features a flash, 'Brewed in Dorpat'. This combines English with the German name for the town of Tartu.

Huguenot background. The Courage group stopped brewing in London in 1980, but its imperial stout is still made, at the group's John Smith's brewery, in Tadcaster, Yorkshire. Brews are vintage-dated, and the label is now rendered partly in Russian. Courage is now owned by Foster's of Australia.

The Estonian connection

In 1869, the Danzig-registered Prussian vessel *Oliva* (487 tons) left London laden with Barclay's Stout and finished its journey on the Baltic seabed. In 1974, Norwegian divers recovered some bottles, which were embossed with the insignia of a mysterious A Le Coq. He turned out to have been a Belgian who shipped beer between London and the Baltic. His company had continued into the 20th century, and one of its retired directors, Stephen Sillem, was still alive. Mr Sillem showed me a manuscript, the length of a novel, written by his brother James, describing in rich sociological detail his adventures in the London-Baltic beer trade.

It begins with James Sillem recalling his father's memories of the British general who had been entertained with London stout by the enemy at the end of the Crimean War; and of tin soldiers, Cossack cavalrymen, brought by his father as gifts from Saint Petersburg during the war between Russia and Japan.

'At this time, Le Coq made large gifts of stout to Russian military hospitals, and for this the firm was later rewarded with the Imperial warrant, of which my father was very proud.'

In the early 20th century, increased import duties persuaded Le Coq that it should brew its own stout within the Russian Empire. The company bought the Tivoli brewery in the old university town of Tartu, then in Livonia and now in Estonia. There had been a brewery on the site since 1823, and Tivoli, established in 1895–8 to produce lager, was adapted by Sillem in 1910–12 to make porter (an unusual reversion). Sillem's account of his life in Livonia is full of black comedy, and stretches to personal encounters with both the SS and the Red Army, before the brewery was finally nationalized. He had also taken photographs of the brewery.

The brewery last produced porter in 1969. When *glasnost* came to the former Empire, I made a snowy pilgrimage to Tartu. The outside of the brewery looked exactly as it did in Mr Sillem's photographs, and I do not think the inside had changed much either. The interesting-looking circular tower turned out to be a maltings, with the grains raked in the kiln by a rotating arm. The director said that his last porter had been made from a gravity of 1080 (20 Plato), bottom-fermented and matured for 75–90 days. I sampled some dryish lagers and asked him whether he could envisage ever again making porter. With independence in sight, and perhaps the end of a command economy, he thought yes, it might be possible.

Just outside the capital, Tallinn, I visited another brewery, among pines by the Saku River. It traced its origins to the brewhouse on the estate of a German landowner in 1820, but had been expanded on an

Tartu brewery, Estonia, on a snowy day in 1990. The round tower accommodates a circular maltings, which was working when this photograph was taken.

Tartu brewery, Livonia, on a snowy day in 1912 or '13. It survived the Russian Revolution, two World Wars and decades behind the Iron Curtain.

industrial scale in 1876. It had its own maltings, and a kettle made in Dresden in 1909. I sampled a sweetish Vienna-style lager and a malty Munich type, and learned that the brewery made a bottom-fermenting porter at Christmas. When the season came, I asked the brewery to send me a bottle, but the mail via Moscow could not deliver. By the next Christmas, Estonia was independent and I was able to sample my first Estonian porter. At 17–20 Plato (1068–80), with 5 percent alcohol by weight, 6.25 by volume, it had a tawny to dark brown colour; both malt and caramel in the aroma; the same notes in the palate, with some coffee; a full body; and a sweetish finish. The Saku brewery has since entered into a collaboration with Hartwall of Finland, and it is to be hoped that its Christmas Porter survives.

Finland

A Russian, Nikolai Sinebrychoff, founded Finland's oldest extant brewery in 1819. Despite past Russian rule in Finland, or perhaps because of it, such names are deemed hard to pronounce; Sinebrychoff is often abbreviated to Koff. The brewery originally produced mead, top-fermenting beer and porter. In 1853, lager was added. From the turn of the century, there was Prohibition in Finland, during which time the brewery made near-beers and malt drinks.

After the two World Wars, Koff reintroduced its porter, perhaps to coincide with the 1952 Olympics. No top-fermenting yeast had been stored, and a starter sample was allegedly removed from a bottle of

Brewed in Britain, but clearly labelled Imperial Russian Stout. This example was for many years the only product to use the designation.

Guinness. No one can provide evidence that this story is true, but the way in which the yeast behaves does seem to correspond with that at Guinness. Koff is a very scientifically minded brewery, but not without a sense of tradition. In its brewhouse, I noticed that its angular, stainless-steel kettle had been decorated with a plastic hop-vine.

In the Baltic countries, porters are now regarded as rather quaint, but the story of their origins has re-kindled interest in the English-speaking world. Koff Porter was for a time exported to the United States under the name Imperial Stout, and perhaps will be again – if it survives the company's move to a new brewery just outside Helsinki.

Koff Porter is very much in the imperial style: big, intense, very dry, smooth and oily, full of flavour, with lots of roastiness, definite but restrained fruit, and more hop than many in the region. It is made with four malts, Northern Brewer and Hersbruck hops. The beer has a gravity of 17 Plato (1068), 5.5–5.8 per-cent alcohol by weight, 6.8–7.2 by volume, a colour of 250–300 EBC, and 50 BU. It is warm-conditioned in tanks for six weeks, not filtered, but flash-pasteurized.

In Estonian, *olu* means beer. It is linked to the English word ale.

This Polish porter, at 22 Plato, would qualify as an imperial stout.

Estonia is a small country, with a splintered history, but it has a rich folk art concerning brewing. This stained-glass window in the Tartu brewery is an example. The facial features are a reminder that these are not Slavic people, but a Uralic group related to the Finns and Lapps. The Russian-sounding Sinebrychoff Porter (far right) is well worth an imperial crown.

Scandinavia

The Baltic had many Scottish settlers in the late 1700s and early 1800s, and one named Carnegie established a porter brewery in Gothenburg. This later merged with Pripps, which became the largest brewing company in Sweden, and Carnegie Porter is now made at Pripps' brewery near Stockholm, still as a top-fermenting brew.

For a time, Carnegie Porter was available only by doctor's prescription, as a tonic, and then for a period only in Sweden's 'Class II' strength, at 9 Plato (1036; 2.8; 3.5). In 1985, the Class III version was reintroduced, at 15.5 Plato (1061–2; 4.5; 5.6). The following year, Pripps started to release an annual vintage edition, with six months' maturation in tank. Although the beer is filtered and pasteurized, the brewery feels that its flavours meld and give it notes of port or Madeira. It has a very dense head; a soft body; and a very deep flavour, with notes of roasted coffee, toffee and the promised Madeira. In 1992, the Class II version was voted the world's best top-fermenting beer of its gravity in the annual competition judged by working brewers in Britain.

Alone among its neighbours, Norway does not seem to have a tradition of this style of brewing, but it has in recent years gained the odd example. In 1991, I tasted a top-fermenting imperial stout at the Oslo Mikro Bryggeri (which, despite its name, is not a micro but a brewpub). This was very smooth, creamy and chocolaty, with some fruitiness and a dry, hoppy finish (14–15 Plato, 1055–60).

Several breweries in Denmark make examples, usually bottom-fermenting, and variously described as porter or stout. Albani, of Odense, has a distinctively, firm, malty porter (20; 1083; 6.2; 7.8). Carlsberg's version is described on the label both as Gammel ('old') Porter and Imperial Stout. It has a deliciously chewy 'burnt toffee' character (18.8; 1075; 6.1; 7.7). Carlsberg's sister company Tuborg has a similar porter, slightly creamy and oily, burnt-tasting and dryish. Ceres, of Aarhus, has in different markets labelled its entrant as Gammel Jysk ('Jutland') Porter, Stout and, with phonetic helpfulness, Stowt. This has a very distinctive character, with fruitiness, spiciness, hints of licorice (though none is used) and iron. Very aromatic Munich malt seems to be the keynote. This beer has 18 Plato (1072), and 6.1 percent alcohol by weight, 7.7 by volume.

Britain

The growth of interest in this style led the British brewery Samuel Smith to introduce an example in the 1980s. This is now easily available in Britain, though it was originally made for the United States market. Like so many of this brewery's beers, it is an excellent product. It has perhaps the best 'burnt currants' character among the imperial stouts, and is full of flavour and complexity without being the heaviest in body. It is brewed with pale ale and crystal malts, roasted barley and sugar, and hopped with Fuggles and Goldings. Its gravity is 1072 (18; 5.6; 7). It is one of history's quirks that a style associated with London should be made by two breweries, both originating from the same Smith family, in the tiny town of Tadcaster, in rural Yorkshire.

A variation on the theme has been created by brewer Jim Pryor, who has over the years worked for Bass, Courage and Whitbread. Pryor became involved in the establishment of English-style pubs in Russia, and encountered nostalgia among some drinkers for the porters and dark beers of the distant past. His researches in Russia led him to believe that these had been made with brown malt, and he was able to obtain in central Europe a yeast that he felt might help to impart an authentic character. In 1993, he launched in Britain a product called Vassilinsky's Black Russian Beer, made under contract at the McMullen brewery in Hertford. At 1048 (12 Plato), this is less of an imperial stout than a porter in the modern sense, but it is surprisingly big, complex, smooth and warming for its gravity. It is almost solid black, with ruby highlights; has both sweetness and dryness, lots of bitter-chocolate notes; and finishes with a yeasty spiciness. This beer is also unusual in that it is bottle-conditioned.

North America

In Canada, I have greatly enjoyed a lightly chewy, somewhat herbal imperial stout from Wellington County, of Guelph, Ontario. This was experimentally brewed to 5.2 percent alcohol by weight, 6.5 by volume, then dropped to 4.4, 5.5. Another Ontario microbrewery, Conner's, has used the term imperial stout to describe a smooth, roasty, dry product at 4 percent alcohol by weight, 5 by volume. In Calgary, the Big Rock micro has a rich, powerful porter called Cold Cock, at 4.8, 6. The Okanagan Spring brewery, in Vernon, British Columbia, has a full-bodied, rounded Old English Porter (6.8, 8.5), with a depth of fruity, rummy and coffeeish flavours.

In the United States, Grant's Imperial Stout is one of the classics made at the microbrewery in Yakima, Washington. Grant's depicts the Imperial palace on the label, and proclaims this brew 'a favorite of the

Samuel Smith's Imperial Stout is an outstanding beer, first brewed in the 1980s.

Czar's court.' It is unusual in that it is made with honey as well as pale, crystal and black malts. Whether the honey lingers in the flavour is hard to say, but there is plenty of bitter-chocolate and a dash of burnt fruit, with some tongue-coating oiliness and alcoholic warmth (17–17.5; 1068–72; 4.8–5.3; 6–6.5). I once tasted an even more intense version made as an experiment for the brewery's tavern. I loved it, but the customers thought it was too much of a good thing.

Japan

Across the Pacific in Japan, the country's biggest brewer, Kirin, makes a strong stout with a full, smooth body and lots of treacle-toffee flavour (18; 1072; 6.4; 8). Asahi produces a top-fermenting stout that is distinguished by an intentional *Brettanomyces* fermentation, a remarkable survival; Asahi, like its rivals, is among the world's most technologically advanced breweries, and is better known for the dubious achievement of having invented an almost-tasteless product called Dry Beer. The astonishing Asahi stout has a whisky-like, smoky aroma; a soft, smooth body (the label rightly, and charmingly, refers to satin); a palate reminiscent of fruit cake doused in Pedro Ximénez sherry; and a lingering dryness (17; 1068; 6.4; 8).

This brew is made only once every couple of years, though it can look after itself long enough to remain available between times. If the market requires such infrequent batches, why does the brewery persist? A brewer at Asahi cheerfully told me: 'We brew it less for our customers than for ourselves, to keep up our techniques. With each brew, we get together to taste it and discuss it. Inside the brewery, we know each batch by the name of the individual brewer who made it, and we like to compare them.'

Tropical stouts

Singapore is best known for its Tiger beer, a lager not a thousand miles from Heineken (the Dutch brewers have a share in the company). Tiger's producers, Malayan Breweries, also make a strong (1073; 18.2; 6.5; 8.1), bottom-fermenting stout, with a toffeeish palate. Similar stouts are made in several tropical regions of the world, typically in Africa and the West Indies. They are clearly a vestige of British Imperial rule, but do not have quite the character of some made in colder countries. Some could be described as strong dry stouts, but others are too sweet for that designation. Around 1060 (15 Plato), it becomes

difficult to produce a true dry stout, as the malty fullness and the fruity esters take charge.

Two of the most interesting tropical stouts I have tasted were in Sri Lanka. Just outside Colombo, the McCallum 'Three Coins' Brewery looks across a valley of banana trees and coconut palms to Adam's Peak, where the first man is said to have left his footprint. Islam and Buddhism have similar legends concerning the same mountain. In this Garden of Eden, I once enjoyed a chocolaty, smooth, full-bodied stout (1060, 15) named after Sando (Eugene Sandow), a circus strong-man from the Baltic, who became internationally famous in the 1890s under the management of Florenz Ziegfeld. This stout was made with pale, crystal and chocolate malts from Scotland, and German and Czech hops.

Farther into the mountains, the Buddhist holy city of Kandy was the unlikely location of my first encounter with cask-conditioned stout, in the mid-1980s. Both there and in the tea-planting town of Nuwara Eliya, where it is made, the stout was soft, fruity, fresh and quite delicious. This was the top-fermenting Lion Stout (1060; 15; 5; 6.2), from the Ceylon Brewery. The Lover's Leap Waterfall provided the first ingredient for this brew, with malt from the Czech Republic, Britain and Denmark; Styrian hops; and an English yeast; and the stout was

The beer house of UKD Silva in Kandy, Sri Lanka. Inside, strong stout is kept in wooden casks.

The Beer Shop, in Nuwara Eliya, is also a very basic bar, on the lines of a frontier saloon. It too, keeps Lion Stout in the cask and serves it on hand-pump. The condition of the beer varies; at its best, it is delicious.

being fermented in wooden vessels. The brewery dates from the late 1800s, and was built to quench the thirsts of tea-planters. At 3,500 feet, and seven hours by precarious roads to the capital, it can have few rivals in remoteness from both raw materials and major markets. In Britain in 1992, I tasted Lion Stout again. It was bottle-conditioned and had an extraordinarily chocolaty, mocha, liqueur-like character.

Sri Lankan fishermen are said to warm themselves with stout laced with the local arrack, distilled from coconut. This combination is one of the world's most potent and delicious drinks. With a lacing of arrack, Lion Stout is a wonderful accompaniment to creamy coconut desserts.

Of the many richer styles that go well with desserts, especially chocolate, the very strongest porters and imperial stouts are the champions. In Seattle, I was once served chocolate truffles in which the ingredients had been bound with imperial stout. This sweetmeat was presented as Imperial Truffles.

Classic producer

COURAGE
John Smith's Brewery, Tadcaster, North Yorkshire LS24 9SA, England Tel: (0937) 832091

Courage still uses the designation Imperial Russian Stout, with a reference to Empress Catherine, on its label. Early allusions to such strong brews mention gravities just into the 1100s (around 25 Plato). Modern

John Smith's, best known for its Magnet bitter, has in recent years made Courage's Imperial.

gravities of Courage's Imperial Russian Stout have hovered around that figure. When I visited the brewery, the stout was being collected into the fermenter at at 1106.8. After the addition of a fining solution, it was being declared for excise at 1102. Some bottlings have been labelled 1098, though this seems a minimum estimate. Alcohol by volume has varied between 7.6–8.5 percent by weight, 9.5–10.5 by volume.

In London, and for as long as anyone can remember (although it cannot be earlier than 1842), this beer always contained a proportion of Pilsner malt, and still does, perhaps a vestige of its Continental destinations. It also contains pale ale, amber and black malts, and some cane-derived invert sugar. It is hopped with Targets, in just one addition.

It begins with a conventional top-fermentation, at 23–24°C/73–75°F, for five or six days, with the John Smith's house yeast, and 'goes like a bomb' according to the brewer. It then has a further two weeks of warm conditioning in the same tank. After this, it is moved to another tank for several weeks' maturation. It is fined in the tank, then bottled without filtration or pasteurization. It has around 50 units of bitterness and a colour of 235 EBC.

In London, it used to be kept at the brewery for 18 months or two years before being released. Now, the consumer is left to do the laying down. I kept a sample of the first Tadcaster batch and sampled it ten years later. When I compared a bottle fresh from the brewery with the ten-year-old, the latter was still remarkably lively, but had become much leaner, drier, more coffeeish and more warming.

The two Smith breweries in Tadcaster originate from the same family, and their sites interlock. The present John Smith's brewery was built in 1883, and is a magnificent Victorian construction, with a dray (minus horses) outside as a reminder of its history. The original brewhouse was augmented by a second in 1976, then replaced by a third (stainless steel, in traditional shapes) in 1984–5. The brewery formerly used slate Yorkshire Square fermenters, and a couple of these are kept in a small but interesting museum. An item in the museum shows that John Smith's once produced an imperial stout under its own name, though the brewery is better known for its nutty-tasting Magnet bitter.

LAGERS

To lager is to lay down. In German, a *Lager* means a bed, a camp, a stockade or a storehouse. A lager is a beer which is fermented with a yeast that works at cool temperatures – then laid down for cold maturation, or 'storage', at close to 0°C/32°F in tanks at the brewery. Once filtered and bottled or kegged, this type of beer is not intended for further laying down. It will not improve in character, and may deteriorate. Lager yeasts produce beers that are characteristically clean and rounded, though not always complex.

The odd very strong lager has a period of cold maturation running to nine months. Three is traditional, and two or one more common. Even in Germany, some breweries now cold-mature their beer for less than a month. In the English-speaking world three weeks is thought respectable and a fortnight acceptable.

A lager fermented at classically low temperatures (5–9°C/41–48°F), and cold-matured for months rather than weeks, has a foamy, soft, delicious drinkability that cannot be matched by hastier products. It is argued that lesser maturation is required for lagers made with a high proportion of corn or rice, but that is to heap one inadequacy upon another.

The cold-storage was originally a means of conserving beer in summer, when it was impossible to brew. The Bavarians took beers in the cask to icy caves in the foothills of the Alps, and they learned empirically that this not only prevented the beer from souring but also built in stability.

In the regions traditionally associated with this type of brewing, the term lager is used by the consumer to some extent in the Czech Republic, and widely in Austria and Switzerland, but rarely in Germany, the Netherlands or

Scandinavia. A German drinker will be more specific. If he requires a basic golden lager, he will ask for a *Helles* (light or pale). This request is likely to bring forth a well-balanced, but lightly malt-accented, lager of about 11.2 Plato (1044–5) with an alcohol content of 3.7 percent by weight, 4.6 by volume, and 20-plus units of bitterness. Although this is a Bavarian style, none of Munich's breweries regards it as a speciality, and it is being superseded in many beer-halls by the Pilsner and Export types.

A Pilsner lager is also golden, but has a slightly higher gravity and is clearly accented toward hop bouquet and dryness. The Export style, especially associated with Dortmund, is slightly higher still in gravity, well-balanced, with a slight tilt toward dryness.

The lagers of Vienna are on the sweet side, but no longer have the full maltiness or reddish colour associated with the city. This style is still found in some of the most traditional Märzen-Oktoberfest beers in Germany, and from some American microbrewers.

The original lagers of Munich were dark brown, and this style is identified as a *Dunkel* or a *Dunkles*. Some notably dark examples are classified as *Schwarz* (black). In the Netherlands, the term lager traditionally meant a dark, sweet style known as Oud Bruin ('old brown').

In many countries a strong lager is known as a bock. An extra-potent example is known as a doppel ('double') bock.

Some British drinkers think, wrongly, that lager is not beer. The North Americans take the opposite view. Unless he is an enthusiast, a North American drinker talking of 'beer' probably has in mind a lager. His understanding is that 'beer' does not include ale.

Two outstanding brews of the new generation in America do identify themselves as lagers, without specifying a style. Samuel Adams Boston Lager has the hop aroma and character of a Pilsner. Brooklyn Lager has the colour and malt character of a Vienna-style lager, but with much more hop aroma and bitterness.

Outside the traditional brewing nations, most of the world's everyday beers are lagers, usually blandly distant derivations of the Pilsner type.

Dark lager

Was it dark beer that had once filled the amphorae dating from 800 BC and subsequently found in a burial site at Kasendorf, in Upper Franconia, northern Bavaria? At that time, it is somewhat unlikely to have been anything else. These oldest relics of beer-brewing in Germany lay almost equidistant from Lichtenfels and Kulmbach, Bamberg and Bayreuth, an area that is still a heartland of dark brews.

Today, most of them are dark lagers. There are also several beers in this style across the nearby border in Bohemia. At its most sophisticated, this style combines the dryish, coffee and licorice notes of dark malts with the roundness and cleanness imparted by a lager yeast.

There are more breweries per kilometre, more dark lagers, and there is more idiosyncrasy (a rare quality in Germany) in Franconia than anywhere else in the country. This is the area in which to explore some of Germany's oldest and smallest breweries, often

making beer just for their own tavern and beer garden. These country brews, many of them to varying degrees dark, are full of grainy, hoppy, yeasty charm. They will never be seen in the cities, let alone the export markets.

The first Franconian town to develop a reputation far beyond its boundaries was Kulmbach, which has been a brewing centre at least since monks made beer there in 1349, and which stands at the meeting point of two branches of the Main, one of Germany's principal rivers. Kulmbach competed as a brewing centre with the university town of Erlangen and with Munich until the advantage began to swing to the bigger, more sophisticated city. Near Kulmbach is Berndorf, the birthplace in 1842 of Carl von Linde, whose pioneering work on refrigeration did much to help lager-brewers in Munich refine their art.

Kulmbach had a reputation for the heaviest and darkest lagers, followed by Erlangen, then Munich. Erlangen still has the odd brewery, but Kulmbach remains one of Germany's biggest beer-making towns. At the edge of the town, Kulmbach announces itself with an arrangement of huge barrels (restored wooden lagering tanks?), each bearing the name of one of the town's breweries. Kulmbacher Mönchshof is the brewery most associated with dark lager, though its malt-accented Kloster Schwarz-Bier is hardly black, with a colour of 55 EBC (12.5 Plato; 1050; 4 percent alcohol by weight, 5 by volume; 26 BU).

The term 'Kulmbacher' is still occasionally used by brewers in other parts of the world to indicate a very dark lager. In 1987, Ed and Carol Stoudt made malty Kulmbacher Lager in the brewery and restaurant that bears their name, in Adamstown, Pennsylvania. Perhaps they will make it again one day. Not far away in Pittsburgh, the Allegheny pub, in the former Eberhardt and Ober brewery, has made a smooth, chocolaty, burgundy-brown Penn Dark. In New Orleans, the wonderfully antique Dixie brewery came late to the craze for Cajun food with its Blackened Voodoo beer, a dark lager with a treacle-toffee taste. In the unlikely location of a former copper quarry in Bisbee, Arizona, electrician-turned-microbrewer Dave Harvan has made his own contribution to the style. While his cleverly named Electric Light is a golden lager, his Electric Dark is a chocolaty brew that might be

The Ayinger range includes a dark lager called Altbairisch Dunkel, with a hint of coffee.

Before golden lagers existed, there were dark ones. What the Germans call simply a *Dunkel* is usually a dark brown lager. This is a traditional style in Munich and has historical associations with Erlangen and Kulmbach. The best examples have a spicy maltiness that is neither sweet nor roastily dry, with the clean roundness that derives from the use of a lager yeast, working at low temperatures.

regarded as a Kulmbacher. Presented with it blindfold, I might identify as a Kulmbacher-style Xingu beer, from Brazil. This has a spicy, licorice-like taste, but I doubt its purportedly Amazonian origins.

The designations 'Bavarian' or 'Munich-style' are much more widely employed, from Scandinavia to the Americas. Most Norwegian breweries include a Bayer ('Bavarian') lager in their portfolios; because this style has declined in popularity in recent decades, enthusiasts have started their own appreciation society in an effort to protect it.

These allusions date from the heyday of dark lager in Bavaria, from around 1840 to the 1890s. Although the lagering technique had been mentioned 400 years earlier, in the minutes of the Munich town council, it was not until that period that brewers began to understand it beyond an empirical level. The leader of this movement was Gabriel Sedlmayr II, at the Spaten brewery. After studying brewing in many other European countries, he returned to Munich in 1834. Sedlmayr's first celebrated lager was dark, and that product is remembered today in Spaten Dunkel Export: light to medium in body, lightly malty, with some spicy, coffeeish notes, but neither excessively sweet nor roasty, and with a light underpinning of hop (12.7 Plato; 1051; 4 percent alcohol by weight, 5 by volume; 47 EBC; 20 BU). Despite its name, the Export is not widely available in overseas markets.

When drinkers in the Americas talk of a 'dark beer' they most often mean a lager of the Bavarian style. It may be a domestic example such as the modestly malty Michelob Classic Dark, from America's (and the world's) biggest brewer, or one from a microbrewery, or it may be an import from Europe, or even San Miguel Dark, from the Philippines.

Although most of the Bavarian brewers still have a dark lager (a *Dunkel* or *Dunkles*) in their range, few do anything to promote these products locally. Some have done more in export markets, although the 'Munich dark' lagers sold abroad are often of the stronger bock type (see pages 224–231).

Dark lagers have probably survived best in this part of Germany because Franconia especially, and Bavaria as a whole, are very conservative, each in their own way. Franconia became a part of Bavaria only after the Napoleonic Wars. The Franconians are regarded as quiet, perhaps taciturn, the rest of the Bavarians more given to flag-waving. Some brewers elsewhere argue that dark lagers lingered because it was difficult to make pale brews; Bavarian barleys were too high in protein. That is no longer the case, but it may explain the tradition of the intensive, triple-decoction mash. Many brewers retain this method for their dark lagers, though not necessarily for the golden brews.

Spaten produced its first pale lager in 1894, and its Munich rival Paulaner claims to have popularized the golden style in the 1920s and 1930s. After World War II, dark lagers lost further ground to the more 'modern' golden ones, but in recent years there have been the stirrings of interest in the earlier style.

A conspicuous revivalist has been the energetic Prince Luitpold of Bavaria, whose castle, with a

Countryside near Kulmbach, where mountain streams become rivers, and meet the forests.

brewery at its heart, is on the hill called Kaltenberg, near the village of Geltendorf, 30 miles west of Munich. 'Berg' means hill, and 'dorf' village. What of Kalten or Gelten? Both probably derive from the word Celt, which identifies the original settlers in the area. At the beginning of this millennium, the site had become a monastic community. By the 1200s, a castle had been built by Duke Rudolph of Bavaria. The site passed back and forth between religious, royal and secular hands, and castles were built then destroyed in various conflicts. The present castle was established in 1670, but owes much of its current shape to a remodelling in the neo-Gothic vein around 1848. Parts of Kaltenberg were designed by the architect who created Neuschwanstein Castle for 'Mad' King Ludwig II of Bavaria. (Ludwig retreated into mythology, Wagnerian fantasy and grandiosity when Bavaria seemed in 'danger' of being absorbed into a unified Germany. Neuschwanstein was later an inspiration to Walt Disney.)

All big houses of the time would have had breweries, but in the late 1800s Kaltenberg opened its own tavern, and in 1872 began to brew for other local inns.

The royal family of Bavaria, the Wittelsbachs, ruled from 1180 to World War I, and their kingdom flowed with beer. There is, in these old provinces of Upper and Lower Bavaria, a sense of natural order. The Alpine snow melts, providing brewers with both water and well-irrigated barley for malting, and the ripening sun coaxes a thirst from the god-fearing, churchgoing people. As early as 1260, it was recorded that Duke Ludwig had 'a fine brewery'. Another Wittelsbach, Wilhelm IV – who ensured at the time of the Reformation that Bavaria remained Roman Catholic – initiated the Beer Purity Law (Reinheitsgebot) in 1516. He thus secured the place of hops, which grow well locally, as the only seasoning in German beer. Duke Albrecht is believed to have founded a Royal Court Brewery (Hofbräuhaus), and Wilhelm V to have established the present one in 1589. In 1810, the betrothal of Prince Ludwig (who became King Ludwig I) to Princess Theresia inspired the Munich Oktoberfest (although it was no doubt based on earlier, less grand, end-of-summer celebrations).

As the Hofbräuhaus is now owned by the State of Bavaria, part of the modern republic of Germany, the royal family no longer has a major brewery within the city limits of Munich. This means that Prince Luitpold's beers do not qualify to be offered at the festival commemorating his forebear.

Prince Luitpold has no other difficulties with the role of royals in a republic; he believes they should

The castle of Kaltenberg was built in a high, defensible position. Its lagering cellars are cut into the hillside underneath.

The steel tanks are used for fermentation, and sometimes lagering. Most of the lagering is in horizontal tanks, some in wood.

The Kings Ludwig were Prince Luitpold's ancestors. His Dunkel, a 'modern' dark lager, is his house speciality.

work for a living, and he has done so by running Kaltenberg's brewery since he was in his mid-20s.

When he took over, in 1976, he decided that a small brewery needed a speciality. The range already included a dark lager, and he decided to develop this. To give it the possibility of more malt flavours, he increased the original gravity from 11.5 to 13.2–3 Plato (1053), but also attenuated it further, so that it would not be full-bodied or especially sweet.

Traditional dark lagers in Bavaria have an attenuation of 65–70 percent, producing a fullness which I feel suits the style. Prince Luitpold's speciality, called König Ludwig Dunkel, is taken to 79 percent, and is thus only medium in body. On one visit, I politely suggested that it was perhaps lacking in texture, and next time noticed that it had gained more malt character. This turned out to be due to the introduction of a more aromatic dark malt, from Belgium. The beer has a tawny-to-dark colour, of 40 EBC.

A triple-decoction mash is employed, and the brew is hopped three times in the kettle, with Hallertau-Hersbruck and Tettnang (the beer has 26 BU). A Weihenstephan yeast is used, and the brew is *kräusened* to give it just a touch of spritziness.

An unusual feature of the production method is dry-hopping. Many German brewers do not like this 'English' practice, because they feel it can introduce oxidation or infection (a counterargument is that the hops form a barrier against intruders). Prince Luitpold takes the precaution of blanching his hops in boiling water before adding them to the lagering vessel. Lagering is for five to six weeks.

König Ludwig Dunkel starts with that characteristic spritziness, then rounds into a firm maltiness, and finishes with dryish notes of coffee and figs. It is filtered, but not pasteurized.

When Prince Luitpold took over, the brewhouse could make 25,000 hectolitres a year. It can now produce 85,000, and he has plans to expand it to 120,000. The brewhouse, central to the main fabric of the castle and facing onto the courtyard, is still small and neat, with copper vessels and blue tiling.

The castle has a restaurant, serving excellent German food, called the Bräustüberl. There is also in the grounds a tavern, called the Ritter Schwemme (*Ritter* is German for knight, and *Schwemme* is a colloquial term for a busy bar), and a beer garden with space for 2,000 people. All the draught beers in the garden are dark styles: besides the König Ludwig Dunkel, there is, during Lent, a dryish but rounded and malty Ritter Bock, and a dark wheat beer (Dunkles Weissbier) with a sherbety palate.

The caves at Kaltenberg are very typical of early lagering cellars. The vessels, each holding 5,000 litres, were bought second-hand in 1870. There are about 60 of them, and some are still used, for seasonal beers. They are lined with pitch, and the brewery employs a cooper to keep them in good condition. The cellars are reached by a seemingly endless, narrow, steep spiral of stone steps in the walls of the castle.

There are still locals to talk politics in U Fleků, despite the fact that every visitor to Prague quite sensibly wishes to see this famous pub. Like all such institutions, it is a place to be explored. Its many paintings and frescos, inside and out (in the beer garden), include a magnificently tragic work called *The Last Beer*, by turn-of-the-century artist Lad'a Novak.

The Kloster is no longer the cloister of a monastery, but the lager-house still lives up to its name. The dark lager made here has a full flavour and a dry maltiness. This is one of nine breweries in Bamberg, Bavaria. It dates its foundation to 1533, which would narrowly make it the town's oldest. It was founded as the Prince-Bishop's Brown Beer brewery.

The notion of all the beers being dark did cause some complaints at first, the Prince conceded, but it soon became a talking point. 'People began to say: "That place is famous for its dark beer".'

Almost all of the castle brewery's output is dark lager. Kaltenberg's golden lagers and wheat beers are made at a larger brewery in the nearby town of Fürstenfeldbruck, on the River Amper. Products there include the 'diet' Pils type known in Britain.

Frustrated at his brewery's exclusion from the Munich Oktoberfest, Prince Luitpold holds an annual jousting tournament in the castle grounds. Over three weekends in July, there are now seven performances in an arena seating 10,000 spectators. The jousters are skilled horsemen who do not mind taking falls at high speeds; the rest of the year, they work in circuses or as film stuntmen. Their encounters at Kaltenberg are based on the rules of tournaments in the days of chivalry. With falconers, tumblers, jugglers, troubadours and trinket-vendors pressing their trades, dusk falls and the flames of an ox-roast play on the castle. The crowds gather over the dusty earth and straw, and it is easy to imagine the heady atmosphere on the eve of a medieval battle. The moment calls for an historic brew, something dark and satisfying. The beer served there is König Ludwig Dunkel.

Schlossbrauerei Kaltenberg, *8 Schloss Strasse, 8085 Geltendorf, Germany. Tel: (08193) 8071. Reservations for jousting: (08193) 5055.*

Dark lager producers

Bohemia and Bavaria are the homelands. Elsewhere, a beer simply labelled 'dark' is often an undistinguished example, but the new brewers of Middle America are rediscovering the region's lager heritage.

ALTSTADTHOF

Hausbrauerei Altstadthof, 18 Berg Strasse, 8500 Nuremberg, Germany
Tel: (0911) 20 39 84

Visitors to Franconia who do not get beyond its biggest city, Nuremberg, should make sure to visit the Old Town (in German, the *Altstadt*). In the Old Town Courtyard (*Altstadthof*), off Berg Strasse, is a tiny 'house brewery' making dark lager and selling it in swing-top bottles.

The buildings date from the 1500s, and the Hausbrauerei Altstadthof presents the brewing techniques of the 1700s, but it was established in 1984. It has a copper brewhouse, open wort-cooler, and wooden fermenters and lagering vessels. Its beer has a malty, yeasty aroma; a creamy head; a deep tawny colour, almost opaque; a yeastily dry, smooth palate, becoming rich and malty, with hints of licorice in the finish. It is made with organically grown barley malt and hops, and has a gravity of 12–12.5 Plato (1048–50).

The beer can be sampled on draught in the *Altstadt*: with sweet steamed puddings at a nearby lunch spot called the Dampfnudel, or in the evening at the tavern Schmelztiegl.

AYINGER

Brauerei Inselkammer, 1 Zornedinger Strasse, 8011 Aying, Germany
Tel: (08095) 8815

This country brewery, taking its name from its home village in the foothills of the Alps, just outside Munich, makes a wide range of typical Bavarian beers. Its dark lager, Altbairisch Dunkel, is a good example. This beer is almost opaque, with tawny tinges when it is held up to the light. It has a warm aroma, a malty start and a coffeeish finish. The beer is made from two malts, with a dark kilning much in evidence, and is only lightly hopped (13 Plato; 1052; 3.9 percent alcohol by weight, 4.9 by volume; 21 BU; 52 EBC).

There is believed to have been a tavern since the 1300s on the site where the clutch of Ayinger buildings now stand: the tiny maltings, the brewery, its beer garden, restaurant and small hotel. The oldest surviving buildings date in part from the 1550s, though there is more evidence of the 1870s. The guesthouse was built, in traditional style, in the 1920s. Outside stands the maypole traditional in Bavarian villages, decorated with scenes of forestry, farming, brewing and baking. Inside, the range of beers can be paired with some serious dishes. I have greatly enjoyed the dark lager with apple pancake.

The Inselkammers, who own the brewery, have been farmers in Aying since 1804, and still grow some of their own barley. Franz Inselkammer is a respected figure in the Bavarian brewing industry.

U FLEKŮ

Pivovar U Fleků, 1 Kremencova, Prague 1, Czech Republic
Tel: (02) 296417

The most famous of the several dark lagers made in the Czech Republic is the house beer at the brewpub U Fleků, in Prague. This establishment is itself the most famous tavern in the city. It was founded in 1499, and in part dates from the 1700s, but nonetheless contrives to be in the quarter known as the New Town. The tavern is named after its one-time owners the Flekovske family.

The large, protruding clock of U Fleků is a Prague landmark, but the tavern's exterior does little to hint at the number of rooms, or the hidden beer garden overlooked by the brewery. The copper brewhouse, renewed in the 1980s, is set into smart green tiles. On the wall is decoratively painted the homily, 'God bless the mother who gives birth to a brewmaster', with a painting of the incumbent (recognizably so) receiving the gift of barley and hops from the good Lord. That personal touch survived some of Prague's darker days.

Four malts are used, to a gravity of 13 Plato (1052), in a double-decoction system, and the beer is hopped three times, with Saaz. The beer emerges with 3.6 percent alcohol by weight, 4.5 by volume. It has a fruity-malty aroma (a fresh 'cellar' character); a very dense, rocky head; a deep brown, almost black, colour; a soft, light, malty start; a light but smooth body; and a hint of licorice in the finish.

An order for *Pivni Syr* brings an accompaniment of a very salty, creamy, smelly 'beer cheese', served with rye bread. This combination is known as a 'miner's breakfast'. In the evenings, one of the larger rooms presents a cabaret, in Czech, for which tickets must be booked.

Other dark lagers can be found in Prague, among them the drier Branik, the sharper Rakovanka, the more

Old lagering vessels, seen through U Fleků's brewery arch.

After the tavern U Fleků, Prague's best-known landmark is probably the Charles Bridge over the River Vltava (in German, Moldau). The bridge has breathtaking cityscapes on both sides – and walks on either side lead to a beer.

caramelly Regent, and the splendidly malty Krušovice. As these have pale counterparts, it is necessary to specify dark (*Tmavé*, in Czech). Not all taverns stock dark lagers, and some consider them suitable only for women.

LAKEFRONT

Lakefront Brewery, 818A E Chambers Street, Milwaukee, Wisconsin 53212, USA
Tel: (414) 372-8800

A Milwaukee policeman, his brother and their home-brewing partner founded this tiny business in 1987, initially as a part-time venture. With a two-barrel batch size, it was one of America's smallest breweries, though it has grown since.

The brewery is in a 1911 bakery building, part of an old Polish neighbourhood that has begun to attract some arty inhabitants.

Klisch Dark Lager Beer, named after one of the partners, is reddish-black, almost opaque. It is firm-bodied, slightly syrupy, with some aromatic maltiness and a hint of chocolate, especially in the long finish. It is bottled with a yeast sediment.

Lakefront makes a wide range of flavourful, beautifully balanced beers.

SPRECHER

Sprecher Brewing Co, 730 W Oregon Street, Milwaukee, Wisconsin 53204, USA
Tel: (414) 272-2337

Randy Sprecher once worked for the then-mighty Pabst, in Milwaukee. Since 1986 he has had his own microbrewery, in the same city. One of his most popular beers is a dark lager.

The beer has an original gravity of 15 Plato (1060), closer to that of a bock, and emerges with only 4.8 percent alcohol by weight, 6 by volume, but is called Black Bavarian. It could be regarded as a black beer, or as a Bavarian dark. Perhaps it is a true example of the old Kulmbacher style.

That was the note I made when I tasted the first batch, out of the lagering tank. More recent tastings have not changed my mind. Black Bavarian is very dark, almost opaque; soft, smooth, with hints of treacle toffee toward its very big, dryish finish.

Sprecher makes a wide range of other styles, including sweetish, fruity wheat beers. The brewery has no pub, but it does have a shop, selling beer and cheese. It is not easy to find, reached by a drive across a web of railroad tracks.

Vienna-style, Märzen/Oktoberfestbier

For mouthwatering succulence, there is no type of beer to compare with the Vienna style: the amber-red, bronze or copper-coloured lager with the soft maltiness of aroma and palate.

The malty sweetness and spiciness of this style make it the perfect accompaniment to sweetly spiced dishes and relatively sweet-tasting meats. No beer is more sympathetic to the potato, dumpling and noodle dishes of Alpine Italy, Austria, Bavaria and Swabia, fennel-spiced sausages, the spit-roast chicken of the German beer festival, or an equally succulent stew of pork. Unless the brew is of the Vienna style, the partnership of beer and pizza is merely Italian-American popular romance. With this superbly suited style, it is a love affair consummated.

After I first wrote about Vienna lagers, in 1977, brewers in that city accused me of having imagined the style. This was because my description exceeded in character anything they were producing.

I had pieced together my account from my understanding of the style of lager created by Anton Dreher when he introduced bottom-fermentation to his famous brewery in Schwechat, a district of Vienna, in 1841; the adaptation of that style by the Munich brewing family Sedlmayr and others to create a special beer for the Oktoberfest; and the continued use, especially in Belgium, of the term 'Vienna malt' to describe a kilning to an amber colour. (I later came across a 1957 reference to the style from the Belgian brewing scientist Jean De Clerck, who thought it had vanished.) Similar beers survive in Scandinavia, one (from Carlsberg) under the nostalgic brand name 1847. There are other examples elsewhere in the world.

Dreher had moved on to brew in other cities in the Austrian Empire, including Michelob, Bohemia, and the port of Trieste (now a part of Italy, where his brand name resides as a local offshoot of Heineken). His former brewery in Vienna was in different hands, but its beers did still tend to be sweet and vaguely malt-accented, even if they were in general gold rather than bronze or amber. They had faded, but so had the Austrian Empire. There was a clear relationship of colour, aroma and palate between Sedlmayr's Spaten Märzenbier at the Oktoberfest, its many imitators in Bavaria and elsewhere, and the Easter and Christmas lagers made in Scandinavia.

In the briefly Austrian Imperial outpost of Mexico, I have over the years tasted reddish and tawny lagers such as (in roughly ascending order of character) Dos Equis, Indio Oscura, Tres Equis Oscura (a classically malty example that has been discontinued), Negra Modelo and Leon Negra, and Christmas brews such as Conmemorativa and Nochebuena. These represent, surely, a progression from Vienna to Munich in inspiration, although they are lighter in body and palate, and less malty, than the Germanic originals.

While the golden lagers of Mexico do nothing more than wash down its spicy foods, these darker, sweeter brews can marry the flavours. They work well with the corn used in broths, tarts and breads, with the pumpkin flour and the shredded chicken and pork stews. The chocolaty Negra Modelo is perfect with chicken *mole*.

These bronze, amber-red or copper-coloured lagers, with their accent toward a sweetish maltiness, are perfect with pizza, noodles and spicy foods. Their history touches northern Italy, Austria, Munich and Mexico. One version was the original style of the Munich Oktoberfest. Other versions are made by several Scandinavian brews as Easter and Christmas beers.

Oktoberfest and similar events originally called for a Vienna-style lager. Today, the colour may have diminished, though the strength often remains.

The term Märzen is used by the Californian brewpubs of Gordon Biersch. Theirs is a good example of the style, in a dryish interpretation.

It did not occur to me at the time of my first writings that immigrants from the Austrian Empire had probably taken the style not only to Mexico but also across the border to Texas. There is plenty of evidence of their breweries there, but less to indicate the precise style of their beers. There surely must have been Vienna-style lagers in the United States before Prohibition. Something not a thousand miles away survived at the Bavarian-accented Spoetzl brewery in Shiner, Texas, until the 1970s. (More recently, the same brewery briefly produced under contract a lightly malty lager called Pecan Street.) Farther north, a light, dryish, amber-red 'Bavarian Dark' survived at the Geyer brewery, in Frankenmuth, Michigan, until the mid-1980s. I well remember enjoying it.

Rediscovering the style
However romantic the brewers of Vienna thought my interpretation of their style, the city's proudly local brewer Ottakringer produced a bronze-red (25 EBC), malt-accented (13–13.5 Plato; 1052–4) lager to mark its 150th anniversary in 1987. This excellent beer had a light, sweet, soft start and a dry, rounded finish. Ottakringer appends the name of the city to its Gold Fassl Spezial, a golden beer with a soft, well-rounded, sweetish malt character.

In Munich, Spaten still produces a reddish Märzenbier but also has a paler Oktoberfest. The tradition that many beers for festivals had a fuller colour has greatly diminished. This is not merely a question of colour, of course. If the beer is paler, it will lose the aromatic, 'juicy', flavour notes that derive from the kilning that puts the colour into the malt.

The good news in Germany is that several of the new-generation 'house breweries' make malty lagers with some colour and the consequent flavours. I have, for example, enjoyed the gold-to-bronze, slightly raisiny, malty Luisen Brau, at the house brewery of the same name in Berlin; and the bronze, more malt-accented, drier Salonbier at Borbecker in Essen.

In Scandinavia, apart from the Danish examples, there remain some excellent Christmas beers in this style from Norway. The Jule Øl of the Aass brewery in Drammen is a good example. (The name might directly translate as yule ale. In fact, Øl is Norwegian for any type of beer, and almost all of the country's brews are bottom-fermenting.) The brewery used its tawny, nutty Christmas beer of 15 Plato (1060) as a model in 1991 for a smooth new brew of a more conventional gravity, called Aass Amber, with a very perfumy malt character, for the Swedish market.

Among Vienna-style lagers from Sweden, in 1988 I encountered a memorable Pripps Julöl with a full red colour and a markedly sweet maltiness.

Finnish brewers had begun around this time to introduce Christmas beers, all in broadly the Vienna style. The first was the Sinebrychoff brewery, in 1987, with its Jouluolut: amber-red, with a firm, medium body and a good clean maltiness. The rival company Hartwall later produced a relatively light, slightly oily and grainy, caramel-tasting Joulo at its brewery in Lapland; and a somewhat dry, biscuity Juhlaolut at its plant in Karelia. The smaller Olvi brewery has a malty, toffeeish beer of 13.4 Plato (1054), in a very full golden colour, called Vaakuna, that it regards as a Märzen type. It also has a sweetish, very malty winter beer, in a bronze-red colour, called Herttua ('duke').

How do the terms Vienna-style, Märzen and Oktoberfest relate to each other? The answer is that the amber-red, malty style of lager originally made by Dreher in Vienna inspired the Märzen-Oktoberfest created by Sedlmayr in Munich. Where both the terms, Märzen and Oktoberfest, are combined on the label of a beer in Germany, it is likely to be in this style. The best examples have a gravity in the range 13–14 (1052–6), and an alcohol content of 4–5 percent by weight, 5–6 by volume. If just one of the designations (or the term Fest) is used, it may be a paler interpretation, in a bronze or full gold colour. Or a Festbier may simply be a slightly higher-gravity and more flavourful version of whatever is the brewery's usual style. In Germany, especially the south, many such beers are produced for various festivals.

The linking of the terms Märzen and Oktober implies that the beer was brewed in March and lagered for many months. September sees the beginning of the Oktoberfest, which runs into the month after which it is named.

These traditions date from the time when March was the last month in which production was possible, because brewers had no refrigeration with which to counteract the wild yeasts of summer. Beer was laid down in icy cellars as a provision, drawn upon during the summer, and finally exhausted in September or October. There were no doubt many September-October beer festivals before the Crown Prince's wedding institutionalized Munich's famous event.

A long lagering, especially with modern controls of temperature and microbiological environment, makes for a very clean, smooth palate. Few Märzen or Oktoberfest beers today have more than three months' lagering, at the most, but it would be a shame if the term altogether lost its meaning in the Old World at a time when it is so enthusiastically being rediscovered in the New.

In the New World

In 1985, the American brewer Gary Bauer produced what he branded as Vienna-style Lager Beer. Bauer, who had won many awards as a home-brewer, was at that time turning professional. In the launch material for his beer, he noted that his choice of style had been inspired by my writings on Vienna lagers. His was the first revivalist example in the United States. It was a good, malty lager, very complex in aroma and palate, and nicely underpinned by a subtle hop character; a fine example of the style (see page 209).

This stained-glass window is at the Ayinger brewery. Ayinger's Fest-Märzen is of the paler type, but it manages to retain a remarkably rounded maltiness.

The name soon caught the attention of Carling O'Keefe, of Canada, producers of Old Vienna lager, who were anxious to protect their trade name. Old Vienna is a vaguely sweet golden lager that may in the distant past have borne a hint of Austrian origins, and there seemed little likelihood of confusion between the two, but Bauer was persuaded to change the name of his product.

He called it Ambier; the red and white stripes of Austria and the illustration of the Emperor Franz Josef on the label remained as an indication of the brew's inspiration.

In the mid-1980s, amber lagers of varying character began to proliferate in the United States: a thinnish example from Chesbay in Virginia Beach; the fruitier New Amsterdam from New York; the malty but light and dry Rhomberg from Dubuque, Iowa. Even the confusingly named, golden, Erlanger (at the

The Viennese Anton Dreher was a leading figure in the world of brewing science when his work led to an early lager with an amber-red colour.

time being brewed by Stroh in Detroit) had decided to call itself a Märzenbier.

By the late 1980s, a lightly malty and coffeeish Amber Lager was being made in Abita Springs, Louisiana; Albany Amber, from New York state, seemed to have settled into broadly a Vienna style; there was Portland Lager, from Maine; the country's biggest brewer, Anheuser-Busch, was market-testing the pale bronze, lightly malty Anheuser Märzen; the full-coloured and rather hoppy amber Steinbeer was emerging from the tiny Lakefront brewery in Milwaukee; in the same city Sprecher made the well-balanced Special Amber; a relatively light Vienna lager, Schild Brau, was being made by Millstream, in the Amana Church colonies of Iowa; and the national brewer Coors had launched its malt-accented, pale amber Winterfest.

By the early 1990s, an aromatically malty Oktoberfest was being produced in Nashville, Tennessee; Olde Heurich, of Washington DC, was calling itself a Märzenbier; Pennsylvania Brewing was making a malty, smooth, dryish Märzen Fest more than worthy of the description; Stoudt, in the same state, had a creamy Adamstown Amber; a rounded, Vienna-style lager called Eliot Ness came from the gangbuster's home town, Cleveland; an Amber Lager with a

pleasantly malty finish was produced by Hoster, at Columbus, Ohio; Capital, in Madison, Wisconsin, came up with a malty, toasty Märzen; and in California, the Palo Alto brewpub Gordon Biersch was making a classic Märzen, slightly dry for the style. In Vancouver, Canada, at around the same time, I tasted a dry, malty Island Märzen.

In 1991–2, coincidentally using an Austrian-designed brewhouse, the new Zip City brewpub in Manhattan, New York, began to produce, unfiltered, a very soft, malty, slightly sweet, Vienna-style lager, in a full amber colour at 13.5 Plato (1054), with 4.2 percent alcohol by weight, 5.3 by volume, and a heftier Märzen (15.5–16; 1060–4; 4.8; 6). Chef Peter Spinelli came up with some perfectly complementary chicken, noodle and dumpling dishes.

In 1991, I was asked to devise a beer to accompany wood-oven, thin-crust pizzas at the Palomino restaurant in Minneapolis. I suggested an unfiltered, Vienna-style lager, which was produced for the restaurant by the local James Page brewery. It proved popular. Later, in Washington state, the Kemper brewery produced something similar for the Palisade restaurant in Seattle. The malty spiciness of these beers did the trick with the pizzas.

In Australia the next year, I found a pizza restaurant that had gone one stage further. The Australian Pizza Kitchen, in Canberra, was using its oven to roast malt with which to brew a darkish amber lager in a kettle behind the bar. The beer had a hint of malty chewiness, and some bitterness in the finish.

Around the same time, after years of making all their lagers golden, the major Australian brewers were beginning to introduce amber-red styles. Curiously, all of these were beers with a lower-than-usual alcohol content, with a sales pitch aimed at drivers. The idea was to add a little malty flavour (and perhaps a dash of visual machismo?) to compensate for the diminution in alcohol. The original example, a runaway success, is a reddish beer with the confusing name Toohey's Blue (9 Plato; 1036; 2.2; 2.7). Despite its lightness, it does have a dryish maltiness in the start and a dash of juiciness in the middle. For lack of any other term, this might be described as a light Vienna-style lager, although the brewery nonsensically termed it a light bitter.

Vienna-style lager producers

The Austrians still make sweetish, malty lagers, but few are in the classic Vienna style. The example first made by Gabriel Sedlmayr for the Munich Oktoberfest continues to be produced by his successors. Ambier signalled the revival of the style in the United States. Among Mexico's more characterful lagers, Negra Modelo is readily available.

AMBIER

Ambier Brewing Company,
5325 West Burleigh Street,
Milwaukee, Wisconsin 53210, USA
Tel: (414) 449-9705

Having been created in 1985 to restore the tradition, this is the definitive revivalist Vienna-style lager. It is an outstanding beer, brewed only occasionally, hard to find, but worth the effort. Its creator, Gary Bauer, was a chemist in a plastics company before his family's brewing history led him to join the beer renaissance.

Bauer, who traces his family back to Koblenz, in the Rhineland, lives in Milwaukee. He produced his first batches in the 1870s' brewery that had variously been Olinger's, Walter's and Hibernia, in Eau Claire, Wisconsin. Batches have since been produced under contract at Huber (Monroe, Wisconsin), Rhomberg (Dubuque, Iowa) and elsewhere, and Bauer has become a sought-after consultant to small brewers.

It is an all-malt beer. The initial brew was made to a gravity of 13.5 Plato (1054), from five malts: six-row pale (Dreher would not have approved), dextrin, Vienna, crystal and Carapils. The hops were Spalt and Hallertau Mittelfrüh, in three additions. Lagering was for six to eight weeks. The beer had 4.1 percent alcohol by weight, 5.2 by volume, a colour somewhere in the 40s EBC and 28 units of bitterness.

Every time I have sampled this beer, I have been struck by its lacework, its malt character and its balance. On some occasions, I have noted earthy characteristics, grainy touches, a hint of coffee, and sometimes a suggestion of roastiness.

NEGRA MODELO

Cerveceria Modelo, 156 Lago Alberto,
Mexico City 11320, Mexico
Tel: (5) 54 60 60

Mexico is said to have had the first commercial brewery in the New World, in the mid-1500s; 300 years later the country began to produce lager beers, under the influence of brewers who arrived from the German-speaking world.

The Modelo brewing company has a wide range of lagers, not all as interesting as its Negra ('La Crema de la Cerveza'). This deep russet (upper 40s EBC) beer has a sweetish start, developing to a lightly herbal, bitter-chocolate, roasty dryness in the finish. The chocolate character is very distinctive, and the beer does become quite creamy if it is not served too cold. An original gravity of just over 13 Plato (1052) means that it can retain some body, despite the use of a high proportion of adjuncts. This beer is *kräusened*, and perhaps that contributes to a spritzy softness. Bitterness is low (19 BU), and there is 4.15 percent alcohol by weight, 5.3 by volume.

Is it a Vienna-style lager or a Münchener dark? Just south of the border perhaps.

SPATEN

Gabriel Sedlmayr
Spaten-Franziskaner-Bräu, 46-48
Mars Strasse, 8000 Munich, Germany
Tel: (089) 51221

This famous company traces its origins to a house brewery on Neuhauser Strasse, in 1397. Its present identity, with its spade emblem, perpetuates the name of George Spaeth, who became owner in 1622. The Bavarian royal court brewmaster Gabriel Sedlmayr I took over in 1807; his son Gabriel II became one of the greatest innovators of the industry. In 1851, construction of a new brewery began on the site that is today Spaten.

In 1858–61, Gabriel's brother Josef acquired the former Franciscan monastery brewery in Munich, and made his own innovations. At that time, the beers served at the Oktoberfest were dark brown. In 1871–2, Josef Sedlmayr introduced the translucent, copper-red style at the festival, and it became the speciality brew of the event. The Sedlmayrs had often collaborated with Anton Dreher, and the new beer was acknowledged as being in the Wiener (Vienna) style. In 1922, the brothers' businesses were united, and eventually assumed their present name.

The Sedlmayr family still has a substantial stake in what is now a public company. On a visit to the brewery in 1985, I was told that Ernst Sedlmayr, then more than 70 years old, was still in the office every day, and that Hans Sedlmayr, of a similar age, lived in a house on the site. Parts of the original buildings still stand, but there has been constant modernization and expansion.

Spaten's Ur-Märzen Oktoberfest has an excellent malt aroma; a malty but rounded body; and a delicate underpinning of hop. It has a gravity of 13.75 Plato (1055); is (naturally, being Bavarian) an all-malt beer; is lagered for 14 weeks, and emerges with 4.48 percent alcohol by weight, 5.76 by volume. Its colour is 32.5 EBC, and it has 21.5 units of bitterness. It is a classic.

Pilsner

All beers were dark or cloudy until 1842. At that time, using the lager method, a newly founded brewery in Pilsen, Bohemia, introduced a beer that was golden and clear. It was not the first lager beer, as is sometimes claimed, but it was the first to be golden and clear. Within the family of lagers, the Pilsner style has ever since been by far the most widely produced. Sometimes the designation is spelled Pilsener. Or it may be abbreviated to Pils. In many parts of the world today, distant, diluted derivations of this style are the only form in which beer is known.

The term Pilsner should indicate not only a lager that is golden but also one that resembles the Bohemian original in its gravity, its softness of malt character and, more especially, in the balancing dryness and bouquet of its hop.

The original Pilsner had (and still has) 12 degrees Balling (an early measurement of gravity, roughly equivalent to the Plato system), with a relatively restrained attenuation. The best followers of the style are within a narrow band of 11.25–12.5, and this usually produces an alcohol content of just under, or around, 4 percent by weight, 5 by volume.

The original is brewed from barley grown in Bohemia and Moravia, and so are some followers. Purists might argue that a true Pilsner should always be aromatized with the Saaz hop variety, from the Žatec area of Bohemia. Many distant breweries import this hop, to provide that Pilsner touch. Others use similar German varieties from the Hallertau

> **Whether they proclaim it or not, the majority of the world's beers are golden lagers that distantly imitate a great Bohemian brew. 'Pilsner' should mean more than just a golden lager. A true Pilsner-style lager has a good malt character, but is accented toward the hop, in its floweriness of aroma and dryness of finish.**

region. Certainly, a Pilsner should have a notable degree of both bittering and late-hopping. The original aims for a bitterness of not less than 40.

Although some excellent Pilsners are made in Germany and other countries, this style has also become the basis for a blandified, cheapened adaptation, the standard golden lager of no particular character that is an international form of beer, sometimes further degraded by being made 'light' or 'dry'. Whether or not they say Pilsner on their labels, and some have the impertinence to do so, that is the remote inspiration of these products.

They are as close to the original as an American 'Chablis' is to the great white wine made in the Burgundian town of that name from the Chardonnay grape. What a true Chablis is to the world of wine, a real Pilsner is to the universe of beer. Like a Chablis,

Behind gates of Napoleonic pride are a water-tower like a lighthouse, a brewhouse with as many funnels as an ocean-liner, a loading bay that is part-railway, part-castle. Pilsner Urquell is not so much a brewery as a tableau.

a Pilsner makes a fine accompaniment to fish. An elderly emigré in Canada once told me that his most evocative memory from his homeland was of buying on the streets of Prague live carp from the lakes near Trebon, and cooking the fish like schnitzels to be served with Pilsner beer for Christmas dinner.

The name simply means 'from Pilsen'. In a more sophisticated time, the name Pilsner would have been trademarked, instead of being adopted as an imprecise designation of style like a Hamburger steak or a Frankfurter sausage.

The original brewery still operates, and its beer is sold in many parts of the world, under the brand name Pilsner Urquell. The second word, added in 1898 in a late gesture to protect the product's identity, means 'original source'. There can only be one original in the matter of Pilsner beer, and this is it.

The region of origin

Bohemia was the kingdom of Wenceslas, of the Christmas carol. He was the first King Wenceslas, whose promotion of Christianity, and struggles against German power in the region, led to his being canonized. A later King Wenceslas tried to protect Bohemia's assets by forbidding the export of hop cuttings. There are records of hop-growing in Bohemia as early as AD 859, and brewing may well predate that. Wheat, oats, herbs and spices were also used. Another King Wenceslas granted brewing rights to the town of Pilsen in 1295.

At the time of the introduction of Pilsner lager in 1842, Bohemia was a province in the Austrian empire, which was German-speaking. After the collapse of the Austrian Empire, the Czech lands, Bohemia and Moravia, formed a republic with Slovakia. After the disintegration of the Communist bloc, this union broke up. Pilsner Urquell is a German-language rendition; in Czech, Plzeňský Prazdroj is the spelling. Wenceslas is a German rendition; in Czech, the spelling is Vaclav, as in the name of the first post-Communist President, who formerly worked in a brewery (as well as being a playwright).

At this meeting point of Germanic and Slavic cultures, there is much contention as to who should take credit for this famous beer. The town of Vilshofen, near Passau, Bavaria, and close to both the

The birthplace of Pilsner lager

Today's Czech Republic comprises Bohemia and Moravia. During the Austrian Empire, České Budějovice was known by its German name, Budweis; the hop-growing town of Žatec was called Saaz.

Austrian and Czech frontiers, supplied the brewer. Vilshofen has had a brewery since 1542. A Vilshofen brewer called Josef Grolle was employed in Pilsen when the owners of that town's brewpubs decided to collaborate. Facing competition from Bavarian dark lagers, they got together to build a 'Burghers' Brewery', using bottom-fermentation. Grolle was said to be a rough, country fellow, but he is honoured as the first brewmaster on a plaque at Pilsen.

It is said that Grolle planned a dark lager, and that the pale result was an accident. Similar stories attend many famous drinks, foods and inventions, but this one is absurd. The ability to control malting temperatures made for the golden colour, while the selection and manipulation of the yeast ensured the clarity.

As dark and cloudy beers can be delicious, and continue to be made, why did a golden, clear brew become so famous? Colour and clarity had not been an issue until opaque drinking vessels of metal, stoneware, wood or leather began to be superseded by glass. Clear, golden beer was visually attractive, exciting and novel. The revolution in technical and industrial knowledge that fostered a better understanding of malting and fermentation also brought the ability to mass-produce glasses. It laid the foundations for steam power, the mechanized production of beer, in bigger breweries, and railways that made for wider distribution. The Austrian empire, already a large single market, made trading links with Bavaria and Prussia. Soon, Pilsner beer was the toast of imperial Vienna and Berlin. Just as soon, a new wave of emigrants was taking it to the new world. Chicago even has a neighbourhood called Pilsen.

The Czechs regard Pilsner as an appellation of origin. In their view, a beer called Pilsner must be made in the city whose name it bears. The Czechs include in this appellation the beer of the Gambrinus brewery (see page 218), which stands on a site adjoining Pilsner Urquell (see page 219). One or two other countries take the same view, and therefore permit only those imported products to use the designation.

Almost all of the other Czech breweries include in their range a premium golden beer in a similar style, but label it simply with their own name and the legend 12. I have, for example, greatly enjoyed the soft, malty Staropramen and the firmer Branik examples, from Prague, and the hoppier-tasting Velké Popovice made just to the south, in Central Bohemia. Yet farther south, near the German border, I have tasted hoppy and well-attenuated brews in broadly the same style from Protivín and Strakonice. Thus far, my greatest favourite is the very bitter but creamy Krušovice, from the hop country. I felt this was even hoppier than the local beer of the growing town, Žatec, when I tasted them on the same day.

At Krušovice, a brewer once told me his beer was so creamy that a coin could be rested on its foam, without sinking. He then demonstrated: 'See...our beer keeps our currency afloat.' With their vaulted floor maltings and flagstoned lagering cellars, the old breweries of Bohemia are proud places. It is to be hoped that their character is not destroyed by the stainless steel of capitalism.

Visitors to the Czech Republic are more likely to spend time in Prague than Pilsen. The latter is an industrial town, albeit with charming architecture. Pilsner beer is widely available in Prague's taverns.

Across the border, the Germans insist that the term Pilsner be hyphenated with the town of origin, or brewer's brand, to avoid 'passing off'. This seems to originate from a court case of 1912–13, between Pilsner Urquell and Bitburger. The hyphen has not prevented some German Pilsners gaining great renown: the firm-bodied Radeberger-Pils and the dry Wernesgrüner from the old East Germany; the soft, beautifully balanced Bitburger (see page 217); the intense Jever (see page 218); the fuller, rounded König; the robust Veltins; the milder Warsteiner, and many others from the West. Most, though not all, German brewers have a beer in this style.

The Germans regard Pilsner as a clear designation of style, and expect such beers to have an appropriate gravity and an emphatic hop character. The hoppiness of Pilsner Urquell and Gambrinus is often exceeded by that of its German followers.

Within Germany, there tend to be some differences of regional emphasis. The Bavarian Pilsners often have quite a big, malty middle. Those of Baden-Württemberg and Hesse are lighter all round. The Rhineland has several famous Pilsners, especially from the Sauerland district, and they tend to be light but dry. Those from the far north are more attenuated and hoppy. Perhaps it is fanciful to imagine that this northern taste for bitter brews has its origins in the days when hops were exported from Bohemia down the Elbe to a market in Hamburg, but I have been offered no better theory.

'Diet' Pils

In Hamburg, the Holsten brewery has for many years made not only a conventional Pilsner but also one adapted for diabetics. This beer is fermented further than is usual, in order more thoroughly to convert its malt sugars. The brewery chose its Pilsner as the product to which it would apply this treatment, but it could equally well have done so with some other style. There is no connection between the designation Pilsner and the extra conversion of sugars. Furthermore, this version, labelled Diat (meaning diet) Pils, and distinguished by a green foil, was created for diabetics, not slimmers. Some people are more susceptible than others to gain weight through drinking beer, but no one ever became slimmer by this means.

The water-tower, which is no longer used, is one of Pilsner Urquell's odder architectural features. The brewery has its own springs, producing very soft water. It also uses some city water, which it softens.

Holsten's Diat Pils was the first such product to be exported to Britain, and has developed a huge following there, surely based on the belief that it is a beer for slimmers. In the British market, it no longer carries the word Diat, but the suggestion has stuck in the minds of drinkers. To these consumers, that is what Pils means: a lager made for slimmers and always bottled with a green foil.

Pilsners of the world

Beyond the Czech Republic and Germany, Pilsner-style beers tend to be considerably less malty or hoppy. The next most characterful Pilsners are those of Belgium, such as Stella Artois, Maes and Cristal Alken (see page 218), all of which use Saaz hops to varying degrees. The Artois brewery, which traces its history to 1366, launched its Stella (Latin for star) as a Christmas beer in 1926, and this popularized the Pilsner style in Belgium. Among the Belgian Pils-brewers, Maes has also been significant in its loyalty to Czech malt. Belgian brewers are inclined to be

A *Pivnice* is a beer tavern, and *Prazdroj* means 'original source'.

Beck's affiliate Haake offers an unfiltered interpretation in its home town, Bremen.

By American standards, the Czech Budweiser Budvar is a small brewery, but it is hardly micro. Kettles do not get much grander than the Czechs' giants. The brewer in the picture provides a sense of scale.

traditionalists, and this has ensured in their Pils a reasonably high malt content (often 75–85 percent or more), a passable level of bitterness (perhaps lower 20s to lower 30s) and an adequate lagering time (one to three months). These standards are under great pressure as Belgium faces competition and influence from countries where beer is made more cheaply.

In the Netherlands, a typical 'Pils' is considerably milder. As a small, densely populated nation on the seaboard of Europe, the Netherlands lives by its

exports: it has made easily drinkable Pilsner-style beers from Heineken and Grolsch internationally known. Heineken has a faintly grassy tinge, and Grolsch a softer aroma of new-mown hay. Visitors to the Netherlands will find more hop in some of the lesser-known beers, notably Brand-Up and Christoffel (see page 217), and in the outstanding Plzen from the Amsterdam microbrewery and tasting room t'IJ.

Denmark is another coastal nation that lives by trade. Its Pilsner-style beers are very mild indeed,

A TOWN CALLED BUDWEIS

Pilsen is not the only Bohemian city which has been brewing since the 13th century. Another is the city known in German as Budweis and in Czech as České Budějovice, once the home of the royal court brewery of Bohemia. In the 1500s, Budweis had 44 breweries. Not long after Pilsen created its golden lager, Budweis added its own interpretation. In what might be regarded as a variation on the Pilsner theme, the breweries of Budweis have over the years produced slightly sweeter golden lagers.

In the days before trademarks, any beer from the city would have been described as a Budweiser brew. Today, the city has two breweries. One, dating from 1795 but rebuilt in the mid- to late 1800s, is known as Samson (with Crystal as a brand name). The other, dating from 1895, is called Budvar. The two breweries make similar lagers, but the latter's Budweiser Budvar is a little fuller and softer, with a more pronounced sweetness. It is an all-malt beer, with an original gravity of 12 (1048; 4 percent alcohol by weight, 5 by volume) and a delicate hop character (19–24 units of bitterness). The brewery claims this beer is lagered for 60 days for the Czech market and 90 for export. It has been exported since its early days.

While the term Pilsner was taken up by brewers throughout the world, the Anheuser-Busch brewery, of St Louis, Missouri, decided to call its premium beer Budweiser. The St Louis brewery has its origins with a man named Schneider in 1850–52, and was acquired in 1860 by Eberhard Anheuser (from Bad Kreuznach, south of Mainz, Germany), whose daughter married Adolphus Busch (from Mainz). In 1875, Anheuser-Busch was incorporated. The company began to produce a beer called Budweiser soon afterward, though there were subsequently legal wrangles over the rights to the name.

American Budweiser is also a sweetish lager, marginally lower in alcohol (11.25; 1045; around 3.4; 4.5) and far lighter in body and flavour. It is not an all-malt beer (it contains about 30 percent rice), and has a much gentler hop character (10–15 units of bitterness), though a complex blend of varieties is used, in the form of blossoms. The company's yeast produces a faintly fruity, apple-like character. Maturation is for not more than 21 days, though there is a touch of tradition in the use of beechwood chips as a means of clarification. This is an old Bavarian technique (I have only ever seen it at one other brewery, in the Bohemian Forest), in which the surfaces of the wood attract yeast and protein sediment. The chandeliered, 1891 brewhouse in St Louis is a protected building.

After the 'velvet revolution' in Czechoslovakia, the American company opened negotiations to acquire a minority stake in Budvar.

often with short lagering times. The examples in the Carlsberg range have a light malty-sweet tinge; those from Tuborg are slightly hoppier.

The Norwegians have a Beer Purity Law similar to that of Germany, and their Pilsners are in general the cleanest and driest in Scandinavia.

Almost all British lagers are very loosely in the Pilsner style, though few have serious aspirations to an authentic character, and the same is true of mass-market lagers in North America, Australasia and the rest of the world.

In general, many British lagers have an inappropriately fruity character; the North American examples

Lion shows just how geographically distant Pilsners can be. It uses Czech malt, but is light and sweetish.

tend to be sweet, with a taste of corn; Australasian versions can be stronger than some elsewhere, but are also sweet, with a tinge of caramelized sugar.

It is not that these countries cannot make a good Pilsner. Most brewers worldwide feel that a true example of the style would be too characterful for easy drinking. They are seeking to produce simple re-freshers, and to do so inexpensively.

In both North America and Australasia, there are micros and brewpubs making serious Pilsners. In Philadelphia, the Dock Street brewpub even offers a choice of a soft Bohemian style and a more attenuated German Pilsner. Such offerings should be sampled. Elsewhere, it is tempting to assume that, the farther from Bohemia, the more remote the character.

There are always exceptions. New Zealand's Kiwi

Lager, despite a pitifully low level of bittering, has a wonderful hop aroma when it is really fresh. This arises from New Zealand's relatively new hop variety, Green Bullet. 'Doesn't the bouquet remind you of a New Zealand Sauvignon Blanc?' asked the man responsible for the brew. I had to agree, it did. Kiwi's local rival Steinlager has less aroma but more dryness.

Although their Pilsner-style lagers are said to be 'light', the Japanese brewers, especially Kirin and Sapporo, do like a good malt and Saaz hop character. The lighter in weight a golden lager is, the more the brewer has probably replaced barley malt with rice or corn. The loss of malt means a diminution in flavour. This is one reason why very light lagers are often served extremely cold. The sensation of coldness is a substitute for taste.

The older brewhouse at Pilsen was built in 1949–52. The newer one, from 1970–71, is also copper.

Pilsner producers

Most German Pilsners have an appropriate malt and hop character; Bitburger and Jever are just two good examples. Elsewhere, single-minded Pilsners are hard to find, but either in their choice of malt and hops, or the bitterness of their beers, some brewers make the effort.

BADERBRAU

Pavichevich Brewing Co, 383 Romans Road, Elmhurst, Illinois 60126, USA
Tel: (708) 617-5252

A wholeheartedly Bohemian-style beer created at the end of the 1980s as the first product of a new micro-brewery in the Chicago suburb of Elmhurst. The beer is named after a man called Bader, a friend of the brewery's founder, Ken Pavichevich. Like many Chicagoans, Pavichevich is of Central European origin. He became entranced by the beers of Bohemia on visits there.

Something of an extrovert, he had worked as a policeman, an oilman and a male model before setting up the brewery, in what was formerly an olive-packing plant. The white-tiled brewhouse, with a trim of Italian decorative tiles, accommodates a stainless-steel mash tun that can tip to disgorge the spent grain, and a gas-fired, direct-flame, copper kettle. Pavichevich engaged as a consultant and vice-president Douglas Babcock, formerly of Stroh. Babcock has helped several of the new generation of American brewers.

The beer was created from both two- and six-row malt, and both Saaz and German hops. In early samples I noted a remarkably creamy head; a flowery, almost talcum-powder, aroma; a early surge of hoppy flavour; a soft, malty middle; and a light hop bitterness in the finish. It is to be hoped that this newcomer can maintain such high standards.

In the matter of a truly serious American Pilsner beer, Baderbrau's rivals are both neighbours: the aromatic, firm, malty Legacy Lager, from Chicago Brewing; and the hoppy Gartenbrau Special, from Madison, Wisconsin.

BITBURGER

Bitburger Brauerei Theo Simon, P O Box 1164, 5520 Bitburg/Eifel, Germany
Tel: (0 65 61) 140

One of the best-known and widely marketed Pilsners in Germany is made in the small town of Bitburg, in the Eifel lake country of the Rhineland Palatinate.

Bitburger, founded in 1817 as a farm-based brew-pub making top-fermenting beers, was one of the first German brewers to produce a Pilsner, in 1884. Its location is out of the way, but the lakes' ice was a valuable resource in the early days of lagering. Bitburger gained a means of wider distribution when a rail line was built to send cannon from the steelworks of Saarbrücken to the Prussian army. The company was also one of the first German brewers to create a strong brand image: personified by 'The Connoisseur', in his Victorian-style smoking cap.

It is an intensely proud company, still run by the Simon family, who are distantly of Tyrolean origin. They have clearly reinvested profits on a great scale to maintain the success of their beer.

The company still has office buildings from the last century, and a copper brewhouse from the 1950s, in the middle of the town, but its principal production is on another site two miles away. The new brewhouse, opened in the 1980s, is an attractive, spot-lit showpiece. Wort and finished beer are pumped between the sites, via underground pipes.

Only spring barley is used, all grown in Germany, about a third in the Rhineland Palatinate. A double-decoction mash is employed, and the company is hesitant to elaborate – perhaps the precise procedure is a key to the soft malt character of the beer. The beer has 11.2–3 Plato (1043–6), and around, or just under, 4 percent alcohol by weight, 5 by volume.

Bittering hops are mainly Northern Brewer, with Perle, Hallertau Mittelfrüh and Tettnang for aroma. There is a tiny growing area, called Holsthum, to the west of Bitburg, and its harvest, of several varieties, is entirely taken up by the brewery. There are three hop additions, and the beer has 37–38 units of bitterness.

The same yeast has been used as long as anyone can remember. 'It is ours, not a library yeast, and you will not find it anywhere else,' a brewer told me. He felt that it imparted a well-rounded, clean character. It works slowly, at classically low temperatures (5–7°C/41–44.6°F). The brewery says the beer is lagered for six to eight weeks. It is not pasteurized. Filtration is sterile for export.

The beer has an emphatic malt note, as well as hops, in the nose; a soft, malty middle; then a rousingly hoppy finish that subsides but gently lingers. I have sometimes felt that it could be hoppier, but a member of the family disagreed: 'We consider it to be definitely dry, but we want the hop bitterness to be at the back of the tongue, not in the throat. We want the drinker to remember the dry finish, but not be gripped by it.'

Bitburger Pils is a very good apéritif, and an excellent accompaniment to the trout from lake Eifel.

CHRISTOFFEL

Bierbrouwerij St Christoffel, 14 Brede Weg, 6042 GG Roermond, The Netherlands
Tel: (04750) 15740

Saint Christoffel is the patron saint of Roermond, a former coal-mining town in Dutch Limburg. The brewery is a micro established in 1986 by

Leon Brand, a member of a well-regarded Dutch brewing family. Other members owned the Brand brewery at Wijlre, near Maastricht, until it was acquired by Heineken.

Leon Brand was educated at Weihenstephan, and worked in the industry in Germany before establishing his own brewery in his home country. He lives in a modern house in front of the brewery, which is utilitarian but for the handsome brick cladding on the copper-domed kettle.

His Christoffel Bier, all-malt, firm-bodied, extremely dry, is a truly assertive Pilsner, hopped with Perle and Hersbruck, and with 43–44 BU. Brand is a quietly serious brewer. 'Some people say the beer is too bitter for them,' he once told me, 'but I am not trying to brew for everyone. Plenty of brewers already do that.'

CRISTAL ALKEN

Brouwerij Alken, 2 Station Straat, 3820 Alken, Belgium
Tel: (011) 31 27 11

Allusions to 'crystal', in various local spellings, were used by several breweries in the early days of golden, clear beers. This example was created in the village of Alken, in the province of Limburg, Belgium. (The region of Limburg also spreads into the Netherlands, and there is a city of the same name not far away in Germany.)

The beer, and the brewery, were created to cater for the coal-mining industry that grew up in Limburg during the 1920s and 1930s.

Cristal has traditionally been paler in colour, cleaner in palate, and more assertively hoppy, than other Belgian Pilsners. Its signature is Saaz, though German and Belgian hops are also used. The yeast was originally obtained from the König Pils brewery in Duisburg, Germany.

The Alken brewery has over the years been run by a succession of respected Belgian brewmasters, and it is to be hoped that its standards are

Cristal's partner, Maes.

maintained now that it is, together with its compatriot Maes (in Waarloos, between Antwerp and Brussels) under the ownership of Kronenbourg, of Alsace, France.

For its Pils, Maes makes a point not only of using Czech malt but also of double-decoction, a two-stage fermentation, natural cooling and two to three months' maturation. The beer has a flowery, 'white wine' bouquet, and a light, soft palate.

GAMBRINUS

Pivovar Gambrinus, 7 U Prazdroje, 30497 Plzeň, Czech Republic
Tel: (019) 22515

The legendary King of Beer, Duke Jean I of Brabant ('Jan Primus', corrupted to Gambrinus) provides the name for Pilsen's second brewery.

Sharing a site with Pilsner Urquell, Gambrinus is, in all senses, the closest to the original. It is the only other beer that is literally a Pilsner. Were it not for 'PU', Gambrinus might be regarded as a classic.

Gambrinus was founded in 1869, and still has the tiled brewhouse of that period. Its iron vessels, painted cream, work on a double-decoction system (as against the triple at Pilsner Urquell); its beer has 32 units of bitterness (as against 40); and it has its own strain of yeast. The finished beer is very aromatic, perhaps firmer-bodied, slightly lighter and cleaner than Urquell, but still with plenty of hop character.

JEVER

Friesisches Bräuhaus zu Jever, 17 Elisabethufer, 2942 Jever, Germany
Tel: (04461) 131

The small town of Jever is in the far northwestern corner of Germany, in Friesland (a region which also straddles the Netherlands and Denmark). It is a base for tourism on the Frisian coast and islands, a market town for the dairying industry, and the proud location of a famous brewery. The town boundary has a sign announcing: 'The home of Jever Pilsener'.

Jever Pilsener typifies the very dry style of Pils made in the far north of Germany, and even exceeds its immediate competitors in that respect. The Frisians are said to like intense tastes, and have one or two powerful liqueurs and herbal or spicy foods. It is a maritime region, and may have picked up this taste in the days of the spice trade. However, the word 'Herb' on the label does not indicate any spicing, which would in any case defy the *Reinheitsgebot*, the German Beer Purity Law. In German, *herb* means dry or bitter.

Malts from the Netherlands, France and Germany are used, with Hallertau and Tettnang hops added in two stages, and a yeast that has been employed since 1936. The beer is said to have 42–44 BU. Lagering is for three to four weeks. The beer has 11.7 Plato (1047) and 3.75 percent alcohol by weight, 4.7 by volume.

Jever Pilsener has an emphatic hop aroma; a dry start; a firm, slightly yeasty palate; and a long, bitter finish. It has been marketed by the British retailer Marks & Spencer as an own-brand beer. It is a splendid apéritif.

Although the brewery is known as a Pils specialist, it does make other styles, including a German interpretation of a light beer. It is owned by Hamburg's Bavaria-St Pauli brewery, itself a part of a national grouping.

MATILDA BAY PILS

Redback Brewery, 75 Flemington Road, North Melbourne, Victoria 3051, Australia
Tel: (03) 329 9400

This noteworthy Australian lager was created by Janice McDonald, one of the country's new generation of beer-makers, originally for the Matilda Bay microbrewery, in Fremantle. Matilda Bay, which also makes Red-back wheat beer, later established a small brewery and pub in Melbourne. Today, the Redback brewery in Melbourne makes the Pils, which still bears the name Matilda Bay. The brewery is now owned by Foster's, and Ms McDonald has moved on to other things.

Matilda Bay Pils is an all-malt beer of 11.2 Plato (1045) and 3.9 percent alcohol by weight, 4.8 by volume. It is made with a multiple-step infusion mash; hopped with Saaz, in two additions; fermented with a yeast from Berlin (most Australian beers use Danish yeasts); and has respectable (although varying) lagering times. It has 30–33 units of bitterness, as against the 18–20 common in Australia. It is unfiltered, shipped in refrigerated transport, and available only on draught.

The beer has a 'warm' malt aroma; a dense head, leaving good lacework; a soft, clean, malty middle; with a definite but restrained hoppiness in the finish.

PILSNER URQUELL

Plzeňský Prazdroj, 30497 Plzeň, Czech Republic
Tel: (019) 227283

Tasted fresh in Pilsen or Prague, this classic beer has a wonderfully appetizing aroma. It is almost the smell of fresh air – a suggestion of ozone. This is Saaz hops at their freshest. In this condition, the beer has an inimitable softness of malt, too, and a finish that sends the consumer's hand beckoning

another one. In Prague, drinkers argue as to which tavern serves the best Pilsner Urquell, and that will vary with changes in management. In my years of drinking in the city, the title has switched between U Salzmanu, U Pinkasu, U Zlatého Tygra and U Kocoura.

No beer really enjoys travel, and Pilsner Urquell certainly does not, but it sometimes maintains a hoppy freshness, and manages to remain soft and soothing: it almost seems to act as a stomach-settler.

The sweetness of the Bohemian barley no doubt contributes to the softness. So does the malting regime. Although malting is no longer on site, its specifications no doubt owe something to the heritage of the first Pilsner production: the malt is fuller in colour (about 3.8–4 EBC) than 'Pilsner malts' made in Germany and elsewhere. This will also make for a slightly fuller taste.

A triple-decoction mash is used, in a long row of vessels of a traditional shape, ranged at two levels on either side of a central platform.

The brewery has its own springs on the site, producing very soft water, though it also uses some from the city supply. The latter is softened. There are three hop additions, all Saaz, in the form of flowers. The boil lasts for two and a half hours, or longer, rather than the more usual 90 minutes. The extra time, perhaps another touch of heritage, is considered necessary for clarity and sterility.

Of the many remarkable features of the brewery, one of the most astonishing is the antiquity and number of its open fermenters, made of uncoated oak from the Bohemian Forest. The brewery has more than 1,000 of them, each with a capacity of 30 hectolitres, mounted at a slight angle on what look like raised railway lines. Although the wooden vessels are circular, they are reminiscent of old railway wagons, and to be among them is like being in a great underground marshalling yard of

fermenting beer. In another touch of heritage, five variations on the same strain of yeast are used, each pitched into separate vessels, the contents of which are later blended.

The fermentation system is matched in visual drama by the maturation vessels, huge, pitch-lined oak casks of 30–35 hectolitres, of which the brewery has more than 3,500, in underground galleries stretching along six miles of damp, dripping, crumbling, sandstone tunnels. This type of maturation vessel was once used in all lager breweries, and the odd battery of them survives elsewhere, but nowhere on such a scale or in such an atmosphere. It is as though the beer were being mined from the rock.

Both systems are cooled by brine, running in pipes along the walls and ceilings. The fermenting areas are held at 4–6°C/39–42.5°F, the lagering cellars (which are naturally cool) at 1°C/33.5°F if possible. The beer is said to be lagered for between two and three months.

Neither of these systems any longer represents the whole story, as both, especially the lagering vessels, are augmented, and increasingly replaced, by stainless steel. Since the 'velvet revolution' in Czechoslovakia, this process has gained in pace. Inevitably, this will change the character of the beer, though it will have the benefit of making it more stable. After years of insufficient investment, many at Pilsner Urquell may welcome the chance to modernize. The sensible thing would be to retain part of the old system, and make a Pilsner Classic. Even in fast-changing Bohemia, such sophistication may not arrive in time.

It would be an outrage if Pilsner Urquell, behind its Napoleonic arch, with its yard full of railway lines, its haunting industrial architecture, and its odd corner of Imperial elegance, were to become, instead of a château, just another brewery, making just another beer.

Dortmunder Export

The appellation Dortmunder appears in the names of all five of its major breweries, and together they make it one of the world's biggest beer-producing cities. Each of these breweries produces a wide range of classic styles of beer – including the one that in modern times made the city famous.

It has been argued that the Dortmund brewers were loyal to their local style too long after it had gone out of fashion in Germany, and lost sales in consequence – now, they almost hide it. Like many brewers who see their traditions as a mixed blessing, they seem unaware that the Dortmunder style is well regarded by many serious beer-lovers elsewhere in the world for its tastiness and balance.

The Dortmunder style, always labelled as Export in its home city, is a golden lager, but a little fuller in colour and body than a Pilsner. It is less aromatic, hoppy and bitter than a Pilsner, but drier and firmer than the malty pale (*helles*) lagers of Munich. It is also slightly lower in carbonation, and less foamy.

The typical gravity is greater than the traditional 12 of a Pilsner, and may be as high as 13.5 Plato (1054), with alcohol at around 4.4 percent by weight, 5.5 by volume. Colour may be around 10.5 EBC, and Munich-style malts were once the norm. The water contains both calcium carbonate and sulphate, drawing more flavour from the malt.

The mash for Dortmunder beers typically leaves sufficient unfermentables in the brew to provide that firmness of body. The hop is intended to be evident, but without elaborate combinations of varieties and additions (20–25 BU).

The first documentary evidence of brewing in Dortmund is from 1266, at a time when the city was gaining in political importance. The aristocracy granted brewing rights to the citizens soon afterward. A medieval carving in the choir stalls of the Marienkirche (St Mary's Church) shows a man drinking from a cask.

The cities of Dortmund and Münster, and the region of Westphalia, have historically been pivotal in

> Less fragrant than a true Pilsner, but still dry; firmer in its maltiness than a Munich lager; slightly stronger than either: Dortmund's own style of golden lager was once widespread in Continental Europe. Today, it is less obviously evident in its home city, but is being taken up by some brewers in the New World.

In Japan, Sapporo remains faithful to the Dortmunder style with its highly regarded Yebisu beer. The original brewery was in the city of Sapporo, but this one is on Tokyo Bay.

This American example has a very firm start; a notably malty palate; and a light, fresh finish.

relationships with the Netherlands and Scandinavia. In medieval times, Dortmund supplied beer to many other towns in Westphalia, and this is the origin of the term Export. These were originally top-fermenting wheat beers, seasoned with herbs and spices.

The city is at the point where the small River Dort flows into the larger Ruhr. With the development of industry in the early 19th century, Dortmund grew tremendously as the capital of the coal and steel region along the Ruhr, and this large and thirsty population made it Germany's biggest brewing city.

In the 1800s, there were several local styles, some bottom-fermenting after that technique was introduced. This is said to have happened as early as 1843–5, although it was not until the 1870s that the modern style that became known as Dortmunder Export began to take shape.

After World War II, industrial recovery spread the name of Dortmunder beers, and the breweries rebuilt and expanded. In so doing, they perhaps made themselves hostages to fortune, not least those that became linked with breweries in other cities. They lost some of their local appeal – and national groupings have not been a great success in Germany.

With its industrial background, and having been heavily bombed and then hastily rebuilt, Dortmund does not have the instantly evident romance of some other brewing cities in Germany. It lost even some of its utilitarian impact when the bigger breweries, once concentrated in the centre, began to move out. Two that stayed have attempted to highlight their presence by adding brewpubs, a very welcome move.

Being so large, the Dortmunder breweries found life difficult when the coal and steel industries began to shrink. Beers made for miners and steelworkers seemed unsuitable to a generation preoccupied with more fashionable pursuits.

Thus far, the Dortmunder brewers have not found a way of turning their beer's muscularity into macho, in the way that the northern English mining city of Newcastle-upon-Tyne has done with its famous Brown Ale (or, to a lesser extent, Pittsburgh, with its Iron City Beer, or Pottsville, Pennsylvania, with its Yuengling Porter). The matching of food with wine, let alone beer, is not a great issue in Germany, but a true, medium-dry Dortmunder Export has enough

This 1913 postcard advertising the Dortmunder Actien Brauerei stylishly presented an image that was both potent and apt – at least while the coal and steel industries flourished.

character to accompany the region's sustaining dishes, featuring a variety of Westphalian hams and bacons, beef with onions, stews and hotpots.

The term Export sounds ironic today, when the style can scarcely be found outside its home region. When the Dortmund brewers do export, they are inclined to send their Pilsners, which are perfectly acceptable but of no great distinction.

A beer in broadly the same proportions as a Dortmunder is made by many brewers elsewhere in Germany, with the designation Export. Several far stronger pale lagers are produced in Belgium and the Netherlands under the abbreviation Dort, with alcohol contents from 4.8–5.6 percent by weight, 6–7 by volume. In Denmark, the Ceres brewery has one that is slightly stronger still. Some of the most enthusiastic essays into a more traditional Dortmunder Export style are today being made in the United States.

Dortmunder Export producers

The big brewers of Dortmund all make beers in the traditional Export style, but no longer promote it. Some of the new generation of brewers in the United States are doing a better job of sustaining this regional classic. Sapporo's Yebisu has long been popular in Japan.

DORTMUNDER ACTIEN BRAUEREI
DAB, 20 Steiger Strasse,
4600 Dortmund 1, Germany
Tel: (0231) 84000

One of the best-known Dortmund brewers, the company was founded in 1868, by a family named Fischer, then went public in 1872. Actien indicates a company issuing shares on the stock market, as in 'a piece of the action'. The brewery likes to recall that it won a gold medal for its Dortmunder-style beer at the 1900 World Fair in Paris, but it also pioneered the city's move to Pilsners, in 1971. In 1979, the company acquired Dortmunder Hansa. I was lucky enough to see both companies' handsome brewhouses (Actien's with brass-railed staircases and stained-glass windows, and Hansa's Art Nouveau) before the two marques moved out of the city centre at the beginning of the 1980s. The merged breweries are part of a national group with Binding of Frankfurt, and Berliner Kindl.

The company's Export, with the brand name DAB, is pale for the style, on the sweet side, with some maltiness in the middle and balancing hop in the finish. Its Hansa counterpart seems softer and slightly less sweet. The Hansa beers are produced as competitive brands for the supermarket trade.

DORTMUNDER KRONEN
Kronen Brauerei, 1 Kronenburg Allee,
4600 Dortmund 1, Germany
Tel: (0231) 54130

Privately owned, proud of that, and said to be the oldest brewery in Westphalia, this enterprise traces its history to a brewpub mentioned in city documents in 1430. It began to serve other outlets in 1517, and was acquired by Johann Wenker in 1729. His sons-in-law took over and their family, called Brand, still run the business. It moved to its present site in the district of Kronenburg in 1873. It sits on a foundation of rock that provided excellent lagering cellars.

Much of the 1870s' building was destroyed in World War II, and most of the brewery structure dates from the 1960s. The equipment is modern, but the company has elaborate procedures at every stage of production. The control systems permit very detailed interventions by the brewers. 'Automation teaches you nothing. Experience is the sum of your blunders,' a brewer once told me.

Kronen's beers are typically very clean and soft, with a fresh, delicate hop aroma. The Kronen Export is an excellent example.

Kronen has also recently acquired two other Dortmund breweries: Stifts (which no longer brews on its own site); and Thier (which does). Kronen has two brewpubs (see Gazetteer).

The Thier brewery is on a site where the city wall once stood. A patrician family called von Hövel is said to have had brewing rights there in the 1500s, and a von Hövel founded the Thier brewery, in 1854, along with a man named Sonnenschein and Gustav Thier. Thier's Export is the fullest, firmest and smoothest, with the most emphatic malt character.

DORTMUNDER UNION BRAUEREI
Brau und Brunnen,
2 Rheinische Strasse,
4600 Dortmund 1, Germany
Tel: (0231) 181702

Dortmunder Union's 'U' logo is a landmark in the centre of the city: it is 55 feet (17 metres) high.

The other very widely known Dortmund brewer, often identified as DUB. The union refers to a merger of ten or a dozen breweries which formed the present company in 1873. An initial 'U', illuminated at night, stands on the roof of the present brewery building, which dates from 1927. In 1973, the brewery linked with Schultheiss of Berlin to form a national grouping. In more recent years, this group has adopted the corporate name Brau und Brunnen. The second word refers to a well or spring, and the company owns a number of mineral water brands, including the internationally renowned Apollinaris.

The Dortmunder Union brewery is itself a landmark, with the look of a 1920s' power station, but there has for some years been speculation as to how long it will operate. Were it to cease, some other use would have to be found for the protected building, and that might be difficult. The logic would be for DUB to share the less central site of its subsidiary Dortmunder Ritter.

DUB's Export is malt-accented and medium-bodied. The Ritter Export seems slightly fruity. DUB's products are widely marketed, while those of Ritter have their strongest following in the Ruhr region.

GORDON BIERSCH

Gordon Biersch, 640 Emerson Street, Palo Alto, California 94301, USA
Tel: (415) 323-7723

Dan Gordon worked as a labourer in the brewhouse for Anheuser-Busch in St Louis, Missouri, then went to Germany to study at Weihenstephan. After he graduated, he was apprenticed at Spaten in Munich. He has since set up several highly regarded brewpubs in California with Dean Biersch. Despite his name, Biersch is not a brewer – he trained in beverage and food management at the Hilton in Beverly Hills. They established their first brewpub in the former Bijou Cinema, in Palo Alto, the university town south of San Francisco. This was so successful that it was soon followed by another in San Jose (33 East San Fernando Street), then in San Francisco itself (2 Harrison Street, at the Embarcadero).

The company has fitted its pubs with sizable, made-to-order brewhouses, constructed in Bavaria, and has chosen to specialize in German styles of lager. It is unusual in that its principal pale lager has, from the start, been an Export type, identified as such. This is an all-malt beer, with a gravity of 12–12.5 Plato (1048–50) and about 25 units of bitterness.

The first Gordon Biersch Export I sampled, at Palo Alto in 1988, was a good example of the style. It had a very fresh aroma, excellent lacework, a lightly malty accent, a firm body, and a very late but emphatic hoppy dryness. At San Jose in 1990, the Export was again very fresh in aroma, malty and soft, but with less hop character. In San Francisco in 1992, it had an excellent malt character,

though it seemed on the light side, and the hoppiness had returned.

These three brewpubs also make a nutty Märzen, a chocolaty, roasty Dunkles, and seasonal specials such as wheat and bock beers. There are plans to open further brewpubs, in Walnut Creek and Pasadena, Los Angeles.

Any brewpub wishing to match its beers with contemporary cuisine could take a lesson from Gordon Biersch. Without pronouncing this as a policy, the menus often feature ingredients and seasonings typical of the great brewing countries in combinations that are surprising but sympathetic. If it were to add an ale or two it would surely have a beer for every dish.

SAPPORO

Sapporo Breweries, 7-10-1 Ginza, Chuo-ku, Tokyo, 104 Japan
Tel: (03) 3572-6111

Some Japanese beer-lovers feel that, among that country's golden lagers, the one with the most character is Yebisu; the name is that of a Shinto deity. The beer was first made before World War II, and is intended to be in the Dortmunder style.

Yebisu has a perfumy maltiness of bouquet; a firm, slightly oily body; and a malty dryness in the palate. It is hopped with Hallertau Mittelfrüh and Hersbruck. The draught version, which enthusiasts especially prize, is softer, with excellent lacework. The beer has a gravity of only 11.7 Plato (1047), with an alcohol content of just over 4 percent by weight, 5 by volume, and a colour of 9–10 EBC.

SARATOGA

Saratoga Lager, 412 Tenafly Road, Englewood, New Jersey 07631, USA
Tel: (201) 568-0716

While working as an advertising executive on the Lufthansa account, Chuck Schroeder regularly visited Germany, and developed a taste for some of the northern beers. Later, he worked on advertising for Stroh and Miller, and decided he would like to make beer himself. He collaborated with Bill Newman, a pioneer microbrewer in upstate New York.

Inspired by Schroeder's interest in German beers, the two created Newman's Brand Saratoga Lager, in the Dortmunder style. This has a gravity of 12.5 Plato (1050), and is brewed from pale and crystal malts, with Hallertau Mittelfrüh, Hersbruck and Saaz hops. It is produced under contract at the Catamount brewery, in White River Junction, Vermont.

STOUDT

Stoudt's Real Beer, Route 272, Adamstown, Pennsylvania 19501, USA
Tel: (215) 484-4387

The Steud family came to the United States from Germany in 1733; in the 1960s, Ed Stoudt went into the restaurant business. In 1987, while Ed ran the restaurant, his wife Carol toured breweries in Bavaria, took a course at the University of California in Davis, then set to work brewing.

Export Gold has a very bright colour; a firm, malty middle; and a dry finish. It has a superbly fresh, aromatic malt character, and is beautifully balanced. It is brewed from a gravity of 12–12.5 Plato (1048–50), with 15 percent Munich malt and three percent crystal, in a decoction mash, with three additions of hops (German-grown Hallertau Mittelfrüh, Tettnang and Saaz). Other styles have included a Kulmbacher, an Eisbock, a very clove-like Weizen, a raspberry beer, and even a stout.

Bock beer

By no means every beer-lover is familiar with Ein-beck, an historic town of only 25–30,000 people, near the old Saxon cities of Hanover and Brunswick (Braunschweig), in northern Germany; far more have unknowingly raised a glass in its name. This town, pronounced as Einbock or something similar by the southerners of Bavaria, almost certainly gave its sec-ond syllable to describe one of the great beer styles.

Five or six miles away, there are already signs on the road announcing the imminence of 'Einbeck, the Beer City'. At the town boundary, three casks stand as a final reminder, even though Einbeck today has only one brewery (see page 227).

The beers that made Einbeck famous were first produced in the 14th and 15th centuries. They were very strong, because they were made to be sent long distances, fermenting on the way. At that time, they may well have been top-fermenting wheat beers. Today, such a beer would be described as a Weizen-bock; on its own, the word bock usually indicates a strong lager, sometimes dark – often seasonal, as a springtime or winter warmer.

Einbeck's seasonal speciality is its May bock, but some regions and countries wait until summer is over.

Because of its geographical origins, the designation bock is used primarily by brewers in the German tradition. The term occurs in several Germanic lan-guages, each with its own slight variation of spelling. In most of these languages, the word also means billy goat, and that animal is frequently used on labels as a symbol of the style. This has led to several alternative, if unlikely, stories about the origin of the designation. Followers of the zodiac have even described it as a beer for the season of Capricorn, which straddles Christmas, a time when some brewers release a bock. More down-to-earth observers might concede that a good bock has the kick of a goat.

The Dutch produce bock beers (often spelled with-out the 'c', and traditionally dark) primarily for the season of late September and early October, usually in the range of 4.8–5.6 percent alcohol by weight, 6–7 by volume, but sometimes stronger.

The Eggenberg brewery in Austria has made some-thing of a speciality of well-balanced, fresh-tasting bock beers, particularly the creamy but dryish Urbock 23, at 23 Plato (1092), with 7.9 percent alco-hol by weight, 9.9 by volume.

In Switzerland, Hürlimann's Christmas beer Sam-ichlaus is surely a very strong bock, although it is not described as such (see page 231).

Not all strong lagers are bocks, and the designation perhaps should be reserved for all-malt beers with a

The brewery remembers 600 years of tradition, with the city's monogram of barley and hops, malting and brewing equipment.

Beer and prosperity go together, and God's guidance in this direction was celebrated in the carvings on the wood-framed houses of Einbeck. The finest buildings are from the late 16th and early 17th centuries, from the end of the Gothic period to the beginning of the Renaissance.

respectable lagering time. The Danish Carlsberg Elephant Beer (5.7; 7.1) does not call itself a bock, but does have some malty smoothness. The stronger Carlsberg Special (6.8; 8.5) is not designated as a bock either, and is too sweet and fruity to be regarded as one. This is true of several similar beers from northern countries. Their flavours suggest that fermentation and maturation have taken place too quickly and at temperatures that are too high to produce the clean, smooth character of a true bock.

Almost all of the Norwegian brewers produce a dark *bokkøl*, at around 4.8 percent alcohol by weight, 6 by volume, and some are very good examples of the style. I have especially enjoyed the malt character of the bock from the Aass brewery (see page 227).

The French and Belgians, confusingly, used to apply the term bock to weak beers; perhaps these were served in large vessels like those used in Munich.

Bock was once a major seasonal style among brewers of German heritage in North America, but after Prohibition and World War II these products declined in authenticity and character until some were little more than standard lagers with a dash of sweetness and colour; now, with the spread of microbreweries, a new generation of serious bock beers is emerging. In Milwaukee, the Lakefront microbrewery, which produces beautifully balanced beers full of flavour, invites a local priest to conduct a blessing of the bock at a small festival in mid- to late March.

The 'malt liquors' of the United States are generally lagers of an above-standard strength, but with a poor malt character (some contain a great deal of sugar).

One of the most interesting survivors of German influence is the Maibock (4.8; 6) made by Namibia Breweries, in the former colony of South West Africa. This has a reddish, tawny colour; a medium to full body, rather carbonic; a hint of iron, some syrupiness, and a tinge of caramel in the finish.

Einbeck

At the point where a smaller river meets the Leine, Einbeck lay at a crossroads of trading routes in the days when the major cities of northern Europe formed the Hanseatic League. This early European Community perceived each member as having its own specialization; Einbeck was the brewing centre.

Paulaner's Salvator Doppelbock shows hints of deep amber when it is held up to the light. Other extra-strong bock beers have similar-sounding names.

Bock beers are strong lagers – though not all strong lagers are bocks. The term is best applied to a smooth, malty beer with a hint or more of sweetness, and bock, along with its even stronger cousin double bock, is usually enjoyed as a warming drink from late autumn through to spring. The richer examples can be served as dessert beers.

To either side, the Harz mountains and Solling hills provide water. Einbeck today grows sugar beet, potatoes and corn, but barley is cultivated between Hildesheim and Braunschweig, and probably was in medieval times. Even in those days, the town had links to the ports of Hamburg and Bremen. Einbeck beers were said to be shipped to Hanseatic towns in Scandinavia and the Netherlands.

The oldest evidence of the industry in Einbeck is a receipt for beer from the ducal court in 1378. Citizens had brewing rights at an early stage. They did their own malting, spreading the grain in lofts and drying it by natural ventilation. Hops are also said to have been dried in this way. In the old centre of the town, every other house seems to have vents in the roof, looking like very shallow dormer windows, set one above the other into the pitch of the tiling. The city had its own public kettle, which was taken to each house in turn.

The Hofbräuhaus Maibock can nourish 4,500 people at the brewery's tavern on the Platzl, in Munich.

In order to admit the mobile kettle, the houses in Einbeck had arches the height of one storey or more, and these remain – another remarkable visual testimony to the preoccupations of the town. A statue on the market square commemorates a town joker who is said to have immersed his dog in the brew-kettle. The dog's name was Hops.

The order in which the kettle went from one house to another was determined by a public lottery on 1 May. One brewing season had ended, and now was the time to reschedule for the next. The timing of this lottery, coinciding with the celebration of spring, is said to be the origin of Maibock. Because they were made when all beers were dark, Maibocks were originally full in colour. Some still are but others, including that of Einbeck, are paler, perhaps in deference to their arrival in springtime.

The people brewed for their own use and sold the excess to the city for 'export'. This made the town prosperous, and the burghers displayed their wealth in ornate carvings on the visible wooden frames of their homes. A fire destroyed the town in 1540, but many houses built by burgher-brewers after that time, in the late Gothic style, survive, their carved facades painted in terracotta, yellow ochre and deep, leafy greens. The carvings feature motifs such as rosettes, cords and trapezoidal patterns. Some also bear classical and religious figures, Biblical texts and aphorisms: 'God is with us…He makes men happy…his advice is good.'

Kulmbach and Munich

The Duke of Brunswick is said to have taken several casks of Einbeck beer for his wedding party when he married the daughter of a southern aristocrat in the 1600s, and that is how the style is supposed to have become associated with Bavaria and its great brewing centres, especially Kulmbach and Munich. One argument has it that Einbeck's success as a brewing town had already inspired Duke Wilhelm of Bavaria to build the Munich Hofbräuhaus. Like the Einbeck brewery, the Hofbräuhaus regards bock beer as its speciality, and highlights the Maytime version.

Doppelbock

Bock beers are meant to be strong, and in Germany have a minimum gravity of 16 Plato (1064). This is likely to produce an alcohol content of not less than 5.3 percent by weight, 6.7 by volume, but bocks can be far stronger.

Traditionally, monks made extremely full-bodied and strong beers to be consumed as 'liquid bread' during Lent. A famous example was made in Munich by followers of Saint Francis of Paula. (These monks were not Franciscans, though their founder, born in Paula, Calabria, had been. The Franciscan order was founded by Saint Francis of Assisi.)

The Pauline monks, who established a brewery in Munich in 1634 and began to sell their beer commercially in 1780, made an especially strong bock named Salvator ('saviour'). The Paulaner brewery was secularized during the time of Napoleon, but still ceremonially taps the first new season's brew of Salvator shortly before Easter every year (see page 230).

Over the years, other brewers in Bavaria launched extra strong bocks and gave them names ending in -ator. Augustiner has Maximator, Spaten has Optimator, Löwenbräu has Triumphator, Hacker-Pschorr has Animator, and there are a great many more. The Ayinger brewery has Fortunator in Germany, although the same beer is called Celebrator in the American market.

These beers are known as doppel ('double') bocks, though they are not actually twice as strong. In Germany, they are required to have a gravity of 18 Plato (1072), probably producing an alcohol content of not less than 5.4 percent by weight, 6.8 by volume.

Eisbock

As gravities become higher, alcohol content does not follow in proportion. This is because fermentation becomes more difficult; the alcohol begins to stun the yeast. One means of achieving higher strengths is to concentrate the brew by freezing it and removing ice. Water freezes before alcohol, so the latter survives the process.

The freezing technique is said to have been discovered by accident: a feckless apprentice left casks out of doors, the contents partially froze, and the remaining beer was especially strong and delicious.

This technique is well known in Bavaria, but only one brewery makes a point of it. Reichelbräu, of Kulmbach, produces a beer in this way and has registered the name Eisbock (see page 229). This is a neat allusion to Germany's Eiswein, made from grapes picked and pressed immediately after a frost has concentrated their juice.

Dessert drinks

Just as Eiswein is likely to be served as a dessert drink, so some bock beers, especially the darker, richer, maltier types, can fulfil the same function. With their warming alcohol content, they seem to do the job, especially after the hearty dinners of the far north.

In Alaska I have been served a bock with a crème caramel which was also flavoured with the beer. One of the best combinations I have enjoyed was bock beer with marzipan cake, which I first sampled at the Aass brewery, in Norway. At a dinner of the wryly named Norwegian Society for the Furtherance of Beer and Other Culture, I was served bock laced with port, again with marzipan cake.

Bock producers

Many long-established Bavarian producers maintain Einbeck's tradition of strong seasonal brews, with names that give a clue to the power within. Switzerland's contender for the world's strongest beer hides behind the jovial name of Samichlaus, 'Santa Claus'. The style emigrated to North America with German brewers, and appeared more recently in Australia. In Norway the beer is known as *bokkøl*.

AASS

P Lauritz Aass, Post Box 1107, Drammen, Norway 3001
Tel: (03) 832580

The name, mercifully pronounced 'orse', is a Norwegian word for a summit. Perhaps the Aass family came from the mountains. A ships' supply company, lumber and grain merchants gave rise to this family brewery, in the port of Drammen, near Oslo, in the mid-1800s. Drammen once had enough brewers to form a guild, but now has only one. The Aass family villa of 1892 was restored in the 1980s to serve as a Guild House, to which the public are invited for evening events.

The 1921 tower brewery still stands, though the vessels are now in another building on the same site, and Aass has constantly modernized.

The brewery produces a Pilsner, an Export, Vienna-style Amber and Christmas beers, and a Bavarian-style dark lager as well as its Aass Bock (17 Plato; 1068; 4.9; 6.1), rendered in Norway as Bokkøl. This beer is dark brown, with a rich, creamy body and a hint of licorice. For its bock, the brewery uses a double-decoction mash, a long boil, and five to six months' maturation.

EINBECKER

Einbecker Brauhaus, 4–7 Papen Strasse, 3352 Einbeck, Lower Saxony, Germany
Tel: (05561) 7970

The town of beer-makers built a public brewery in 1794. This was replaced by a steam-powered brewery in 1844, and in 1880 shares were sold to raise money for public works. The brewery was rebuilt, on the same site, between 1967 and 1975, and a controlling interest is now held by the national brewing group Brau und Brunnen.

Just behind the main street of timbered buildings, the modern brewery building rises, its looming tower finished in a sympathetic terracotta colour, and bearing a legend that claims the style for its home-town: 'Ohne Einbeck gäb's kein Bockbier.'

(If it was not for Einbeck, there would be no bock beer.)

The company makes a Pils as well as its three bock beers. The latter are produced, all to a gravity of 16.3 Plato (1065–6), by double-decoction, with a relatively short boil, under pressure. The water is soft, from deep springs in the Solling nature reserve. Hops are added twice, as pellets and extract from the Hallertau Northern Brewer, Perle and Hersbruck varieties.

The aim at Einbeck is to have in the bock beers an aroma leaning toward a soft maltiness rather than hop. The maltiness is intended to be aromatic rather than sweet, syrupy or full in the palate, and the hop bitterness to be evident. The brewery argues that the original Einbecker beers would have largely fermented out during transport, and would have been well hopped to survive the journey.

The Maibock has only six weeks' maturation, with the intention that it should have a faintly estery, more bubbly and refreshing character. The Hell (pale) and Dunkel (dark) are matured for eight to ten weeks.

The Hell is very pale (15 EBC), with a fresh maltiness in the aroma and palate, and a light hop character eventually developing to become pronounced and long in a late finish (38 BU). The Dunkel is tawny to dark brown (40 EBC), with a smooth, dry, quite intense malt character, rounded off by a balance of hoppiness in the finish (again 38 BU, but against a maltier background). The Maibock has a bronze colour (25 EBC), a softer malt character, and a less assertive hoppy dryness (36 BU). It is released at the end of March, and the last bottles leave the brewery in early to mid-May. Curiously, there is no festival set around the Maibock.

Visitors to the brewery can see a small museum, and enjoy a beer while sitting inside an old wooden lagering vessel in the cellars. The brewery's 'tap' is the 1552 'Brodhaus' on the Market Square. Specialities include ham boiled in the Dunkel.

The EKU brewery in nocturnal mood.

EKU

Erste Kulmbacher Actienbrauerei,
1 EKU Strasse, 8650 Kulmbach,
Germany
Tel: (09221) 8821

The 'First' Kulmbach Brewery was formed from the merger of two smaller companies in 1872. The 1890s' maltings, a classic of its period, still stands, albeit with more recent equipment working inside.

From the post-modernist structure one has a view of the rival Reichel brewery in the distance. Kulmbach has a third brewery, Mönchshof (a fourth, Schweizerhof, has closed, but a brewpub is planned) and five maltings, all in a town of only 29,000 people. As a very old brewing town, it is known for its dark and strong specialities.

The town's water comes from the conifer-covered granite mountains of the Fichtel range and is softened for brewing. EKU uses barley from Upper Franconia and Thuringia, in a single-decoction mash, and makes three additions (in its Pils, four) of Perle, Hersbruck and Tettnang hops, in the form of pellets and extract.

The brewery is especially well known for its Kulminator (19.2; 1077; 6; 7.6+) double bock and a yet-stronger version with the imprimatur '28' (after its original gravity, now boosted to 30, or around 1120). The '28' usually has an alcohol content of 9.2–9.6 percent by weight, 11.5–12 by volume, but I have seen analyses as high as 11.1 by weight, 13.7 by volume. This brew, inspired by an old specification, was launched in 1954, and was for a time listed as the world's strongest.

Kulminator has a colour reminiscent of dark cherries (65 EBC); a creamy, malty character with some whiskyish notes; and a very restrained hop character (24 BU).

The '28' is made entirely from pale malt but, at such a gravity, develops some colour. It is pale amber, with a pink tinge (35 EBC). Sampled fresh, it is rich and malty without being overwhelmingly cloying, and has very complex perfumy esters reminiscent of orange skins. These provide a dryish finish. Again, the hop is restrained (30 BU), but there is a surge of warming alcohol. Some enthusiasts consume the beer at room temperature, as a bedtime drink or a cold remedy. The brewery also suggests a cocktail of one part '28', two of orange juice and a dash of rum: a Bock's Fizz?

The brewery claims it lagers the '28' for nine months, at temperatures from 0 to -2°C/32–28°F. For the last two or three weeks, ice forms in the tanks. The brewery says this is to clarify and stabilize the brew, and that the ice left behind is insufficient significantly to concentrate the strength of the beer.

FRANKENMUTH

Frankenmuth Brewery, 425 South Main Street, Frankenmuth, Michigan 48734, USA
Tel: (517) 652-6183

'Franconian courage' is the translation of the town's name. It was originally settled in 1845 by Lutheran missionaries from Neuendettelsau, near Nuremberg. The first Frankenmuth Brewery was established in 1857, and there has been production since 1862 on the present site.

In 1986, the castle brewery of Lauenstein, in the extreme north of Franconia, on the border with Thuringia, ceased production, and its kettles were shipped to Frankenmuth. They were installed on the brewery site, but in new buildings, and under new management, though with some of the same staff. The brewery is now run by Fred Schumacher, of the Düsseldorf brewing family. The head brewer is Fred Scheer, a German who has worked in several American small breweries old and new, and been active in the beer renaissance.

Frankenmuth has a range of well-made German styles, and is one of several new-generation American breweries known for its bock beers. Frankenmuth Bock has a dense, rocky head; a tawny colour (32 EBC); a malty nose and palate, with some toffeeish notes; and a warming finish. It is made from six specifications of malt. The brewery, built in rustic style, welcomes visitors...and sells them its products.

HOFBRÄUHAUS

Hofbräuhaus am Platzl, Munich 2
Tel: (089) 221676

Staatliches Hofbräuhaus, 1 Hofbräu Allee, 8000 Munich 82, Germany
Tel: (089) 921050

The world's most famous 'brewpub', the Munich Hofbräuhaus, was built in 1589–91 by Duke Wilhelm V of Bavaria, and at first made what was described as 'brown beer'. In 1614, a new brewmaster introduced a strong beer modelled on those made in Einbeck. This style attained such a reputation that, as with wheat beer, the aristocracy retained a monopoly of its production for 200 years. Several other cities or towns each had their own Hofbräuhaus ('royal court brewery'), and some of these still exist.

The Munich Hofbräuhaus stands on a small square called the Platzl, in the centre of Munich.

The beer hall and garden has been renovated several times, most comprehensively in 1897, gaining more arches, turrets and balconies with age. The range of beer styles has grown, and their production moved first to a handsome 19th-century brewery elsewhere in the city centre and more recently to an uncompromisingly modern plant on the edge. Both the Hofbräuhaus and its brewery are owned by the State of Bavaria.

On a sunny day, the galleried courtyard garden, shaded by chestnut trees, can be a delight, its folding tables brightened with check cloths, glasses of hazy Weissbier, golden Export and ruby bock, and snacks of *Weisswurst* or *Leberkäs* (a meat loaf made from beef and pork).

The vaulted chambers on the ground floor have their moments, too, though sometimes they smokily evoke the battlefield imagined by the travel writer Patrick Leigh Fermor in 1932. In the centre of the main hall, a band periodically strikes up, urging drinkers to recharge their vessels. In one private chamber, duelling clubs

still spill blood. Depending upon business, three floors can be opened to guests, and around 4,500 people can be seated at a time. Last orders are at 11.30.

The great 'feast hall' upstairs, decked with flags and coats-of-arms, hosts a formal lunch in the last week of April, at which a thousand of Bavaria's social elite are invited to witness a member of the state or federal government tap the first barrel of Maibock.

The Hofbräuhaus Maibock has a very full amber colour; a malty fruitiness in its aroma and palate, without being excessively sweet; and is remarkably soft and easily drinkable. It has a gravity of 16.2 Plato (1072–3), and 5.8 percent alcohol by weight, 7.2 by volume. The Hofbräuhaus also has a slightly darker winter bock, with a very faint hint of roasted malt and some yeastiness (18.3; 1073–4; 5.9; 7.4). This is known as Delicator. There is also, at this same higher gravity and strength, the pale Bock Hell, malty and relatively dry for its weight. These beers are said to have three months' lagering.

KULMBACHER REICHELBRÄU

Reichelbräu Aktien-Gesellschaft, 9 Lichtenfelser Strasse, 8650 Kulmbach, Germany
Tel: (09221) 7051

By a small margin, Reichelbräu is the second of Kulmbach's brewers in output, but its beers are more evident locally.

The brewery takes its name from a man named Reichel who was one of its founders in 1846.

There was a natural lake on the site, from which ice was cut to cool the lagering cellars. The lake is now a lawn, but the ice-house still stands. Wooden lagering vessels sit decoratively by the road. A new brewhouse

Kulmbach's colours, seen as the beer is filtered.

was fitted in 1970, in a white-painted tower, which is one of the several beery landmarks of Kulmbach.

The brewery has a wide range of more conventional products with higher volumes, but its speciality is its Eisbock, subtitled Bayrisch G'frorns ('Bavarian frozen'). This complex brew has a deep reddish-brown colour; a malty nose; a remarkably smooth palate; and a hint of a whisky-and-coffee liqueur in its warming, alcoholic, faintly bitter finish. The beer has 8 percent alcohol by weight, 10 by volume.

It is made to a gravity of 24 Plato (1096) from five malts, including one that has an intentionally sour, lactic character. A dark malt of 21–33 EBC provides a lot of the aroma and palate, while the lactic one helps avoid excessive sweetness. The finished beer has 130 EBC. The malt character is more significant than the hop, but there are nonetheless three additions, of Brewers' Gold, Perle, Hersbruck and Tettnang (27 BU).

After a conventional fermentation of eight to nine days, the beer is frozen for 11–14 days. Between five and seven percent of the volume remains behind as ice when the brew is removed. It is *kräusened* in the lagering tank. Brews of the Eisbock are made for only a couple of weeks, at the end of August and beginning of September. The beer is then introduced at an Eisbock Festival in Kulmbach's town hall on the last Saturday of March. The ceremony begins at around 7 pm with the cracking open of a frozen cask.

NIAGARA
Niagara Falls Brewing, 6863 Lundy's Lane, Niagara Falls, Ontario L2G 1V7, Canada
Tel: (416) 374-1166

An Italian family making equipment for the wine-makers of Niagara built this brewery as something of an experiment. Eiswein is a local speciality, so the Crivellers decided to make its beery counterpart, an Eisbock.

The brewery opened in July 1989, and brewed its Eisbock early in November. The beer was put on the market in mid-December, and had sold out before the end of January. In subsequent years, brewing began in July, and the beer was launched at the beginning of October, then kept on the market until late February.

I sampled the first batch, and found it remarkably delicate and surprisingly dry. It had a clean, fresh bouquet; a peachy colour and palate; a light, soft maltiness; a smooth body; and a dry finish. It seems since to have become even more complex.

The idea, which I believe succeeded, was not to achieve the highest possible strength but simply to use the freezing technique as a means of concentrating flavours. The first Niagara Falls Eisbock was made from four malts to a gravity of 15.3 Plato (1061–2), hopped with Hallertau Mittelfrüh and fermented to 4.8 percent alcohol by weight, 6 by volume. After a good two weeks' lagering at -1°C/30.2°F, its temperature was reduced until it reached -15°C/5°F.

The ends of the traditional wooden lagering vessels are often carved. This retired vessel is at Paulaner.

It was held at that temperature for a further week or so, until more than a quarter of the volume had frozen. The ice was left behind, and the finished beer had an alcohol content of 6.4 percent by weight, 8 by volume.

The brewery has made several other products, including a conventional lager, a brown ale and an extra-strong bitter.

PAULANER
Paulaner-Salvator-Thomasbräu, 75 Hoch Strasse, 8000 Munich 95, Germany
Tel: (089) 480050

The monks who established the brewery originally called their strong Lenten speciality 'Holy Father Beer'. In the early 1800s, the secular brewer Franz-Xaver Zacherl took over, and began to promote the strongest beer under the name Salvator. Other brewers borrowed this as a generic name for a strong beer, but a trademark law of 1894 allowed the Paulaner brewery to protect the term.

The first new Salvator of each season is tapped with some ceremony at the brewery's cellar and garden on a Thursday afternoon three or four weeks before Easter. This period is known in Munich as 'the strong beer season'. People talk about 'taking the beer cure'. After a long winter's hibernation, the citizens wish to get out into the beer gardens, but the weather may still be cool: a double bock is a springtime warmer, though the beer is now available year-round.

Like many such communities, the Paulaners' monastery was built on a hillside, defensible and at the time remote from the city. On the same hill, a banker named Nockher had built a country house. The hill is still known as Nockherberg. Zacherl expanded the brewery, and dug lagering cellars into the hillside. Paulaner became a lager brewery, pioneering the use of refrigeration and steam power. It still has one or two wooden lagering vessels, its original von Linde ammonia compressor and a donkey engine, as museum pieces. In 1923, Paulaner acquired the Thomas brewery (which no longer operates separately) and more recently Hacker-Pschorr (which still does).

From the modern office block, a tunnel runs under the hillside to Paulaner's own maltings, brewhouse (with traditional copper kettles) and cellars. The brewery has its own springs, giving relatively hard water, and its beers are dry by the standards of Munich. The Salvator double bock is a dark beer, with a malty aroma and palate, rounding out to a relatively dry finish. It is made from three malts and Hallertau hops. Its gravity is 18–18.5 (1072–4), with an alcohol content of 6 percent by weight, 7.5 by volume. Lagering is from ten to 12 weeks, sometimes much longer.

SAMICHLAUS

Brauerei Hürlimann,
150 Brandschenke Strasse,
8002 Zurich, Switzerland
Tel: (01) 288-2626

The world's strongest lager, named after the Swiss-German dialect for Santa Claus, is made by the Zurich brewery Hürlimann. It is truly a seasonal beer. Samichlaus is brewed annually on Saint Nicholas' Day, then lagered until it must be bottled for the next year's celebration. It is not labelled as a doppelbock but, with 11–13 percent alcohol by weight, 14–16 by volume, fits that category.

This corner of Switzerland has a long history of brewing. The abbey of Saint Gallen, founded by an Irish monk after the Dark Ages, was one of Europe's greatest brewing monasteries. The Hürlimann brewing company was established by the family of the same name in 1836. Thirty years later, the brewery moved to its present site, southeast of the city and in the foothills of the Alps, which provided ice for lagering.

Hürlimann's work on the isolation of yeast strains has led to its supplying cultures to around 200 breweries throughout the world. In studying yeasts' abilities to tolerate high levels of alcohol, the company bred the culture that ferments Samichlaus.

Samichlaus was first made in 1980, initially in both pale and dark versions. In a beer so dense (original gravity more than 30 Plato, around 1120), the 'pale' had a markedly ruddy complexion, and the brewery eventually decided to leave the field to the reddish-brown 'dark' (65–75 EBC). From barley grown in the Czech Republic, Germany and France, one pale malt and three dark are used, with a double-decoction mash.

Hops are added three times, as both extract and pellets. The fourth generation of Hürlimanns introduced hop-growing, on a small scale, to Switzerland, fearing that World War II might interrupt supplies from Germany. A variety similar to Hallertau Mittelfrüh, called Stammheim, is grown at Schaffhausen, not far from Zurich. This is used along with Tettnang and Hallertau Northern Brewer from Germany (25–30 BU).

Samichlaus is fermented for up to two weeks, at relatively high temperatures, then lagered for nine or ten months. The beer has a densely malty creaminess, with some yeast notes. Its fullness is relieved by a smooth firmness of body, and its richness by the soothing surge of warming, brandy-like alcohol in the finish.

SCHARER'S

George IV Inn, 180 Old Hume
Highway, Picton,
New South Wales 2571, Australia
Tel: (046) 771415

The Scharers, from the Zurich area of Switzerland, emigrated to Australia four generations ago. Publican's son Geoff Scharer runs the George IV, a historic bar and hotel, in the coal town of Picton, 50 miles southwest of Sydney.

The George IV, said to date from 1819 but officially opened in 1839, comprises a verandah, two bars and a dining room. Behind are a number of bedrooms, arranged like an early counterpart to a modern motel. Convicts and road gangs were once its guests, and more recently passing drivers, then Picton was cut off by a new highway. Scharer decided to add a brewery in the hope of attracting weekend visitors from Sydney.

In 1978, he made the first move in Australia's beer renaissance by applying for a licence to brew. He finally received this in 1981, and subsequently engaged the German consultant Otto Binding to help him with equipment. He started brewing in 1987. Scharer clearly feels passionately about the quality of his beers, and is joined in this perfectionism by his brewer, the spendidly named Deo Gratias Lule, who was born in Uganda and graduated at Heriot-Watt University, Edinburgh.

At Scharer's, I have tasted a full-bodied, hoppy, resinous, pale lager and the outstanding Burragorang Bock. The latter, taking its name from a nearby stretch of countryside, has a dense, creamy head; a very dark ruby colour; a remarkably smooth, silky palate; and a clean malt character, with hints of treacle toffee. It is a very deceptive beer, with no obvious alcohol taste. Three malts are used, to a gravity of 16 (1064), in an upward infusion mash, and the hops are Spalt blossoms. Maturation is for seven weeks to three months.

EXTRA SPECIALITIES

While it is helpful to divide beers into classic styles and families, no such categorization can be the last word on the subject. A handful of specialities are difficult to categorize. Arguably, this applies to whimsical products such as pepper or ginger beers, or those flavoured with various herbs and spices, but there are also classic styles that for one reason or another resist being placed within a family.

Some, such as the classic Anchor Steam Beer, use a lager yeast at ale temperatures. Yet the words 'steam beer' do not necessarily guarantee a brew in this style.

Another elusive term is black beer. It is usually applied to very dark lagers but also embraces the odd top-fermenting speciality. Here again, the same name is being used for different styles, although in this instance they have their colour in common.

The classic smoked beers of Bamberg in Bavaria are lagers, but several similar specialities elsewhere are made with top-fermenting yeasts, and some have established a considerable following.

The best-known rye beer is an adaptation from a wheat beer, but others are harder to classify.

These are all by now established terms, but more new styles are developing as brewers become more adventurous and eclectic. Some of their new creations work well, like a brewers' counterpart to Italian-Californian cuisine, others have been concocted without any thought for the harmony of elements, like Thai pizzas, or bagel-shaped tacos.

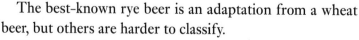

Steam beer

It is not surprising that the term steam beer excites the imagination. People have never ceased to be fascinated by steam power. Its machines are superhuman in their visible strength and throbbing potency. They were the engines of the industrial revolution, and their users were proud of a technology that was in today's cliche 'state of the art.' The legend 'steam beer brewery' can still be seen in the brickwork of some buildings of the mid- to late 19th century in Europe.

The pioneering breweries in California also had a product that came to be known as 'steam beer'. It has been argued that in California this description alluded not to the source of power but to the hiss of natural carbon dioxide that issued from the casks when they were tapped. This sounds like legend, but the idea was advanced in print as early as 1898, in an article in the *Western Brewer*. It is true that the beers made on the West Coast in the early days would have been unusually high in carbonation.

While the breweries in the East and Midwest had access to an industrial infrastructure, those on the Pacific were improvised affairs, hastily set up to quench the thirsts of the Gold Rush.

At a time when lager brewing was the 'new' technology, many Eastern and Midwestern breweries obtained ice from the Great Lakes with which to cool their fermenters. The Californian coast is not known for its ice, so its brewers tried to use lager yeasts without ice. One method was to employ very shallow fermenting vessels: with more of the brew exposed to the air, it would cool faster. Without ice, these brewers could not employ long, slow periods of fermentation and maturation; this would have made for a continued secondary fermentation in the barrel, and a very lively beer, emerging with a hiss. The Californian method created a specific type of beer, described as 'steam beer' in the *Western Brewer*'s article.

One or two American microbreweries have attempted to produce beers of this type. All have been inspired by Anchor, the last survivor among the 'steam beer' breweries of San Francisco Bay. Its flagship product is Anchor Steam Beer (see page 235),

> **European breweries proclaimed their pride in their steam engines, but America had something else in mind. The Anchor brewery has developed a world classic based on its own hybrid system of fermentation.**

American pride flies the flag at Anchor, a very small brewery in a handsome building.

No other brewery has quite the same shallow fermenters as Anchor, and they are a secret of the Steam Beer's character. It is Anchor's original product and its flagship brew, protected with great resolve.

Fritz Maytag is a shirtsleeve brewer as well as a proprietor. The original Anchor belonged to one generation of breweries and inspired another. The bar facing the brewhouse offers not only Anchor Steam but the brewery's full range of beers.

and it has been most fastidious in legally protecting that brand name.

In 1991, at a microbrewery in Norwalk, Connecticut, on the East Coast, I tasted a beer intended to have something of the Californian character. This was New England Atlantic Amber, made from British pale and American crystal malts, with Cascade hops, and fermented with a 'top' yeast in a cylindro-conical vessel. This product was created for the New England Brewing Company by Phil Markowski, one of the young generation of adventurous American beer-makers. I found it sweetish in aroma and palate, with a lightly malty accent, a very good fruitiness, and a soft body.

European 'steam beers'

Some European breweries that perhaps once had 'steam beer' in their name have in recent years sought to restore the soubriquet, but these producers are not using the Californian method.

In Bavaria, the Bayreuth company Maisel Brothers has maintained its 1887 brewery pristine and shining, with 1930s' steam engines alongside the early 1970s' plant it now uses. Among its extensive range, its biggest-selling products are its fruity, appley wheat brews, but it also has a Dampfbier (steam beer) as a house speciality. This was introduced in the late

1970s, 'because all beers in Bavaria were beginning to taste alike,' Oscar Maisel told me. The name Dampfbier is protected.

The peach-coloured (20 EBC) Dampfbier is assertively fruity, with a touch of vanilla, and soft in body. It has a gravity of 12.2 Plato (1048–50), and just over 4 percent alcohol by weight, 5 by volume. It is made from four barley malts, with a triple-decoction mash, hopped with Hallertau Hersbruck and Tettnang (26 BU), top-fermented in open (but deep) vessels, and lagered at 0°C/32°F for five or six weeks. It is filtered but not pasteurized.

In Britain, some of the earliest steam engines were built by Thomas Newcomen (1663–1729) and Richard Trevithick (1771–1833), for use in tin mines in Cornwall. A brewery established in Redruth, Cornwall, in 1792 adapted this heritage to launch a range of 'steam' beers in the 1980s. These were named after Newquay, the nearby port from which beers were once shipped. Although the brewery did not make anything in the Californian style, it did use some distinctive techniques, employing lager and ale yeasts in the primary and secondary fermentations of each product. For a time, these beers were widely available, but a management buy-out of the brewery led to the brands being sold to Whitbread. They have since been produced in more conventional breweries.

Classic producer

ANCHOR
Anchor Brewing Co, 1705 Mariposa Street, San Francisco, California 94107, USA   Tel: (415) 863-8350

Anchor was arguably the last speciality brewery of any kind in America, and the smallest, when it was set to close in 1965. What happened instead is a legend in American brewing.

Fritz Maytag, a member of a Swiss-German family from Iowa, was living in California as a student of literature at Stanford University. He was a regular at a bar and restaurant in San Francisco, where Anchor Steam Beer was served. One day he ordered an Anchor Steam and was told the brewery was due to close at the end of that week. Maytag's family own one of the United States' principal washing-machine companies, and he thought he might be able to provide some business experience to help the brewery. Instead, he found himself selling some shares in his family's company in order to become a partner, and subsequently owner, at Anchor Steam.

In the early days, Maytag did his own deliveries. On sales calls, he would introduce himself as the owner of Anchor Steam to be told by the owner of a bar or store: 'That brewery closed years ago.'

The brewery was underneath a freeway, employing only one person, using baker's yeast, and producing only draught beer, in the absence of a bottling line.

It took Maytag ten years to put the brewery into the black, soon after which he moved it into a stylish 1930s' building that had formerly accommodated a coffee-roasting company. The location, Potrero Hill, has since become a fashionable spot for art galleries and shops.

Maytag ensures that the company remains in touch with its raison d'être. Once a year, he takes a party from the brewery to see the barley harvest, in the far north of California. Back at Anchor, all offices face on to the copper kettles, lest anyone forget what the business is about. For a drink after work there is a traditional back-bar decorated with memorabilia, within sight of the fermentation vessels (safely behind glass).

The inspirational Anchor is one of the world's most handsome breweries, and its flagship product is a classic acknowledged by beer-lovers internationally. Anchor Steam Beer is an all-malt brew. It is produced from pale and crystal malts, at a gravity of 1048–51 (12–13 Plato), with around 4 percent alcohol by weight, 5 by volume, and is hopped three times, with Northern Brewer. The brewery still uses the uniquely shallow fermentation vessels, two feet deep. (Those used for Anchor's top-fermenting products are six feet deep.) The beer is fermented with a lager yeast, at 'ale' temperatures, from 16–21°C/ 60–72°F, and has three weeks' warm-conditioning, with *kräusen*. The beer is flash-pasteurized, both for bottling and kegging.

Anchor Steam Beer has the roundness and cleanness of a lager, but some of the complexity of an ale. It has a bronze colour; a refreshingly persistent natural carbonation (2.85–3 volumes of carbon dioxide); a clean, firm, malt character; a very light fruitiness; and an emphatically dry, crisp hoppiness (30–35 BU) in the finish. In a city known for its bars and restaurants, it is the definitive beer over which to socialize and develop an appetite.

I once asked Maytag if his persistence in protecting his trademark had not prevented a recognition of steam beer as a style. He pointed out that no one else had used the term for decades when he took over the brewery, and that, with his colleagues at Anchor, he had put in a great deal of time and effort to save and foster a unique way of brewing. Though he never intended to spend his life as a brewer, Maytag has developed a comprehensive love of beer's mysteries, and this is reflected in the brewery's range.

Anchor's regular products also include the famous Liberty Ale (see page 161) and Old Foghorn Barley Wine (see page 104), a light-tasting wheat beer, and a rich, sweetish, faintly herbal-tasting porter of 1068 (17; 5; 6.25). Anchor's 'Our Special Ale' is available after Thanksgiving and until the New Year. Each year's brew is different, but they are usually spiced. Tasters feel that in various years' 'vintages' they have tasted cloves, cinnamon, nutmeg, allspice, coriander, licorice and zest of lemon, but the brewery likes to keep the spices secret. 'Our Special Ale' bears on the label each year a different variety of tree, 'the ancient sign for the winter solstice, when the earth appears born anew.' Anchor has also on occasion made a resiny-tasting Spruce Beer. In the late 1980s and early 1990s, the brewery began its experiments to explore the methods of the Sumerian brewers (see page 10).

Maytag lives at York Creek, on Spring Mountain, in the Napa Valley of northern California. There, he grows Cabernet Sauvignon and other grape varieties, which appear under the York Creek name from the Ridge winery. He also grows olives. Maytag Blue, one of America's best-known cheeses, is produced on the family's dairy in Iowa.

Maytag's rescue of Anchor preceded the microbrewery movement by ten or a dozen years, though his example was inspirational. Despite its growth, Anchor is still a very small brewery, but not a micro.

Smoked beer

The appetizingly dry smokiness that characterizes the most traditional Scotch whiskies can also be found in a handful of speciality beers. It is a result of the kilning of the malt over fire.

When grain is malted, it has to be dried to arrest its germination at the optimum point, and traditionally this could be done only by wind (in an open attic) or over fire. In the latter method, the grains are spread out on a fine mesh in a kiln, and a fire is set some distance beneath, so that warm air passes through – so does smoke. Once, many whiskies and beers must have picked up some smokiness in this way. In modern maltings, an enclosed source of heat warms the air. It is the difference between heating a house with an open fire or with radiators.

In the world of spirit-distilling, Scotland is the one traditionalist nation that has continued, at least in part, to kiln malt over fire. In the universe of brewing, Germany and Poland have traditional beers both made with smoked malts, and there are several more recent examples in the New World. Wind-drying and

The classic smoked beers from Bamberg employ beechwood, and are lagers. Others use oak or alder. Some are ales or porters. All are distinctive, and are a natural accompaniment to smoked foods.

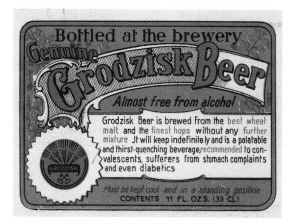

The very rare Grodzisk, of Poland, in its lower-alcohol form. This delightful label is still in use.

smoking are both methods of preserving foods, and such distinctively flavoured products go well with beers that have been treated in the same way: a 'whisky malt' beer or its Alaskan alder-wood counterpart with smoked salmon or venison (or, in the New World, caribou); a German Rauchbier or Polish Grodzisk with smoked ham or sausages.

Peated beers

Perhaps because of the popularity of Scotch whisky in France, a brewer there pioneered in the early 1980s the production of beer with a similar character. This creation came from the Adelshoffen brewery, a subsidiary of the large independent Fischer/Pêcheur in Schiltigheim, near Strasbourg, Alsace. The product is called Adelscott Bière au Malt à Whisky. In this instance, peat-smoked malt is used, and the beer is bottom-fermenting. It has a pale amber-red colour (18–22 EBC) and a malty palate, with just a slight suggestion of smokiness (16.2 Plato; 1065; 5.2; 6.4; 20–22 BU). In 1993, the brewery added Adelscott Noir, an almost black beer made with peated malt. It has a daringly grey head and just faintly dark-red highlights. It is still only lightly smoky, but with more assertive complexity and notably peaty-grainy flavours, especially toward the finish.

A bronze-coloured 'Whisky Malz Bier', with a dense head, a malty palate and a hint of dryness, is made by the Eggenberg brewery, between Linz and Salzburg, Austria. It is called Nessie, after Scotland's legendary monster. The beer has 17 Plato (1068; 6; 7.5), and is said to have six months' maturation. Another, with lots of malt and fruit, is produced by top-fermentation at the brewpub in Nussdorf, Vienna.

Half way across the world, the Pike Place brewery, of Seattle, Washington, uses peated malt to subtle effect in its lusty Old Bawdy barley wine. Seattle's Redhook brewery employed peated malt more assertively in what it described as a Scotch Ale, launched in 1993 as the first in a series of limited edition beers. The intention was that the best-liked of these would reappear from time to time. It is to be hoped that the Scotch Ale does. It had a luscious maltiness, quickly developing to an aromatic smokiness and dryness.

Brewer Trum, producer of Schlenkerla, in Bamberg, Bavaria. The beechwood logs stacked outside are used to smoke the malt for this classic beer. The maltings and the brewery are in the same premises.

Beechwood at Rauchenfels fires the rocks that flavour the beer – in the boil and the lagering.

Redhook's Scotch Ale was inspired by a similar Whisky Malt Beer made at Spinnakers brewpub in Victoria, British Columbia, Canada. I have not tasted that beer but am inclined to believe the good reports of it, judging from the many excellent brews I have enjoyed at Spinnakers.

Wood-smoked beers

The region of Franconia, and notably the town of Bamberg, has traditionally persisted in malting over fire, using fuel from the local beech forests. People in other parts of Germany, even the rest of Bavaria, are often unaware of this style, or dismiss it as hopelessly eccentric, but the dark, bottom-fermenting Bamberger Rauchbier is the world's greatest smoked beer, from one of the oldest brewing towns.

A former abbey founded by Benedictines in 1015 on a hill overlooking a division in the River Regnitz, and a cathedral established at the same time, are Bamberg's landmarks. The cathedral is Romanesque and Gothic, with famous sculptures and a Papal tomb; the abbey is Baroque, as is much of the town. The abbey's former brewery is now a museum of beer-making.

Within 30 or 40 miles of Bamberg, there are around 100 breweries: this is the most densely breweried part of the world. Bamberg itself has no fewer than nine breweries to serve 70,000 people, and is also a centre of malting. The breweries make a range of lager beers, often with a characteristic dry maltiness. These include an excellent bock (mid-October to December) from the Fässla brewery and a popular dark lager from Kloster. Two of the town's breweries, Spezial and Heller, specialize in Rauchbier.

Not far from the railway station, in a half-timbered building, the Christian Merz Spezial brewpub, founded in 1536, makes only Rauchbier, with a soft but insistent smokiness and a treacle-toffee finish. The regular version has a conventional gravity and strength, but there are also seasonal Märzen and bock interpretations. In a galleried courtyard behind, the brewery has its own tiny drum maltings. Brauerei Spezial has the atmosphere of a basic tavern but it offers hearty food and unelaborate bedrooms (10 Obere König Strasse, Tel: 0951 24304).

A small proportion of Spezial's smoked malt is used in the faintly phenolic golden lager that is the house beer of the Greifenklau brewpub, on Laurenzi Platz, on the edge of the ecclesiastical part of the town. A band sometimes plays in this little square, and there are views across the valley to Altenburg castle. Greifenklau describes itself as an inn, but the bedrooms are in an adjoining small, modern hotel.

Also in the ecclesiastical part of the town, on the hill of Saint Stephan's Protestant church, the

As well as being one of the world's great brewing cities, little Bamberg is an architectural delight. This is the old town hall.

Heller-Trum brewery dates from 1678. Its dry, smoky, long Rauchbier represents 95 percent of its production. Even its Helles Lagerbier, the remaining five percent, tastes faintly smoky. This brewery's tap is just down the road, at the Schlenkerla tavern, where Dominikaner Strasse meets Sand Strasse. One of the two main rooms has magnificent vaulting. This is a busy tavern, offering good regional food.

A third Bamberg brewery, Kaiserdom, is known in some export markets for its Rauchbier. It has a brewery in the town, making a variety of styles, but its dry-ish Rauchbier is produced nearby in Eltmann. A lighter-tasting Rauchbier is made in the area by Goller, at Zeil, and an unfiltered example at the Heller brewery at Herzogenaurach, nearer to Erlangen.

Another little-known style of wood-smoked beer is traditional to the town of Grodzisk, near Poznań, in Poland. This very aromatic brew is said to have been produced since 1301. It is known simply as Grodzisk beer, and is made with a significant proportion of malted wheat, smoked over oak. The beer is top-fermented, perhaps with some wild yeast influence, and bottle-conditioned. Grodzisk is made in both a low-alcohol and a conventional-strength (4 percent by weight, 5 by volume) version. It is an extremely pale golden beer, with a faint haze, a dense white head, and a surprisingly light body. It has a sourish, sappy, oaky aroma (like a box that had held smoked herring), and a smoky, very dry, crisp palate. After a period of storage, it begins to develop a tart, quenching acidity. Grodzisk is a smoked counterpart to Berliner Weisse or the old style of low-gravity wheat beer once made around Leuven, Belgium.

Some of the new American brewers have begun to wood-smoke malts in recent years, in typically adventurous style. The Vermont Pub and Brewery in Burlington, Vermont, has used apple, hickory and maple woods to make a smoked porter. This style was pioneered by the Alaskan Brewing Company, in Juneau. The Alaskan micro uses alder (the twigs of which were traditionally employed as a filter and flavouring agent by rustic brewers in Scandinavia).

In one of the world's more remote industrial estates, Juneau's single-storey, pine-clad brewery sits opposite a similar building that houses the Taku fish smokery. Together with another fish smokery and coffee-roaster, they are dotted in an inlet between a curtain of mountains. The brewing company treats the malts for its porter at the Taku Smokeries. The malts – pale, crystal, chocolate and black – are spread on sieve-like racks in a small oven that normally accommodates salmon. Chinook and Willamette hops are used (54 BU).

Alaskan Smoked Porter is brewed from a gravity of 1055 (around 14 Plato) but fermented down only to around 4 percent alcohol by weight, 5 by volume. It has a pronounced smoke character but is also very complex, with mellow woodiness, roastiness, oiliness, hoppiness, acidity, fruitiness and sweetness. It is hardly a breakfast beer, but it was once presented to me at an early-morning picnic, with lox and bagels, in the middle of an icefield around 15 miles from Juneau. Happily, I was not driving the helicopter.

Stone beer

When Germany was divided, the frontier between East and West stood a few hundred metres from Ewald Werner's brick-built tower brewery, in the small town of Neustadt, north of Coburg, Bavaria. The division cost the brewery much of its market. Eventually, the brewery was acquired by Gerd Borges, an entrepreneurial Franconian with several similar investments in Bavaria. Borges decided that the Neustadt brewery needed a speciality.

He is a brewer himself, and had read of beer being made with the aid of heated stones. This method derives from the days before the skills existed to make sufficiently large brew-kettles from metal. A fire could not be placed under a wooden kettle, but hot stones could be shovelled into the brew. 'Boiling stones' were widely used by rustic home-brewers in northern Europe until the mid-1800s, and this has been well documented by anthropologists Eilert Sundt and Odd Nordland.

Borges found a quarry once used for this purpose by two breweries in Weidmannsdorf, near Klagenfurt in southern Austria. At least one of these breweries continued to work in this way in the 20th century, according to an article in *Tageszeitung für Brauerei* (1906, No. 243). I believe the brewery continued to make 'stone beer' until World War I. Although the technique had long been superseded by copper kettles, it was retained for its influence on flavour. The quarry yields graywacke, a type of sandstone, grey-green in colour, that can carry very intense heat, and cool without shattering.

In 1982, Borges decided to reintroduce stone beer. Stones the size of small boulders are taken to Neustadt, where they are rendered white-hot in a beechwood oven built in the brewery yard. This takes 12 hours, and the stones are said to reach 1,200°C/2,192°F. A crane fitted with claws then hoists the stones through a hatch into the brewhouse and lowers them into a conventional copper kettle. Inside, the brew has been heated almost to boiling in the normal way; the hot stone finishes the job. As the stone is lowered in, the brew foams and rages, filling the room with steam, and some of its sugars are caramelized.

When the stones cool, they are left coated with caramelized malt. The stones are then placed in the

Alaskan Smoked Porter makes a wonderful pairing with the state's many variations on smoked fish. This salmon fillet was cold-smoked over the same alder wood as that used in the production of the porter. The brew was conceived for the winter season. It is one of several fine products from the Alaskan Brewing Company, whose range also includes an Altbier called Alaskan Amber.

lagering vessels, so that the caramel primes the maturing brew. By the time the stones are returned to the brewery yard, they resemble large pieces of coal.

The basic product, Rauchenfels Steinbier, is brewed from equal proportions of pale barley malt and wheat malt, to a gravity of 12 Plato (1048), hopped with Hersbruck and Tettnang (27 BU), and top-fermented. The brewer told me that it took a year to breed a suitable yeast for this beer, and that the lagering brew did not really begin to attack the rocks until they had been in the tank for 50 or 60 days. The beer has a smoky, treacle-toffee palate, less dry than smooth, and a long, rounded finish. A version called Rauchenfels Steinweizen, made with 60 percent wheat, is very lively, a little less hoppy, with just slightly more sharpness. It forms a huge head, and has a very sustained bead. Both beers are tawny in colour (around 32–33 EBC), with an alcohol content of just under 3.8 percent by weight, 4.7 by volume. The Steinweizen is bottle-conditioned.

Classic producer

SCHLENKERLA
Brauerei Heller-Trum, Schlenkerla,
6 Dominikaner Strasse,
8600 Bamberg, Germany
Tel: (0951) 56060

The world's classic smoked beer has a confusion of names on its label, and still regards its home address as the Schlenkerla tavern. The Hellers were early tenants of the Schlenkerla when it was a brewpub. The present owners, whose name is Trum, have been there for five generations.

From the early days, the beer was taken to nearby caves, in the hill called Stephansberg, for lagering. Eventually, the need for space led to the brewhouse being moved to Stephansberg. The brewery is easily missed. The narrow, winding hill of Stephansberg is now residential, though it once had seven breweries.

What looks at a glance like three adjoining houses, smartly painted in cream and brown, bears a discreetly gilded plaque whispering the presence of Heller-Trum.

Everything inside is equally smart, and just as compact. In a barn in the brewery yard are neat ricks of split trunks of beechwood, fetched from forest around ten miles to the east. Below ground level, in a cramped corridor, a set of gauges and controls, and a cast-iron hatch in the wall, reveal the beechwood fire. It looks like the firebox of a small locomotive, or of a mad inventor's steam-powered submarine. Above, a small whitewashed building resembling a chapel turns out to be the smokehouse. Inside that, the grains sit on a mesh and the smoke rises through, swirling like a mist and smelling like an autumn bonfire.

The malt is made twice a week,

germinated in a system that uses both boxes and a drum, and only the smoked type is used in the Rauchbier. The brewhouse is in copper, with brass rails, white-tiled walls and a quarry-tiled floor. A double-decoction system is used. The beer is brewed from a gravity of 13.5 Plato (1054), hopped with extract (a rare departure from tradition), fermented in open squares – releasing the fragrance of smoked ham – and lagered for six to eight weeks. It emerges with an alcohol content of around 4 percent by weight, 5 by volume, 29–32 units of bitterness and a colour of 52 EBC.

A seasonal bock version is also produced. The Heller Schlenkerla beers are smoky from the first moment right to the end of their long finish.

'We don't try to make a beer for everyone,' the owner told me. 'You like it – or you don't.'

For all that the malting process is very old, the classic brewhouse at Schlenkerla is pristine. The lagering cellars are beneath the brewery.

Aecht is old German for 'real', Rauch means smoked – the fire is shown at the top. The beer also carries the designation Märzen, because of its gravity.

Rye beer

With its fruity, slightly bitter, spicy, oily, sometimes almost pepperminty notes, rye has the most assertive flavours of all the cereal grains. This is evident when it is made into bread. It is largely neutralized in some classic Russian vodkas and in Dutch gin (where it plays a supporting role), but it blossoms beautifully in the whiskey that was once traditional to Pennsylvania and Maryland. It is less often put to the test in beer.

As a grain that grows in poor soil, it has been a staple in some of the hardier climes of eastern and Baltic Europe, and is cultivated less in beer-brewing countries than in the spirits belt. Perhaps because it is associated with some economically poor, rustic regions, it is seen as somehow a less exalted grain than wheat or barley. It is relatively high in calcium and iron, and in beta-carotene and vitamin E, and in Germany is fed to billy goats 'to make them potent'.

Rye bread or flour (perhaps with buckwheat, oats and other less tasty grains), is used as the basis of kvass and similar beer-like fermented drinks that were, and sometimes still are, traditional in many parts of eastern, central and Baltic Europe.

It is not an easy grain with which to work in large proportions, in that, like wheat, it has no husk. It also absorbs and retains water more than other brewing grains, and that poses further problems in mashing.

The traditional Estonian and Finnish brew sahti is often made with rye or oats. One or other of these grains, or a blend of both, may comprise half the mash in very traditional examples, the remainder being malted barley. Juniper is the traditional seasoning, although hops are also used.

The most important occasions for sahti-brewing are weddings, the midsummer festivities (when, even at this latitude, it scarcely gets dark), the potato-picking season and Christmas. Helpers at the potato harvest were traditionally refreshed with a meal of rye bread, fish and new potatoes, accompanied by sahti.

The drink is ceremonially served from two-handled vessels like miniature buckets, or half-barrels, made from juniper wood. Similar vessels occur in several parts of Europe's far north, among them the quaich (at its finest, made from silver) in which Scotch whisky is served.

Originally, sahti was made only on farms, and production was often carried out in the sauna, usually by the woman of the house, but since the mid- to late 1980s this traditional beverage has also been produced by commercial brewers.

> Once the brewing grain in only the coldest corners of Europe, rye is finding a new place in speciality beers. Perfect with a pastrami and rye bread sandwich, or perhaps to chase down a North American rye whiskey.

The sahti of Estonia and Finland, often made with rye, is filtered through juniper twigs and straw.

The trough-shaped filter vessel is so characteristic as to be a symbol of sahti brewers.

This wooden vessel is the emblem of Lammin Sahti, one of the commercial producers.

The number of sahti home-brewers in Estonia is not well documented, but in Finland estimates run to thousands, making the best part of four million litres a year. In the past, a proportion of raw rye was used, although the grain was malted for the finest brews. Malting was carried out at home, and it is said that no one does this any longer – but some sahti does have a smoky taste, suggesting a primitive kilning. The malted and milled rye is supplied by local farm stores, dairies or grocers.

Traditionally, the brew is filtered through straw, reeds and juniper twigs, in a distinctively shaped wooden trough, called a *kuurna*. This is how the juniper aromatizes the sahti. The brew is often fermented in milk churns, and baker's yeast is typically employed. One or two enterprises produce unfermented sahti, to which the consumer can then add yeast, but there are also five commercial producers of finished sahti.

In Estonia, sahti is most commonly made on the islands, and there is some cottage-industry production. In Finland, some sahti is made around Helsinki, but the two heartlands are between 100 and 200 miles to the northeast and northwest, to either side of Tampere. The Finns call this 'the North', though their land stretches for more than 500 miles farther.

To the northeast, it is around 100 miles to the town of Lammi, in the county of Häme. The Lammin Sahti made there is the best known of the commercial examples. While none of the commercial producers uses a great deal of rye, perhaps because of the difficulties in mashing, Lammi's does have some taste of the grain. Close to Lammi, there is a second commercial sahti brewery at Sysmä, again using the the name of its location as its brand. The same distance farther north, and slightly to the east, is a commercial sahti brewery at Joutsa. In the northwest, there is one commercial producer taking its name from the community of Honkajoki and another nearby called Mafia, the latter name intentionally tongue-in-cheek.

Lammin Sahti blends a small proportion of rye with both pale and dark barley malts, uses plenty of juniper and a very small proportion of hops, brews in 13-hectolitre batches, and has a large traditional *kuurna*. The brewery uses a top-fermenting culture derived from a baker's yeast. The sahti is brewed from a gravity of 20–25 Plato (1080–1100), and has 6–7 percent alcohol by weight, 7.5–8.75 by volume.

The sahti is marketed in a three-litre vessel like that used for 'wine in a box'. It has a rusty, reddish-brown colour, with a considerable haze; a relatively low, but lasting, head and carbonation (like a British cask-conditioned ale); a slightly sticky, oily, but soft body (reminiscent of a fortified wine); and a winy, spicy, almondy palate. I have enjoyed this sahti on several occasions, and find it very drinkable. Finnish enthusiasts say that sahti makes them feel relaxed and sleepy, but is deceptively moreish. Too much, and it leaves the unsuspecting drinker wondering what happened to his legs.

In recent years, the use of rye in speciality beers has begun to interest conventional brewers elsewhere in the world. I have tasted a couple of examples.

One is produced from time to time in that crucible of brewing innovation, the city of Seattle, Washington. The Big Time brewpub's beer is made from a small proportion of flaked rye, along with pale and Munich barley malts (13–13.5 Plato; 1052–4; 3.7; 4.6), hopped with Mount Hood and Centennial in two additions, fermented with the house ale yeast, and served unfiltered. It is called, neatly, Hefe-Ryzen. It has a remarkably dense head; a ripe, yellow colour; a rounded, chewy, cereal-grain character; and a very full, complex flavour, with a light, very clean spiciness and lots of fruit.

At least one other brewery in the Pacific Northwest, Steelhead, of Eugene, Oregon, makes a rye beer, and there are no doubt others. Steelhead's, created by well-regarded brewer Teri Fahrendorf, also employs English crystal malt. It is called Riley's Rye, and I have yet to taste it.

The only rye beer that is at all easily obtainable is Schierlinger Roggenbier (*Roggen* being German for rye). This is marketed as a speciality in Germany, and exported to several other countries.

Another rye beer from the German-speaking world, which may become more widely available, is Goldroggen, from the monastery brewery of Schlägl, in Upper Austria. This has a very full gold colour, only the faintest hint of rye flavour, an emphatic hop character and a very slight fruitiness reminiscent of that in a Kölsch.

Classic producer

SCHIERLINGER

Fürstliche Brauerei Thurn und Taxis,
15-17 Haupt Strasse, 8306 Schierling,
Bavaria, Germany
Tel: (09451) 412

Schierling is south of the important Bavarian city of Regensburg. The brewery at Schierling has its origins in a 13th-century convent. After the Napoleonic period, it was acquired by the aristocratic family Thurn und Taxis, among the longest-established, wealthiest and most colourful of German nobility. The family's fortune was based on the world's first postal service, which they devised in 1490 and operated throughout the Holy Roman Empire. In the 1820s the service was sold to the state and profits invested in agricultural businesses, including brewing.

Schierling was the first brewery to be owned by the family, but they later acquired and merged various breweries in their home city of Regensburg (including the Carmelite and Jesuit breweries), and are now headquartered there. Today, the Regensburg brewery makes lager styles while Schierling produces top-fermenting speciality beers.

Under this arrangement, Schierling originally produced only a conventionally pale Hefe-Weizen, and pioneered that style on draught. As the style grew in popularity, there was discussion as to whether a Dunkelweizen should be introduced. It was decided instead to make a greater distinction. 'Wheat is a pale grain, rye dark,' the director of the brewery told me. 'These beers look, and taste, as different as white bread and black.'

He felt it reasonable to assume that rye had been used for brewing in Bavaria before the *Reinheitsgebot*, but could find no 'recipes'. Rye grown in Franconia is malted in Erlangen, and constitutes 60 percent of the grist. The remainder comprises barley malt, in equal proportions of pale and crystal, with a small proportion of yet darker specification. The darkest malt is dehusked, in order to avoid a burnt taste.

The beer originally had a colour of a little over 35 EBC, but this was deemed not to be sufficient for a beer claiming to be 'dark'. This decision was propounded by the head of Trading Standards for Northern Bavaria, whose name is Dr Misere, the brewery director was amused to tell me. Dr Misere felt that a dark beer should have at least 40 EBC. The brewery now aims for 45, in order to leave no room for doubt.

The original gravity is 12 Plato (1048), with just under 4 percent alcohol by weight, 5 by volume. In order to avoid the problems caused by rye in mashing, the grain bed is kept very shallow, there is an intensive system of lauter 'knives', and carbon dioxide pressure in the vessel. A double-decoction mash is used.

From the outside, the brewery still bears hints of its origins, and most of the buildings appear to be from the late 1800s. It used a coal-fired kettle until 1987, but has now installed steam-heated stainless steel vessels, in traditional shapes.

From the kettle, the brew is circulated through a hop percolator filled with Perle. There are two additions.

In the brewhouse, the rye aroma is evident, and in the open square fermenters the Roggenbier has a more pinkish head than batches of wheat beer alongside. A wheat beer yeast is used, and a proportion of unfermented wheat beer is used to prime the rye brew during a period of tank-conditioning.

Schierlinger Roggenbier, which was launched in 1988, has a reddish-brown colour; a very big, dense head; a typically phenolic, acidic, 'wheat beer' aroma; a distinctly dry, grainy texture; and a soft, rounded, fruity, spicy palate, finishing with a rye bitterness.

The beer can be sampled in a delightfully unpretentious taproom behind the brewery. This is a bar, not a restaurant, and I have yet to see rye beer matched with food in Germany.

Central Europe gave us not only rye bread, but also pastrami, the spiced beef of Romania. Put them together with rye beer and you have a lunch for the hungriest New Yorker.

Bavarians might find it surprisingly cosmopolitan, but that New York classic, pastrami on rye, is a natural with Roggenbier. On the West Coast, they might prefer the Hefe-Ryzen from the Big Time brewpub in Seattle.

Black beer

In the lore of the drinker, several beers might be called black, but the soubriquet has most strongly attached itself to one style. The classic example, right down to its name, is the Schwarzbier made by the local brewery at Bad Köstritz, in Thuringia, in the former East Germany. Schwarz simply means black. This once-famous beer retained its life-force in the shadows, and has recently emerged, blinking slightly, into the open air of a new Europe. There is an obdurate quality to black beers, as reflected in the German style's survival across the world in Japan, where each of the four national brewers has an example. Although the term black may crop up elsewhere, the examples of Köstritz and Japan most clearly define this style.

The first mention of brewing in the Köstritz area is in 1505, and there are more specific allusions to the town in 1543. Given such antiquity, it is reasonable to believe that the first Köstritzer Schwarzbier was top-fermented, but the product has probably been a lager since at least 1878. Without clear reference to the Schwarzbier, the company's history talks of the introduction of a bottom-fermenting yeast at that time. The black beers of Japan, which date from at least 1892, have probably always been lagers.

I once asked the head brewer at Köstritz what was the difference between his beer and dark lagers from other German cities. 'Ours is darker – ours is black – virtually opaque,' was his first thought on the subject. He then went on to discuss fuller body and a distinctive palate, reminiscent of bitter chocolate. Mashing temperatures were kept high enough to give the beer some 'mouth-feel', he observed, and fermentation was restrained. There was also more underlying hop character than in many dark lagers.

I would describe the body of his beer as rounded (Köstritz's well water is quite hard, but is softened), and strongly endorse the comparison with bitter chocolate, perhaps also a hint of relatively dry toffee. This tangy dryness is very important in the finish. These characteristics are to varying degrees found in the Japanese examples, too. Black beers make a sustaining drink, and a good accompaniment to a dessert based on a truly robust-tasting chocolate.

Why should such a distinctly German style have leapfrogged to Japan? Although an American founded the first beer-brewery in Japan, in 1869, and the successor enterprise was briefly run by Englishmen, it was under German instruction, around the turn of the century, that it metamorphosed into Kirin, today one of the world's biggest brewing companies.

The original brewery at Sapporo in Japan was founded in 1876 as a state enterprise. It was privatized in 1887. The brewery still stands, and parts of it (right) have been turned into a beer hall and garden. It was advertising a black beer in 1892. After the end of World War II, the company was divided to form Sapporo and Asahi.

The classic black beer is the one made in the town of Bad Köstritz, in the former East Germany. It probably began as a top-fermenting brew, but has been for at least a century an unusually dark lager, with a distinctive bitter-chocolate palate. It may well have been the inspiration for the black beers that are still made in Japan.

Black beer is clearly signposted among the 12 taps at the gleaming restaurant in Kirin's Beer Village, a theme park attached to the company's Yokohama brewery. There is a separate brewpub on the site.

In the 1870s, German breweries were toured by a researcher from Japan, who in 1876 helped establish the Sapporo brewery. Perhaps he visited the town of Köstritz on his travels, but the geography need not have been that precise.

Just to the east of Gotha, Erfurt, Weimar and Jena, and six or seven miles from the city of Gera, the town of Bad Köstritz is by no means distant from old brewing centres farther south, across the Bavarian border, such as Kulmbach, Bayreuth, Bamberg, Erlangen and Munich. There are still many good dark beers to be found in this area. In the great days of dark beers, the region was full of variations on the theme, many of which were lumped together by people beyond Germany's borders under the umbrella of Bavaria's biggest city, Munich. 'Was it Köstritzer Schwarzbier that inspired these black beers?' I have asked several Japanese brewers. 'Köstritz? Never heard of it! I think Munich beers were the inspiration,' came the reply.

Outside Germany, few people have heard of Bad Köstritz. It is a small town, with a population of only 4,000. On the 'wrong' side of a divided Germany, its name became even more obscure.

The name is Slavic, and Köstritz may originally have been a Bohemian village. The Thuringian Forest finds its continuation in the Bohemian Forest.

In feudal times, licences to brew commercially were at the disposal of local aristocrats. There seem at one stage to have been two breweries in Köstritz, bearing the heraldic emblems of the lion and the crane, both of which are incorporated in the arms of today's enterprise. Although the reference in 1543 is imprecise, by the 1690s there is an allusion to a

The position has been adopted by Uncle Sam, Britain's Lord Kitchener, and more than one brewer. Here, a healthily hirsute German points out that Köstritzer Black is the beer for you.

brewery in the castle of the local count, and the history is certainly continuous since then. At one stage, the beer was sent through wooden pipes to cellars cut into a hillside half a mile away for fermentation and maturation. It could be argued that this was an empirical lagering process.

Even in those days, when all beers were dark, the product of Köstritz seems to have gained a reputation for being especially rich in colour and sustaining. Students from Jena, about 25 miles away, were said to ride their horses to Köstritz to sample the beer at the tavern near the brewery, and not return for three days. One is quoted as saying: 'I wish I had been born in Köstritz.' There is still a tavern opposite the brewery gate. Like many of the buildings in the cobbled town, it is half-timbered, with its woodwork painted in an ox-blood colour.

For many years, the beer was sent by horse and dray the 170 miles to Berlin. In 1748, a high-school teacher in Berlin is on record as commending the beer, and remarking that it looked like red wine (a very dark Burgundy, perhaps?).

When Germany's greatest writer, Johann Wolfgang von Goethe (1749–1832) was ill, a friend wrote: 'He is not eating, but fortunately we have some Köstritzer beer.' Goethe seems to have taken beer very seriously. When he moved to Leipzig in 1765, he wrote: 'I am getting used to the beer.' Several rhymes in German suggest Köstritzer Schwarzbier as the drink of the nursing mother. It was sometimes recommended that a raw egg be stirred into the beer, perhaps with some sugar.

Similar drinks existed in other brewing nations, often using nutmeg. In his book *The Curiosities of Ale and Beer* (1889), John Bickerdyke talks of an ale enriched with Malaga wine, beef gravy and eggs. The blending of ale and wine sounds odd, and there seems less conflict in the addition of rum, as in the Yorkshire black beer combination suggested below. There have been stranger prescriptions for the sake of health.

In the era of the grand tour, when spas became popular, Köstritz came to be known for sand-baths, which were said to ease rheumatism. The water washing along the sandy banks of the River Elster, on its way to the Elbe, apparently had magical properties. A 'cure house' was built in 1865, and extended half a century later; the town became known as Bad ('bath') Köstritz. The local landowner had by now been elevated from count to earl, and his tenant ran both the brewery and the Kurhaus. Minerals in the area helped Gera (which now has a population of about 150,000) to become an industrial city making filtration materials and chemicals for the photographic industry, as well as textiles.

The present Köstritzer brewery, built in 1907, is a majestic red-brick structure of four storeys, with a tower reaching a further three, topped off with a spire

A BLACK VARIATION

In the days when all beers were dark, and very dense examples were made to ferment out on long journeys, several such specialities were produced in ports, whether on rivers or the sea. This may explain a now-extinct style called Mumme, once brewed in Braunschweig (Brunswick), Germany, but also known as far away as England in the 1600s. It certainly accounts for the unfermented, but heavily-hopped, Seefahrt Malz ('Sea Journey Malt') still made for an annual dinner in Bremen, Germany, and the low-alcohol, faintly smoky, Skibsol ('Ship's Ale') of Scandinavia.

In Britain, the voyages of the explorer Captain James Cook are suggested as the origin of a black beer made in his native county of Yorkshire. When Cook landed in New Zealand in 1769, he recorded that beer had been made for the crew from a mash of spruce tips. I found the reference to Captain Cook's spruce beer in a booklet sent to me in the late 1970s by Mather's of Leeds, West Yorkshire. The same publication refers to black beers having been made in Baltic cities. It also suggests that the product can be used in a soup made with a typically Baltic and German ingredient, rye bread (the other ingredients being lemon peel and sugar).

Spruce has never been used in the Black Beer made by Mather's since 1903, though the ingredient is employed in a soft drink in the United States (in the same family as birch and root beers). Mather's

Black Beer is made from malt extract, barley syrup and brown sugar, to a gravity of 1210 (52–3 Plato) and fermented with a wine yeast to an alcoholic content of 6.5 by weight, 8 by volume. Surprisingly, hops are not used. Because of its high density, it is rich in protein and vitamins. The beer is sometimes made into a shandy with lemonade (this is known as a 'Sheffield Stout', after another Yorkshire city), mixed with milk as a children's drink or restorative, or served half-and-half with rum.

Mather's is now owned by a company that also makes mead and liqueurs.

bearing a weather vane in the shape of a lion and a crane. After World War II, the newly formed East German Government turned the Kurhaus into a sanatorium, and nationalized the brewery.

There is enough left of the tiled brewhouse to show that it was a classic of its period, but the kettles no longer stand. In the 1970s, the state management fitted an extremely ugly brewhouse into a building across the yard. An unusual feature is a system in which wort is pumped through a cooler during fermentation. This technique is said to have been imported from Japan in the 1960s, completing the circle of influences. It does not appear to be in use in Japan any longer.

The Köstritz brewery can make 500,000 hectolitres a year. Throughout the 45 years of East German Government, the brewery was permitted to continue producing its speciality as long as it also met quotas of more conventional beer for the region. It still makes two beers of the Pilsner type: the thinnish, fairly dry (with 30 BU) Köstritzer Edel (noble) and the firmer, more hoppy (35 BU) Köstritzer Kranich (crane). To the possible confusion of the drinker, there is also a

Pilsner type called Ur-Krostitzer (note the different position of the 'r') from a brewery near Leipzig, also in the former East Germany.

In 1989, the Berlin Wall began to crumble, and in 1990 Germany was reunified. In that year, the sanatorium closed, possibly to be reopened as a resort hotel, and the brewery was acquired by Bitburger, with the intention that its Schwarzbier once more become available throughout Germany.

One of the principals of Bitburger and a member of the founding family, Dr Axel Simon, recounts that his mother drank Köstritzer Schwarzbier before his birth and when she was nursing him. He reckons he knew the taste of the Schwarzbier before he encountered the family's own Bitburger Pils.

Bitburger regards its Pils as a speciality, and sees Köstritzer Schwarzbier as complementary. Bitburger is in the western part of the country, Köstritz in the east (and their latitude is almost the same); both have built reputations despite being in very small towns; and both are in regions where the local people are said to pride themselves on being responsible and hard-working.

Nutritious and tasty, warming in winter, and a nightcap – advertisements from the brewery's archives.

Black beer producers

It may belong to folklore in Yorkshire, England, and be the subject of rediscovery in Thuringia, Germany, but the only country where all the national brewers make a black beer is Japan.

ASAHI

Asahi Breweries, 23-1 Azumabashi
1-chome, Sumida-ku, Tokyo, 130
Japan
Tel: (03) 5608-5129

Among the Japanese national brewers, Asahi makes the least traditional of the black beers. It is nonetheless gratifying that this company, which strongly emphasizes the youthful fashionability of its high-tech products, should persist with the style.

Asahi Black Beer has a gravity of just under 11 Plato (1044), and an alcohol content of 4 percent by weight, 5 by volume. Its colour was reduced in the 1960s to 60 EBC, which provides for a reddish-brown hue. The beer has an aroma and flavour reminiscent of caramel and a surprisingly rich malty sweetness. While older people in Japan drink it 'straight', the young prefer it half-and-half with a conventional lager or 'dry' beer.

Despite its somewhat old-fashioned image, the beer is available in an uncompromisingly post-modernist environment at the Flame d'Or restaurant, next to the company's corporate headquarters in Tokyo. This Asahi showpiece was designed by Philippe Starck, celebrated for having created the interior of the Royalton Hotel in New York. The denizens of the Royalton famously drink designer mineral waters. The loss is theirs.

KIRIN

Kirin Brewery Company, 26-1,
Jingumae 6-chome, Shibuya-ku,
Tokyo, 150 Japan
Tel: (03) 5485-6170

The entrant from Japan's biggest brewer may also have lost a little colour over the years, but it is still relatively black, with just a tinge of cherry when it is held up to the light. This is a beer of 12–12.5 Plato (1048-50), with an alcohol content of 4 percent by weight, 5 by volume.

Kirin Black Beer has a faintly smoky aroma; a licorice-toffee palate; a smooth, firm body; and a light finish. Like its contemporaries, it receives little promotion, but it is available in the brewery's chain of Kirin City pubs, and in the restaurant at the Yokohama brewery's Beer Village theme park.

KÖSTRITZER

Köstritzer Schwarzbierbrauerei,
Heinrich Schütz Strasse, Bad Köstritz,
6514 Thüringen, Germany
Tel: (0377) 095830

This beer was available only on draught until the 1950s, but customers could fill jugs to take home and sweeten the brew to their taste. After the introduction of bottling, two versions were made, without and with sugar.

The basic product was brewed to a gravity of 12 Plato (1048) from two malts: a Munich type and a roasted version, the latter, at a dark 1,200 EBC, representing 20 percent of the grist. The malts came from Saxony and the Erfurt area, and were made from a blend of varieties of winter barleys.

The beer was attenuated to only 2.8 percent alcohol by weight, 3.5 by volume. Protein and yeast were given time to precipitate during lagering, but the beer was not filtered. It was stabilized by pasteurization.

It had a creamy beige head, and the beer was a solid black colour (100 EBC). It had the aroma of malt bread; a slightly oily body; and notes of bitter chocolate, dry toffee and coffee, with some roastiness in the finish. East German hop varieties, grown near the Polish border, were used, and the beer had 40 units of bitterness.

A second version was based on the same beer, with white sugar added, boosting the gravity to 14 Plato (1056). This version was also pasteurized, before the sugariness had fermented out. It was, of course, sweeter, but also gentler and lighter in taste, with more malt loaf and less of the other flavours. This was created to save consumers the trouble of adding sugar themselves (though they still had to take responsibility for the egg if they wanted one).

The sugaring of the beer was possible because East Germany did not impose the Purity Law, the *Reinheitsgebot*. When Germany reunited, it was decided that this law would apply in the former East from the end of 1992. The sweetened version therefore had to be dropped.

Faced with having only one version, the brewery tried to achieve a balance between the previous two. They developed a new version which had 12.5 Plato (1050), and used three malts: 50 percent pale lager, 43 percent Munich (40 EBC), and seven percent roasted, of 900–1,000 EBC. The pale malt was from Erfurt, the other specifications from Bamberg, all made from summer barley. The hops are Hüller for bitterness and Hallertau Mittelfrüh for aroma. The beer then had 35 units of bitterness and a colour of 90 EBC. Its alcohol content remained at 2.8 percent by weight, 3.5 by volume.

This version was still almost opaque, and had all the taste characteristics of its predecessors, especially the bitter chocolate, but with less richness and a dash less roastiness.

However, it presented problems of stability, and the brewery made yet a further change, to an alcohol content of 3.9 percent by weight, 4.6 by volume. It still retained its black chocolate character, and a new firmness seemed to offset the slight loss of richness.

The resilient Köstritzer Schwarzbier has experienced greater changes over the years, but I cannot help regretting its reduction from two versions to one. The consumer who wants a sweet Schwarzbier can still add sugar, but what of those who liked the drier versions? On the other hand, how splendid that such an old speciality should re-emerge.

SAPPORO

Sapporo Breweries, 7-10-1 Ginza, Chuo-ku, Tokyo, 104 Japan
Tel: (03) 3572-6111

Given that dark lagers were still a major style in Germany when companies like Sapporo were established, it seems logical that they would have been made in Japan from the very beginning of beer-brewing there. Perhaps they were, but history is vague, not least because brand names did not become an issue until competition increased. Sapporo's production began in 1876, but there is no mention of a brand until 1892, when a Black Beer was launched. This is described in the company's history as Japan's first black beer.

Sapporo Black Beer still lives up to its proclaimed colour. It is almost opaque (100 EBC), with a tawny tinge when it is held up to the light. When really fresh, and especially on draught, it has a dense, cream-coloured head; a wonderful aroma, like coffee caught in the act of being roasted; a slightly fig-like palate; a firm, round, faintly grainy-oily body; and a pronounced finish, with notes of malt, toffee and perhaps even licorice. It has 13 Plato (1052); is made from four malts (pale, crystal, Munich and chocolate) and a small amount of rice; and exclusively aroma hops, both domestic and imported (25 BU); it emerges with 4 percent alcohol by weight, 5 by volume. Because it is a characterful product, of some historic interest, I have always been keen to see one of the breweries where it is made.

Sapporo has ten breweries, only a couple of which produce the black beer. Like all the Japanese brewing companies, it is intensely proud of its technological achievements. When I asked to visit one of the breweries that made black beer, the company's management in Tokyo was worried. The nearest of the two breweries making this product was very old – would I get the impression that the company was backward? Nonetheless, they agreed.

The brewery was about an hour northwest of Tokyo, in green onion country, at the village of Nitta, in Gunma Prefecture. By American or European standards, it was hardly a creaking veteran: the buildings had the look of the 1950s, and turned out to have been constructed then, by a company that left beer-brewing in 1968 to concentrate on *shochu* (the native hard liquor of Japan). In the fifties, no one worried unduly about ugly pipes and tanks, but these had been masked with cherry trees, arbors, topiary and hydrangeas. Next to the brewery was a brand-new maltings, designed by fashionable architect Irie Miyake. Its line reminded me of a Shinto shrine.

The brewery had copper kettles, being used in a double-decoction system, overlooked by two stained-glass windows depicting the brewers' star. (A five-pointed star is the company's logo, but it very probably derived from the traditional symbol for brewing, the six-pointed star.) There were at least two dozen open fermenters still in place, but having been retired five or six years earlier. In another hall, half a dozen open squares had been covered, and were still being used for the black beer.

When it came to tasting, the brewer clearly enjoyed this beer. I asked him what he looked for in the black beer, and he said he wanted a good malt character, especially in the finish.

SUNTORY

Suntory Brewery, 1-2-3 Motoakasaka, Minato-ku, Tokyo, 107 Japan
Tel: (03) 3470-1104

This company, Japan's leading whisky producer, did not move into the beer market until the 1960s. Its early essays were into light and mild-tasting lagers, but these enjoyed mixed fortunes. In recent years, it has begun to look more at the speciality market. Its black beer was launched not in 1890 but in 1990.

This product has an almost solid black, opaque colour; a dryish palate, with lots of bitter chocolate; a soft, gentle texture, light without being thin; and a touch of milk chocolate in the finish, perhaps with some vanilla notes. It is an all-malt beer of 13 Plato (1052), 4 percent alcohol by weight, 5 by volume, and 23 BU.

Suntory Black Beer is not widely available, but can be found in some of the company's own bars and beer gardens. There is a well-known beer garden on the roof of the company's Tokyo headquarters.

Cooking with beer

Cuisine à la bière owes its existence as a recognized style of cooking to the French and Belgians, people at the geographical meeting point of the passions for good food and fine beers. In recent years, several chefs elsewhere in Europe, and more especially in the United States, have taken up the idea with gusto. For them, wine no longer has a monopoly, either as an accompaniment or an ingredient.

Particular styles of beer have been chosen as accompaniments to certain dishes because their flavours either complement or contrast; regional foods that traditionally are served with beer, or simply go well with a local brew, have been rediscovered; and dishes have been created to highlight the use of beer as an ingredient. Beer can be used as a marinade; to tenderize, baste or glaze meat; as the basis for soups, stews, sauces and mustards; and to aerate or leaven soufflés, doughs and puddings.

Edouard Manet's model Bellot is said to have held monthly banquets featuring dishes made from beer as early as the 1870s. Escoffier proposed several such dishes in his classic *Le Guide Culinaire* of 1903, but the true diversity of beer cuisine was not set out until the work of Raoul Morleghem, who cooked for heads of state in Belgium during the 1950s. His work led to a comprehensive book of 300 recipes, compiled by more than 20 Belgian chefs, called *La Cuisine au pays de Gambrinus*. In 1960, a group of French gastronomes founded the order of the Chope d'Or (golden tankard), to further 'the gastronomic appreciation of beer'. Over the years, their events have been illuminated by such stars as Paul Bocuse, the Troisgros brothers, and Emile Jung.

In 1984, four Belgian chefs, with six Michelin stars between them, prepared a lunch featuring ten beers at the Pierre Hotel, New York. *Cuisine à la bière* had arrived in the New World.

In 1989, a more modern book, called *Cuisine légère à toutes les Bières*, was produced by Michel David, who has made a speciality of this cuisine in several restaurants in Brussels. Other less elaborate books have appeared in the English-speaking world. The odd restaurant in Paris or Brussels emphasizes *cuisine à la bière*, but many more feature one or two such dishes on the menu. The same is true from Mayfair to Manhattan, with beer dinners a popular event at restaurants such as Windows on the World, New York's Brasserie and Nosmo King.

At its simplest, *cuisine à la bière* is based on a solid foundation. Beer, like any drink, is a part of our gastronomic heritage. Beer itself is regarded as a food in Bohemia and Bavaria, and is a normal element of everyday meals in those regions. The northern French and Belgians have a richer cuisine, and love to

In New York, Zip City's Peter Spinelli offers herbed pork with the brewpub's Vienna-style lager.

At Watou, near Poperinge and Ypres, in Belgium, the cosy restaurant Hommelhof has a name that means 'hop garden'. It cooks with beer, and serves a range of local brews to accompany meals.

unwrap and uncork a beery bottle of something special. In England, Evelyn Waugh recalled having beer with his breakfast at Oxford (did not Somerset Maugham say that the beginning of the day was the only time the British ate well?), and several breweries made dinner ales until recent years. Bass occasionally revives the habit with a fruity-tasting special brew.

At its most sophisticated, *cuisine à la bière* can be ambitious. A good example is a dinner I enjoyed in Paris, at a restaurant called L'entre-siècle.

First came an apéritif comprising equal proportions of a framboise lambic and a dark, sweet, abbey-style beer, served in a large cocktail glass.

The first course was a terrine of trout, layered with parsley and other herbs, in a vinegary sauce flavoured with Hoegaarden, and accompanied by the same beer. The herbs in the terrine seemed to be accentuated by the coriander note in the Hoegaarden, and the vinegar was balanced by the beer's sweetness.

There followed mussels and prawns on a bed of diced cucumber, carrots and peppers, in a sauce made from one of the drier abbey-style beers, St Feuillien, with mustard and coriander. The delicate flavours of the fish were perhaps overpowered by the beer, which was also the accompaniment.

Fillets of red mullet, fried crisply in their skins, were served in a sauce of Rodenbach Grand Cru. Here, the strong flavour of the skins was echoed in the iron-like notes and acidity of the beer. A wonderful combination, again washed down with the same beer.

A palate-clearing sorbet was flavoured with the very dry Orval beer and a genever gin from the Belgian town of Namur. The sorbet was served with Orval. Perhaps because it once entertained juniper as an ingredient, beer seems to enjoy the company of gin. (The same could be said of beer and coriander.)

Veal sweetbreads and kidneys were braised in the chocolaty, fruity-tasting Rochefort Trappist beer, with juniper berries, served with wild mushrooms, and again accompanied by the same brew. The sweetness of the beer coaxed out the gentle flavours of the meats, and the aroma was irresistibly appetizing.

Pheasant in a sauce of old lambic was served with Belgian endive and chestnuts and a glass of the sweet, dark, abbey-style Leffe Radieuse. In this instance, the dish was almost too big for the beer.

The pungent, soft Hervé cheese of Liège was served with 'French toast' and an apple and pear syrup, beautifully accompanied by the fruity Chimay Grande Réserve, with its cinnamon spiciness.

Finally, mocha mousse flavoured with malt whisky was accompanied by a creamy St Sixtus '8'.

All of those dishes were taken from the restaurant's standard menu. Here is the menu for the best beer meal I ever had. Perhaps I enjoyed it because I had a hand in its planning, with itinerant Belgian chef Pierre Fonteyne. There are two more sample menus on the pages that follow.

Restaurant Le Bruegel, Damme, near Bruges, Belgium

Terrine of pork with cherries marinated in kriek, served with a salad dressed in lambic and accompanied by gueuze

Fillet of cod in a sabayon of abbey-style tripel, served with hop shoots and accompanied by Duvel

Wild rabbit, simmered in Liefmans' Goudenband, accompanied by Rodenbach Grand Cru

Blue cheese marinated in Gouden Carolus, accompanied by Rochefort 10

Pear poached in Hoegaarden, accompanied by faro

In London, England, the restaurant Belgo offers the cuisine of Flanders and Wallonia, prepared by chef Bobby Gutteridge.

Matching beer with food

Wine's acidity is often an asset in cutting the richness of food. I have heard it argued, and tend to agree, that beer performs less well in this respect – but no brew is wholly lacking in acidity, and some are distinctly sharp. (I have also heard the opposite argument: that beer is too acidic.)

Beer has an obvious affinity with malt vinegar and I know of one brewing company, Gulpener, in the Netherlands, that makes both. Before the invention of refrigeration, beer that turned sour was sold as vinegar; afterward, a vinegar brewery was established to continue the tradition. The rival yeasts are kept well apart: the beer and vinegar breweries are separated by the major road that links Copenhagen with Madrid. Many breweries market a mustard flavoured with their beer, among which my favourite is the sweetish, if verbose, Beautiful Aunt Edie's Blessing of the Bock, from the Lakefront brewery in Milwaukee.

Chefs often worry that the hoppiness of beer used in the preparation of food will make the dish too bitter – a problem not encountered with wine. It is a matter of taste, but most beer dishes I have sampled could have accommodated a little more of the hop flavour. It is, indeed, bitter – but it also has elements of resemblance to mint, coriander and other herbs. As a marinade, beer will not render food too bitter, but it may if it is reduced to make a sauce.

The yeastier elements of the beer provide tartness, fruitiness, acidity and sometimes savoury notes, and the malt gives sweetness, nuttiness and occasionally spiciness. Beer is very aromatic, and sometimes seems to have the property of arousing the flavours of the raw materials. Beer-yeast extracts such as the British Marmite and Australian Vegemite may not be culinary triumphs, but they awaken the taste-buds.

Some dishes that make classic marriages with wine might enjoy an occasional flirtation with beer. Others go well with either. Certain ingredients – asparagus and chocolate spring to mind – defy a wine to please them but respond beautifully to beer. The foods of southern Europe seem to call for wine and those of central and northern Europe for beer, but these cultural strands become intertwined when they are transplanted to California or Australasia. In Sydney, at the Lord Nelson Hotel, I enjoyed the roastiness of Coopers Stout with the caramelized flavours of sun-dried tomatoes in a *focaccia*; the fruity tartness of Redback wheat beer with aubergine in a beer batter; and the richness of Burragorang Bock with beer-marinated kangaroo in a mushroom and herb ragout.

In California, the Gordon Biersch brewpubs' menus feature eclectic combinations of ingredients and seasonings: Belgian endive, walnut and Gorgonzola salad in a balsamic vinaigrette; *andouillettes* with shrimps and celery, in a Creole sauce; pizzetta with wild mushrooms and Westphalian ham; lamb shank with leeks, carrots and polenta, seasoned with coriander leaves. Three of these dishes I feel go very well with beers from the house: salad with wheat beer, *andouillettes* with Märzen, pizzetta with Export. If this lager brewery ever decided to make an ale, surely that would be perfect with the lamb.

Some diners are put off beer because of its bulk and its own food value, but there is no need to consume a whole bottle with each course. At the very least, it can be shared. Nor is a (reasonably hearty) wine glass inappropriate to hold beer. At the table, the quantity is perfect, the plain glass will show off both the head and the colour, and the shape of the vessel will retain the aroma of the beer. The Belgians serve many of their beers in Burgundy samplers, and the Germans prefer their Pilsner in a small, stemmed glass (although the cone-shaped Pilsner glass is still used).

Servings of beer need not be overwhelming: try a sampler glass for a bière de garde.

Framboise offered in a slender flute glass makes an elegant apéritif or party drink.

The beer that gives a Flemish flavour to the carbonade also makes the perfect accompaniment. This is not an infallible guideline: the question is, complement or contrast?

The simplest of classics: mussels cooked in gueuze, accompanied by a glass of the same.

Apéritifs

In Alsace, local lagers are sometimes laced with the aromatic orange and gentian bitters Amer Picon to make an apéritif. In Belgium, I have been served a cocktail made from gueuze, a berry-fruit brandy and a splash of tonic. My own preference is for one of the drier examples of lambic, kriek or framboise. A very dry Pilsner such as Jever, or a hoppy ale, especially Belgians such as Orval, Chimay White or Duvel, or Young's Special London Ale, or a new-generation American IPA, arouse the appetite like nothing else.

Soups

Beer-flavoured soups are a standard item in American cooking, sometimes also using onions, cheese or, in more recent years, black beans or shrimp. The choice of beer depends upon the flavour desired. Yeasty beers such as Chimay Red or the drier Chimay White, and similar abbey brews, add a distinctive spiciness. They can also be a good accompaniment, although soup is as tricky to marry with beer as it is with wine.

Asparagus

Not an everyday food, perhaps, but one that is almost impossible to match with wine and superbly accompanied by beer. In the beer lands of Alsace, Switzerland and southern Germany, the asparagus season, in May, signals great feasts. Often, the asparagus is served with ham or scrambled eggs. The beers tend to be conventional lagers, but a coriander-tasting, fruity Belgian Trappist *tripel* does the job much better: Westmalle's Tripel seems to be made for asparagus.

Pâtés and terrines

Fruit beers can be used to flavour a sauce or marmalade to go with this type of dish. As an accompaniment, a very rich double bock, Trappist ale or barley wine is the beer world's answer to a Sauternes. Rather than this complement, I prefer the contrast afforded by a more acidic beer, perhaps a dry lambic or kriek, or a Rodenbach.

Shellfish

Stout and porter sound like hefty flavours to pit against oysters, and the two met by chance in Victorian London, but they are a marriage made in heaven. If the stout is dry enough, its tanginess seems to tickle the salty flavours of oysters. Some would argue that Guinness is even better than champagne with oysters; others choose a black velvet, the best of both worlds. The combination works almost as well with clams and other molluscs, and with crab and lobster. One of the most memorable meals in my life was a salty, peppery crab feast, with the crustaceans piled on brown paper

A stylish approach to country cooking at the rustic inn of the Ayinger brewery, near Munich.

on the table, and washed down by Guinness, at a pub called Brady's in Baltimore. This was not the original Irish Baltimore, but the slightly larger one in Maryland, where feasts of crabs from Chesapeake Bay are a seasonal ritual.

Raw, pickled or smoked fish
Very acidic beers such as Belgian lambics or red ales, or Britain's Strong Suffolk, are natural partners for these dishes. If the fish is smoked, the beer could be, too. A splash of dry stout, or a rich, hoppy ale, can add an edge to soy sauce, ginger and horseradish dips served with shellfish or sushi.

Fish
Just as a dry white wine would be the obvious choice with most fish, so would a hoppy Pilsner, whether the beer is an ingredient in a sauce, or an accompaniment. This is especially true with some of the firmer fish eaten in northern Europe, such as cod, or freshwater examples such as pike and carp in central Europe. A Dortmunder Export might better stand up to salmon and heavier fish. The dryness and refreshing characteristics of these beers seem to sharpen the flavours of the fish. At a beer dinner in Kentucky, I wanted to feature southern ingredients, and persuaded the chef to use a tart lambic beer as the 'vinegar' to make *ceviche* of catfish.

Pizza
A pizza's most obvious accompaniment is a red wine from southern Italy, but beer is often prescribed in

America. A good pizza has too much cooked-tomato sweetness and basil spiciness for an everyday lager. Northern Italy borders on Austria, and that is where the answer should be found: a Vienna-style lager, with its own malty spiciness and sweetness.

Chicken, pork
These sweetish meats are best prepared with, or accompanied by, a reasonably malty lager, perhaps a Dortmunder for chicken and a Festbier or Vienna-style lager for pork. Such beers are especially good with spit-roast meats (as served at the Munich Okto-berfest) and stews. The south Germans, Swiss and Austrians are keen on dumplings and noodle dishes (probably due to northern Italian influence), and these also seem to work well with malty lagers, even Munich-style dark lagers. When the Austrian-Californian chef Wolfgang Puck was one of the owners of a brewpub in Los Angeles, his beers could be sampled as an accompaniment to barley dumplings in a chicken broth.

Lamb, beef and game
Red meats are better partnered by full-coloured, fruity ales. A classic 'pale' ale does the job perfectly. With the roast beef of old England, Yorkshire pudding is essential. A split second before the batter is placed in the oven, a splash of lively pale ale into the mixture will both raise and aromatize the pudding. Pale ales are also the natural accompaniment to British classics such as steak and kidney (whether in a pie or pudding). An Oudenaarde brown ale, or a heavier-bodied ale from the Ardennes (Chimay Red, Rochefort) or Scotland seems the perfect accompaniment to game. Beer mustards add relish.

Stuffings
With chicken, veal or pork, moisten nutty stuffings with a dark lager or a British-style brown ale. With game, possibly a fruit stuffing, with kriek.

Spicy foods
It is often argued that because wine is too subtle, and lacks the cultural empathy, beer should be assigned to spicy foods. There is an element of condescension to this suggestion, which is also rather vague (which

beer?). Mexico does make the odd Vienna-style lager, and a Dos Equis or more robust Negra Modelo will go better than most with chicken *mole* or a Texan chili. With the latter, a chili beer is even more fun. By chance, Thailand has quite a dry, hoppy, flavourful lager, Singha, to go with its delicately spiced foods. It seems appropriate to have a Chinese beer with the dishes of Canton or Beijing, but which could stand up to the hot and sour flavours of Hunan and Szechwan? Tea is at least as good a match. The British say lager (again, which one?) should be served with curry. The sweetness of most Indian lagers does harmonize with many of the subcontinent's dishes, but arguably the yogurt drink *lassi* is more suitable.

Barbecues
Smoked beers are the obvious choice, and the most fun, but could be overbearing. A dryish, burnt-tasting porter or stout is an alternative. An American or Australian one would seem especially appropriate.

Sausages, smoked meats
Very delicate sausages, such as the classic *Weisswurst* need one of the gentler south German golden lagers or wheat beers. Kölsch and Altbier are often served with *Mettwurst* or black pudding, although the latter gains more from the tartness of a good gueuze. Italian

sausage needs the spiciness of a Vienna-style lager. Smoked sausages, once again, are delicious with smoked beers. Some British sausage-makers add a dash of ale to their products. A spoonful of hoppy beer can add piquancy to the accompanying mustard.

Salads
The most extremely acidic styles of beer, such as Berliner Weisse or a true gueuze, can be used instead of vinegar or lemon juice in salad dressings. A framboise makes an interesting raspberry vinaigrette. Sometimes the beers are just not sour enough, and need helping along with vinegar (malt, of course). This style of beer might also make an interesting accompaniment, but not to the crisper, nuttier type of salad. If nuts, or their oils, or simply very crisp salad ingredients have been used, try a brown ale of the northern English type, such as Newcastle, Samuel Smith's Nut Brown or Brooklyn Brown.

Cheese
If the great Italian and French cheeses go so well with their native wines, should not the German, Belgian, Dutch and British examples be offered with beer? British wine-writer Andrew Barr unearthed a 19th-century manual for butlers, which recommended that wine glasses be removed from the table when cheese is

The north-south divide in food and drink is not always clear cut. Chili goes well with Vienna-style lager. Here, the ingredients have headed northward to meet the cooks and drinkers of Munich.

In a café called The Old Prune, at Beersel, near Brussels, black pudding comes with gueuze.

served; 'beer is taken by some'. In Belgium, Michel David has put together a list of more than 70 cheese-and-beer marriages, using only his own country's products in each category. A more manageable list has been proposed by another culinary author in Belgium, Sonia De Kimpe, who writes in Flemish. I was one of Ms De Kimpe's tasters, sampling our way through a dozen cheeses and three times as many beers at the Hopduvel café in Ghent. Strong northern European specialities such as Limburger, mature Gouda or Cheddar, need a beer that is potent and reasonably hoppy. Belgium is full of such products, the Netherlands has a hefty barley wine called Arcener Grande Prestige, and Britain some hearty old ales.

America does not make a cheese that is quite the match for Anchor's Old Foghorn or Sierra Nevada's Big Foot. Stilton best displays its creamy, buttery flavours when it is enjoyed with a Chimay Grande Réserve or any bottle-conditioned strong brew that evinces port-like notes with age. The best combinations are those where both the cheese and the beer have some acidity. Softer cheeses can be blended with beer to produce a spread, mousse or dip. Some cheeses, such as Rutland and Somerton in Britain, and Ireland's marbled porter cheese, are made with beer.

Desserts

Diners may think dessert is the least obvious place for a beer, yet this is where John Barleycorn is at his most versatile. Many wheat beers have just the right blend of tartness and sweetness to accompany pies and other fruit dishes. Belgian 'white' beers, with their orangey flavours, are splendid in this role. The sweeter examples of fruit beers are, naturally, excellent (kriek with cherry desserts, for example). The biggest surprise is the willingness of the sweeter double bock, Trappist and abbey beers, barley wines and especially strong porters and sweet (or imperial) stouts to accompany (or flavour) dried-fruit cakes and puddings, marzipan, chocolate and anything creamy.

The Oregonian beer-writer Fred Eckhardt once ran a tasting where he matched six examples of chocolate with the most appropriate beer. A dark lager was a good partner for Tobler nougat chocolate, and the Belgians did predictably well in both departments. If it has a few years' bottle-age, Thomas Hardy's Ale, with its Madeira notes, is better than any (even fortified) wine as an accompaniment to chocolate. The Swiss beer Samichlaus is so rich and creamy as to perform wonderfully in this role, too.

I have had many chocolate desserts, especially

The heartiest and most traditional of German food is on the menu at the Schneider Weisse beer hall and restaurant, in the centre of Munich. Like many such establishments in German cities (and in Milwaukee), it has a faintly baronial rusticity, but Schneider's is more convincing than most. It is less brash than many, and at least as favoured by locals as by visitors.

The bittersweet flavours of black chocolate blend beautifully with those of the right dark brew, but it must be very rich and potent to do the trick. A Scotch ale of the dark, strong type might be a contender, but it seems even more fitted to being an after-dinner drink, especially if it is served in the thistle-shaped glass favoured by the Belgians.

mousses, made with beer, but the best was in the brewing city of Strasbourg, in Alsace, France. Chocolatier Christophe Meyer made the mousse at his family's Patisserie Christian, at 10 Rue Mercière, opposite the Twelve Apostles beer café, near the cathedral. The chocolate was moistened with La Cuivrée, a strong, malty-fruity Vienna-style lager from Madame Rina Muller's brewery Schutzenberger, in the Strasbourg suburb of Schiltigheim.

Patissier Meyer has also made sorbets with the brewery's strong golden lager Jubilator (with no other flavouring, just a dash of lemon), and chocolate truffles with the Flemish brown ale Gouden Carolus. The truffles were shaped like beer tankards, with a marzipan handle. I have even heard of the Belgian spiced strong ale Forbidden Fruit being served with mango-flavoured *kulfi* (a very dense, sweet, Indian dessert similar to ice cream).

Digestifs

The best after-dinner beers are those which are strong, perhaps sappy, but on the sweet side. (Dryness and hops arouse the appetite.) The strongest of double bocks, the sweetest of Trappists, barley wines, old or Scottish ales, are ideal. The Wynkoop brewpub in Denver takes sweet wort from its mash tun and laces it with Scottish whisky to produce a Colorado 'coffee'. After a beer dinner, any spirit served should be a whisky, preferably a malt Scotch.

The menus described on page 251 used only Belgian beers, the most versatile in the kitchen. Here are two more cosmopolitan examples.

East India Club, London, England

Savarin of calves' liver prepared with framboise and served with Chimay Red

Supreme of salmon prepared with Duvel and served with Pilsner

Oranges in Belgian 'white' beer, served with kriek

Croquettes of Stilton and Chimay Grande Réserve, served with Young's Old Nick Barley Wine

Fournou's Ovens, Stanford Court Hotel, San Francisco

Grilled prawns marinated in smoked beer, served with a jalapeño chilli salsa, and accompanied by Guinness

Duck prosciutto, Arkansas ham, venison sausage and sliced rabbit, marinated in Pete's Wicked Ale, served with mustard flavoured with Young's Special London Ale and a salad of haricots verts and yellow peppers in a Berliner Weissbier vinaigrette, accompanied by Anderson Valley Boont Amber Ale

Apple bread pudding made with Samuel Smith's Imperial Stout, accompanied by Thomas Hardy's Ale

Recipes

Some of these recipes are traditional to the European brewing regions, others have been created more recently for celebrations of beer with food; some use beer as an ingredient, others seem to me to form ideal partnerships with a specific style of beer. I have included some ideas that you will be able to recreate with a minimum of specialist shopping – and others in which either the beer or the other ingredients demand a certain amount of hunting. So here are just a few of the dishes that I have enjoyed with beer, beginning with hop shoots, known as a salad since ancient times.

Hop shoots with poached eggs, a variation of a classic Belgian springtime dish.

JETS DE HOUBLON
Hop Shoots

Pliny's *Natural History* described their use as a salad, long before there is clear evidence of the hops' blossoms having been employed in beer. There are vestiges of the tradition in several hop-growing areas, but it is best known in Belgium. Like many delicious dishes, it had humble beginnings in the farm kitchen's desire to waste nothing. The shoots had to be thinned, so why not eat those that were taken from the ground?

In Belgium today, hop shoots are such an expensive delicacy that they are cultivated under glass, and are available from New Year to spring. The more tender, naturally thinned shoots have a short season in March.

Hop shoots resemble a nuttier bean sprout. They can be eaten raw, but are traditionally steamed, then served with poached eggs and butter, cream and nutmeg or a béchamel sauce. A fancier touch might be a very light mustard sauce made with a hoppy beer. Escoffier recommended 'cockscomb-shaped' croutons of fried bread. Modern refinements in Belgium are the use of quails' eggs, and the addition of a few slivers of smoked salmon, or duck or goose liver. Hop shoots are eaten as a first course or a light lunch or supper dish, like asparagus or eggs Florentine.

In the main hop-growing region of Belgium, Poperinge, near Ypres, the shoots are often accompanied by the local Hommelbier – although any very hoppy beer will do the trick. Hommel is a local way of saying hop, sounding more like the Czech *chmel* than the French *houblon* or Flemish and English hop. This recipe is served by chef Stefaan Couttenye, at the restaurant Hommelhof, in Watou.

Serves 4

400 g / 14 oz hop shoots	For the mousseline sauce:
pinch of salt	2 egg yolks
juice of ½ a lemon	salt, freshly ground black
4 tablespoons cream	pepper
4 eggs	200 g / 7 oz butter, clarified
croutons and parsley, to garnish	

1 Wash the hop shoots and trim off the hard tips. Plunge the shoots into a pan of boiling water, with the salt and lemon juice, and boil until tender, 5–10 minutes. Drain well and divide between 4 plates. Pour a tablespoon of cream over each plate of hop shoots, then place in a warm oven while you prepare the eggs and sauce.
2 Poach the eggs lightly, then keep them warm in a bowl of hot water.
3 For the sauce: whisk the egg yolks with the salt, pepper and a few drops of cold water over a very low heat until the mixture is frothy. If the eggs become too hot they will curdle; to prevent this happening, you may need to remove the pan from the heat from time to time – but keep whisking. Very gradually add the clarified butter (there will be about 125 ml/4 fl oz), whisking continuously until the sauce is thickened and mousse-like. Add a few drops of lemon juice and check the seasoning, then pour over the poached eggs on their beds of hop shoots. Garnish with croutons and a sprig of parsley.

POTAGE A LA BIERE
Beer Soup

Beer soup is well known in the United States, but not featured as often as it might be in Europe. I rather like this simple recipe from the Belgian chef Michel David (from his book *Cuisine légère à toutes les Bières*). I would suggest a good, flavourful Pilsner as the main ingredient. This dish emphasizes the bitterness of the hop, and is something of an acquired taste; you might like to add more sugar – up to 1 or 2 tablespoons.

Serves 4

50 g / 2 oz butter	salt, freshly ground black
25 g / 1 oz flour, sifted	pepper
1 litre / 1¾ pints Pilsner	150 ml / ¼ pint crème fraîche
lager	4 slices French bread,
pinch of freshly grated	toasted
nutmeg	snipped chives, to garnish
2 pinches of sugar	

1 Melt the butter in a heavy-based pan over gentle heat. Stir in the flour, beating vigorously with a wooden spoon.
2 Pour in the beer, holding the bottle at an angle to prevent it from frothing, and stirring constantly to avoid lumps. Add the nutmeg, sugar, salt and pepper. Simmer gently for 20 minutes, stirring occasionally.
3 Just before serving, whisk in the crème fraîche. Put a slice of toasted French bread into each bowl and pour the soup over the bread. Sprinkle with snipped chives.

For a subtle variation, try making this soup with rye beer, replacing the nutmeg with cinnamon, and using 1–2 tablespoons of sugar.

Another version, more like the classic French onion soup, begins with finely chopped onions and garlic softened in the butter; the soup is simmered for 45 minutes and served without the addition of cream, but accompanied by grated cheese to sprinkle on the toast.

An American version is a thick beer and cheese soup, in which onion, carrot and celery are softened in butter, sprinkled with flour, and simmered with single cream and beer. Plenty of grated cheese is stirred in until it melts, and the soup is finally enriched by mixing a little hot soup with beaten egg yolks and stirring them back into the soup.

FROMAGE DE CHEVRE CHAUD CASTELAIN
Warm Goat Cheese on Sautéed Spinach with Castelain

I have seen several variations of salads of cheese with beer. Here, using a fruity *blonde* French bière de garde, is a dish in this style from Pierre Cauvin, chef at New York's Brasserie (100 East 53rd Street), created for a beer and food festival. The use of beer to flavour the pears is subtle, but is accentuated by an accompaniment of the same beer.

Serves 4

2 pears	1 tablespoon cider vinegar
75 g / 3 oz butter	4 slices of bread, lightly
salt, freshly ground black	toasted
pepper	4 round slices of goat cheese,
200 ml / 7 fl oz Ch'ti blonde	about 2.5 cm / 1 inch
700 g / 1½ lb fresh young	thick
spinach	freshly grated nutmeg

1 Peel and core the pears and cut in half lengthways. Sauté in 25 g / 1 oz of the butter, season, then pour in the beer, stirring the bottom of the pan with a wooden spatula. Simmer until the pears are tender. Leave to cool in the beer.
2 Wash the spinach thoroughly, discarding large stems. Pat dry. Sauté in the remaining butter, stirring frequently,

Toasted goat cheese on a bed of spinach.

until the spinach wilts. Pushing the spinach to the edge of the pan, pour in the cider vinegar and stir well with a wooden spatula, then mix the spinach with the vinegar. Season to taste.

3 Meanwhile, cut circles of bread, a little larger than the cheese slices, and place on a baking sheet. Put the cheese on the bread and place under a hot grill for 3–4 minutes, until the cheese just begins to melt.

4 Divide the spinach between 4 plates. Slice the pears and place on the spinach, sprinkled with nutmeg. Add the cheese toasts and serve immediately.

MOULES A LA GUEUZE
Mussels cooked in Gueuze

The great brewing nations all have their famous foods, and one of Belgium's is mussels. Here is a simple recipe from the café In De Rare Vos, at Schepdaal, near Brussels. I have also enjoyed this dish in some of the beer cafés of Paris.

Serves 4

2 kg / 4½ lb mussels	*6 shallots, or 2 onions, diced*
50 g / 2 oz butter	*300 ml / ½ pint gueuze*
2–3 sticks celery, diced	

An aromatic dish of freshly steamed mussels.

1 Clean the mussels thoroughly in plenty of cold water, discarding any that are cracked or broken.

2 Melt the butter in a large casserole and soften the celery and shallots over gentle heat for about 5 minutes.

3 Add the beer and bring to the boil, then immediately add the mussels and cover the pan. Cook for 5–7 minutes, stirring or shaking the pan a few times, until most of the mussels open.

4 Discard any that remain closed and serve at once, with plenty of bread to mop up the delicious juices. A large plate of French fries is the traditional accompaniment.

ESCAVECHE

Wherever the Spanish ruled, there are variations on *escavèche* (the spelling as well as the dish), a cold hors d'oeuvre in which fish are 'pickled' in a marinade. In Belgium, I have often been offered this treat with Chimay Capsule Blanche and this recipe comes from the Auberge de Poteaupré on the Chimay abbey estate. Eels feature in several of Belgium's national dishes. If you would like to use a more delicate fish such as trout, the chef suggests that you reduce the amount of onions and vinegar.

Serves 4–6

1 kg / 2¼ lb fresh eels	*2 bay leaves*
4 tablespoons plain flour	*few sprigs of tarragon*
4–6 tablespoons olive oil	*salt, freshly ground black*
5 onions, sliced	*pepper*
2 lemons, sliced	*1–2 tablespoons cornflour*
600 ml / 1 pint vinegar	*(optional)*
300 ml / ½ pint white wine	*1–2 tablespoons chopped*
200 ml / 7 fl oz water	*parsley*

1 Cut the eels into 6–7 cm / 2½–3 inch pieces, coat with flour, and fry in hot oil until golden brown. Transfer to a deep dish, using a slotted spoon.

2 Fry the sliced onions and lemons briefly in the oil, then add the vinegar, wine, water, herbs and seasoning. Bring to the boil and thicken with cornflour if the sauce seems too thin, then pour over the eel pieces. Leave to cool, then leave overnight in the refrigerator.

3 Serve cold, sprinkled with parsley, with salad and French fries.

In Spanish and Provençal cooking the dish is usually known as *escabèche*, and is made from small fish such as sardines, anchovies, whiting or red mullet. A greater proportion of olive oil is used for the marinade, which is flavoured with garlic and pimentos.

The term was taken by the Spanish to the West Indies and from there it found its way into some old English cookery books, under the name of caveach.

In South America the dish changed its name to *ceviche*. In this version the fish is not cooked at all, but is marinated in lime or lemon juice; the acidity of the fruit 'cooks' the fish.

KAPR SMAZENY NA STROUHANCE
Carp fried in Breadcrumbs

Some Czechs argue that Moravian white wine goes best with fish, and Bohemian beer with meat. I cannot agree. There is nothing like a good Pilsner or Budweiser Budvar with carp, one of the freshwater fish that are so widely consumed in landlocked central Europe. At a single meal in Bohemia, I have eaten carp prepared in three ways, and of course it is also the classic ingredient of *gefilte fish*.

Serves 6
6 pieces of carp, cleaned and scaled, weighing about 150 g / 5 oz each	2 eggs, beaten
salt	150 g / 5 oz dried white breadcrumbs
250 ml / 8 fl oz milk	fat for shallow frying
50 g / 2 oz flour, sifted	lemon slices, to serve

1 Soak the fish in salted milk for 15 minutes, then pat dry.
2 Place the flour, eggs and breadcrumbs in 3 separate shallow bowls. Sprinkle the fish with salt, then dip each piece first in flour, then in the eggs, then in breadcrumbs, making sure the fish is evenly coated at each stage.
3 Heat the fat (lard is traditional, but butter and oil, or just butter, have a better flavour) in a large frying pan. Fry the fish over gentle heat until both sides are golden.
4 Serve at once with lemon slices, and grated Emmental cheese if you like. Boiled potatoes are the traditional accompaniment, or a selection of salads, such as potato, bean and celery.

Milena Grenfell-Baines, who provided this recipe, had several more at her fingertips – carp in a sour cream and paprika sauce, carp on a bed of carrots and celery with a mayonnaise-based sauce, marinated carp. Lady Grenfell-Baines remembers carp in aspic as a set piece for special occasions in her Prague childhood, and suggests that other edible freshwater fish, such as trout, could replace the carp.

FILETS DE ROUGET A LA RODENBACH GRAND CRU
Red Mullet with a Sauce of Rodenbach Grand Cru

Fillets of mullet in the style of chef Olivier Simon, at the restaurant L'entre-siècle, not far from the Eiffel Tower in Paris, is one of my favourite beer dishes.

Serves 4
6 fillets of red mullet	1 tablespoon brown sugar
1 tablespoon olive oil	50 ml / 2 fl oz raspberry vinegar
pinch of freshly grated nutmeg	50 ml / 2 fl oz sherry vinegar
	1 bottle (33 cl) Rodenbach Grand Cru
For the sauce:	400 ml / 14 fl oz fish stock
75 g / 3 oz celeriac	1 tablespoon jus de veau
1 stick celery	(well-reduced veal stock)
1 carrot	sprig of thyme
50 g / 2 oz butter	1 bay leaf
50 g / 2 oz shallots, finely chopped	salt, freshly ground black pepper
1 tablespoon finely chopped parsley stalks	

1 Scale the fish fillets, taking care not to tear the skin. Remove any small bones with a pair of tweezers, rinse the fish and pat dry. Rub all over with the olive oil.
2 For the sauce: cut the celeriac, celery and carrot into fine dice. Melt half the butter in a saucepan and sauté the shallots, diced vegetables and parsley stalks until they are golden brown. Add the sugar, both vinegars and the beer. Simmer until slightly reduced, about 10 minutes.
3 Add the fish stock and jus, thyme, bay leaf, salt and pepper. Reduce to the consistency of a light syrup by simmering gently for about 30 minutes.
4 Heat the oven to 180°C/350°F/gas mark 4. Heat a non-stick frying pan and cook the fish, skin side down, over

Red mullet with a sauce of Rodenbach Grand Cru.

Coq à la bière, a northern French classic.

high heat for 4 minutes. Finish cooking in the preheated oven – this should take no more than 1–2 minutes.

5 To finish the sauce, strain it into a clean pan, reheat and whisk in the remaining butter and nutmeg to taste.
Serve the fish surrounded by the sauce, with fresh pasta and spinach, or other vegetables.

COQ A LA BIERE
Chicken in Beer

Why should coq always be 'au vin'? In northern France and Belgium, it is often 'à la bière', using a dark bière de garde or other local brew. Here is a recipe from the café Les Brasseurs in Lille, France, where the traditional accompaniments are French fries and braised chicory.

Serves 4

2 tablespoons oil	225 g / 8 oz button mushrooms
25 g / 1 oz butter	bouquet garni
16–20 baby onions	salt, freshly ground black
1 x 2 kg / 4½ lb chicken, cut	pepper
into 8 pieces	50 ml / 2 fl oz crème fraîche
50 ml / 2 fl oz gin	or double cream
1 tablespoon flour	1 tablespoon chopped
300 ml / ½ pint dark beer	parsley

1 Heat the oil and butter in a wide, heavy-based casserole. Sauté the baby onions until they just begin to brown, then remove with a slotted spoon. Brown the chicken pieces in the same fat over moderately high heat, then lower the heat and flame with the gin.

2 Sprinkle the flour over the chicken and cook for 1–2 minutes, stirring frequently. Return the baby onions to the pan with the beer, mushrooms, bouquet garni, salt and pepper. Bring to the boil, cover and simmer until the chicken is tender, 40–45 minutes.

3 Discard the bouquet garni, skim off excess fat and stir in the cream. Bring back to the boil and check the seasoning. Serve sprinkled with parsley.

MOLE POBLANO DE GUAJOLOTE
Chicken in Chili and Chocolate Sauce

In Mexico, this festive dish is classically made with turkey. It is famous as one of the few dishes in which meat and chocolate meet, although the Norwegians have been known to do something similar with lamb. The chilies specified are all dried red varieties, each with their own subtle contribution to the piquancy of the *mole*, or chili sauce. Its slight sweetness goes well with Vienna-style lager, whether a Mexican version or one made in North America or Europe.

Serves 4–6

6 ancho chilies
4 mulato chilies
4 pasilla chilies
2 whole cloves
4 black peppercorns
pinch of anise or fennel seeds
4 coriander seeds
2.5 cm/1 inch piece of
   cinnamon stick
2 tablespoons sesame seeds
1½ onions
6 cloves garlic
2–3 tablespoons lard or oil

50 g/2 oz blanched
   almonds, chopped
50 g/2 oz shelled peanuts
50 g/2 oz raisins
450 g/1 lb tomatoes, peeled,
   seeded and chopped
1 stale corn or wheat
   tortilla, shredded
1 large chicken, cut into
   serving pieces
1 tablespoon salt
40 g/1½ oz dark bitter
   chocolate

1 Using a sharp knife, slit the chilies open lengthways and discard the stems and seeds. Tear the chilies into pieces, place in a bowl and add enough boiling water just to cover them. Leave to soak for around 30 minutes while you prepare the sauce.

2 Toast the cloves, peppercorns, anise and coriander seeds, cinnamon and 1 tablespoon of the sesame seeds until they are fragrant, then grind in a spice grinder or pound to a powder with a pestle and mortar.

3 Chop 1 onion and 3 cloves garlic and sauté in the lard or oil for 3 minutes. Using a slotted spoon, transfer the onion and garlic to a blender or food processor. In the same fat, sauté the almonds, peanuts and raisins for 3 minutes, then lift out of the fat into the blender, along with the tomatoes,

tortilla, spice mixture and drained chilies. Blend to a coarse, thick purée, adding a little of the chilies' soaking water if necessary.

4 Reheat the fat in the pan and cook the purée, stirring constantly, until the oil begins to rise to the surface. (Traditionally the sauce is prepared 2–3 days ahead, to allow the flavours to blend.)

5 Put the chicken in a pan with the salt, remaining ½ onion and 3 cloves garlic, and add water to cover. Bring to the boil and simmer until the chicken is cooked and tender, about 1 hour. Drain, reserving the stock.

6 Reheat the spicy purée in a large casserole, and when it comes back to the boil, add 300 ml/½ pint of the chicken stock and the chocolate. Taste, and correct the seasoning if necessary. Add the chicken pieces, cover the pan and simmer over gentle heat for 20–30 minutes, stirring occasionally and adding more stock if necessary.

7 Toast the remaining sesame seeds until fragrant, and sprinkle over the *mole* before serving.

8 Serve with hot tortillas, guacamole, rice and *frijoles refritos* (a chunky purée of red kidney beans, pinto or black beans, with onions and lard).

AGNEAU A LA BIERE ET AUX COEURS D'ARTICHAUTS
Lamb with Beer and Artichoke Hearts

Lamb goes well with fruity ales. This dish uses a Belgian saison, although a good English or American ale could easily be substituted. The recipe comes from Brussels beer merchant Rene Van Autenboer and his culinary collaborator Annita Smet.

Serves 4

8 globe artichokes
1 lemon, cut in half
700 g/1½ lb lean lamb, cut
   into strips
1 clove garlic, chopped
1 teaspoon chopped fresh
   thyme

freshly ground black pepper
750 ml/1¼ pints ale
100 ml/4 fl oz crème
   fraîche
1 tablespoon flour
2 tablespoons chopped fresh
   parsley

1 Trim the artichokes' bases and all the leaves with a sharp knife, rubbing the cut areas with half the lemon. Cook in a large pan of boiling water with the squeezed juice of the

Mole poblano, a festive Mexican dish.

Lamb cooked with artichoke hearts in a sauce of cream and a fruity ale.

lemon, until the hearts are just tender, then drain and refresh with cold water. Scrape out the prickly 'chokes' with a teaspoon and discard.

2 Heat a wide, heavy-based pan over moderately high heat and add the strips of lamb, stirring frequently until they are just browned, but still pink inside.

3 Add the garlic and thyme, then add the artichoke hearts and brown them in the lamb fat. Add freshly ground black pepper to taste.

4 Gently pour in 500 ml/18 fl oz of the ale, stirring the bottom of the pan with a wooden spatula. Turn down the heat slightly and allow the beer to reduce until only a few tablespoons remain.

5 Add the remaining beer and the crème fraîche, blended with the flour. Allow to boil for a further 1–2 minutes, stirring constantly, until the sauce thickens. Serve in a warmed earthenware casserole, sprinkled with parsley.

HERB-CRUSTED LOIN OF PORK

In New York, the Zip City brewpub (3 West 18th Street) offers this dish, created by chef Peter Spinelli. It goes well with the soft, sweetish, slightly grainy Vienna-style lager made there.

Serves 4

1.5–1.75 kg/3–4 lb loin of pork
750 ml/1¼ pints white wine
200 g/7 oz fresh white breadcrumbs
5 tablespoons clarified butter
2 large onions, chopped
3 sticks celery, chopped
2 carrots, chopped
2–3 cloves garlic, crushed
50 ml/2 fl oz ruby port
sprigs of fresh rosemary, to garnish

For the spice mixture:
1½ teaspoons ground cinnamon
1 teaspoon ground cloves
1 bay leaf, crushed
1½ teaspoons ground nutmeg
1½ teaspoons dried thyme
1½ teaspoons ground allspice
1 tablespoon white peppercorns, crushed
1½ teaspoons cayenne pepper
2 teaspoons salt

For the herb coating:
2 cloves garlic
2 sprigs fresh rosemary
large handful fresh thyme
small handful fresh oregano
½ teaspoon salt
2 tablespoons Dijon mustard
1 tablespoon coarse-grained mustard
2 tablespoons lemon juice
3 tablespoons olive oil

1 Bone the pork, or ask your butcher to do this for you, reserving the bones. Trim the pork and tie into a neat roll, cutting cross hatches into the sides. Mix all the spices together and rub 2–3 teaspoons of the mixture over the pork. Chill overnight.

2 To prepare the herb coating: combine the garlic and herbs in a blender or food processor. Add the salt, mustards and lemon juice. With the machine running, add the oil slowly, so it forms a thick emulsion.

3 Heat the oven to 240°C/475°F/gas mark 9. Place the pork bones in a deep flameproof roasting tin with the wine. Brush the herb coating over the pork and set on top of the bones. Roast for 10 minutes.

4 Reduce the oven heat to 180°C/350°F/gas mark 4. Take the pork out of the oven and roll in the breadcrumbs. Brush with the butter, then return to the oven for 1½–2 hours, or until the pork is cooked through.

5 Transfer the pork to a warm plate and leave to rest for 15 minutes before slicing.

6 Add the onions, celery, carrots and garlic to the pan with the bones and brown over moderately high heat, stirring frequently, adding more wine if the pan seems dry before the vegetables are thoroughly brown. Deglaze with the port and strain the sauce.

7 Slice the pork and serve with the sauce, cranberry relish and sweet potato and apple galette. Garnish with rosemary.

Cranberry Relish

1.5 kg / 3 lb cranberries
finely grated zest of
*   3 oranges*
finely grated zest of 1 lemon
350 ml / 12 fl oz fresh
*   orange juice*

500 g / 1¼ lb sugar
2 tablespoons grated fresh
*   root ginger*
3 tablespoons cider vinegar
2 cinnamon sticks

1 Place all the ingredients in a large pan, and simmer over gentle heat until the cranberries have split and are tender.

Sweet Potato and Apple Galette

2 teaspoons butter
135 g / 4½ oz brown sugar
3 sweet potatoes, peeled and
*   sliced 3 mm / ⅛ inch thick*

4 large cooking apples, cored
*   and sliced 3 mm / ⅛ inch*
*   thick*

1 Generously butter the bottom and sides of a 23 cm / 9 inch cast-iron frying pan. Sprinkle evenly with 2 tablespoons of the sugar. Arrange alternate slices of sweet potato and apple in a spiral, completely covering the bottom of the pan. Top with the remaining sugar. Place over gentle heat and leave undisturbed for 45 minutes.
2 When the pan juices look thick and give off a nutty aroma, the galette is ready (test the potatoes with a skewer to make sure they are tender). Invert the galette onto a plate and wipe away any excess juices. Cut into quarters.

Herbed pork, served with sweet potato galette.

CARBONADE FLAMANDE
Beef stewed in Beer

Even diners who have never heard the phrase *cuisine à la bière* probably know carbonade of beef. There is much more to beer cuisine than this one dish, but it remains a simple classic. This recipe is from Madame Rose Blancquaert, of the café De Mouterij, in Oudenaarde, Belgium, where she makes it with Liefmans' Goudenband, the classic Flemish brown ale. The same beer is served as an accompaniment.

Serves 4

4 shallots, or 2 onions
50 g / 2 oz butter
900 g / 2 lb beef, cubed
salt, freshly ground black
*   pepper*
good pinch of ground
*   coriander*

2 sprigs of thyme
½–1 litre / 18 fl oz–1¾ pints
*   Liefmans' Goudenband*
2 tablespoons flour
1 tablespoon Dijon mustard
*   (optional)*

1 Chop the shallots or onions and fry them in the butter in a casserole. Add the beef and brown for about 5 minutes. Season with salt, pepper, ground coriander and thyme. Pour in enough beer to cover the meat completely, and simmer gently for 1½ hours.
2 Lift out the meat with a slotted spoon, and set aside. Rub the sauce through a sieve and return it to the pan. Blend the flour with a little of the sauce and add to the pan, adding mustard if you like. Simmer, stirring, until the flour is cooked, about 2 minutes.
3 Return the meat to the sauce and heat through. Serve with steamed or boiled potatoes and sweet onions.

Madame Rose suggests an alternative using kriek, a variation I reserve for a carbonade of pork. In this version, black cherry preserve replaces the mustard, with stewed apples as an accompaniment. If the sauce is too sweet, a dash of malt vinegar can be added just before the dish is served.

Some cooks add a few ounces of lean cubed gammon to the beef version. Some specify various cuts of beef (boned neck, top shoulder, thin flank, topside, bottom round, chuck steak), or suggest deglazing the frying pan with the beer, adding a brown roux, then cooking the meat, covered with more beer, for 2–3

An authentic carbonade flamande, as served in Flanders, with French fries, fresh from the pan.

hours in a casserole in the oven. Escoffier's recipe has alternate layers of beef and finely sliced onions. In another variation, slices of French bread, spread with mustard, are browned on top of the stew for about 15 minutes at the end of cooking: the top of the bread becomes crisp, while the bottom absorbs some of the delicious juices.

STEAK AND KIDNEY PUDDING

A British classic, but this recipe has an especially beery accent. Not only is it made with English bitter, it was devised by cookery writer Rosemary Ruddle, whose family once owned the brewery of the same name in Oakham, Rutland. The filling can also be cooked separately (brown the meat first, then simmer for 1½ hours), and topped with shortcrust or puff pastry.

Serves 4

For the suet crust:
275 g / 10 oz plain flour
1 heaped teaspoon baking
  powder
large pinch of salt
150 g / 5 oz beef suet

For the filling:
700 g / 1½ lb steak
225 g / ½ lb ox kidney

2 tablespoons plain flour
salt, freshly ground black
  pepper
1 clove garlic
1 tablespoon chopped fresh
  basil
1 teaspoon chopped fresh
  thyme
1–2 bay leaves
450 ml / ¾ pint Ruddles
  bitter

1 Sift the flour, baking powder and salt into a large bowl. Mix in the suet and add just enough water to make a fairly soft dough.

2 On a floured surface, roll out the dough until it is about 5 mm / ¼ inch thick. Cut away one third of the dough in a fan shape and set aside. Sprinkle the remaining two thirds with flour and lift into a greased 1.5 litre / 2½ pint pudding basin. Press gently into the bowl, joining the cut edge carefully to seal.

3 Cut the steak into 1 cm / ½ inch cubes, trimming off gristle and excess fat. Skin, core and chop the kidney. Toss all the meat in seasoned flour.

4 Place the garlic in the pudding basin and add the meat, interspersed with the herbs. Pour in the beer.

5 Roll out the remaining dough into a circle about 2.5 cm / 1 inch larger than the top of the bowl. Wet the edge, then cover the pudding with the dough round, pressing well to seal.

6 Place a piece of greaseproof paper on top of a piece of kitchen foil and pleat them down the centre. Grease the greaseproof paper and use to cover the pudding; tie a piece of string tightly around the rim of the basin to keep the paper and foil in place.

7 Place in a large pan of boiling water and boil for about 4–4½ hours, topping up with more boiling water from time to time.

FAISAN A L'ECOSSAISE
Pheasant in Scottish Ale

The hearty flavours of game are splendidly accompanied by an equally robust beer. This recipe combines pheasant with Scottish ale and single-malt whisky.

Serves 4

3 tablespoons oil
50 g / 2 oz butter
2 pheasants
1 onion, chopped
1 stick celery, diced
2 carrots, diced
75 ml / 3 fl oz single-malt
   whisky

2 bottles (33 cl each)
   Scottish ale
600 ml / 1 pint chicken stock
2 cloves garlic, crushed
300 ml / ½ pint double cream
salt, freshly ground black
   pepper

---

1 Heat the oven to 220°C/425°F/gas mark 7. Heat the oil and butter in a deep, flameproof roasting tin, add the pheasants and coat in the hot fat. Roast the birds on their sides for 25 minutes, turning after 12 minutes. Remove from the oven and leave to cool.

2 When cool, cut off the breasts and legs (bone the legs if you like) and set aside.

3 Chop the carcasses and add to the roasting tin with the vegetables. Brown well over moderately high heat, stirring with a wooden spatula. Flame with the whisky, then add the beer, stock and garlic. Reduce the heat and simmer for 1 hour, skimming occasionally.

4 Strain the sauce into a clean pan, add the pheasant breasts and legs and simmer for 30 minutes.

5 Remove the meat and keep warm while you reduce the sauce by half.

6 Skim, then stir in the cream and boil until thickened slightly. Season to taste and serve with the pheasant, accompanied by roast potatoes, shredded red or green cabbage, or other seasonal vegetables.

Pheasant with a Scottish accent.

Serves 4

4 x 75 g / 3 oz steaks cut
   from a saddle of venison
1 tablespoon brandy
salt, freshly ground black
   pepper
2 tablespoons rendered pork
   fat or oil
2 tablespoons butter
3 tablespoons finely chopped
   shallots
50 ml / 2 fl oz cider vinegar

120 ml / 4 fl oz porter
250 ml / 8 fl oz beef or game
   stock, reduced to a demi-
   glace
2 tablespoons huckleberries,
   lingonberries preserved
   in sugar, or cranberry
   sauce
3–4 gingersnaps, crumbled
freshly grated nutmeg

SEARED MEDALLIONS OF VENISON WITH ANCHOR PORTER, HUCKLEBERRIES AND GINGERSNAP PAN SAUCE

An inspired combination created by Rick Moonen, executive chef at The Water Club, New York (500 East 80th Street) for a lunch exploring the possibilities of Anchor's range of beers. It began with crisp fried calamari served with Anchor Steam Beer; a pheasant chili and a seafood and andouillette gumbo were offered with Liberty Ale; and this venison dish was served with Anchor's spicy 'Our Special Ale'. The cookies thicken the sauce, and the sweet berries and butter balance the bitterness in the porter to make a rich, full-bodied sauce.

1 Flatten the steaks to 2 cm/¾ inch thick, moisten with the brandy, season and set aside.

2 Heat a heavy-based frying pan for 1 minute, add the fat until it sizzles, then add the steaks. Brown quickly on each side, then remove from the pan and keep warm.

3 Discard the fat, add half the butter and the shallots and cook over medium heat until softened. Add the vinegar, scraping the meat residue from the bottom of the pan.

4 When the vinegar has reduced to a thick syrup, add the porter and stock and reduce by half.

5 Add the berries, gingersnaps, remaining butter and any meat juices. Stir until smooth, and season to taste.

6 Spoon the sauce over the steaks and serve with hot potato dumplings and apple and turnip purée.

Potato Dumplings

3 large potatoes, peeled
1 large onion, finely
    chopped
1 tablespoon butter
1 egg, beaten
50 ml/2 fl oz milk

50 g/2 oz plain flour
salt, freshly ground black
    pepper
freshly grated nutmeg
melted butter and chopped
    parsley, to serve

1 Boil the potatoes until tender. Meanwhile, sweat the onion in the butter for 5 minutes. Drain the cooked potatoes and mash with the egg and milk. Mix in the onion and butter, and just enough flour to make a very soft dough. Season with salt, pepper and nutmeg.
2 Form the mixture into small balls and drop into simmering salted water for 10 minutes. Serve drizzled with melted butter and sprinkled with chopped parsley.

Apple and Turnip Purée

3 turnips, peeled and sliced
5 tablespoons butter
salt, freshly ground black
    pepper

3–4 red-skinned apples,
    cored and chopped
1 tablespoon lemon juice

1 Put the sliced turnips in a small pan with 2 tablespoons of the butter, 2 tablespoons of water, salt and pepper. Cover and cook until tender. Add the apples and lemon juice and cook over gentle heat until very soft, and most of the moisture has evaporated.
2 Pass through a food mill (to extract the colour from the apple skins), then add the remaining butter and beat over medium heat until the purée is light and just firm.

LEEK PUDDING

Leeks are grown in several brewing regions. Although the British know them as the emblem of Wales, they also have almost cult status in the northeast of England, where growers compete to cultivate the biggest. Small leeks have more flavour, for this Northumbrian savoury pudding. It is customarily served with a stew, perhaps of lamb, made with a splash of brown ale in the northern English style, which would also accompany the dish. Or try it with a bière de garde from northern France.

Serves 4–6

450 g/1 lb self-raising flour
225 g/8 oz beef suet
salt, freshly ground black
    pepper

450 g/1 lb leeks, roughly
    chopped
225 g/8 oz onion, sliced
50 g/2 oz butter

1 Mix the flour, suet, salt and pepper with just enough cold water to make a soft dough.
2 Put the leeks, onion and butter in a pan with water to cover. Bring to the boil and boil for 2–3 minutes, then drain and season. Grease 4 small pudding basins (10 cm/4 inches in diameter) and line with the suet pastry. Fill with the leek mixture, then cover with suet pastry, greaseproof paper and foil, as for Steak and Kidney Pudding (see page 266).
3 Place in a large pan, with boiling water two-thirds of the way up the sides of the basins, cover and boil for 1½–2 hours.

'SOUR' BEER BREAD

In Germany and elsewhere, brewpubs often take a little 'spent grain' from the mash tun to make a beer bread for their diners. If you do not have your own brewery, you do not have recourse to this delight. An alternative is to add beer when you make bread; both the malt and the hops enhance the flavour. Here is a recipe from America's best-known pastrycook Jim Dodge, Senior Vice-President of the New England Culinary Institute in Vermont. Beer-lover Dodge used a Munich dark lager.

For the starter:
150 ml/¼ pint water
100 g/4 oz wholemeal flour
pinch of active dried yeast

For the bread:
125 ml/4 fl oz warm beer
450 g/1 lb strong plain
    flour
1 sachet active dried yeast
50 ml/2 fl oz warm water
2 teaspoons salt

1 Prepare the starter a day before making the bread. Mix all the starter ingredients in a bowl, cover with plastic wrap and set aside in a warm place for 24 hours.
2 To make the bread: put the starter into the bowl of a mixer fitted with a dough hook; stir in the warm beer. Add 175 g/6 oz of the flour and mix until evenly blended; about 2 minutes. Add the yeast and continue to mix for a further

5 minutes. Add the remaining flour, the water and the salt, and mix until a dough forms.

3 Knead the dough on a lightly floured surface for about 10 minutes, until it is smooth and elastic. Place in a lightly oiled bowl and cover with a damp cloth. Leave in a warm place until doubled in size.

4 Turn out and shape into a round loaf. Place in a shallow, round, well-floured basket or bowl, cover loosely and leave in a warm place until more than double the original size.

5 Heat the oven to 230°C/450°F/gas mark 8. Grease a baking sheet and dust with cornmeal or flour.

6 Turn the loaf out of its mould onto the baking sheet and score the top with a sharp knife. Fill a deep roasting tin with boiling water and place in the hot oven. Put the loaf on the shelf above the water and bake for 10 minutes.

7 Reduce the oven temperature to 200°C/400°F/gas mark 6, remove the water and bake for 35–45 minutes.

Sweet, sugary beer tart.

TARTE A LA BIERE
Beer Tart

It sounds unlikely, but beer tart is a standard dessert in northern France. It is also known as *tarte à la cassonade* or *tarte vergeoise*, referring to the unrefined cane sugar which imparts its faintly rummy taste. A bière de garde would be pleasingly authentic.

Serves 6–8
135 g/4½ oz butter
200 g/7 oz flour, sifted
1 tablespoon caster sugar
pinch of salt

2–3 tablespoons iced water
200 g/7 oz soft brown sugar
2 large eggs

1 Cut 100 g/3½ oz of the butter into pieces and rub into the flour with the sugar and salt. Mix in just enough water to bind the dough smoothly. Chill for 30 minutes.

2 Heat the oven to 220°C/425°F/gas mark 7. Roll out the pastry on a lightly floured surface and line a 23 cm/9 inch tart tin. Sprinkle the brown sugar over the pastry base.

3 Break the eggs into a bowl and beat in the beer. Pour through a sieve directly onto the sugar, then cut the remaining butter into slivers and scatter over the tart.

4 Cook for about 35 minutes, until the filling is just firm to the touch. Leave to stand for at least 10 minutes before serving warm, or allow to cool completely and serve cold.

BIERSCHAUM
Beer Foam

Many very strong beers, especially those with a secondary fermentation in the bottle, have similar flavours to fortified wine. Instead of Marsala, try a strong ale in that delightfully simple dessert, zabaglione. This version, from the Bräustüberl restaurant attached to Kaltenberg castle in Bavaria, is made with König Ludwig Dunkel dark lager.

Serves 4–6
4 whole eggs and 4 yolks
4 tablespoons caster sugar
8 tablespoons dark lager

1 tablespoon Jaegermeister
(a dark red, bitter,
herbal liqueur) or
Angostura bitters

1 Put the eggs, yolks and sugar into a large heatproof bowl and beat with a balloon whisk or electric mixer until they are very thick and pale.

2 Place the bowl above a pan of simmering water, and slowly add the beer and liqueur, whisking constantly. The mixture will begin to swell; it is ready when it holds its shape for a few seconds.

3 Serve immediately in small beer glasses, accompanied by crisp biscuits, or use as a sabayon sauce to go with a dish of poached pears.

Kriek ice cream (top) and beer and cherry sorbet.

Iced walnut soufflé with orange custard sauce.

SORBET A LA BRUNE GRIOTTINE
Dark-beer Cherry Sorbet

There are many recipes for sorbets made with beer. Here is one from the eminent chef Emile Jung, of Le Crocodile, Strasbourg, France.

Serves 6

250 ml / 8 fl oz dark beer	75 g / 3 oz puréed morello
50 ml / 2 fl oz Amer Picon	cherries
75 g / 3 oz caster sugar	

1 Mix all the ingredients together until the sugar is completely dissolved. Pour the mixture into an ice-cream freezer and process until firm.

CREME GLACEE A LA KRIEK
Cherry-beer Ice Cream

Ice creams flavoured with fruit beers are another favourite. This was created by Bruno Loubet of The Four Seasons restaurant at Inn on the Park, London.

Serves 6

6 egg yolks	2 x 450 g / 1 lb tins pitted
500 ml / 18 fl oz milk	black cherries in syrup
	1½ bottles (33 cl each) kriek

1 Whisk the egg yolks until thick and light. Bring the milk to the boil and pour onto the egg yolks, whisking constantly. Return the mixture to the pan and cook over gentle heat, stirring constantly until it thickens to a light coating consistency. Cool over ice.
2 Reduce the cherries and their syrup with 1 bottle of the beer until the liquid is very thick.
3 Place in a blender or food processor with the cooled egg mixture and the remaining ½ bottle of kriek and blend until smooth. Pour the mixture into an ice-cream freezer and process until firm.

ICED WALNUT SOUFFLE
WITH BOCK BEER

This iced soufflé was devised by chef Pierre Labrot. He made it with Thomas Hardy's old ale, but a bock beer such as the spicy Aventinus wheat double bock would add a sharper, less sweet note.

Serves 4

75 g / 3 oz walnuts	For the orange crème
200 ml / 7 fl oz Doppelbock	anglaise:
or Weizenbock	600 ml / 1 pint milk
150 ml / ¼ pint double cream	6 egg yolks
100 g / 4 oz caster sugar	100 g / 4 oz caster sugar
4 eggs	grated zest of 1 orange

1 Soak the nuts in the beer overnight.

2 Whip the cream until it is thick but not stiff; chill.

3 Put the sugar in a small saucepan with 150 ml/¼ pint of the beer and boil until it reaches the soft ball stage, 115°C/239°F on a sugar thermometer.

4 Beat the eggs until thick, then pour the sugar syrup onto the egg mixture, whisking constantly. Continue whisking until the mixture is cool.

5 Fold in the remaining beer and nuts, then the whipped cream, and pour into 4 individual soufflé dishes. Freeze until firm, at least 2 hours.

6 To make the crème anglaise: bring the milk to the boil. Whisk the egg yolks and sugar until thick and pale. Add the orange zest, then pour the hot milk onto the mixture, whisking steadily. Return the mixture to the pan and cook gently, stirring constantly with a wooden spoon, for 5–10 minutes, until it thickens slightly.

7 Pour the sauce onto 4 plates and turn out the soufflés onto the sauce. Decorate with peeled orange segments, sprigs of mint, and extra walnuts if you like.

ATHOLL BROSE

Another version of Atholl brose is served as a drink in its own right, but this rich Scottish dessert is an excellent partner to a glass of oatmeal stout.

Serves 4
2–4 tablespoons honey
4 tablespoons whisky
2 tablespoons oatmeal
300 ml/½ pint double cream

1 Gently heat the honey with the whisky until it dissolves; leave to cool slightly. Toast the oatmeal until it begins to release a nutty fragrance.

2 Whip the cream until it is thick. Sprinkle with most of the oatmeal, reserving 2 teaspoons. Fold in the oatmeal, honey and whisky, then spoon into 4 whisky tumblers. Sprinkle with the remaining oatmeal and chill.

YORKSHIRE PARKIN

A moist, spicy cake which makes a good accompaniment to a glass of its local brew, Theakstons Old Peculier, or indeed any rich, slightly sweet old ale.

Makes 12–15 pieces
225 g/8 oz plain flour
1 teaspoon bicarbonate of soda
2 teaspoons ground ginger
1 teaspoon mixed spice
100 g/4 oz medium oatmeal
225 g/8 oz black treacle
100 g/4 oz butter
50 g/2 oz soft brown sugar
1 egg, beaten
50 ml/2 fl oz milk or beer

1 Heat the oven to 180°C/350°F/gas mark 4. Sift the flour, soda and spices into a large bowl. Stir in the oatmeal.

2 Place the treacle, butter and sugar in a saucepan over gentle heat, stirring frequently, until the butter melts and the sugar dissolves. Pour into the dry ingredients, then add the egg and the milk or beer, stirring to form a thick batter.

3 Line an 18 x 28 cm/7 x 11 inch tin with buttered greaseproof paper, pour in the mixture and bake for 45–55 minutes, until the cake is firm to the touch and has begun to shrink away from the edge of the tin. Parkin is usually made 2–3 days before it is needed, which allows the flavours to develop and makes it easier to cut into pieces.

HULASTRÄUBLA
Elderflower Fritters

In early summer in south Germany, frothy, scented clouds of elderflowers are often gathered and made into fritters. The Ayinger brewery makes these with its dark wheat beer or Celebrator double bock and serves them with its fruitily acidic wheat beer.

Serves 6
100 g/4 oz plain flour
pinch of salt
1 egg
400 ml/14 fl oz beer
oil for deep frying
elderflower heads
icing sugar, to serve

1 Sift the flour and salt into a bowl. Break in the egg and work into the flour, adding the beer a little at a time, until you have a fairly thick batter.

2 Heat the oil until a light haze forms.

3 Shake the elderflower heads gently to remove insects, then, holding the stalks, dip the heads into the batter, turning to coat them evenly. Deep fry until golden brown, then drain well. Trim away the bottom of the stalks, then sprinkle the fritters with icing sugar and serve at once.

Hunting the classic brews

People often tell me that they just returned from a holiday or business trip in this country or that and could find no interesting beer. Sometimes, their visit was to a nation or region with many fine brews, the pleasure of which they missed. The difficulty is that, even in great brewing countries, the most interesting of beers are often a minority taste – they have to be hunted. Some are also seasonal, and may be unavailable, or past their best, at the wrong time of year.

In most countries, bartenders often assume that foreigners want well-known international or national brands. On principle, I always ask: What do you have that is local? It may not always be better, but it might be different. Restaurants and hotels in chains are the least likely to have local brews, although some in North America are beginning to take a more adventurous line. If he has the products of a local brewery, the bartender will almost always offer its blandest beer. I ask, politely but tenaciously: Don't they make anything with a bit more flavour?

The custom of the country
The broader approach to beer-hunting varies, according to the culture of the country. Hot regions tend to regard beer as a thirstquencher, and are not likely to offer specialities, although a surprising number of African countries and Caribbean islands have strong stouts. In the heartlands of the grape – the southern parts of Italy and France, and much of Spain – the discerning drinker will be busy with wine, and will regard a good beer as a bonus.

In northern Italy, especially Milan, many bars offer an extensive range of beers, one or two local but more from Germany, Belgium and Britain. Beer is becoming more popular in Spain, but specialities do not extend much beyond the odd Dortmunder or Munich-style dark lager (ask the bartender if he has a *birra especial* or *extra*). In France, the more sophisticated cities have bars offering the odd bière de garde and perhaps a few Belgian beers, and in Paris and points north the selections can be more extensive.

In central and northern Europe, it should be easier to find unusual beers, but this can still require tenacity. The local drinkers may have strong opinions about quality, but do not necessarily appreciate variety. In some countries, dark beers are deemed 'for women'. This perception, which seems odd to a Briton or American, is based on the idea of malty brews for nursing mothers.

Belgium and the Netherlands have the most knowledgable and best-run speciality beer bars in the world, and it is possible to offer only a sampler here. It is now relatively easy to find good cask-conditioned ale in Britain, but harder to locate specialities, although there is an increasing number of speciality beer retail shops. Many North American cities have a bar or shop offering 'the most beers in town', but there is also a growth of more serious outlets.

Beer-lovers like to be aware of establishments with a large selection, but will treat such places with caution. Does the selection represent variety of style, or merely of brand or country? A list of two dozen famous-name Pilsner-derivatives from different countries is really offering beers that are very similar. Nor is there any special joy in tasting a standard lager just because it comes from Ruritania. Does the establishment have a fast turnover? If that beer from Erewhon has been on the shelf for a year, it may taste of damp cardboard. Darker and stronger beers have longer shelf-lives, but only those that are bottle-conditioned can be treated as vintage brews, and even those must be properly cellared. How well-informed is the staff? That is a good guide to the establishment's seriousness of intent.

Consumer campaigns
Beer-lovers who wish to protect their nations' most interesting products have formed consumerist organizations in several countries, and some of these publish or support guides to good outlets, as well as organizing tastings and festivals.

Official industry associations may find it less easy to help the hunter of unusual beers. These bodies are usually funded by member-brewers in proportion to size (and the biggest brewers' products are already the easiest to find). Sometimes, maverick brewers with interesting products are not members.

The following represents just a small sample of places where I have enjoyed good beer. Pubs and breweries do change their policies, or even close, so please phone before attempting a visit. When calling overseas, please be aware of time differences.

AUSTRIA

Country breweries in Austria often have attractive taverns attached, and a new generation of brewpubs is beginning to add some diversity of style. Some taverns and brewpubs do not open until mid-afternoon.

KEFERMARKT In this small town, north of Linz in the direction of Ceské Budejovice, the castle of Weinberg has had brewing rights since the 14th century. Inside is a new brewpub *(Tel: 07947-7111)*.

SALZBURG Die Weisse, *9 Virgil Gasse (Tel: 0662-872246)* is an old-established brewery and beer garden offering unfiltered wheat beer. Off the tourist track, and popular on Sunday mornings, it opens at 11am. Augustinerbrau, *Kloster Mülln (Tel: 0662-31246)*, is the beer garden of a former monastery brewery. Stigl Keller, *10 Festungs Gasse (Tel: 0662-842681)*, a beer garden facing the cathedral.

VIENNA In addition to Nussdorf, described on page 151, the capital has the following brewpubs: Fischer, *17 Billroth Strasse (Tel: 0222-316264)*, in the suburb of Döbling, on the edge of the Vienna Woods, making a soft, malty, golden lager in the Munich style, and seasonal specialities: Wieden, *5 Waag Gasse (Tel: 0222-5860300)* in the Wieden district produces a flame-coloured lager in broadly the Vienna style.

Medl, *275 Linzer Strasse, Penzing (Tel: 0222-944340)* is a lager brewery in the style of a Vienna wine-garden.

In town, the oldest-established speciality beer bar is Krah-Krah, *8 Rabensteig (Tel: 01-533 8193)*. This is in a touristy area where prices can be high and pickpockets are active.

For a large selection of bottled beers, head to the suburb of Hernalse, to Schwaiger's Bier-Besel, *212 Haupt Strasse (Tel:*

0222-458657). Popular with locals; few tourists.

ZWETTL Gasthaus Schwarzalm, *43 Gschwendt (Tel: 02822-53173)* is a quality hotel with a restaurant to match, serving the local brew with beer-oriented food.

BELGIUM

Even the non-specialist café in Belgium will offer a reasonable range of beer styles. In addition to establishments mentioned elsewhere in this book, several Brussels restaurants offer *cuisine à la bière*. A good example is Beguine des Beguines, *168 Avenue des Beguines (Tel: 02-425 77 70)*.

ANTWERP Kulminator, *32 Vleminckveld (Tel: 03-232 45 38)*, a famous specialist beer café, with many vintage brews; Taverne Bierland, *28 Korte Nieuw Straat (Tel: 03-231 23 40)*, in the old town, is known for the size and quality of its range, including De Troch gueuze in traditional form.

BRUGES 't Brugs Beertje, *5 Kemel Straat, near Simon Stevin Plein (Tel: 050-33 96 16)*, with a speciality gin bar next door; Straffe Hendrik Brewery Tavern, *26 Walplein(Tel:050-33 26 97)*, a brewpub producing a very hoppy golden ale.

BRUSSELS Two famous Art Nouveau cafés at either side of the Bourse (Stock Exchange), just behind Grand' Place, are Falstaff, *17–23 Rue Henri Maus (Tel: 02-511 87 89)* and Cirio, *18 Rue de la Bourse (Tel:02-512 13 95)*. Also behind Grand' Place, Café de la Bécasse, *11 Rue de Tabora (Tel: 02-511 00 06)* has sweetish lambic blends and intense cheeses. A short walk away, the 1920s-style café A la Mort Subite, *7 Rue Montagne aux Herbes*

Potagères (Tel: 02-513 13 18), serves gueuze. Still in the centre of town, the L'Ultième Hallucinatie, *316 Rue Royale (Tel: 02-217 06 14)*, in an Art Nouveau building, has under one roof a studenty café, formal restaurant and late Saturday disco. Jazz-lovers may prefer Bierodrome, *21 Place Ferdinand Cocq (Tel: 02-512 0456)*.

Specialist beer bars in the near suburbs: Le Père Faro, *442 Chaussée d'Alsemberg, Uccle (Tel: 02-347 39 01)*, has more than 100 . 't Narrenschip, *185 Rue Rogier, Schaarbeek (Tel: 02-217 22 27)*, also has around 100. Le Miroir, *24–26 Place Reine Astrid, Jette (Tel: 02-424 04 78)*, is both a specialist beer café and a brewpub; highly recommended.

CHARLEROI Beau Lieu, *3 Rue du Commerce (Tel: 071-32 89 69)*, also specializes in cheese.

GHENT De Hopduvel, *10 Rokerel Straat (Tel: 091-25 37 29)*, is tricky to find, but an outstanding beer tavern in a city with many; good selection of gueuze and Trappist beers. Another good one, more central, is Het Waterhuis aan de Bierkant, *9 Groentemarkt (Tel: 091-25 06 80)*, with a gin bar next door.

LEUVEN Domus, *8 Tiense Straat (Tel: 016-20 14 49)*, speciality beer bar and brewpub, with its own honey ale; Gambrinus, *13 Grote Markt (Tel: 016-20 12 38)*, local favourite with 1890s' interior, modest selection of beers.

LIEGE La Vaudrée, *149 Rue St Gilles (Tel: 041-23 18 80)*; nearly 1,000 beers, with restaurant.

MONS L'Alambic, *25 Place du Marché aux Herbes (Tel: 065-34 60 07)*; an outpost for lambic.

NAMUR L'Eblouissant, *108 Rue des Brasseurs (Tel: 081-22 69 28)*, also has other regional drinks and foods.

Information: the consumerist organization is De Objectieve Bier-proevers, *Postbus 32, 2600 Berchem 5, Belgium.* Flemish-speaking, but multilingual.

Further reading: the author's *The Great Beers of Belgium* (published by Coda, of Antwerp), with separate editions in English, Flemish and French, is an extended essay and memoir on the Belgian themes explored in this book. *Bier Jaarboek* by Peter Crombecq (Kosmos, of Antwerp and Utrecht) is a comprehensive guide to beers, brewers and speciality cafés in Belgium and the Netherlands. It is in Flemish, but not difficult to follow. The *Good Beer Guide to Belgium and Holland* by Tim Webb (Alma Books, *Campaign for Real Ale, 34 Alma Road, St Albans AL1 3BW, Hertfordshire, England*) is highly recommended as a tourist handbook for the English-speaking beer-lover.

BRITAIN

The great joy for the beer-drinker in Britain is its cask-conditioned ales, and these are available at a majority of pubs, although the standard of cellaring, which is critical to the quality of this living product, varies. Pubs offering exclusively the ales of a nearby independent brewery are often the best in this respect, although the national groups do encourage their landlords to look after the beer properly.

Seekers of the best brews always carry the *Good Beer Guide*, which is published in a new edition each October by the Campaign for Real Ale, *34 Alma Road, St Albans AL1 3BW, Hertfordshire, England (Tel: 0727-867201).* This guidebook provides details, by county and city, of around 5,000 pubs throughout the British Isles, recommended for their beer by local branches. The campaign, known as CAMRA, also

organizes the annual Great British Beer Festival and acts as a consumerist lobby. Anyone, in any country, can pay a modest fee to join, and members receive a monthly newspaper reporting on beer events and new brews.

In a country with wonderful ales, there is no point in ordering lager, especially as the products offered are almost all international standard brews, often made under licence to lower specifications for the British market, and usually badly served. Only a handful of British pubs serve well-kept and interesting brews from other countries.

For anyone wishing to have a drink at home, national retail chains do offer some interesting imports. The best is Oddbins, but the major supermarkets are also quite adventurous. Several towns have speciality beer shops, where the selection is far wider and the staff knowledgable. Here is a small selection of such shops:

LAKE DISTRICT The Masons Arms (also a brewpub), *Strawberry Bank, Cartmel Fell, Grange-over-Sands, Cumbria CA11 6NW (Tel: 04488-486).*

LEEDS The Ale House (also a brewpub), *79 Raglan Road (Tel: 0532-455447).* Also in West Yorkshire, The Ale Shop, *205 Lockwood Road, Huddersfield (Tel: 0484-432479).*

LINCOLN Small Beer, *91 Newland Street West (Tel: 0522-528628).*

LONDON The Beer Shop, *8 Pitfield Street, near Old Street (Tel: 071-739 3701).*

PRESTON (Lancashire) The Real Ale Shop, *47 Lovat Road (Tel: 0772-201591).*

SHEFFIELD Small Beer, *57 Archer Road (Tel: 0742-551356).*

YORK York Beer Shop, *28 Sandringham Street, off Fishergate (Tel: 0904-647136).*

It is also possible to order speciality beers by mail, from:
The Beer Cellar, *Unit 10, Thame Park Business Centre, Wenman Road, Thame, Oxfordshire OX9 3XA (Tel: 0844-260500);* Belgium Bière, *23 Monarch Way, West End, Southampton, Hampshire S03 3JQ (Tel: 0703-470277);* The Elite Beer Company, *Jubilee Estate, Foundry Lane, Horsham, West Sussex RH13 5UE (Tel: 0403-261554).*

FRANCE

Establishments identified as restaurant tend to concentrate on wine. The word brasserie derives from brewery, and usually promises fresh draught beer, although the choice may be very limited. The famous Brasserie Lipp, in Paris, has only one but, for its ambience, should not be missed.

Tavernes, bars and cafés usually offer beer. References in their names to the north, or Belgium, are promising. Here is a small selection of specialist establishments:

LILLE Le Pub McEwan's, *15 Place de la Gare (Tel: 20 55 11 26);* also branches in other northern towns. Les Brasseurs, *22 Place de la Gare (Tel: 20 06 46 25);* a brewpub with *cuisine à la bière.*

PARIS Restaurant with *cuisine à la bière:* L'entre-siècle, *29 Avenue de Lowendal, Paris 15 (Tel: 47 83 51 22).*

Specialist beer bars: L'Abbaye, *1 Place de la Bastille (Tel: 42 72 16 39);* Gambrinus, *62 Rue des Lombards (Tel: 42 21 10 34);* Au General Lafayette, *52 Rue Lafayette (Tel: 47 70 59 08);* Taverne St Germain, *155 Boulevard St Germain (Tel: 42 22 88 98);* La Gueuze, *19 Rue Soufflot, near Boulevard St Michel (Tel: 43 54*

63 00); Hall's Beer Tavern, *68 Rue St Denis (Tel: 42 36 92 72)*; Le Mazet, *61 Rue St André-des-Arts, St Germain (Tel: 43 54 68 81)*; L'Oiseau de Feu, *12 Place de la Bastille (Tel: 40 19 07 52)*; La Taverne de Rubens, *12 Rue St Denis (Tel: 45 08 14 59)*; Le Sous-Bock, *49 Rue St Honoré (Tel: 40 26 46 61)*; Au Trappiste, *4 Rue St Denis (Tel: 42 33 08 50)*.

STRASBOURG Aux 12 Apôtres, *7 Rue Mercière (Tel: 88 32 08 24)*, in a street facing the cathedral. Patron Bernard Rotman is knowledgable about the beer scene in Alsace.

Information: for further information about beer in Lille and the North, write to: Les Amis de la Bière, *Les Sept Muids, 36 Route de Valenciennes, Haspres 59198, France* (please enclose postage, and expect answers in French).

GERMANY

The Germans can be understandably chauvinistic about their beer, their Purity Law and their great number of breweries (more than 1,200), but do not necessarily take advantage of the variety of styles available, except perhaps for seasonal specialities. Not only do many taverns sell the products of only one brewery, but sometimes in only one style. Specialities can be hard to find.

In the South, especially among the young, unfiltered wheat beers are popular, but at the expense of dark lager, Märzenbier or bock, for example. In the North, many drinkers seem to know only Pils, although this is less true in Cologne and Düsseldorf.

Almost every town and village in Bavaria (and, famously, Franconia) has its own brewery, sometimes several. Often, the brewery is behind, or next door to, or opposite, its principal outlet, or *Ausschank* (what the British would call its 'tap'). The best of these are beautifully kept, and they very often serve rustic food of very good quality and value. Some also act as inns, with bedrooms.

While there have been many closures among small and medium-sized breweries in recent years, around 150 new brewpubs have opened since the late 1970s. There is one in almost every town of any size, from Aachen to Würzburg. Ask for the local *Brauhaus, Hausbrauerei* or *Gasthausbrauerei* ('guest-house brewery'). Many of these specialize in unfiltered beers, often top-fermenting, frequently wheat brews. Few have been as innovative as brewpubs in other countries, but most are worth a visit.

In a country with so many breweries and taverns, exploration can be endless. For the traveller wanting a quick sampler, here are notes on major cities:

BERLIN Brewpubs have opened and closed in Berlin, but the excellent Luisenbräu, near Charlottenburg Palace at *1 Luisenplatz (Tel: 030-341 0232)*, seems to thrive. Its speciality is a soft, sweetish, malty-fruity, Vienna-style lager. Several cities have bars that describe themselves as 'The House of a Hundred Beers', or something similar; Berlin's, at *45 Mommsen Strasse (Tel: 030-324 2580)*, is called Mommseneck am Brunnen.

BREMEN The Erste Bremer Gasthausbrauerei, *12-13 Hinter dem Schutting (Tel: 0421-337 6633)*, in the old town, opened in 1990. In the same little street, the Kleiner Ratskeller serves the unfiltered Kräusen Pils from the local Haake-Beck brewery.

COLOGNE In addition to the establishments mentioned in the Kölsch chapter (see page 153), a newcomer is *Weiss-Brau, 24 Am Weidenbach (Tel: 0221-247993)*.

DORTMUND The Hövels Hausbrauerei, *5-7 Hoher Wall (Tel: 0231-141044)*, is recommended for its misnamed Bitterbier, its excellent German food and its comfortable ambience. The Kronen brewery's Wenker's Brauhaus, which serves a top-fermenting, unfiltered, pale beer, has a more pubby atmosphere. It is on the market square, at *10 Am Markt (Tel: 0231-527548)*. Both bring a little colour to the workaday city centre.

DÜSSELDORF In addition to the excellent old brewpubs (see page 147), two new ones have been trying to establish themselves: Johan Albrecht, part of a chain, makes Pilsner and Vienna-style lagers at *104 Nieder Kasseler Strasse (Tel: 0211-570129)*; Ober Kasseler is in the old railway station of that name, *2 Belsen Platz (Tel: 0211-555158)*.

FRANKFURT Two big companies, Henninger and Binding, dominate the local market, but there are several brewpubs. The city centre has Zwölf Apostel, *1 Rosenberger Strasse (Tel: 069-288668)*, making an unfiltered Pilsner-type.

At Eltville, west of Frankfurt, between the towns of Wiesbaden and Mainz, is the pioneering Kleines Brauhaus, *41-43 Schwalbacher Strasse (Tel: 06123-2706)*, set up by Otto Binding in 1984. It offers an interestingly malty, 'organic' dark brew, and free-range pigs' knuckles.

HAMBURG Another city with several new brewpubs. The pioneer was Dehn's, *47 Ost-West Strasse (Tel: 040-330070)*, making a dryish dark lager.

HANOVER Again, several brewpubs, the pioneer being Ernst August, *13 Schmieder Strasse (Tel: 0511-13000)*, making a wheat-tinged unfiltered Pilsner, and offering breakfast.

HEIDELBERG Brauhaus Vetter, *9 Steingasse (Tel: 06221-15850)* is notable for an intensely hoppy, bitter beer.

MUNICH The beer capital. The best time to visit Munich and taste beers is spring, perhaps March or early April. At this time of year, there are bock beers as well as the everyday lagers and the more summery wheat brews, the weather is usually pleasant, and the city is not yet overrun with tourists, as it certainly will be for Oktoberfest, which is no time for contemplative sampling.

Visits to the Paulaner Keller beer cellar and garden at Nockherberg (see page 230) and the Hofbräuhaus (see page 229) are a must for the beer-lover. The latter can be smoky, noisy and touristy, but its garden is a delight. Among golden lagers, the locals favour the malty examples from Augustiner, especially at the Keller on Arnulf Strasse, the Hirschgarten public park, near Nymphenburg Castle, or the 1890s' Augustiner Restaurant on Neuhauser Strasse. The Spaten brewery's beers are very well served at the Osterwaldgarten, *12 Kefer Strasse,* near the Münchener Freiheit metro station. Nearby is Haus der 111 Biere, *3 Franz Strasse.*

For wheat beer, try the Aventinus at the Schneider restaurant in the street called Tal, in the city centre.

Take a trip out of town to the nearby Andechs or Ettal monastery brewery beer gardens, but be aware that the bock beer may not be available at weekends (too strong for casual drinkers).

The most characterful brewpub beer is the St Jacobus Blonder Bock at the *Forschungs Brewery, 76 Unterhachinger Strasse (Tel: 089-670 1169),* in the outer suburb of Perlach; well worth the journey, but do not drive. Forschungs opens only from late February or early March to late October.

STUTTGART This modern industrial city (albeit overlooked by vineyards) has two new brewpubs: Calwer Eck, *31 Calwer Strasse (Tel: 0711-226 1104)* and Tü 8, *8 Tübinger Strasse (Tel: 0711-291090).*

ITALY

'English pubs' often have big selections not only of British, but also of Belgian and German beers, and the speciality café is well established. These are just a few examples.

MILAN La Fontanella, *6 Alzaia Naviglio Pavese (Tel: 02-282 0931)*; Matricola, an 'Irish pub' at *43 Viale Romagna (Tel: 02-236 3498)*; El Tumbun, *20 Via San Marco (Tel: 02-659 9507).*

ROME Birreria l'Orso Elettrico, *64 Via Calderini (Tel: 06-324 0523).*

VENICE Devil's Forest, *Calle Stagneri, 5185 Via San Marco (Tel: 041-520 0623).*

THE NETHERLANDS

The Dutch are beginning to brew a great many more speciality styles, but their beer bars also heavily feature Belgian products. Several towns have bars in the Beiaard group, and an unconnected bar, De Beyerd, was a pioneer in the old brewing town of Breda, at *26 Bosch Straat (Tel: 076-214265).*

ALKMAAR This tourist town, better known for cheese, has the national beer museum, called De Boom, with its own café, at *1 Houttil (Tel: 072-115547).* Ask for the house special beer.

AMSTERDAM In De Wildeman, *5 Nieuwezijds Kolk (Tel: 020-638 2348),* off Nieuwendijk pedestrian

shopping street in the city centre, is a classic beer bar in a former gin tasting-room; hard to find, but well worth seeking out. 't IJ Proeflokaal, *7 Funenkade (Tel: 020-622 8325),* a brewpub under a windmill, within sight of the central railway station, has outstanding Pilsner and abbey-style beers. Brouwhuis Maximilaan, *6–8 Kloveniersburgwal (Tel: 020-624 2778),* is a brewpub with some *cuisine à la bière,* in the old inner city. De Zotte, *29 Raam Straat, near Leidseplein (Tel: 020-626 8694)* is a lively bar, specializing in Belgian brews.

THE HAGUE Den Paas, *16a Dunne Bierkade (Tel: 070-360 0019),* in the old town.

MAASTRICHT La Vièrge, *2 Corten Straat (Tel: 043-217550).*

ROTTERDAM Cambrinus, *4 Blaak (Tel: 010-414 6702),* near the Blaak metro station; the name is a variation on Gambrinus, and there is some cooking with beer. The old-established and well-respected beer café Locus Publicus, *364 Oostzeedijk (Tel: 010-433 1761),* is next to the Oostplein metro station. There are sometimes dishes cooked with beer at Het Weeshuis, *76 Hoog Straat, Schiedam (Tel: 010-426 1657),* an old gin-distilling town now part of the Rotterdam metropolitan area.

UTRECHT Jan Primus, *27 Jan van Scorel Straat (Tel: 030-514572),* pioneering speciality beer bar.

Information: The specialist cafés have their own organization, Alliantie van Bier Tapperijen, and produce a guide. The chairman of the ABT, Piet de Jongh, owns the café De Beyerd, *26 Bosch Straat, 4811 GH Breda, The Netherlands.* The consumerist organization is PINT, *Postbus 3757, 1001 AN Amsterdam, The Netherlands (Fax: 020-411 6915).*

Further reading: see the *Good Beer Guide to Belgium and Holland* and *Bier Jaarboek*, recommended under Belgium.

SCANDINAVIA

While Denmark sees itself as a brewing nation, and has liberal laws concerning the serving of beer, the other Nordic countries have many restrictions. They also impose high taxes with a view to making drink an expensive pleasure. Denmark has the most breweries, though the industry is dominated by Carlsberg. Norway has a Purity Law based on the German *Reinheitsgebot.*

Information: the Nordic Beer Association is an informal, voluntary, consumer body. Please contact the association by fax: Denmark *(Fax: 31 22 14 55)*; Norway *(Fax: 66-982452)*.

DENMARK

AALBORG Queen's Pub, *25 Vingårdsgade (Tel: 98 10 15 99).*

AARHUS St Clemens, *10–12 Kannikegade (Tel: 86 13 80 00)*, is a brewpub under the same ownership as Copenhagen's Apollo. Chas E Vinhandel, *5 Rysegade (Tel: 66 12 14 11)*, is a beer shop.

COPENHAGEN The city has one brewpub, The Apollo, *3 Vesterbrogade (Tel: 33 12 33 13)*, producing unfiltered beers. Café Sommersko, *6 Kronprinsengade (Tel: 33 14 81 89)*, has a large selection of Danish and imported beers in the bottle. Rosie McGee's, *2 Vesterbrogade (Tel: 33 32 19 23)*, is a huge theme pub with imported beers, and dancing. At the corner of the square of the same name, the Gammel Strand beer and wine shop has sold drink since 1796 and has the

biggest selection in Scandinavia, at *6 Nabolos (Tel: 33 93 93 44).*

ESBJERG You'll Never Walk Alone, *10 Kongensgade (Tel: 75 45 40 60).*

ODENSE Hot News Café, *Grand Hotel, 18 Jernbanegade (Tel: 66 11 71 71).*

FINLAND

HELSINKI Kappeli Brasserie, *11 Etelä-Espanadi (Tel: 90-179242)* is a brewpub producing unfiltered lagers and seasonal specials. Vastarannan Kiisk, *15 Salomon Katu (Tel: 90-694 1383)* is a beer bar with Belgian and Dutch brews. William K, *3 Annan Katu (Tel: 90-680 2562)* has Finnish and imported beers and whiskies.

NORWAY

OSLO The Oslo Mikro Bryggeri, *6 Bogstadveien (Tel: 22-569776)* is a brewpub offering British and American style. Johan Albrecht is a German-accented brewpub at the Studenten café, *45 Karl Johansgt (Tel: 22-425680)*. The oddly named Lorry is a delightful beer café at *12 Parkveien (Tel: 22-696904)*. Mjodhuset is a beer shop at *11 Youngsgt (Tel: 22-207003).*

SWEDEN

STOCKHOLM Nora Brunn, *33 Surbrunnsgatan (Tel: 08-166180)*, is a shop with a large selection of beers, and is a good source of information. Unfortunately, it closes in June, July and August.

NORTH AMERICA

UNITED STATES

It is all too easy to miss the truly distinctive beers of America – yet there are hundreds of them. The old south and small-town America can be deserts, but the bigger cities of the north, especially on the two coasts, and the Chicago area, have a great many fine brews.

Devotees in several regions of the United States have started newspapers, usually bi-monthly, carrying listings of beer bars, shops and breweries. Piles of these can be found in the best beer bars. From the scores of such bars in America, there is room to list only a handful – but these are key sources of information. There are several guidebooks to American brewpubs, and the most comprehensive is *On Tap*, from WBR Publications, *Clemson, South Carolina (Fax: 803-654-5067)*. The Association of Brewers is parent of the American Homebrewers' Association, the Institute for Brewing Studies, Brewers' Publications and the Great American Beer Festival: *P O Box 287, Boulder, Colorado 80306 (Tel: 303-447-0816, Fax: 303-447-2825)*. It publishes the Classic Beer Styles series and produces a directory of brewpubs, micros and contract brewers.

All About Beer, a magazine widely available throughout the United States, is published from Durham, North Carolina *(Tel: 919-490-0589).*

EAST *Ale Street News* covers New York and other cities from a base in Bergenfield, New Jersey *(Fax: 201-387-1850)*.

In addition to Zip City, *3 West 18th Street, Manhattan (Tel: 212-366-6333)*, New York has now regained another brewpub, at *40–42 Thompson Street and Broome, SoHo (Tel: 212-925-1515).*

New York's leading speciality beer bars are the Peculier Pub, *145*

Bleecker Street, Greenwich Village (Tel: 212-353-1327, and Brewsky's, *41 East 7th Street, in the East Village (Tel: 212-982-3006).* Guidebooks can be bought at Little Shop of Hops, *15 West 39th Street (Tel: 212-704-9797).*

The Washington–Baltimore area has the newspaper *BarleyCorn*, published in Falls Church, Virginia *(Tel: 703-573-9870).* Capitol City is a brewpub at *1100 New York Avenue NW, Washington (Tel: 202-628-2222).* The capital's most famous beer bar is The Brickskeller, *1523 22nd Street NW (Tel: 202-293-1885).*

MIDWEST In Chicago, the key brewpub is Goose Island, *1800 North Clybourn (Tel: 312-915-0071).* The Chicago Beer Society can be reached by mail at *600 Albion Lane, Mount Prospect, Illinois 60056.* In Minneapolis, the key brewpub is Sherlock's Home (see page 110). Minneapolis also has a newspaper, *Midwest Beer Notes (Tel: 612-861-1562).*

SOUTH-EAST No newspaper yet, but the guide book *On Tap* (see above) is published from South Carolina. Florida has the most brewpubs, though several produce rather bland beers. Those that have established the strongest reputations are McGuire's, *600 East Gregory Street, Pensacola (Tel: 904-433-6789)* and Sarasota Brewing, in the town of that name, at *6607 Gateway Avenue (Tel: 813-925-2337).*

SOUTH-WEST *Brewing News (Fax: 512-282-4936)* is published from Austin, the most beer-friendly city in Texas. The Celis brewery there (see page 65) is well worth a visit. So is the Dog and Duck, *406 West 17th Street (Tel: 512-479-0598).* In Houston, The Gingerman, *5607 Morningside (Tel: 713-526-2770)* is a classic beer bar, and there is now a branch in Dallas. That city also has the Dallas Brewing

Company, *703 McKinney Avenue (Tel: 214-871-7990).*

Visitors to New Orleans should not miss the Crescent City brewpub, *527 Decatur Street (Tel: 504-522-0571).*

Colorado has many brewpubs, and the best base from which to explore is the Wynkoop Brewing Company, *1634 18th Street, Denver (Tel: 303-297-2700).* The newspaper is *Rocky Mountain Brews*, published in Fort Collins *(Tel: 303-493-3387).*

WEST COAST California has about 75 brewpubs and micros, though the south of the state is less well endowed than the north. There are as many again in the Pacific Northwest.

San Diego's pioneer was the Old Columbia, *1157 Columbia (Tel: 619-234-2739).* The most central brewpub in Los Angeles is Gorky's, *536 East 8th Street (Tel: 213-627-4060).* In San Francisco, serious beer-lovers should visit Anchor (see page 235) and dine at Gordon Biersch (see page 223). The city also has the San Francisco brewpub, *155 Columbus Avenue (Tel: 415-434-3344)* and 20 Tank, *316 11th Street (Tel: 415-255-9455).* California has the pioneering *Celebrator Beer News*, published in Hayward *(Fax: 510-670-0639).*

In Portland, Oregon, a good place to begin beer-hunting is The BridgePort brewpub, *1313 NW Marshall Street (Tel: 503-241-7179).* In Seattle, the Liberty Malt Homebrew store, *1418 Western Avenue (Tel: 206-622-6648)* stocks guidebooks and has a very well-informed staff. The most central of Seattle's famous ale houses is The Pioneer Square Saloon, downtown at *73 Yesler Way (Tel: 206-638-6444).* The pioneering Cooper's Ale House is across the ship canal at *8065 Lake City Way NE (Tel: 206-522-2923).* The heartland is the university district and adjoining suburbs such as Fremont,

Greenlake and Wallingford. The beer-lovers' favourite is The Latona, *6423 Latona Avenue (Tel: 206-525-2238).* For beer-sympathetic food: The Triangle, *3507 Fremont Place NE (Tel: 206-632-0880)* and The Maple Leaf, *8909 Roosevelt Way NE (Tel: 206-523-8449).* The Pacific Northwest has *The Pint Post*, obtainable at $1.00 plus postage from The Microbrew Appreciation Society, *12345 Lake City Way NE, Suite 159, Seattle, Washington 98125, USA.*

CANADA

CALGARY The hearty beers of the Big Rock Brewery (see page 113) feature in a good selection at Buzzard's, *140 10th Avenue SW (Tel: 403-264 6959).*

MONTREAL The city's superbly fresh, fruity St Ambroise pale ale is on draught at the speciality beer pub l'Ile Noir, *342 Ontario Street East (Tel: 514-982-0866),* along with a selection of single-malt whiskies. Brewpubs include Le Cheval Blanc, *809 Ontario Street East, near Rue Berri (Tel: 514-522-0211);* and La Cervoise, *4457 St Laurent, near Rue Mt Royal (Tel: 514-843-6586).*

TORONTO Many brewpubs, including the excellent Rotterdam, *600 King Street (Tel: 416-868-6882).* Very good beer selections at C'est What, *67 Front Street East (Tel: 416-867-9499),* and Allen's, a New York saloon in a Greek neighbourhood, *143 Danforth Avenue (Tel: 416-463-3086).*

VANCOUVER A wide selection of beers, with pizzas and the like, at the Fog 'n' Suds chain *(Tel: 604-732-3377)* and branches. On Vancouver Island, the city of Victoria has two recommended brewpubs: Buckerfield's (in Swan's Hotel), *506 Pandora Street (Tel: 604-361-3310),* and Spinnakers, *308 Catherine Street (Tel: 604-384-6613).*

Information: CAMRA Canada is a consumerist organization inspired by its British namesake but operating separately: *10 Ontario Street West, Suite 604, Montreal, Quebec H2X 1Y6, Canada (Fax: 514-844-0102).* The Canadian Association for Better Ale and Lager is headquartered at *294 Logan Avenue, Toronto, Ontario M4M 2N7 (Tel: 416-466-5696).* *Bière* magazine is published three times a year from Hull, Quebec *(Tel: 613-737-3715).*

AUSTRALASIA

AUSTRALIA

After a very promising start, the brewpub and microbrewery movement in Australia was devastated by economic recession. There have been many closures. Apart from establishments mentioned elsewhere in this book, the following are of interest: Sail and Anchor brewpub, *64 South Terrace, Fremantle (Tel: 09-335 8433);* Reflections Café and Moonshine Brewery, Wildwood Road, Yallingup, on a vineyard in the Margaret River area of Western Australia *(Tel: 097-552277);* Bull

and Bear Ale House, *91 King William Street, Adelaide (Tel: 08-231 5795);* the Geebung Polo Club, *85 Auburn Road, Hawthorn, Melbourne (Tel: 03-882 7388);* Rose and Crown beer bar, *309 Bay Street, Port Melbourne (Tel: 03-646 3580);* the Rifle Brigade brewpub, *137 View Street, Bendigo, Victoria (Tel: 054-434 092);* The Lord Nelson, *corner of Kent and Argyle Streets, The Rocks, Sydney (Tel: 02-251 4044)* – the Lord Nelson is a good source of information in Sydney; The Real Ale Café (although it has nothing cask-conditioned) at *King Street and George, Sydney (Tel: 02-262 3277);* Kelly's brewery and restaurant, *251 Stanley Street, Mater Hill, Brisbane (07-844 9777);* Sanctuary Cove brewpub, *Casey Road, Hope Island, Gold Coast (075-308400).*

NEW ZEALAND

There are now many brewpubs. In Auckland, The Shakespeare, *61 Albert Street (Tel: 09-373 5396)* is recommended. Christchurch has Dux de Lux in the Arts Centre at *Hereford and Montreal Streets (Tel: 03-666 919),* and the Loaded Hog at *39 Dundas St (Tel: 03-666 674).* The Brewer's Hop home-brew store, *801 Colombo Street,* Christchurch, is a good source of information.

JAPAN

The national giants have some well-done 'theme pubs' and beer gardens, but there is also a growing number of bars offering a greater diversity of products, often with Belgium heavily featured. A guide is in preparation by Bryan Harrell, an American living in Tokyo *(Fax: 03-3481-0947).* Jazz pianist Masaharu Yamada, who spent some years in Belgium, features piano and beer at Bois Cereste, *2-13-21 Akasaka (Tel: 03-3588-6292).* There is also a chain called Beer Bar Brussels, with a reasonably central branch at *75 Yarai-cho, Kagurazaka (Tel: 03-3235-1890).* British beers can be found at the restaurant "1066", *3-9-5 Kami Meguro, in the suburb of Meguro-ku (Tel: 03-3719-9059).*

Elsewhere in Japan, Sapporo's famous beer garden is at *North 6, East 9, Higashi-ku (Tel: 011-512-4774).* Sapporo also has a renowned basement bar run by Californian Phred Kaufman, at the Onoda Building, *South 9, West 5, Chuo-ku (Tel: 011-512-4774).*

Glossary

Adjunct: Fermentable material used as a substitute for traditional grains, to make beer lighter-bodied or cheaper.

Aroma hops: Varieties of hop chosen to impart bouquet.

Attenuation: Extent to which yeast consumes fermentable sugars (converting them into alcohol and carbon dioxide).

Balling, degrees: Scale indicating density of sugars in wort. Devised by C J N Balling (see page 27).

Barrel: A unit of measurement used by brewers in some countries. In Britain, a barrel holds 36 imperial gallons (1 imperial gallon = 4.5 litres), or 1.63 hectolitres. In the United States, a barrel holds 31.5 US gallons (1 US gallon = 3.8 litres), or 1.17 hectolitres.

Bittering hops: Varieties of hop chosen to impart bitter and dry flavours.

Bottle-conditioning: Secondary fermentation and maturation in the bottle, creating complex aromas and flavours.

Brewpub: Pub that makes its own beer. Also known in Britain as a homebrew house and in Germany as a house brewery (*Hausbrauerei*).

BU: Bitterness units. A system of indicating the intended hop bitterness in finished beer (see page 23).

Carbonation: Sparkle caused by carbon dioxide, either created during fermentation or injected later.

Cask-conditioning: Secondary fermentation and maturation in the cask at the point of sale. Creates light carbonation.

Conditioning: Period of maturation intended to impart 'condition' (natural carbonation). Warm conditioning further develops the complex of flavours. Cold conditioning imparts a clean, round taste.

Decoction: Exhaustive system of mashing in which portions of the wort are removed, heated, then returned to the original vessel (see page 18).

Dosage: The addition of yeast and/or sugar to the cask or bottle to aid secondary fermentation.

Dry-hopping: The addition of hops at a late stage (see page 23).

EBC: European Brewing Convention. An EBC scale is used to indicate colour in malts and beers (see page 17).

Ester: Volatile flavour compound naturally created in fermentation. Often fruity, flowery or spicy.

Fining: An aid to clarification: a substance that attracts particles that would otherwise remain suspended in the brew.

Grist: Brewers' term for milled grains, or the combination of milled grains to be used in a particular brew. Derives from the verb to grind. Also sometimes applied to hops.

Hogshead: Cask holding 54 imperial gallons (243 litres).

Hop back: Sieve-like vessel used to strain out the petals of the hop flowers. Known as a hop jack in the United States.

Infusion: Simplest form of mash, in which grains are soaked in water. May be at a single temperature, or with upward or (occasionally) downward changes (see page 18).

Kräusening: The addition of a small proportion of partly fermented wort to a brew during lagering. Stimulates secondary fermentation and imparts a crisp, spritzy character.

Lagering: From the German word for storage. Refers to maturation for several weeks or months at cold temperatures (close to 0°C/32°F) to settle residual yeasts, impart carbonation and make for clean, round flavours.

Lauter: To run off the wort from the mash tun. From the German word meaning to clarify. A lauter tun is a separate vessel to do this job. It uses a system of sharp rakes to achieve a very intensive extraction of malt sugars.

Mash: (Verb) To release malt sugars by soaking the grains in water. (Noun) The resultant mixture.

Microbrewery: Small brewery (see page 9).

Original gravity: A measurement of the density of fermentable sugars in the mixture of malt and water with which a brewer begins a given batch (see page 27).

Pasteurization: Heating of beer to 60–79°C/140–174°F to stabilize it microbiologically. Flash-pasteurization is applied very briefly, for 15–60 seconds, by heating the beer as it passes through a pipe. Alternatively, the bottled beer can be passed on a conveyor through a heated tunnel. This more gradual process takes at least 20 minutes and sometimes much more.

Plato, degrees: Refinement of the Balling scale (see page 27).

Priming: The addition of sugar at the maturation stage to promote a secondary fermentation.

Reinheitsgebot: 'Purity Law' originating in Bavaria and now applied to all German brewers making beer for consumption in their own country. It requires that only malted grains, hops, yeast and water may be in brewing.

Squares: Brewers' term for a square fermenting vessel.

Tun: Any large vessels used in brewing. In America, 'tub' is often preferred.

Units of bitterness: See BU.

Wort: The solution of grain sugars strained from the mash tun. At this stage, regarded as 'sweet wort', later as brewed wort, fermenting wort, and finally beer.

Index

Figures in **bold** refer to producer profiles

ACKNOWLEDGMENTS

Commissioned photography
Sally Cushing: 7 left; 9 left; 76 top; 77; 88 top; 109; 149; 159; 160; 161 left; 162; 163; 165; 206; 233 left

Ian Howes: 20 left; 46 right; 68; 69 left; 70; 71 bottom; 75 right; 82; 89; 91 bottom; 93; 94; 95 left; 96; 98 bottom; 134; 146; 152 bottom; 156; 173 top; 179 left; 180 left; 187 right; 189; 195; 198; 205; 207; 214 bottom left; 218 top; 254

Richard McConnell: 11 right; 69 right; 72; 73; 75 left; 76 bottom; 78; 95 centre and right; 100 right; 101; 102; 103 bottom; 104; 105 right; 174 right; 187 left

Alan Williams: 10; 14 right; 18; 19; 20 right; 21; 22; 27; 30–31 (all bottles); 34; 35; 36; 37; 39; 40; 41; 42; 43; 45; 46 left; 48 top left and bottom left; 49 top right and bottom right; 50; 53; 55; 56; 58; 60; 62; 63 left; 64; 65 top; 103 top; 114; 115; 116; 117; 118; 119; 120; 121; 122; 123; 124; 125; 126; 127; 128; 129; 130; 131; 132; 133; 135; 136; 137; 138; 140; 141; 147; 148; 152 top; 154; 155; 199; 200; 201; 202; 203; 204; 210 left; 212; 213; 214 top left and right; 216; 222; 224; 225; 226; 227; 228; 229; 230; 237 left; 238; 240; 250 right; 253; 255; 256; 258; 266

Other pictures
Andrée Abecassis: 25, 233 right, 234; Alaskan Brewing: 84, 239; Bass: 71 top, 86, 100 left; Beamish & Crawford: 181 top; Beer Cellar: 143, 144, 171 bottom right; Bitburger: 217; Boston Beer Company: 47, 161 right; Bridgeman Art Library: 33, 80; Brooklyn Brewery: 92; Bryant Jackson Communications: 232 bottom left; Carlsberg: 24, 26; Chris Chunn: 251; Colorphoto Hans Hinz 85; Coopers: 166, 167, 168; Courage: 191; Dock Street: 161 centre, 196 top left; Edwards, Martin, Thornton: 81; Eric Elmer: 105 left, 196 bottom left, 197 top right and bottom right, 215 top, 218 bottom and right, 246; Fuller's: 74; Guinness: 176, 177, 178, 180 right; Pekka Haraste: 241 left; Hürlimann: 231; Michael Jackson: 7 right, 9 right, 11 left, 14 left, 16, 17 right, 27 right, 65 bottom, 111 left, 151, 172, 173 bottom, 190 left, 192 left, 194, 210 right, 215 bottom, 237 right, 245 top; Marston's: 83; Murphy: 183; David Murray: 48 top right, 51, 63 right, 66 top left, 97, 170 top left, 171 top right, 179 right, 181 bottom, 243, 252, 257, 259, 260, 262, 263, 264, 265, 267, 269, 270; Negra Modelo: 209; Pike Place: 23; Retrograph Archive: 1, 6, 184, 208, 221; Sapporo: 8, 220, 244; Saratoga: 220; Scottish & Newcastle Breweries: 90; Sherlock's Home: 110 left; Sillem family: 190 right; Sinebrychoff: 192 right; Samuel Smith: 87, 91 top, 193; Smithwick's: 111 right, 113; Summit: 88 bottom; Suntory: 17 left; Pirkko Tanttu: 241 right; Traquair House: 107, 110 right; Whitbread: 174 left, 185; Zip City: 250 left.

Author's acknowledgments
Countless brewers worldwide, and their national organizations, have helped me in my researches over the years, and I thank them all. My further thanks for help in my most recent work to: Silvano Rusmini, Przemyslaw Wisniewski, Conrad Seidl, Dr Hans Schultze-Berndt, Erich Dederichs, Pierre-André Dubois, René Descheirder, Bernard Rotman, Kari Ylanne, Mikko Montonen, Lars Lundsten, Hans Henschien, Bob Henham, Barrie Pepper, Gary and Libby Gillman, Drew Ferguson, Alan Dikty, Vince Cottone, Willie Simpson and his many beer-loving friends, and the Japanese external trade organization Jetro.

My constant travels, and my desire to discuss and photograph every beer and meal, have made long and hard work for editor Maggie Ramsay and designer Paul Reid, and I greatly appreciate their efforts. I also thank Maggie Ramsay for her enthusiastic collaboration in the recipe section.

The publishers would like to thank A M Heath & Co, the estate of the late Flann O'Brien and Blackstaff Press for permission to reprint an extract from *The Pure Drop* on page 172.